China and Vietnam
The Politics of Asymmetry

In their three thousand years of interaction, China and Vietnam have been through a full range of relationships. Twenty-five years ago they were one another's worst enemy; fifty years ago they were the closest of comrades. Five hundred years ago they each saw themselves as Confucian empires; fifteen hundred years ago Vietnam was a part of China. Throughout all these fluctuations the one constant has been that China is the larger power and Vietnam the smaller. China has rarely been able to dominate Vietnam, and yet the relationship is shaped by its asymmetry.

The Sino-Vietnamese relationship provides the perfect ground for developing and exploring the effects of asymmetry on international relations. Brantly Womack develops his theory in conjunction with an original analysis of the interaction between China and Vietnam from the Bronze Age to the present. The value of asymmetry theory is demonstrated in its illumination of the dynamics of the relationship.

Brantly Womack is Professor of Foreign Affairs at the University of Virginia and has been named an honorary professor at Jilin University in Changchun and East China Normal University in Shanghai. He is the author of *Foundations of Mao Zedong's Political Thought* and *Politics in China* (with James Townsend) and the editor of a number of books, including *Contemporary Chinese Politics in Historical Perspective* (Cambridge University Press, 1991). He has made frequent visits to China since 1978 and to Vietnam since 1985, and he has published articles comparing their politics and exploring their relationship in *World Politics, Government and Opposition, China Journal, Asian Survey, Pacific Affairs*, and elsewhere. His articles on asymmetry in international relations have appeared in *Journal of Strategic Studies, Journal of Contemporary China*, and *Pacific Affairs*.

China and Vietnam
The Politics of Asymmetry

BRANTLY WOMACK
University of Virginia

CAMBRIDGE
UNIVERSITY PRESS

CAMBRIDGE
UNIVERSITY PRESS

32 Avenue of the Americas, New York NY 10013-2473, USA

Cambridge University Press is part of the University of Cambridge.

It furthers the University's mission by disseminating knowledge in the pursuit of education, learning and research at the highest international levels of excellence.

www.cambridge.org
Information on this title: www.cambridge.org/9780521618342

First published 2006

A catalogue record for this publication is available from the British Library

Library of Congress Cataloguing in Publication data
Womack, Brantly, 1947–
China and Vietnam : the politics of asymmetry / Brantly Womack.
p. cm.
Includes bibliographical references.
ISBN 0-521-85320-6 (hardback) – ISBN 0-521-61834-7 (pbk.)
1. China – Foreign relations – Vietnam. 2. Vietnam – Foreign relations – China.
I. Title.
DS740.5.V5W65 2006
327.51059709 – dc22 2005010534

ISBN 978-0-521-85320-0 Hardback
ISBN 978-0-521-61834-2 Paperback

For Ann, David, and Sarah

Contents

Tables, Figures, and Maps

Tables

Figures

Maps

Preface

From 1985 to 1991 I made a number of visits to China and Vietnam and talked to some of Vietnam's China experts and to some of China's Vietnam experts. By that time the hostility that had emerged during the 1970s had become embedded. Not only did I hear different "sides" of the conflict in each country, but the perceptions that each had of the other side struck me as profoundly distorted. The problem was not a lack of information. Each set of experts that I talked to had more information than I did. But the Vietnamese China experts seemed hypersensitive to every gesture and action emanating from China, while the Chinese Vietnam experts seemed overly concerned with "big picture" questions and out of touch with the realities of the place that I had just visited.

After the normalization of Sino-Vietnamese relations in 1991, the distance between the two viewpoints diminished, but the disparity remained and grew more complicated. Now both countries were concerned about developing a peaceful relationship, but "off the record" and in concrete areas of confrontation, the Chinese disparaged the Vietnamese as unreliable, while the Vietnamese were alert to Chinese malevolent inscrutability and bullying. The attitudes were not simply the residual effects of previous hostility. The issues were the peacetime problems of border trade, bridges, rail connections, and so forth, not problems of history. But there was a continuity of roles. Vietnam tended to be overly sensitive to China's actions, while China tended to be insensitive to the effects of its policies on Vietnam.

It would have been easy for me simply to assume that my situation of disengaged observation allowed me to rise above the biases of each side, that I was right and they were wrong. But I have a great deal of respect for the knowledge and judgment of my colleagues in both countries. Moreover, they were directly involved in an interaction to which I was only a bystander. So the question occurred to me, what aspect of the reality of Sino-Vietnamese relations led to the characteristic juxtaposition of viewpoints that I witnessed? Having thought of the question, the answer became obvious.

The great disparity of capacities between China and Vietnam created an asymmetric framework for the relationship that shaped every aspect of it and every phase. Asymmetry was a structural influence so fundamental to the relationship that its influence did not attract conscious notice, but it put the two countries in basically different situations vis-à-vis one another. Vietnam is vulnerable to China, and therefore quick to react to perceptions of risk. China has nothing to fear from Vietnam except in combination with other powers, and thus its perspective was rooted in general strategic concerns. Each perspective was appropriate to the different situation of each country, but by the same token each also tended to misperceive the other. And yet despite the continuing misunderstandings and tensions, the relationship progressed from a cold peace in 1991 to thick and confident ties by 1999. Successful management of the relationship required China to respect Vietnamese autonomy, and required Vietnam to show deference to a mighty neighbor.

Since my background was in the comparative politics of China and Vietnam rather than in international relations theory, I did not know at the time whether my discovery of the importance of asymmetry was really new or was simply the re-discovery of something that was common knowledge. But as I explored international relations theory, I found a pervasive concentration on wars and the competition of great powers, and very little on the structural effects of asymmetry on the interaction of large and small states. Most theorists assumed that such relationships would simply be dominated by the more powerful state, despite the contrary evidence of the American war in Vietnam. Those who did take the situation of small states more seriously were more interested in the room to maneuver available to these states in a world defined by big states. They were addressing the puzzles left unsolved by the paradigm of competitive great powers rather than taking a new approach based on asymmetry. Despite the fact that most international relationships most of the time are asymmetric, and that in the post–Cold War world all of America's relations are asymmetric, there was no sustained reflection on the structural implications of asymmetry.

This book attempts to introduce a general theory of asymmetry on the basis of a sustained analysis of the Sino-Vietnamese relationship from its beginnings to the present. I hope that it will contribute to a better understanding of China and Vietnam, and that it will stimulate other scholars to examine other relations in this light. Although the bilateral, dyadic relation is the basic unit of analysis for asymmetry, I plan to explore more complex patterns as well as regional and global systems of asymmetry in future research, and I invite other scholars to join me in this enterprise.

As the foregoing paragraphs imply, this project has been long in gestation, and many have contributed to its formation and completion. The Center for Southeast Asian Studies at Northern Illinois University made possible my first trips to Vietnam and my study of Vietnamese, and the University of Virginia took up the general burden of supporting my research since 1992. The Luce Foundation and the Social Science Research Council have funded activities that in retrospect were essential to this project. Most important were friendly interactions with institutions and individuals in Hanoi, Ho Chi Minh City, Nanning, Beijing, Kunming, Changchun, Shanghai, and Guangzhou, especially the late Vice Minister Le Mai, Ho Hai Thuy, and Nguyen Huy Quy in Hanoi; Gu Xiaosong and Wei Shuxian in Nanning; Lin Zhonghan, Ding Kuisong, Wu Baocai, and Qin Yaqing in Beijing; Liu Debin in Changchun; Feng Shaolei and Guo Xuetang in Shanghai; and Wang Gungwu in Singapore. Most of my friends in Asia were not able to review the book manuscript, however, so they are certainly not responsible either for its viewpoints or for its mistakes.

Many friends, colleagues, and students have helped to shape this manuscript. The analysis of Vietnam was much improved by John Whitmore, Bill Turley, Alex Woodside, and Alex Vuving. Allen Lynch and Paige Johnson Tan provided particularly fine-toothed critiques that led to many emendations. Jeff Legro and John Echeverri-Gent labored to raise my theoretical level, and the comments as well as the encouragement of Mark Selden, Ben Kerkvliet, and especially Chen Jian were vital for both the project and my confidence in it. Alex Vuving provided invaluable help with the glossary, as did Myungsik Ham with the bibliography and the index. The support of Cambridge University Press, incarnate in Lew Bateman, has been a deeply appreciated *sine qua non*.

My students in many classes have not only provided a patient forum for the emergence of these ideas, but also useful feedback and further stimulation. Especially Sophie Richardson, Leng Tse-kang, Alice Ba, Chen Weixing, Cho Hui-wan, Lin Teh-chang, Ray Hervandi, and Myungsik Ham have been most helpful and encouraging.

Most gratitude expressed to spouses and children in prefaces is in terms of their forbearance at being displaced by a long and lonely project. Not so in my case. I am quite sure that my wife Ann and my children David and Sarah could each give a stimulating disquisition on asymmetry at the drop of a hat. Throughout my research, Ann's expertise in family systems psychology has added a parallel universe of asymmetric relationships between individuals that has been stimulating to my understanding of international relations. David's depth as a thinker and talents as an editor have been of great help. Sarah has contributed as a distinguished historian of Vietnam countering the blunders of her sinophilic father. More important, however, her research on the interactive character of colonial politics in Vietnam provides the basic insight for my treatment of the colonial era, and more generally for my analysis of subjugated asymmetry.

It takes a village to produce an idiot as well as a healthy child, and it is up to the reader to decide whether this book is worth the efforts that have gone into it. Although I can absolve my friends, students, and family of any guilt for the weaknesses that remain, I could not have done it without them.

Introduction

In the first three millennia of their relationship, China and Vietnam have been through almost every conceivable pattern of interaction among neighbors. Even in the past fifty years, the relationship has swung from intimate friendship to implacable enmity, and at each extreme the Sino-Vietnamese relationship became the defining relationship for different phases of Southeast Asian regional politics and a major element of global international relations. Although the success of normalization since 1991 has taken the relationship out of world headlines, the stability of relations between China and Vietnam remains an essential part of the foundation of international order in Asia.

The one constant in relations between China and Vietnam since the unification of the Chinese empire in 221 BC has been that China is always much the larger partner. Regardless of whether the relationship was hostile, friendly, or in between, it has been asymmetric. China has always been a much more important presence for Vietnam than Vietnam has been for China, and Vietnam has had a more acute sense of the risks and opportunities offered by the relationship. Given the great disparity between China and Vietnam, one might expect that either Vietnam would be subservient to China or that China would annex Vietnam. In fact, however, even though Vietnam was formally a part of China for a millennium it was never fully "domesticated," and for most of the last thousand years the relationship has been a negotiated one. The Sino-Vietnamese relationship therefore presents an interesting case of a long-term asymmetric relationship that has moved through a full gamut of possible variations. Moreover, the asymmetry of the relationship can be used to explain its restlessness as well as the methods that both sides have used to define and to manage it.

Asymmetry provides the analytic focus for the book. I argue that asymmetry is more than just an obvious fact about the relationship between China and Vietnam; it has always been its most important structural factor. The disparity in capacity in an asymmetric relationship does not lead inevitably to the stronger side dominating the weaker side, as the case of Vietnam shows. If greater size and strength implied that China could easily dominate Vietnam, Vietnam would not exist today as an independent state. But Vietnam's existence next to China has not been an easy one. A great disparity, especially between neighboring states, always means that the weaker side will be more attentive to the relationship than vice versa because proportionally it is more exposed to its risks and opportunities. It is easy for misunderstandings to arise because the relationship means different things to each side. In times of crisis, the misunderstandings of each side are more likely to lead to a vicious circle than to mutual correction. Therefore asymmetric relations are difficult to manage.

I stress the theory of asymmetric relations in this book because most international relations theory overlooks the matters highlighted here. Since nations are sovereign entities and Western international relations theory arose from the competition of roughly equal powers in Europe and then concentrated on great power conflicts, it is not surprising that relations of disparity are usually treated as temporary disequilibria.[1] It is assumed that either the weaker state will balance its vulnerability by means of alliances with other states or it will be subject to the hegemony of the stronger state. But in fact there exist many long-term asymmetric relationships, and the stronger cannot always impose its will on the weaker. If an asymmetric relationship cannot be "solved" through force, then it must be managed by both sides. China and Vietnam provide a broad spectrum of experiences in managing an asymmetric relationship, and their recent management of normalization has been quite effective. Asymmetry provides a useful approach to understanding their relationship, and the Sino-Vietnamese case provides a rich case study for a general theory of asymmetry.

It is beyond the scope of this book to provide a sweeping analysis of contemporary world politics, but the salience of asymmetry reaches far beyond the case of China and Vietnam and even beyond similar bilateral situations. The post–Cold War world of the lone superpower is a world of asymmetric, non-competitive relations, and in general international relations theory turns a blind eye to the problems of managing and sustaining such relations. The grand boxing match between the United States and the Soviet Union is over, and the key problem of international relations has shifted to the sustainability of leadership. Rather than speculating on the next challenger, international relations theory should attend to the problems of the sustainable leadership of the strong and the factors influencing the compliance of

---

[1] A recent exception is David Kang's theory of hierarchy, which like this work is also based on the East Asian model. See David Kang, "Getting Asia Wrong: The Need for New Analytic Frameworks," *International Security* 27:4 (Spring 2003), pp. 57–85; "Hierarchy, Balancing, and Empirical Puzzles in Asian International Relations," *International Security* 28:3 (Winter 2004), pp. 165–80.

the weak. We live now in a world not of competitive great powers, nor one of master and slaves, but in a world of asymmetry.

The book is intended to be a contribution to the general theory of international relations as well as to the understanding of China and Vietnam, but I give greater priority to "the case" rather than to the theory. This is a deliberate methodological decision. As John Gerring has argued, case studies are especially appropriate when exploring new causal mechanisms.[2] I would argue more broadly that the "case" is the reality to which the theory is secondary. In international relations theory, "realism" is often contrasted to "idealism," but surely a more basic and appropriate meaning of "realism" is to give priority to reality rather than to theory. The philosopher Alfred North Whitehead defined the Fallacy of Misplaced Concreteness as "neglecting the degree of abstraction involved when an actual entity is considered merely so far as it exemplifies certain categories of thought."[3] In effect, the concept is taken as the concrete reality, and actual reality is reduced to a mere appendage of data. Misplaced Concreteness may well be the cardinal sin of modern social science. It is certainly pandemic in international relations theory, where a serious consideration of the complexities of real political situations is often dismissed as mere "area studies." Like the Greek god Anteus who was sustained by touching his Mother Earth, theory is challenged and rejuvenated by planting its feet in thick reality.

I have decided to attempt a comprehensive analysis of interactions between China and Vietnam rather than a narrower analysis of foreign relations for two reasons. First, the most appropriate method for a new approach to a topic is to include all relevant phenomena. It might be more convenient to limit the scope of study, but a limited scope would assume the irrelevance of factors beyond its domain of attention. Second, although questions of war and peace provide the strongest illustration of asymmetric relations, asymmetry affects the full range of external activities. Its influence can be seen in border trade, national development policy, ideology, and so forth. Attention to a broad spectrum of relationships, especially in the current period of normalization, will facilitate both a well-rounded view of the effects of asymmetry and also a better understanding of methods of managing asymmetric relations.

The greatest challenge of a comprehensive analysis is brevity. It is difficult to write less than one knows about a subject, and it is a high art to present a broad and complex reality in as few words as possible. Inevitably simplification occurs, and I acknowledge in advance to the experts reading this book that topics of considerable richness and controversy are reduced to a few sentences. This may be particularly problematic in the chapters dealing with

---

[2] John Gerring, "What Is a Case Study and What Is it Good For?" *American Political Science Review* 98:2 (May 2004), pp. 341–54.
[3] Alfred North Whitehead, *Process and Reality* (New York: Harper, 1929), p. 11.

history. But I would also like to present a challenge to the experts. It is easy to correct simplifications by expanding the text and the research. A more interesting question might be, what would be a better simplification? To the extent that scholarship has a broader audience than the scholars themselves, simplification is a necessary and honorable task. Moreover, brevity sharpens basic issues and judgments, and scholarly progress can be made even if further research and more sophisticated articulations are required. The texture of life and of history is infinitely fine and complex, but it does not preclude the possibility of discerning shapes and patterns in its fabric.

This book has been written with audiences in Vietnam and China in mind as well as audiences in third countries. It inevitably differs from official interpretations of the relationship in each country, and it is written from the point of view of an observer in a third country. However, the ideas embodied in this book occurred to me as I interacted with friends and institutions in both China and Vietnam, and my intent is to be respectful of the interests, intelligence, and dignity of all concerned. Available resources and my language competencies have restricted my research materials to Western language materials (English, German, and French) supplemented by Chinese and Vietnamese materials. I am sure that this has led to obvious mistakes and oversights from the point of view of Chinese and Vietnamese specialists, and I apologize and request their criticisms and corrections. This book is my attempt to learn from my current experience of China and Vietnam as well as from the lessons of the past.

The Book in Brief

The book has a general overview, two major parts, and a conclusion, subdivided into a total of eleven chapters. The underlying reason for its structure is that it is first necessary to consider the general conditions affecting the relationship before analyzing its development over time. It concludes with reflections on the variations in the relationship and the implications of these for the deep structure of asymmetry.

Chapter 1 introduces the relative situations of China and Vietnam, asymmetry theory, and the variety of relationships that China and Vietnam have held in their long history. It is a microcosm of the book. Chapters 2, 3, and 4 comprise the first of the book's two major parts, "Basic Structure," which considers the preconditions to understanding the Sino-Vietnamese relationship. Chapter 2 presents the basic parameters of China's external posture. It argues that there are five parameters – size, centricity, sufficiency of natural resources, the challenge of renewable resources, and history – that set a durable context for all of China's external relations, including its relations with Vietnam. Each of these parameters occurs to greater and lesser extents in other countries as well, but together they give China a unique and self-centered vantage point in external relations. Chapter 3 addresses the parameters of Vietnam's external posture. In contrast to China, Vietnam has never considered itself to be the center of its world, a basic fact that gives its external relations a quite different cast. Vietnam's parameters are geography, an identity that combines both nationalism and cosmopolitanism, resource imbalance, the challenge of integration and diversity, and history.

The preceding pair of chapters sets the stage for the analysis of an asymmetric relationship, but before the specifics of the Sino-Vietnamese relationship are explored it is worthwhile to consider in Chapter 4 the general structural characteristics of asymmetry. Asymmetric relationships must be analyzed in terms of their two sub-relations, that of the stronger to the weaker and that of the weaker to the stronger. The position of the stronger is influenced by the fact that the relationship is less important to itself, and therefore it is less attentive. The weaker side is vulnerable to the greater capacity of the stronger side, and therefore it is more attentive. Characteristic patterns of misperception can develop in which the stronger side makes errors of inattention while the weaker makes errors of overattention, and these misperceptions can amplify one another into a crisis. Asymmetric relationships can be successfully managed, however. The two fundamental techniques are to remove issues from contention by neutralizing them and to control the vicious circle of misperceptions by relying on the common sense of an established relationship and by using diplomatic ritual to acknowledge mutual respect and mutual benefit in the relationship. Meanwhile the tensions inherent in the bilateral relationship can be buffered and reframed by being part of a larger pattern of multilateral relations.

The six chapters of the book's second part, "The Relational Dynamic," present the history of Sino-Vietnamese relations from the beginning to the present. Each chapter combines the narration of a phase of the relationship with reflections on the asymmetric structure of that phase. Chapter 5 begins with the emergence of a sinitic zone of culture and conflict before the establishment of imperial China with the Qin Dynasty in 221 BC. At this time China was not yet China, and Vietnam was not yet Vietnam, and yet the scale of what was emerging in Chinese territory affected what became Vietnam. Vietnam was drawn into northern-oriented zones of influence and eventually became part of China during the Han Dynasty. Vietnam remained part of China for the next thousand years, but its own sense of identity emerged in conflict with consolidation. On the one hand, many fundamental aspects of Vietnam's social and material culture were set during this time. On the other, the memories of resistance to Chinese control and the emergence of local leaders led to Vietnam's independence in AD 968. Chapter 5 concludes with a discussion of two types of asymmetric relations, amorphous asymmetry and internal asymmetry, which are illustrated by the early history of China and Vietnam.

Chapter 6 covers the relations between China and Vietnam as unequal traditional empires, a period of nine centuries from 968 to encroachments by the West beginning with the Opium War in China in 1840. International relations between China and Vietnam began with the Song Dynasty's acknowledgment of Vietnamese autonomy, but there was considerable development in the identities of both parties as well as in the management of the relationship. The watershed of the relationship was the ultimately unsuccessful Ming occupation of Vietnam from 1407 to 1427, after which a stable coexistence was established in the framework of the tribute system. The role-based asymmetry of this era guaranteed the autonomy of Vietnam as well as Vietnam's deference to China, but did so in a patriarchal framework of inequality that limited the utility of the relationship. Role-based asymmetry provided a process for controlling a limited relationship, but it did not provide a venue for exploring and expanding mutually beneficial contacts.

The coming of the West in the modern era led to the collapse of both the Chinese and the Vietnamese empires and created crisis situations in both countries from which fraternal revolutionary movements eventually arose. Chapter 7 covers the period in which, for the first time since China was unified in 221 BC, Vietnam faced a greater threat than China, and China was not the center of its world. China and Vietnam shifted from an unequal face-to-face relationship to a shoulder-to-shoulder relationship of common threat and shared suffering. This situation of distracted asymmetry in the Sino-Vietnamese relationship was complemented by one of disjunctive asymmetry between both countries and the West.

Chapter 8 covers the period from the founding of the People's Republic of China in 1949 to the reunification of Vietnam in 1976. The relationship was driven by China's support for Vietnam's national liberation efforts, but it underwent a major change in the mid-1960s under the influence of the American war in Vietnam, the Sino-Soviet split, and China's internal turmoil during the Cultural Revolution. Because Vietnam was dependent on Chinese aid, the differences remained unarticulated. The major contrast between the dependent asymmetry of China and Vietnam and the dependence of the Saigon government on the United States was that China respected the autonomy of Vietnam's decision making whereas the United States subordinated the Saigon government to the requirements of its containment policy.

Chapter 9 treats the decline of the Sino-Vietnamese relationship from the 1970s to normalization in 1991. The response of both countries to the novel situation of victory in Indochina provides, unfortunately for them, an excellent illustration of the vicious circle of misperceptions in asymmetric relations. The situation was rendered more complex by the role of Cambodia, but the dynamic of misperception between Vietnam and the Khmer Rouge was also deeply affected by asymmetry. The second part of the chapter covers the happier story of the undermining of stalemate in the late 1980s and finally the emergence of normalization in 1990–91. Vietnam's daring diplomatic move in 1985 of announcing a unilateral withdrawal from Cambodia by 1990 shows the frustrations and eventual success of persistent and imaginative small country diplomacy in a hostile environment. In general, though, the period of hostile asymmetry provided a lesson in the consequences of the mismanagement of relations, a "teacher by negative example" that set the sober tone for normalization.

Chapter 10 covers the process of normalization from 1991 to 1999 and the era of relative calm that emerged from normalization. I call this the era of mature asymmetry because the acceptance of the necessity of a negotiated relationship is based on the frustrations of the preceding period of hostility. Normalization is not premised on friendship but rather on the mutual desire for peace and the real possibility of continued hostility. As confidence builds, the initial cold caution is gradually replaced by the attractive opportunities opened by peace. Eventually the weight of the relationship shifts from the defense by peaceful means of conflicting interests to the development of common interests, and the era of normalcy begins. Normalcy remains an asymmetric relationship, but it does not imply the subordination of the smaller to the larger state; rather, it signals the institutionalization of a pattern of management that is based on the autonomy of the smaller state and yet its deference to the capacities of the larger.

Chapter 11 begins by pulling together the variety of asymmetries experienced by China and Vietnam and generalizing them into a picture of possible variations, using the experiences of other states as well. Table 11.1, "Varieties of Sino-Vietnamese Asymmetry," pulls together all of the modalities experienced in the Sino-Vietnamese relationship and links them to analogous relationships elsewhere. The chapter then proceeds to questions of the deep structure of asymmetric relations and the roles of identity, context, and leadership in sustaining and changing relationships. Finally, we return to China and Vietnam and consider the possible challenges that normalcy there might face.

For the convenience of multilingual readers, the appendix provides a glossary of people, places, and important terms in English, Chinese characters and pinyin, and Vietnamese. Occasionally translations are provided in the text in the following format [pinyin, Chinese characters, Vietnamese]. The reason for these linguistic cross-references is that while Chinese and Vietnamese often share the same linguistic roots (and in traditional Vietnamese texts, most of the same characters), the pronunciation is sufficiently different to be confusing to readers with a stronger base in one language or the other. When Vietnamese names and words are used in the text and not as translations, diacritic marks are omitted because they are confusing to non-Vietnamese speakers, and in any case non-Vietnamese speakers would have little hope of pronouncing the words correctly. Similarly, polysyllabic Vietnamese words and names are run together (for example, Vietnam rather than Viet Nam), although in standard Vietnamese syllables are always separated.

I

General Overview

In November 1991 the General Secretary of the Vietnam Communist Party Do Muoi and Chairman of the Council of Ministers of Vietnam Vo Van Kiet visited Beijing at the invitation of Chinese Communist Party Secretary Jiang Zemin and Chinese Premier Li Peng, and a Joint Communiqué was signed on November 10 establishing normal relations between China and Vietnam, ending twelve years of hostility. In one sense this marked the re-establishment of relations, since China had been the first country to extend diplomatic recognition to Ho Chi Minh's government and had been its major supporter during its struggles against the French, the Saigon government, and the Americans. But neither China nor Vietnam viewed the normalization of 1991 as a return to the alliance of 1950–1975. Despite the fact that normalization concluded a decade of bitter hostility in which neither side had triumphed, admitted defeat, or apologized, the era of normalization was immediately accepted by the participants and by external observers as a robust and long-term relationship. Normalization was expected to be a new era of peaceful but not close relations, and from 1999 it has exceeded those expectations by moving from cautious normalization to more integrated normalcy. Why?

The shorter the question, the longer the answer. This book attempts to present a holistic view of China and Vietnam in their relationship, and this chapter is in part an introduction to the subject and in part a microcosm of the book. It will first of all attempt to capture the overall shape, complexities, and tensions of the two countries' attitudes toward one another. Then the contemporary disparity between them will be sketched, outlining the asymmetry of capacities between China and Vietnam. Next, the problems posed by "normal" asymmetry for contemporary international relations theory will be discussed. The chapter concludes with a narration of the major phases of the Sino-Vietnamese relationship, ending with the present era of normalcy.

Relational Attitudes: The Rock and the Giant

The relationship of China and Vietnam is not one relationship but two: the relationship of China to Vietnam and the relationship of Vietnam to China. These two sub-relationships are not simply the same game viewed from the perspective of one or the other player. Each player is playing a different game. Each player interprets the behavior of the other in terms of its own game. As a result each player is often surprised by the actions of the other, and each has a critical opinion of the other. However, since 1999 both sides have been confident that a stronger relationship is advantageous.

For China, Vietnam has been the southern boundary stone of its grand notions of itself. In periods of hostility China has kicked this rock and found it hard and difficult to move. Again and again the power of China has broken on the rock of Vietnam, and although Vietnam has suffered more from these encounters than China has, China has found it necessary to withdraw and thus to acknowledge that China was smaller than it had hoped to be. In times of peace, China accepts the limits that the existence of Vietnam imposes on its sense of regional importance and enjoys the relatively minor advantages of a mutually beneficial relationship. But in neither war nor peace does China regard Vietnam as an equal.

Vietnam does not normally intrude on China's consciousness as either a major threat or a major opportunity. Vietnam achieves major importance in China's eyes only when it appears to be linked to global forces such as imperialism, world revolution, or Soviet "social imperialism." But when China treats Vietnam as an icon or a proxy of these global forces it tends to be frustrated by the outcome. So Vietnam remains a minor mystery to China, one that is often explained privately by references to the duplicity and inconstancy of the Vietnamese character. The Chinese have said of Vietnam that "anyone with milk is her mother."

Vietnam views China as the inscrutable northern giant. Even at peace the giant is feared because the fateful decision of war or peace is largely in the giant's hand. Flushed with victory and allied with the Soviet Union, Vietnam cast off its wartime deference to China in the late 1970s, and it suffered grievously in consequence. With such a neighbor, Vietnam is caught in a standing dilemma. It needs peace with China more than China needs peace with it, but if it allows China to push it around, to move the boundary stone, its loses its national substance and autonomy. Thus Vietnam tends to desire peace and yet to be fearful of uncontrolled contact, and to be allergic to any gesture on China's part that impugns Vietnam's sovereignty.

Vietnam's estimate of China is complex. On the one hand, corresponding to Vietnam's high level of concern and suspiciousness about Chinese behavior, China is viewed as almost diabolically clever in manipulating and pushing Vietnam. On the other hand, China is derided as a global force.[1] Vietnam would rather model its stock markets after New York or Tokyo than after Shanghai or Shenzhen. The existence of a world more attractive and more powerful than China, one in which China is itself a small player, is important to Vietnam's general sense of security. Peace with China offers a favorable environment for Vietnam's development and some opportunities for trade, but Vietnam tends to downplay the salience of China in its future even though they both pursue similar development strategies.

Of course, these sketches are only caricatures of views common in both countries; different people have different opinions, and views change over time. But such views of the other country are not the result of isolation, ignorance, or mistakes. It is certainly not the case that one side is right and the other is wrong, although this is the implicit assumption made by each side. The perspectives are each founded in basic facts: Vietnam is not China's equal, and China is threatening to Vietnam whether or not it intends to be. Nevertheless, there is something dysfunctional here. Regardless of how much their interests coincide or differ, these two perspectives will tend to cause the misinterpretation by each country of the other's actions and intentions, adding to friction in peaceful times and increasing the possibility of confrontation that neither side desires. The divergent perspectives are part of the reality of an asymmetric relationship.

The other reality of the relationship is that despite the disparities of capacities and resulting differences of perspective, neither side can eliminate the other. China's greater power does not imply that it can control Vietnam, as it discovered most recently during the hostilities that lasted from 1979 to 1991. Likewise, there is no conceivable self-strengthening program or alliance that would make Vietnam the equal of China. Not only are China and Vietnam fated to coexist, but they have done so and will do so within an asymmetric relationship. Although Vietnam cannot do to China what China can do to Vietnam, their asymmetric relationship, like many similar relationships around the world, is remarkably stable.

China and Vietnam in Comparison

To the constant frustration of the Vietnamese, external observers are struck with the similarities of China and Vietnam. In general, there is no country more similar to China than Vietnam, and there is no country more similar to

---

[1] These Vietnamese fears and denigrations of China are often combined in interesting ways. For instance, on the occasion of Chinese President Jiang Zemin's visit to Hanoi in November 1994, the local press complained about the flood of Chinese goods in local markets hurting local production. But the reason China was selling these goods to Vietnam, according to the Vietnamese, was that superior Western goods now available in China were pushing China's own products out of their home markets. *Vietnam Investment Review* as reported in *South China Morning Post*, 21 November 1994.

Vietnam than China. In part the appearance of similarity is due to a shared sinitic civilization, but it has other important roots as well.

China and Vietnam are both countries with ancient roots and largely homogeneous populations. The ethnic Chinese [Han汉, Han] comprise 92 percent of the total population of China, and the ethnic Vietnamese [Jing京, Kinh] comprise 88 percent of the total population of Vietnam. In both countries the core cultural area was first located in the north, around the Yellow River in China and around the Red River in Vietnam, and both countries expanded toward the south, displacing, destroying, or absorbing other indigenous cultures. The ethnic minorities in both countries are generally located in the less densely populated peripheral areas, while the ethnic majorities are concentrated in the densely populated wet-rice areas and in the cities.[2] So the overwhelming population of the core areas (rural and urban) of both countries is homogeneous, while the largest concentrations of minorities tend to be in mountainous border areas. The core areas are overwhelmingly rural, but they have a high population density. For example, population density in Vietnam's Red River delta is as high as 1,152 people per square kilometer, while the national average is 231.[3] In China, the population density of Jiangsu Province, a major rice producer, is higher than that of Beijing Municipality.[4] Food production has long been a matter of central concern to both countries, although these concerns have been eased by increasing production and by the diversification of the rural economies.

In the domain of societal institutions and culture, China and Vietnam share a broadly similar and overlapping traditional heritage; also, both have been through protracted rural revolution, which makes their modern experiences more similar to one another than to any third country. Their similarities have continued to develop in post-revolutionary policy. In both revolution and reform China has served as the most important referent for Vietnamese politics. However, Vietnam's learning from China was always grounded in the effort to find appropriate policies for its own similar conditions. If China had figured out how to cope with a certain problem, it would be foolishly nationalistic for Vietnam to ignore or shun the Chinese solution simply because it was Chinese. Vietnam's habit of learning useful things from China has given it an alacrity in adapting to other foreign models and opportunities as well.

[2] The major exception is the ethnic Chinese [Hua ren 华人, Hoa] in Vietnam, who in 1989 comprised 1.5% of the total population but 11% in Ho Chi Minh City. See Vu Tu Lap and Christian Taillard, *An Atlas of Vietnam* (Paris: Reclus, 1994), pp. 110–17.
[3] Calculated from *Niên Giám Thống Kê 2001*[Viet Nam Statistical Yearbook 2001], (Hanoi: Statistical Publishing House, 2002).
[4] Of course, Beijing Municipality does include extensive surrounding areas. See Wang Guixin, "The Distribution of China's Population and Its Changes," in Peng Xizhe, ed., *The Changing Population of China* (Oxford: Blackwell, 2000), pp. 11–12.

There are also important similarities in the relationship of China and Vietnam to the rest of the world. Traditionally each considered itself the center of its regional civilization. China thought of itself as "All under heaven." Vietnam occasionally called itself the "Middle Kingdom," [Zhongguo 中国, Trung Quôc], though Vietnam was part of a larger galaxy of which China was the acknowledged center.[5] The imperial self-respect of both was destroyed in the nineteenth century by the military power of modern Western imperialism, and the progressive and radical movements that emerged in the twentieth century were broadly similar in their targets, ideologies, and methods. After the defeat of Japan, both saw their revolutionary movements as events of world significance, and their victories as decisive steps in the defeat of imperialism and the progress of socialism. Increasingly disillusioned by socialist economic development, both launched bold new strategies of market-oriented development and international openness.

While the similarities between China and Vietnam concern situation, culture, history, and institutional forms, the differences lie primarily in scale. Table 1.1 provides some basis for appreciating the disparity between the two countries. Clearly China is not only much larger in population and territory, but it is considerably more advanced economically and its state structure is more solidly based. All these differences together create a contextual disparity in which even similar policies can have different effects, and the situation of asymmetry is the chief defining characteristic of the bilateral relationship.

Vietnam has only one-seventeenth the population of China, and its territory is one-twenty-ninth as large. There is a similar disparity in the ratio of rural population to arable land, though both countries have high ratios. The United States has only 36 rural residents per square kilometer of arable land, 6 percent of China's ratio and 3 percent of Vietnam's, while Japan has a ratio of 603, somewhat smaller than China's. However, Vietnam began to get control of rapid population growth only in the 1990s, whereas China brought its birthrate down in the early 1970s and decreased it further in the late 1970s. China's current dividend is a smaller juvenile population and a larger percentage of workers. In China, 27 percent of the population is below the age of fifteen, while in Vietnam the comparable figure is 40 percent.[6] This means that Guangdong Province, for instance, has four million fewer people than Vietnam, but three million more workers (not counting thousands of migrants from other provinces). Of course, China's large working-age population is only a temporary advantage. As the generations proceed, China's

---

[5] The classic portrayal of Vietnam's attitude toward China in the early nineteenth century is Alexander Woodside, *Vietnam and the Chinese Model: A Comparative Study of Vietnamese and Chinese Government in the First Half of the Nineteenth Century* (Cambridge: Harvard University Press, 1971).

[6] The average for developing countries is 36%, while for developed countries it is 22%. The United States is 22%. See Li Yongping and Peng Xizhe, "Age and Sex Structures," in Peng Xizhe, ed., *The Changing Population of China*, p. 67.

TABLE 1.1. *China and Vietnam: Some comparative data**

	Vietnam		China		Guangdong**	
	aggregate	per capita	aggregate	per capita	aggregate	per capita
Demographics						
Population (million)	80		1272		77.8	
Vietnam as % of	100		6		105	
Area (thousand square kilometers)	332	244/k²	9600	136/k²	178	408k²
Vietnam as % of	100		3.4			
Arable land (million hactares)	9.35		1240			
Rural population density	1037/k²	arable land	653/k²	arable land		
Dependency ratio 2002		59		44		
Adult literacy	92.7		85.8			
Life expectancy		68.6		70.6		
Infant mortality (per 1000)		31		30		
Production						(1999)
Grain production (million tons)	34.1	426 kg	452.6	356 kg	19.7	271 kg
Electric power (billion kilowatt hours)	23.6	295 kwh	1481	1164 kwh	110	1519 kwh
Coal (million tons)	13	163 kg	1161	1159 kg	2	28 kg
Crude oil (million tons)	16.7	209 kg	164	129 kg	12.8	177 kg
Steel (million tons)	1.91	24 kg	152	119 kg	3.0	42 kg
Cement (million tons)	15.4	193 kg	661	520 kg	32.2	493 kg

(continued)

TABLE 1.1 (continued)

	Vietnam		China		Guangdong**	
	aggregate	per capita	aggregate	per capita	aggregate	per capita
Economics						
Gross Natl Income (billion US$)	32.8	$410	1131	$890	128.6	$1634
Vietnam as % of 100	100%	2.9	46%	26%	25%	
Annual growth rate, 91–01	10.0%		7.7%			
Purchasing power per capita		$2070		$3950		
Vietnam as % of 100		100%		52.4%		
State Budget, (billion US$), 2000						
income	6.41	$80	162	$127		
expend	7.69	$96	192	$151		
Difference as % of income		−20.1%		−18.6%		
Foreign Trade						
Exports (US$ billion)	15.0	$188	266.2	$209	95.8	$1231
Imports (US$ billion)	16.2	$202	243.6	$198	84.2	$1082
% trade surplus/deficit	−3.8%		4.4%		6.4%	

* 2001, unless otherwise indicated.
** Guangdong Province is included because it is a southern Chinese province with roughly the same population as Vietnam. However, in the 1990s Guangdong became one of China's five richest provinces largely as a result of investment and trade with neighboring Hong Kong.
Sources: Calculated from various sources, including *Human Development Report 2003*; *World Development Report 2003*; *Zhongguo Tongji Nianjian 2002*, *Nien Giam Thong Ke 2001*. When necessary, currencies were converted at 1US$ = 8.28 RMB = 14,168 dong (for 2000).

retired population will rise rapidly, doubling its current percentage by 2025, and retired dependents require twice as much in social services as the young.[7] Both China and Vietnam have performed comparably (and quite respectably) in basic services, as indicated by literacy rate, life expectancy, and infant mortality. Both compare favorably with non-communist countries at similar economic levels. However, the introduction of market reforms has led to a reduction of state capacity, and basic welfare services in both countries have suffered. In Vietnam, the number of hospital beds per capita dropped by more than half from 1980 to 2000.[8] On the other hand, both China and Vietnam have seen vast reductions in poverty since adopting market reforms.

Looking at production, it is clear from the quantities listed that China's massive superiority in population and area is reflected in all areas of the economy. Moreover, with the exception of grain production, China is well ahead of Vietnam in per capita production as well. Vietnam produces only 1.9 percent as much electricity as China, and only one-fifth as much per capita as Guangdong. On the other hand, Vietnam produces more grain, coal, and crude oil than Guangdong. This discrepancy highlights China's advantage of scale. While Vietnam might do better in some areas than even a rich Chinese province of similar size, it cannot compete with China as a whole because the best producers within China will raise the national average.

Of course, China has experienced the most rapid economic growth in the world during the past twenty years, so it is worth considering how Vietnam's current per capita production compares with China's production in the past. In grain, Vietnam pulled up to China's level of per capita production in 1995 and then decisively surpassed it in 1999. China achieved Vietnam's 1999 level of per capita production of coal in 1954, cement in 1985, electricity in 1981, and steel in 1970.[9] Even in these areas in which Vietnam lags behind, it made considerable progress in the 1990s. For the foreseeable future, however, the general material strength of Vietnam in comparison to China will be considerably smaller than its 6 percent of population size.

I have somewhat lamely labeled the last category of data "economics" to alert the reader that the figures are not material output, as in the "production" category, and so they are subject to the additional vagaries of price and currency conversion. China in 2001 had the sixth-largest economy in the world, and Vietnam had the fifty-eighth largest.[10] Guangdong's economy is roughly the same size as that of Poland and somewhat larger than

[7] Du Peng and Tu Ping, "Population Aging and Old Age Security," in Peng Xizhe, ed., *The Changing Population of China*, pp. 77–90.
[8] World Bank, *World Development Report 2001* (New York: Oxford University Press, 2001), p. 98.
[9] Chinese figures from *Zhongguo Tongji Nianjian 1993* [Statistical Yearbook of China] (Beijing: China Statistical Press, 1993), p. 30.
[10] World Bank, *World Development Report 2003* (New York: Oxford University Press, 2003).

that of Thailand. The Gross National Income (equivalent to Gross Domestic Product [GDP], the final market value of domestic production) of China is roughly twice the per capita figure for Vietnam, while Guangdong has almost twice the Chinese national figure. Guangdong's figure shows how rapidly economies can grow, since it was below the national average in 1980. But Vietnam is unlikely to gain on China in GDP per capita in the foreseeable future because China's current and projected rate of growth is faster, as is the amount and rate of growth of foreign investment. The actual purchasing power of the GDPs of China and Vietnam is about four times higher than their nominal GDP per capita because, as any American visitor knows, a dollar buys much more in China or Vietnam than it does in the United States. In terms of purchasing power parity China was the second largest economy in the world in 2001, and Vietnam the forty-first largest.[11] However, both China and Vietnam are in roughly the same situation with regard to purchasing power parity, so it does not affect their relative positions.

The figures on the state budget show that China's revenue and expenditures per capita are in line with its GDP advantage. Moreover, the level of deficit suggests what a longer series of data would confirm, namely, that Vietnam has run chronic and severe state deficits, made up in the past by foreign aid and inflation, while China has been less afflicted with red ink.

The figures on foreign trade show that China and Vietnam are in the same league in per capita terms, which means that Vietnam's foreign trade is roughly 6 percent of China's. Of course, there is a striking contrast between Guangdong and both national figures, since Guangdong has been favored by special policies encouraging foreign trade and investment since 1979 and works closely with Hong Kong. Guangdong's foreign trade per capita is almost six times that of China and Vietnam, and it provides over one-third of China's exports.

The comparative data just presented provide a necessary preface to the discussion of the asymmetric relationship between China and Vietnam, but they do not tell the whole story. First, the differences in scale between the two influence each country's general attitude toward the outside world. This question of general posture is addressed in detail in the following two chapters. Here we will just note that China has the self-referenced, centric attitude of a large country toward all its neighbors and assumes that it is on at least equal terms with the world's great powers and with historic trends. Moreover, China's advantages of scale are enhanced by the presence of Hong Kong, providing a front porch to the world market. Because it is located next to China, Vietnam has always been alert to the dangers and opportunities of the external world, making it both more overtly nationalistic and more cosmopolitan than China. But beyond its relationship to China, Vietnam's

[11] Central Intelligence Agency, *The World Factbook 2003*, http://www.odci.gov/cia/publications/factbook/rankorder/2001rank.html

middle-sized demographic scale and low level of development mean that isolation from other countries, which occurred from 1979 to 1990, is far more problematic than it would be for China. Vietnam is both more vulnerable and more dependent on the rest of the world than is China.

Second, the disparity in scale between the two leads to an asymmetric bilateral relationship. Whether the relationship is friendly, hostile, or normal, it is not one between equals, even when both are sovereign states. Of course, Vietnam is hardly unique. Before the arrival of Western colonialism most other Asian countries had similarly asymmetric relations with China, and the general pattern of Asian international relations was based on a patriarchal model of unequal relations. That model was destroyed ideologically as well as militarily by the coming of the West, but the situation of asymmetry persists and has been strengthened in the past two decades by China's internationalization and economic growth.

Asymmetry and International Relations Theory

Although the major focus of this book is the relationship between China and Vietnam, it is also an exploration of the significance of relative power in international relations. The analytic approach of asymmetry theory is fundamentally different from contemporary international relations theory in the West, and especially in the United States.[12] Of course, no one has failed to notice that some countries are more powerful than others. But in general, attention has concentrated on asymmetry as a disequilibrium rather than as a sustained condition.

The two basic theses of asymmetry theory are, first, that disparities in capacities create systemic differences in interests and perceptions between the stronger and weaker sides of the relationship. An asymmetric relationship is not composed of two similar actors who happen to have a difference

---

[12] The most comprehensive article presenting asymmetry theory is Brantly Womack, "Asymmetry and Systemic Misperception: The Cases of China, Vietnam and Cambodia during the 1970s," *Journal of Strategic Studies* 26:2 (June 2003), pp. 91–118. Much of its argument is incorporated into Chapters 4 and 9 of this book. Other articles by Womack exploring various aspects of asymmetry include "How Size Matters: The United States, China and Asymmetry," *The Journal of Strategic Studies* 24:4 (December 2001), pp. 123–50; "China and Southeast Asia: Asymmetry, Leadership and Normalcy," *Pacific Affairs* 76:4 (Winter 2003–4), pp. 529–48; "Asymmetry Theory and China's Concept of Multipolarity," *Journal of Contemporary China* 13:39 (May 2004), pp. 351–66; "The United States, Human Rights, and Moral Autonomy in the Post–Cold War World," in Robert Fatton and Ruhi Ramazani, eds., *The Future of Liberal Democracy: Thomas Jefferson and the Contemporary World* (London: Palgrave, 2004), pp. 255–70; "Ke chixu de guoji lingdao quan: lai zi 968–1885 nian Zhong Yue guanxi de jingyan jiaoxun" 可持续的国际领导权: 来自持 968–1885 年中越关系的经验教训," [Sustainable International Leadership: Lessons from the Sino-Vietnamese Relationship, 968–1885], *Shixue Jikan* [史学季刊], [Collected papers of history studies], pp. 3–14.

in capacities. Rather, mutual perceptions and interactions in an asymmetric relationship will be fundamentally shaped by the different situation of opportunity and vulnerability that each side confronts. In effect, the relationship of A and B is best viewed as a set of two very different sub-relations, A⇒B, and B⇒A. The differences between the two perspectives are developed in Chapter 4.

Second, although asymmetric relations are rarely unproblematic, they tend to be robust. "Stability" might not be the right word to describe asymmetry, because the differences in interests and perceptions between A and B are a constant source of tensions. However, in most cases the basic disparity of capacities between the two is unlikely to change, and the stronger power is unlikely to be able to eliminate the weaker power.[13] Despite all the variations in the Sino-Vietnamese relationship that are analyzed in Chapters 5–10 and that are summarized in Chapter 11, China was not able to "solve" its Vietnam problem, and Vietnam was unable to "solve" its China problem. The failure of China's twenty-year occupation of Vietnam in the Ming Dynasty was proof that Vietnam could not be eliminated or subdued. The learning process in an asymmetric relationship involves the acceptance of the relationship as normal. Asymmetric normalcy remains asymmetric, but both sides manage their affairs with the confidence that the power of the larger side will not be challenged and the autonomy of the smaller side will not be threatened.

Asymmetry theory does not fit easily into the normal categories of contemporary international relations theory, though it has elements in common with each of them. Like classical realist theory, it assumes that capacities matter and that states attempt to maximize their interests.[14] Like neo-realism, it is a structural theory of international relations, although here the structure is a mid-range one composed of bilateral relational patterns rather than the configuration of a whole system.[15] Its concentration on the problems caused by disparities between units is similar to "democratic peace" theories arguing that states with similar forms of government are less likely to go to war,[16] and its emphasis on the different perspectives of stronger and weaker states is analogous to the reshaping of weaker states described by dependency theory. Like hegemonic theories, asymmetry theory emphasizes relational structures

---

[13] It certainly happens that relative strength can change (for example, China and Japan since 1850), and that weaker powers can be eliminated (for example, native American tribes in the United States). It is also the case that China and Vietnam are a remarkably long-standing instance of an asymmetric relationship. However, there are many other such relationships in the world.

[14] See Hans Morgenthau, *Politics among Nations*, 5th ed. (New York: Knopf, 1973).

[15] See Kenneth Waltz, *Man, the State, and War: A Theoretical Analysis* (New York: Columbia University Press, 1959); also *Theory of International Politics* (Reading, MA: Addison-Wesley, 1979); John Mearsheimer, *The Tragedy of Great Power Politics* (New York: Norton, 2001).

[16] See John Owen, *Liberal Peace, Liberal War* (Ithaca: Cornell University Press, 1997).

based on disparities of power,[17] and like interdependence theory it expects mature relations to be peaceful.[18] Asymmetry theory is similar to idealist and constitutional international relations theories in that all assert that there are significant choices in diplomacy and that self-restraint on the part of the powerful is prudent.[19] It is similar to constructivist theories in its stress on perception and interaction.[20] It is similar to the English School of international relations in its attention to the historical development and specific content of relationships.[21]

Despite such similarities, asymmetry theory is not a syncretic sampling of what appears attractive from each of the other theories, but rather a reinterpretation of international relations from a fundamentally different starting point. All the theories mentioned earlier interpret asymmetry as an imbalance of capacities and power, a disequilibrium that creates either subordination or a competition for domination. To take the most obvious case, neo-realism assumes that all states are driven by the security dilemma to seek a predominance of power over other states, and that states too weak to compete for ultimate power will either balance against the more threatening great power or bandwagon with it.[22] Therefore neo-realism concentrates on the competition of the great powers, and the system of international relations is defined by the number of great powers in competition.[23] It would be, in the typically pithy words of Kenneth Waltz, "ridiculous to construct a theory of international politics based on Malaysia and Costa Rica.... A general theory of international politics is necessarily based on the great powers."[24] Even theories that are radically critical of hegemonism, such as Lenin's theory of imperialism or Immanuel Wallerstein's theory of world systems, are based on the assumption that asymmetry is an unnatural, unstable, and/or immoral condition.[25] Theories of international leadership, of world government, and

---

[17] See Charles Kindleberger, *The World in Depression, 1929–1939* (Berkeley: University of California Press, 1973).

[18] See Robert Keohane, *After Hegemony: Cooperation and Discord in the World Political Economy* (Princeton: Princeton University Press, 1984).

[19] See Reinhold Niebuhr, *The Irony of American History* (New York: Scribners, 1962); John Ikenberry, *After Victory: Institutions, Strategic Restraint, and the Rebuilding of Order after Major Wars* (Princeton: Princeton University Press, 2001).

[20] See Alexander Wendt, *Social Theory of International Politics* (Cambridge: Cambridge University Press, 1999).

[21] See Barry Buzan and Richard Little, *International Systems in World History: Remaking the Study of International Relations* (Oxford: Oxford University Press, 2000).

[22] The "security dilemma" is the problem that all states desire security, but a state is secure only if it is strong enough to prevail over all others, thereby rendering all other states insecure.

[23] The "great powers" are the set of states capable of challenging one another's preponderance of power.

[24] Waltz, *Theory*, p. 73.

[25] V. I. Lenin, *Imperialism, The Highest Stage of Capitalism* (1916); Immanuel Wallerstein, *The Modern World System* (New York: Academic Press, 1974).

of the self-restraint of the hegemon come closest to accepting asymmetry as normal, but these approaches are based on the preservation of a world order that happens to be asymmetric rather than on an analysis of the structure of asymmetry.

Likewise, states in an asymmetric relationship are usually viewed as similar actors, plus or minus the disparity in capacities, rather than as actors whose interests and perceptions are shaped by their relative positions. Like card players who might be dealt a good hand at one time and a bad hand at another, it is assumed that the interests and perceptions of states are indifferent to their relative positions, and that misperceptions result from individual mistakes rather than from relational structures. Even theories that deconstruct the state actor or pay special attention to ideology and values tend to do so without regard to the disparities in specific relationships. In the real world, however, states must bloom where they are planted. Stronger states will tend to be less engaged in a particular asymmetric relationship, and their mishandlings will tend to result from inattention and bullying. Weaker states are more at risk and therefore more attentive, but they are prone to paranoia. The realities of differences in capacities are reflected in real differences of perspective and role.

Another major difference between asymmetry theory and most other theories of international relations is that asymmetry theory does not assume that relative power implies control. Most security theories concentrate on victory in war, and it is almost tautological that the more powerful will win, and that only those who think they might have a chance at victory will challenge. Theories of economic hegemony are interested in a larger set of issues, but there is usually the presumption that the most powerful is in control.[26] If, however, the most powerful prevail, why are there so many weaker states still in existence, and why are the powerful so often frustrated? In reality, weaker states can persist, and often can frustrate attempts at subjugation by more powerful states, even if they could never defeat the more powerful state in a "fair fight." There is no better example in twentieth-century history than Vietnam, which frustrated the efforts of France, the United States, and finally China.

Of course, international relations theory has not been blind to a persisting, resilient world of power disparities. Neo-realism has generated more and more complex analyses of structure and interaction.[27] The problem of the limited reach of military power prompted Joseph Nye to coin the term *soft power* in 1990 and to remind the United States of its importance in

[26] David Lake, "Leadership, Hegemony and the International Economy," *International Studies Quarterly* 37 (1993), pp. 459–89.

[27] See, for example, Robert Powell, *In the Shadow of Power* (Princeton: Princeton University Press, 1999). Although Powell accepts what he terms the "stylization" of a Hobbesian anarchic world, his exploration of its dilemmas makes the outcomes more complex.

2004.[28] Annette Baker Fox explored the diplomatic power of five small states in World War Two,[29] and Peter Katzenstein demonstrated the elbow room available to small states in economic matters.[30] James Scott's seminal analysis of the "weapons of the weak" within Malaysian society has been broadly applied to international relations.[31] Typically, however, such efforts are viewed as puzzle solving on the periphery of a generally accepted paradigm of a world in which power prevails.

Why doesn't a preponderance of power translate into control, or even into the elimination of the weak? The answer supplied by the national images of such conflicts is that the heroism and cleverness of the weak defeats the venality, immorality, and clumsiness of the strong. These images are not without foundation, but such a skewed distribution of individual virtues and vices is best explained by the limited and partial interests that the more powerful side has in the conflict compared to the mortal and communal interests of the weaker side. Moreover, even when the strong are able to defeat the weak, as with the French colonization of Vietnam described in Chapter 7, the victor must face the costs of occupation, the necessity of managing local collaboration, and the possibility of new insurgency. Stalemate, in which neither side can secure its aims with available resources, is the most common end state of asymmetric conflicts. To move beyond stalemate, both sides must negotiate. Normalcy in an asymmetric relationship is negotiated; it is not simply dictated by the stronger side.

The virtue of self-restraint on the part of the powerful is thus grounded in the reality that more power does not necessarily mean control. Sustainable international leadership is not guaranteed by the preemption of rivals but rather by the creation of a matrix of unequal relationships, each of which acknowledges the autonomy of weaker states as well as the reality of power differences. The powerful require deference and the weak require autonomy, and while these demands are not incompatible, they are in a fragile relationship. Nevertheless, for most asymmetric relationships most of the time, managing and negotiating the relationship is preferable to hostility.

The international order that results from the bilateral dilemmas of asymmetry is a restless but fundamentally stable pattern of unequal relationships. The stronger states can do things that the weaker ones cannot, and the strong

---

[28] See Joseph Nye, *Bound to Lead* (New York: Basic Books, 1990); Nye, *Soft Power: The Means to Success in World Politics* (New York: Public Affairs, 2004).

[29] Annette Baker Fox, *The Power of Small States: Diplomacy in World War Two* (Chicago: University of Chicago Press, 1959).

[30] Peter Katzenstein, *Small States in World Markets: Industrial Policy in Europe* (Ithaca: Cornell University Press, 1985).

[31] James C. Scott, *Weapons of the Weak: Everyday Forms of Peasant Resistance* (New Haven: Yale University Press, 1985). For applications to international relations, see Stephen Gill and James Mittelman, eds., *Innovation and Transformation in International Studies* (New York: Cambridge University Press, 1997).

will hold central positions of attention and influence in their regions. In the post–Cold War world, the United States occupies the global center. But it is clear from the contemporary case of U.S. pressures on North Korea regarding its nuclear program that commanding attention is quite different from commanding compliance. Incentives will not be attractive unless the autonomy of the weaker side is secure, and sanctions may be counterproductive if they create a sense of mortal threat. Precisely because North Korea is vulnerable to the United States, its perception of the relationship will be fundamentally different, and its reactions will be dictated by its own perceptions rather than by American intentions.

The relationship of China and Southeast Asia since 1991 provides a more positive case of international leadership in a situation of asymmetry, and we will touch on this in Chapters 10 and 11.[32] In conjunction with normalizing relations with Vietnam, China also began to improve its ties to the Association of Southeast Asian Nations (ASEAN). In 2002 a China ASEAN Free Trade Area (CAFTA) was initiated, and in 2003 China and India became the first non-Southeast Asian nations to accede to the region's Treaty of Amity and Cooperation in Southeast Asia.[33] China has shown sensitivity to the feelings of vulnerability of Southeast Asian countries and has been able to create a closer relationship by acknowledging the autonomous interests of the region. Meanwhile Southeast Asia has behaved deferentially toward China, although not at the expense of its relations with the United States, Japan, and Europe. The region was careful in its criticisms of the People's Republic of China's (PRC) actions at Tiananmen in June 1989 and open to developing CAFTA as well as ASEAN plus 3 (China, Japan, South Korea).[34]

In general, the traditional patterns of international relations in East Asia were asymmetric, based on a patriarchal model of unequal roles in which the central power (most importantly China) claimed superiority and the rulers of other states were deferential, but the autonomy and legitimacy of the lesser states was also recognized. In modern times, the experience of colonialism and imperialism in Asia was certainly an asymmetric one, although Western imperialism did break the patriarchal mold of unequal relations. In the era of the Cold War, East Asia was distracted from its regional asymmetries by the

---

[32] See Womack, "China and Southeast Asia"; also Joseph Y. S. Cheng, "China's ASEAN Policy in the 1990s: Pushing for Regional Multipolarity," *Contemporary Southeast Asia* 21:2 (August 1999), pp. 176–202, and Cheng, "Sino-ASEAN Relations in the Early Twenty-First Century," *Contemporary Southeast Asia* 23:3 (December 2001), pp. 420–52.

[33] Alice Ba, "Sino-ASEAN Relations: The Significance of an ASEAN-China Free Trade Area," in T. J. Cheng, Jacques deLisle, and Deborah Brown, eds., *China under the Fourth Generation Leadership: Opportunities, Dangers, and Dilemmas* (Singapore: World Scientific Press, 2005).

[34] The role of regional deference in reshaping the China-Southeast Asia relationship is analyzed in Brantly Womack, "China's Southeast Asia Policy: A Success Story for the Third Generation," *Cross-Strait and International Affairs Quarterly* 1:1 (January 2004), pp. 161–84.

TABLE 1.2. *The general phases of the Sino-Vietnamese relationship*

			Chapter
1.	–221 BC	Pre-imperial	5
2.	111 BC–AD 968	Vietnam as part of China	5
3.	968–1885	Unequal empires	6
4.	1840–1949	Fellow victims of imperialism	7
5.	1949–73	Revolutionary brotherhood	8
6.	1978–90	Hostility	9
7.	1991–99	Normalization	10
8.	1999–	Normalcy	10

tensions of global competition. In the current era, Asian countries have been among the most adroit at adapting their patterns of interaction to the twin realities of protecting a diversity of national interests while recognizing the disparity of national capacities. ASEAN has been a model of regional consensus in both its internal and its external relations. China in the reform era and Japan since the Second World War have each made major contributions to both regional and global stability.

However, Asia's experiences and successes have had little effect on international relations theory, which remains rooted in the modern European experience of competitive nationalism.[35] This book is an attempt to articulate a major part of the Asian experience and thereby to enrich the global understanding of international relations. The purpose is not to establish Sino-Vietnamese relations, or those of Asia more generally, as exceptions to European rules. Rather, competitive nationalism itself should be seen in a larger framework of international relations, of which asymmetric relations are a major part. The course of relations between China and Vietnam vividly illustrates the difficulties, the robustness, and the variety of a general type of international relation that has largely escaped theoretical attention.

The Phases of the Sino-Vietnamese Relationship

The second part of the book (Chapters 5–10) will present in greater detail the historical dynamic of the relationship between China and Vietnam, but a sketch of the development of the relationship is also an essential part of an introductory overview (Table 1.2). Without considering the changes in the relationship over time, a structural overview tends to give a static and overly predictable portrait. The concluding chapter, Chapter 11, will return

---

[35] The challenge of integrating the experience of Asia into social sciences is eloquently presented by Suzanne Rudolph, "State Formation in Asia: Prolegomenon to a Comparative Study," *Journal of Asian Studies* 46:4 (November 1987), pp. 731–46.

to the general theme of variations in asymmetric relations and consider its implications for the future of the Sino-Vietnamese relationship.

Pre-imperial

In the beginning China and Vietnam did not exist as identifiable states, though both were locations of Stone and Bronze Age cultures. The deepest roots of what became Chinese civilization were in the area of the Yellow River in what is now northern China, a long way from Vietnam's place of origin in the delta of the Red River. During the disunity that characterized the Spring and Autumn (770–476 BC) and Warring States eras (475–221 BC), a broader cultural context emerged in China as independent states struggled with one another and also interacted in more positive ways. Vietnam, as the southernmost of the "Hundred Yue " [bai yue百越, Bach Viet], was in the outer orbit of this political-military arena with its own autonomous Bronze Age culture. For our purposes, it is important to note that neither country owed its original existence to the other, and they did not confront each other in a situation of primordial national consciousness. Vietnam was on the edge of the zone of military conflict and cultural interchange that was eventually transformed into the Chinese empire. It was also on the edge of Southeast Asian cultures that never were part of the pre-imperial Chinese arena.

Vietnam as Part of China

To use a term fashionable in the 1990s, China was *reinvented* in 221 BC by Qin Shi Huangdi (who named himself "Qin the First Sovereign Emperor"). Instead of simply conquering his neighboring (also Chinese) states, he integrated them into one polity. The power of political-military scale that this created led to a rapid conversion of a multi-state world into an empire, and Vietnam became the southern fringe of the empire. But the empire was least strong at its periphery. Vietnam was already settled, and the Chinese rulers and soldiers who moved there were absorbed into the local situation. There were rebellions whenever the imperial center became divided or confused. The greatest effort to integrate southern China and Vietnam into the heartland of China came in the Tang dynasty (618–907), and as the dynasty weakened, the most determined efforts emerged to establish an independent Vietnam. Annam, "Pacified South," was the name given by the Tang to Vietnam, and it turned out to be wishful thinking.

Unequal Empires

Vietnam's assertion of independence was by no means a rejection of things Chinese, though successive Chinese invasions and Vietnamese resistance had defined a national consciousness of heroic defensiveness. At the same time, the Vietnamese developed their trait of studying and adopting the useful, and the influence of China as a model of culture and politics increased. The Vietnamese empire [Da Yue大越, Dai Viet] not only was eventually modeled closely on the Chinese empire, but it was also deferential to Beijing's central position in the galaxy of East Asian politics. Even as it defended its autonomy it apologized to Beijing for the inconvenience caused by Vietnam's victories over invading Chinese armies. China did not willingly accept Vietnam as a southern boundary for its power, but even its twenty-year occupation of Vietnam (1407–1427) during the Ming dynasty proved impossible to maintain. From 1427 China accepted Vietnam as an independent tributary state rather than as a lost part of itself. Meanwhile, after Vietnam stopped China's southern advance it began its own advance to the south, destroying the kingdom of Champa in central Vietnam in 1471 and contending with Cambodian influences in the Mekong delta, establishing control in 1622. As Vietnam extended itself geographically, however, it became prey to internal dissension and regionalism. Vietnam showed renewed unity and vigor in the early nineteenth century, but the arrival of French imperialism at mid-century stopped Vietnam's expansion into Cambodia and Laos. Despite pleas to China for help and a creditable Chinese show of force against the French, Vietnam was defeated and colonized.

Fellow Victims of Imperialism

From the Opium War in 1840 to the founding of the People's Republic of China in 1949, China had much more urgent concerns than its southern boundary. The French occupied Danang in 1858, beginning a process of creeping control and consolidation that culminated in China's renunciation of suzerainty claims in 1885 and the establishment of the Indochinese Union in 1898, splitting Vietnam into three parts of the French colony. By 1911 China had collapsed – as an empire, as a domestic order, and as an autonomous civilization. Out of the total crisis emerged radical political currents with the common purpose of opposing imperialism and combating domestic warlordism. Even though China was not a colony, the presence of "treaty ports" [zu jie租界 tô giới] and its submission to a series of unequal treaties gave China common cause with Vietnamese anti-colonialism. Meanwhile, Vietnam could apply its culture of opposition to foreign domination to a new target, France, and the progressive forces in China became sympathetic partners in the struggle. Vietnam helped China, and China helped Vietnam, though each was so beset by its own problems that the aid was not decisive. More important, this was the first period since China had come into existence two thousand years earlier that the relationship between the two was distracted by a more urgent concern. A century of fellow suffering created the impression that China and Vietnam could have a friendly, intimate relationship that would not be threatening to Vietnam.

Revolutionary Brotherhood

With the founding of the People's Republic of China on October 1, 1949, the relationship between the Communist Parties of China and Vietnam remained intimate, but it shifted from one of fellow suffering to a stratified relationship in which the Chinese gave freely of their resources and expertise to their revolutionary brethren in Vietnam, and the Vietnamese expressed their deep gratitude for socialist internationalism. The two were "as close as lips and teeth." The direct intervention of the United States after the Gulf of Tonkin Incident in 1964 brought about even stronger support from China, but ironically it also contributed to an alienation between China and Vietnam. China's interest shifted from helping Vietnam to the war as a global symbol of class struggle. Moreover, the depredations of the Cultural Revolution, which were particularly terrible in the border province of Guangxi, shocked the Vietnamese, and China pressured Vietnam not to accept aid from the Soviet Union. Thus from the mid-1960s the relationship became as close as a scratchy sweater, but the pressure of the war with the United States did not allow a readjustment. The Shanghai Communiqué of 1972, which began the process of normalization between China and the United States, was an especially alienating action from the Vietnamese perspective, and the withdrawal of American troops from Vietnam in early 1973 ended the global threat to China from the Vietnam war even if it did not end the war itself.

Hostility

Victory in 1975 meant different things to China and to Vietnam. For Vietnam, victory meant reunification and the opportunity to set new courses in domestic and foreign policy. In domestic policy Vietnam defined an ambitious program of strengthening socialism in the north and pushing the south to catch up. Given the destruction of the war and Vietnam's habit of relying on foreign subsidies, the country counted on massive aid from China and the Soviet Union as well as on the $4.7 billion in reparations promised from the United States by Richard Nixon. In foreign policy, Vietnam attempted to redefine its international relations from the standpoint of independence and enhanced prestige. China, by contrast, saw the end of the war as an end to the priority that Vietnam had held in Chinese foreign affairs. China expected Vietnam to act as a grateful client and to reduce its ties to the Soviet Union, but without much additional investment on China's part.

As the conflict between these very different ideas of victory became more evident, both countries began to define the other as an antagonist, and each assumed that it could be victorious again. China hoped to prevent a Vietnamese regional bloc by supporting the anti-Vietnamese Khmer Rouge in Cambodia, and Vietnam's status as a problem rose again as Vietnam strengthened its ties to the Soviet Union. Vietnam's mistreatment of its ethnic Chinese was taken as a bilateral issue, and the resulting high-publicity, confrontational diplomacy in 1978 was symbolic of the intransigence of both sides. Vietnam's confidence that with Soviet support, it could prosper as China's enemy was as mistaken as China's assumption that if Vietnam could not be bent to its will, it could be broken. Each side paid dearly for its illusions of victory in the brief war of 1979 and the long period of hostile stalemate during the 1980s.

Although neither side profits from a hostile stalemate, its deprivations are felt more acutely by the smaller side. Hence it is not surprising that Vietnam began its attempts to resolve the Cambodian crisis in 1985, while China did not rethink its position until 1990. Vietnam's declaration of a unilateral withdrawal from Cambodia by 1990 was not taken seriously at first, but after Prince Sihanouk began negotiations with Hun Sen in 1987 a process of endgame was set in motion in Southeast Asia that eventually drew in the United States and China. China and Vietnam came to an agreement in principle for normalization at a secret summit in Chengdu in September 1990 and formalized normalization in November 1991.

Normalization

Normalization is a transition from hostility to a negotiated relationship based on mutual acceptance. Although it involves a "moment" of normalization, in this case November 1991, the distance between war and peace cannot be covered in an instant. The entire period of normalization is characterized by the lessening shadow of war and increasing involvement in trade and in other activities that require the cooperation of both sides. The chief concern in the process of normalization was to prevent continuing differences of interests from causing a reversion to hostility. The initial stiffness of normalization reflected not only the residual coldness and resentment produced by recent hostility but also the desire on both sides to avoid mistakes. Neither side desired continued conflict, but at the same time neither side wanted to surrender in peace the interests that it had fought for so recently. The solid foundation of normal relations was the realization, proven through bitter experiment, that neither country could simply prevail over the interests of the other.

The phase of Sino-Vietnamese normalization extended from formal recognition in 1991 to the adoption of a "16 Word Guideline" for the relationship in 1999. In economics it was characterized by the mushrooming of border trade and the cautious development of more formal trade and investment relations. In diplomacy, neither side opposed or interfered with vital interests of the other side. Although Taiwan has been a major investor and trading partner, Vietnam did not toy with President Lee Teng-hui's "pragmatic diplomacy" and "vacation diplomacy" in the 1990s, as Indonesia and the Philippines did. Vietnam did not show alarm during the Taiwan Straits crisis of 1995–96 and it supported the reversion of Hong Kong in 1997. Likewise, China did not oppose, formally or informally, the admission of Vietnam to the Association of Southeast Asian Nations (ASEAN) in July 1995, and it supported the normalization of relations between Vietnam and the United States in the same month. Both countries supported arrangements sponsored by the United Nations (UN) in Cambodia, and both have supported the post-1991 Cambodian government. Both have supported one another's applications for entry into the World Trade Organization (WTO). Nevertheless, public conflicts continued in the 1990s, especially concerning conflicting claims in the South China Sea.

Besides strengthening the relationship through cooperation and noninterference, the developments just discussed strengthened Sino-Vietnamese normalization indirectly by embedding it in a thicker regional and world context of regulated and multilateral interactions. The most important event in the regionalization of Sino-Vietnamese relations was the Asian financial crisis of 1997–98. Although Vietnam did not suffer as acutely as its neighbors, as a new member of ASEAN it could share in the region's deep appreciation for China's decision to support the Hong Kong dollar and not revalue its currency the renminbi. China's conduct during the Asian financial crisis strengthened its prestige throughout the region as well as its credibility as a reliable economic partner, and the change in China's regional reputation facilitated progress in its relations with Vietnam.

Normalcy

A relationship is normal when both sides are confident that their basic interests will not be threatened and that differences of interests can be managed. These two assumptions undergird the pursuit of increasingly diverse relations of peaceful cooperation and competition. The caution that characterized normalization is replaced by a confidence in the sturdiness of the structure and in the future of the relationship.

Because normalcy evolves from normalization, the official beginning of normalcy is not dramatic. Party Secretary Le Kha Phieu's visit to Beijing in February 1999 was one of a series of increasingly friendly summit meetings. He and Jiang Zemin announced a "16 Word Guideline" for future relations: "long-term, stable, future-oriented and all-round cooperative relations [Changqi wending, mianxiang weilai, mulin youhao, quanmian hezuo, 长期稳定, 面向未来, 睦邻友好, 全面合作 *Láng giềng hữu nghị, hợp tác toàn diện, ổn định lâu dài, hướng tới tương lai*]." The Guideline was fleshed out in a "Joint Statement for Comprehensive Cooperation" adopted in December 2000. These general statements were accompanied not only by a rapid increase in trade and investment, but also by treaties providing official resolutions for disputes on the land border (1999) and maritime rights in the Gulf of Tonkin (2000). The disputes concerning the Paracel and Spratly Islands in the South China Sea are more intractable and more complicated, but the joint agreement between China and ASEAN in 2002 concerning the peaceful resolution of conflicts in the South China Sea provides multilateral assurances against provocations and hostilities. The policy of normalcy survived leadership transitions in both China and Vietnam during its first five years.

Perhaps the best symbol of the difference that normalcy has made is oil. During normalization the most visible dispute between China and Vietnam concerned the Spratly Islands, and most of the incidents concerned unilateral moves by each side to control the area's petroleum resources. The problem was particularly sensitive for Vietnam since almost all its oil production is offshore to the west of the Spratlys. Vietnam was interested in protecting and expanding its most lucrative natural resource; China was interested in supplementing its oil production as its economy shifted from oil export to oil import in 1994. Beginning in 1999, however, China began to import Vietnamese oil, and already in 2000 it was importing 20 percent of Vietnam's total exports. Vietnam's oil has become a significant part of China's oil security strategy – not by seizure, but by purchase. Cooperative arrangements for the exploitation of the Spratlys are not yet on the horizon, but the likelihood of major conflict over the islands has already passed.

As the case of the Spratlys dispute illustrates, normalcy between China and Vietnam is embedded in a supportive regional environment. Vietnam is increasing its linkages to ASEAN and to the rest of the world at the same time that it improves relations with China. Meanwhile, from China's perspective its relations with Vietnam are part of successful regional policies toward ASEAN, and in turn China can look with similar satisfaction at the results of its other "good neighbor" policies in Central Asia (the Shanghai Cooperation Organization, formed as the "Shanghai Five" in 1996) and in Northeast Asia. The larger policy frameworks strengthen the confidence of all participants, and in some cases, such as the South China Sea disputes and Mekong River development, they permit the expansion of normalcy beyond the narrowness of bilateral relations.

Despite progress in regional and global integration, however, the normal relationship between China and Vietnam is not simply a carbon copy of relations with other countries. It remains an asymmetric relationship and therefore a pair of unique sub-relationships. China can be expected to pursue economic opportunities in Vietnam while avoiding becoming the patron in a patron-client relationship. It will be insensitive to the material threat posed to Vietnam by its larger and more prosperous economy and will perceive Vietnamese efforts to control the growth of the relationship as irrational and anti-Chinese.

The political and economic relationships with China will be proportionately much more important for Vietnam, both as opportunities and as threats. The cost of opportunities created by trade with China is the threat posed to Vietnamese production by competition with a much larger and wealthier market. A secondary anxiety is that the terms of trade favor China. In the 1990s these concerns caused a reluctance to maximize trade with China and also occasional attempts to prohibit the import of goods that threatened Vietnamese industries. Although such anxieties are now only part of a larger and more positive trade picture, one can confidently expect Vietnam to remain sensitive to its economic vulnerability to China and to engage occasionally in protectionist measures. Normalcy, therefore, does not imply complete harmony, but rather confidence in the institutional capacity to negotiate the relationship for mutual benefit.

Normalcy can be considered a mature stage in the Sino-Vietnamese relationship for two reasons. First, it is based on the sobering experience of ineffectual hostility. However cold a peaceful relationship, it is not as destructive as a hostile one. Second, normalcy generates self-reinforcing trends. Starting with a formal and distant handshake at the beginning, border trade began to develop, communications improved, and lower-level officials began to exchange visits. Although greater economic, social, and political contact is never without friction, such contacts also generate diverse new interests that could not operate in a hostile environment and therefore are alarmed by crises.

Possible challenges to normalcy will be considered in Chapter 11, but tantalizing as the future is, the feet of this book are planted firmly in the present. The future will be a creative accomplishment of its time, not simply a product of social vectors visible to us now. If this book can illuminate the present era of Sino-Vietnamese relations and in the process develop and apply an analytical perspective that might be useful elsewhere as well, it will accomplish its purpose.

PART ONE

BASIC STRUCTURE

2

The Parameters of China's External Posture

It would be possible to write a book about relations between China and Vietnam without devoting special attention to the structure of the relationship. All information about the relationship can be fit into a narration of its history, and the current situation could be fully described in terms of "China does this" and "Vietnam does that." There are, however, two weaknesses of commonsense description that are important for our subject. The first is that it tends to absolutize the present moment. If Mao Zedong is in power, all history leads to Mao. If Le Duan is in power, he is discussed as if he will be there forever. Without consideration of a deeper structure, the future can only be imagined as an extension of present facts. A structural analysis does not allow one to predict the future, but it can look for the context of the future that is hidden in the present and the past, and in the shape of the general situation.

The second weakness of commonsense description is specific to situations of disparity. If we do not take the different structures and contexts of China and Vietnam into account, it will appear that a particular fact or event would have the same meaning for both. I argue in this book and especially in this first part that the characteristic problem of the relationship is that it is shaped by asymmetry. Simply describing the relationship without observing the assymetry would be like comparing two fractions by looking at their numerators but not at their denominators.

The basic structure of the Sino-Vietnamese relationship is set by the general situation of each of its two actors and by the disparity of their relationship. Thus, this first chapter of the section discusses the parameters of China's external posture, the second discusses the parameters of Vietnam's external posture, and the third discusses the asymmetries of their relationship. The first two chapters have to be general enough to encompass the relationships of each country with any other country. They are thus broader than our current interests require, but they provide essential background to our current interests.

The word "parameters" may require some special attention. I use it to refer to basic realities of a country's situation that help determine how it views relations with other countries. Parameters do not dictate behavior, but they do influence it and set its significance for the actor. For instance, the amount of money that a gambler has is a parameter of his or her behavior, but if he or she is poor he or she may either stop gambling or gamble more desperately. A rich gambler may play as long as he or she finds it interesting, without consideration of wins and losses. They both want to win, and they play by the same rules, but the objective context of their behavior is different, and thus the subjective meaning of their actions is different. Even if both gamblers leave the table at the same time they do so for different reasons.[1] A parameter is a basic second-level reality that influences both the actor's behavior and the significance and consequences of that behavior. A parameter is not something that forces a particular action (the gambler's spouse coming to fetch him or her), nor is it a behavioral habit (always betting low). Therefore it does not simply predict behavior ("the poor will leave before the rich" would be a risky prediction). Countries are rarely as willful as gamblers, so their parameters are better predictors of their behavior, but it is well to remember that the decision makers who take each step of history may kick against necessity as well as conform to it. Parameters do change; they are current contextual givens, not natural laws. After all, the poor gambler could win big and become rich. Indeed, changes in parameters are the most important changes, for they require a reorientation of the framework of action. Should the newly rich gambler quit while ahead, or rely on good luck to continue? One of the questions we will consider below is whether or not the parameters of China and Vietnam are changing.

It is a daunting task to face the question, "what are the general and intractable givens that shape China's attitude toward the rest of the world?" So much has changed in China during its long history, especially in the last 150 years. The five parameters that I will suggest – size, centricity/localism, resource sufficiency, challenge of sustenance, and history – could

---

[1] The response of an actor to parameters has been termed *parametric rationality* [huanjing can-shu lixing 环境参数理性, or, more explicitly, shehui jigou suo rongxu de fanwei yinei de lixing xuanze 社会机构所容许的范围以内的理性选择] in distinction to strategic rationality. To return to our gamblers, both might play the same hand in the same way; indeed, they should. Strategic behavior, action oriented toward a specific purpose (winning the hand, in our example) should be dictated by the most efficient means of achieving that purpose and thus should be the same for whoever adopts the purpose. But the value of goals and the capacities of actors are not the same for all, and parametric rationality addresses these differences. While strategic rationality might dictate a best path to a given goal, parametric rationality cannot be so determinate, because the goal-setting itself is a part of an estimate of what is feasible in the current context. See Zou Dang 邹谠 (TangTsou), Ershi shiji zhongguo zhengzhi: zong xiongguan lishi yu weiguan xingdong jiaodu kan 二十世纪中国政治: 从雄关历史与微观行动角度看 [Twentieth Century Chinese Politics: From the Macro-Historical and Micro-Behavioral Perspectives] (Oxford: Oxford University Press, 1994), esp. pp. 211–12.

be subdivided or rearranged, and they are all interrelated. For instance, I have put the factor of the scale of domestic market in the parameter of resource sufficiency rather than in the parameter of size, because market scale influences the economic value of resources. Moreover, especially in the case of China, it is impossible to separate the parameters of domestic politics from the parameters of China's foreign politics.

Political culture is not treated as a separate parameter. I do not deny the importance of political culture, but it is too powerful as an explanation. It says, in effect, that the Chinese behave in a certain way because they are Chinese. This is not only tautological (anything the Chinese do would be Chinese); it also implicitly separates what the Chinese do from what anyone else would do in the same situation. In my opinion, it is necessary first to analyze the situation before jumping to a cultural explanation. The collection of parameters that I discuss are unique to China, and therefore I would also say that the Chinese external posture would tend to be unique. But the implicit message of my analysis is that anyone in China's situation would behave according to these constraints. I would rather leave culture as a residual explanation for patterns of behavior that cannot be linked to situational constraints.

Size

Clearly, China is a very large country, both in population and in area. Its 2001 population of 1,272 million people is roughly the same size as those of Europe and North and South America combined, four times that of the United States. Its area of 9.5 million square kilometers is half that of the Russian Federation, three times that of India, twice that of Europe. China's economic magnitudes are not as impressive, but in 2001 it passed Italy to become the world's sixth-largest economy and it is estimated that China might attain parity with the United States by 2015–20. Despite such remarkable magnitudes, one rarely reflects on the impact of size on China's world situation. Indeed, the habits of speech in foreign affairs pressure us to ignore size and to stress equal sovereignty when talking of nations. However, when size is brought into the picture, it is often assumed that a country ten times larger than another, all things being equal, will be ten times more powerful. This sort of extrapolation contributes to anxieties about China's current economic growth. When China's size is not ignored, it is used to draw alarmist pictures along the lines of the Burmese saying, "If all Chinese urinated at the same time we would be flooded."

The first effect of large size is to create a disjunction between aggregate and per capita magnitudes. China is, for example, the world's largest producer of grain and cotton, and yet it has been a net importer of both. If China were not the world's largest producer of food, it would be in severe famine. Canada is the world's seventh-largest grain producer, harvesting only

12 percent of China's total, but Canada's per capita production is six times that of China, and wheat is a major export crop. To someone planning to sell fertilizer to China the aggregate may be more important; to someone living there, the per capita figure is more important. In the case of military budgets, the aggregate counts more than the per capita, because it is spent by central authorities for national purposes. However, per capita military expenditure can be useful as a measure of the mobilization of resources. Chinese are often torn between being impressed by their national size and being humbled by per capita rankings. Indeed, He Xin, a prominent intellectual, suspects that per capita figures are part of a plot by Western economists to destroy China's self-esteem and sense of its own power.[2]

It should be remembered that a per capita figure is very artificial – simply the aggregate divided by the population. It can be expected that the larger the country, the more variation there will be in actual distribution. For instance, within China some provinces will be grain exporters and some importers. Jilin Province, for instance, produces 3.7 times as much grain per capita as Guangdong.[3] If we turn to industrial production, China's progress has been enormous since 1949. In 2000 China was the world's largest producer of steel, coal, and cement, second-largest producer of electricity, and fifth-largest of oil. While the per capita figures are still low by the standards of developed countries, these levels of production imply a large industrial base, and this base can support smaller amounts of advanced industrial and technological activity. Of course, the ability to launch a man into space does not mean that the whole economy is advanced, but the whole economy must be big in order to provide an adequate platform for advanced efforts. By comparison, Thailand has a significantly higher per capita GNP than China, but its economic base is not broad enough to sustain an independent space program.

Scale also affects structure. As the naturalist J. B. S. Haldane has observed about animals, advantages, disadvantages, and internal structure differ between large and small.[4] The large animals have the advantage of greater weight for surface area, so they are not as buffeted by winds or frustrated by other surfaces. A dog can drink what it wants; a fly must be careful not to be captured by the surface tension of the water. But greater weight means greater problems of control and coordination. A two-ton gazelle would splinter its graceful legs; in order to run at that weight, it must have legs like a

---

[2] He Xin, *Sikao: Wo di zhexue yu zongjiao guan* [Reflections: My Philosophical and Religious Viewpoint] (Beijing: Shishi chubanshe, 2001), p. 139.
[3] Statistics for 2001. Calculated from *Zhongguo Tongji Nianjian 2002* [*China Statistical Yearbook 2002*], table 12–22.
[4] J. B. S. Haldane, "On Being the Right Size," in *Possible Worlds* (New York: Harper and Row, 1928). This essay is such a classic that it is included in *The Oxford Book of Essays*, ed. John Gross (Oxford: Oxford University Press, 1992), pp. 452–7.

rhinoceros. The huge giant in a fairy tale who was ten times as high and wide as a human would collapse under his own weight.

The basic lesson here is that an increase or decrease in scale does not mean simply a similar increase or decrease in capacity. A flea can jump two feet high, and a human only a few feet more. Moreover, it is a much greater effort for the human, and the flea will be ready more quickly to jump again. On the other side of the coin, the larger animal is advantaged in internal maintenance functions. Haldane points out that five thousand mice weigh as much as one human, but they have to eat seventeen kilograms of food each day to keep warm. Also, large animals have a relative advantage in the case of specialized organs like eyes, which have a narrow range of optimum size. A whale's eye is not much bigger than a human's, while a mouse's smaller eye is less efficient and a larger part of its head.

Countries are very different from animals, and extrapolation can be misleading.[5] Nevertheless, it is interesting to reflect on what the political analogues of these organic features might be. It could be argued that for a large country the task of maintaining internal equilibrium is less dependent on the external environment than it would be for a smaller one, because in general it is less exposed. It follows that domestic affairs will tend to be relatively more important than foreign affairs in national policy, and that domestic political forces might be more important in determining all policy. The larger economy can be unified in its regulations, can be rationalized in its communications, and can suffer a smaller military burden, since the relative border area is reduced. Indeed, this was the justification offered by China's first emperor for his unification of the warring states.[6] It is also the logic of common markets and regional trading systems.

What of the structural problems of large size? As the authors of *Economic Reform in Three Giants* point out in their study of China, India, and the Soviet Union, coordination and control are more difficult, leading necessarily to more administrative layers and the likelihood of social heterogeneity.[7] In domestic politics this could be expressed in federalistic devolutions of power or in tendencies toward regionalism. In foreign affairs, the larger country is less likely to be as quick and internally coordinated in its external actions. Deployment of military power might be less efficient in a larger state than in a smaller one, and the consequences for other relations might be more

---

[5] Haldane himself ventures from biology to politics in the final paragraph of his essay, and opines that while he could imagine a socialist Denmark (on the model of a Henry Ford factory) he could not imagine a large socialist country.

[6] See Szuma Chien (Sima Qian), *Records of the Historian*, tr. by Yang Hsien-yi (Yang Xianyi) and Gladys Yang (Hong Kong: Commercial Press, 1974), pp. 159–96.

[7] Richard Feinberg, John Echeverri-Gent, and Friedemann Müller, *Economic Reform in Three Giants* (New Brunswick, New Jersey: Transaction Books, 1990). See also John Lewis, "Some Consequences of Giantism: The Case of India," *World Politics* 43:3 (April 1991), pp. 367–89.

distracting. On the other hand, the high levels of necessary inputs of some domains of high-technology weaponry might make size a relative advantage, somewhat like the eye in our organic example.

Perhaps the most important structural effect of large size – and its greatest risk – is that the national network of interrelationships extends far beyond the localities and usually displaces or mediates international contacts. As long as the national social network holds, its large scale makes it more efficient. But if it fails, or if the population loses confidence in its government, its economy, its security, and its values, then the larger the network the larger the collapse. I would argue that the fate of Russia in the 1990s in contrast to Eastern Europe was in part a consequence of the former's size. The Chinese fear of chaos [*luan*乱, *luan*] is not only well founded in the national memories of the twentieth century, but it is also related to the scale of disorientation that would occur in the collapse of any extremely large social order. It is a good example of a trait of political culture that is grounded in parametric rationality.[8]

Moving from the abstract consideration of size to China's relative size vis-à-vis other countries, it is clear that a country with one-fifth of the world's population will be a global entity, especially if the other four-fifths are not organized in their own giant countries. Before the world was unified by modernity, China's disparity of size in its realm of Asia was even more pronounced. Currently, one-third of Asia's population lives in China's 30 percent of Asia's territory, and trade with the rest of Asia constitutes more than half of China's total trade. The asymmetry implicit in these figures implies that what might be a small matter for China could be an acute concern for a neighbor. For instance, certainly most Chinese would not want to emigrate to Siberia, but even a tiny number of Chinese businessmen (by China's standards) appears large to the local residents there.

China's status as a global entity, and the importance of size for that status, is best illustrated by its experience in the first half of the twentieth century when it was weak and disunified. More powerful nations took advantage of China, but the group of world powers did not want one of their number controlling all China. Countries that insisted on colonial control elsewhere contented themselves with treaty ports and spheres of influence in China. As China's internal order collapsed into warlordism after 1911, the major powers entered into agreements not to support or supply arms to the various warlords.[9] Japan's attempt to occupy China proved the wisdom of earlier restraint, since even with its military prowess Japan could not finish the

---

[8] There are deep resonances between the Chinese fear of chaos and the Russian fear of a "time of troubles [смутное время]." See Allen Lynch, *How Russia Is Not Ruled* (Cambridge: Cambridge University Press, 2005), pp. 1–17.

[9] Hsi-Sheng Ch'i, *Warlord Politics in China, 1916–1928* (Stanford: Stanford University Press, 1976).

conquest, and even if it had defeated the Guomindang (GMD) government and declared victory in China, the struggle with the Chinese communist guerillas would have continued. Similarly, the invitation to China to join the Security Council of the United Nations in 1945 was not a testimony to China's power at that time, but to its size. So even as a relatively powerless country China remained a world entity because it was too big to swallow and too difficult to divide.

Since 1979 Deng Xiaoping's reform era has transformed China's economy as well as its interaction with the world economy. As China's relative wealth and power begin to approximate its population, it has become an active global entity rather than merely a passive global object of policy. Moreover, it appears to be disproportionately powerful in comparison to its neighbors. Of course, such disparities are not unusual. During the Cold War all countries had an even more asymmetric relationship to the superpowers than anyone had or has with China. Nevertheless, to the extent that national interests diverge, other countries might feel an implicit threat from China's disproportionate presence regardless of China's explicit policy or actions. As we will discuss in Chapter 4, Vietnam is the archetypal example of such a fearful neighbor.

However, China's apparent military superiority against a "normal-sized" opponent is misleading. First, it is inhibited by its stature as a global actor (for example, Japan and the United States would be very concerned about Chinese military behavior toward some other country). Second, many countries also have asymmetric relations with China and they each would feel threatened by a use of force against any one of them. Third, a military confrontation would probably occur on the territory of the smaller country, giving the smaller country the advantages of defense, internal logistics, clear national threat, and probably world public opinion. Of course the cost of such a conflict is more acute for the smaller country. But Vietnam has demonstrated the military advantages of defense against a number of large opponents.

In the light of these considerations, China's most rational policy would be to enhance its prestige but to avoid conflict. However, the greater role of domestic politics in large countries implies that what might appear rational from a cosmopolitan perspective might not be decisive in determining policy.

Centricity and Localism

While size is perhaps China's most obvious peculiarity in a global context, centricity, and the role of localism within centricity, might be called its most Chinese characteristic. Centricity has its essential physical dimensions, but it has also been shaped by the long evolution of Chinese civilization and politics.

"Centricity" is not a completely new word in English, but I am making a new use of it, so it would be best to start with a definition. Centricity refers to a situation in which the awareness, capacity, and control of the center fades as distances become larger, but not as a result of open opposition or confrontation. Effective governance is a constant problem in China, but it is rarely a matter of negotiation with counter-centers. Thus there is a basic tendency of Chinese politics to be self-referenced and to assume that the correct posture of its highest (or most central) leadership is the key to resolving political problems. "Self-referenced" in international relations means that China expects to play the decisive role in bilateral relations and prefers to see itself as a decisive factor in regional and global politics. "Correct posture" implies that the solution to problems of governance lies in one's own appropriate attitude rather than on skill in negotiating or use of force. Because the center is aware of its diminishing power of enforcement as it moves out to the periphery and down to the basic levels of society, leadership is most successful when it is peaceful and realistic rather than constantly relying on force. This situation is not only reflected in the teachings of Mencius[10] and Lao Zi[11], but also in the writings of the military strategist Sun Zi.[12] The boundary of the state is one of a number of concentric circles of control, but it is the most important because within the state boundary challenge to the center must be met by force, while outside the state boundary China does not expect to prevent open political differences.

Centricity has three immediate implications for China's foreign affairs. First, China's external posture is an extension of its internal political posture. Although China does not expect to control external affairs as it controls internal affairs, because of its self-referencing it would be hard for China to act externally according to principles in contradiction to its internal politics. Second, China's external priority is the appearance of authority and leadership rather than the exercise of military power or the expansion of territory. Third, China would not feel threatened by its individual neighbors in bilateral relations, but it would be more likely to be concerned about the presence of counter-centers on its borders, that is, by the presence of other global powers or by the appearance of an alliance among its neighbors that was not a part of its own concentric system and from which is was excluded.

---

[10] See King Hui of Liang, part one: "If Your Highness reforms your policies and practices a policy of benevolence, all the officials in the world would like to come to Qi to assume posts, all peasants would like to cultivate the soil of Qi, all merchants would like to do business in Qi, all travelers would like to travel the roads of Qi, and all persons who hate their own kings would come to complain to you, expecting you to uphold justice and relieve them of their agony. Who could keep you from realizing your great aspiration of unifying the world in such a situation?"

[11] See Chapter 61: "A large state should play the role of the female, just like the lower reaches of the river where all the other streams meet."

[12] See Sun Zi, Chapter 3: "A hundred battles fought, a hundred victories is not the ultimate achievement. The ultimate achievement is to subdue the enemy without battle."

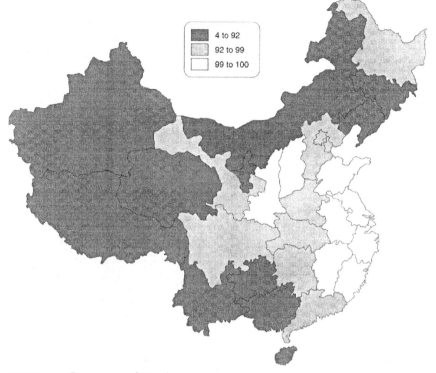

FIGURE 2.1. Percentage of Han by province

Domestic and International Ecology

Centricity is a parameter of China's external relations rather than merely a strategy because it is grounded in basic features of China's geo-politics. Domestically, these include China's ethnic homogeneity, the concentration of population away from borders, and the rural orientation of the economy.

Ethnically, China presents a very different picture from the ethnic diversity of India, Russia, or the United States. China is 92 percent Han Chinese. Moreover, as Figure 2.1 (percentage of Han population by province) illustrates, China's minorities live primarily in the border provinces, so the heartland of China is almost 100 percent Han Chinese. Nine of China's heartland provinces have less than 1 percent minority populations. It is not surprising that with the exception of Tibet and Xinjiang provinces, localism in China does not develop ethno-nationalistic tendencies. On the contrary, when local warlords were in fact independent of any effective central authority in the 1920s they all claimed to want to reunite China.[13] Localism is quite

---

[13] Ch'i, *Warlord Politics*, p. 17. Ch'i claims that "almost all the prominent militarists at one time or another engaged in sweeping attacks on militarism, advocated disarmament, and condemned the very nature of military regimes," p. 194.

FIGURE 2.2. Population density by province

strong in China, but it is more likely to hide from the center than to challenge it. For most of the periphery, localism differs in degree from the heartland but not in kind. Peripheral provinces may feel that they are far from Beijing and that their particular needs and interests are neglected. They also have a greater complexity of ethnic relationships. However, except for Tibet and Xinjiang, ethno-nationalism is negligible.[14]

The concentration of China's population in central and coastal provinces as illustrated in Figure 2.2 (population density by province) combines with ethnic homogeneity to reduce the sense of potential threat from neighbors. The population heartland is surrounded by a vast reach of territory that is under China's control and is relatively inhospitable, and in general the frontier areas face similar but smaller regions in neighboring countries. Thus, demographically the Chinese have not found their own peripheral areas very attractive and are thus even less inclined to pursue *Lebensraum* beyond.

[14] See, for example, Kate Kaup, *Creating the Zhuang: Ethnic Politics in the People's Republic of China* (Boulder: Lynne Reinner Publishers, 2000).

The coastal concentration and hence exposure of China might seem to contradict the notion of a well-buffered heartland, and indeed China proved to be vulnerable from the sea in the nineteenth century. But historically China has been more a river civilization than a maritime one, and its coastal provinces have tended to be inward oriented rather than linked in maritime commerce.[15] Moreover, in general the Chinese coast is not directly exposed to the Pacific (in contrast to the west coast of the United States, for example). Instead it is surrounded by peninsular and island neighbors with shallow coastal seas as buffers.

China's rural orientation may not seem relevant to its centricity, but it is essential to the fact that regions and cities have not emerged as counter-centers of domestic politics. Numerous scholars, perhaps most notably Karl Wittvogel,[16] have argued that the rural need for irrigation and flood control created an authoritarian "hydraulic state." In any case, bourgeois society in the West emerged from fortified cities (*bourg, burg*) under local control, while Chinese cities, as big as they were (the capital of the Tang dynasty, Chang'an – today's Xi'an – had a population of over one million in AD 900, while Paris had a population of 100,000 in the 1100s and 620,000 in 1784), were imperial administrative centers that were the targets of local rebellions rather than the origins. It is thus quite interesting that the Beijing crowds supporting the students in April and May 1989 called themselves "city-people" [shi min 市民, *thị dân* – "bourgeoisie" in the original sense], but clearly the idea was late in coming to China.[17]

Externally, China's geo-political centricity is enhanced by the fact that it is surrounded by neighbors on all sides who are smaller than China and who have little in common other than being neighbors of China. The more comparably sized neighbors, India and the former Soviet Union, are also the ones whose own heartlands are most distant. First the military and then the economic power of Japan in the last hundred years has made Japan something of an exception, but the argument could be made that it is an exception that proves the rule. And, even more clearly, the threat posed by a global power like the United States did not begin at China's border but with the occupation of a neighbor. Much like the possessiveness of the United States toward the Americas expressed in the Monroe Doctrine, China feels threatened by the presence of a global power in its region. However, it is not as aggressive as the United States in requiring the submission of regional states. China aptly termed Vietnam "Asia's Cuba" in 1979 (implicitly putting itself

---

[15] This is eloquently summarized in Wang Gungwu, *The Chinese Overseas* (Cambridge, MA: Harvard University Press, 2000).

[16] Karl Wittvogel, *Oriental Despotism: A Comparative Study of Total Power* (New Haven: Yale University Press, 1957).

[17] See Anita Chan and Jonathan Unger, eds., *Popular Protests in China: Reports from the Provinces* (Armonk: M.E. Sharpe, 1991).

in the position of the United States), but while China reduced its sanctions on Vietnam as Vietnam's relations with the Soviet Union became less salient, the United States continues to increase its sanctions on Cuba in order to bring to heel an unsubmissive government in its region.

Localism

There is a subtle but essential interrelationship of central authority and local discretion in Chinese centricity, and it is quite different from center-local relations in the West. The presumption of the Chinese system is a hierarchical harmony in which all do their parts. The authority of the leader is unbounded, but so is his or her responsibility for the welfare of all. The leader is bound not only by a moral obligation but also by its historical reflection in ritual and good example, its ontological reflection in nature's blessing or rejection, and its societal reflection in peace and prosperity. In the modern Western system, powers are allotted by contract, but the leader is at liberty to use the powers allotted. Authority is carefully aggregated from an egalitarian disharmony of individuals, and constitutional attention is fixed on the propriety of procedure rather than on the appropriateness of conduct or result. It seems as if the Chinese and the Western ideals of politics are the two halves of a human puzzle, one emphasizing harmony, community, and family, and the other emphasizing competition, society, and individual.

In center-local relations, the Chinese model implies that the localities cannot challenge the center, but that the center must provide order to the localities and minimize interference. The Confucian emphasis on ruling through good example rather than through force implies a political style based on mediation and gesture, and even the classic military strategists pointed out the dangers of alienating the people and of maintaining a large army. The emperor's mandate, and the mandate of each lower official as well, was to preserve societal order for the general good. The resulting center-local relationship was hardly Weberian, as the following complaint made in 1872 by Imperial Customs Inspector Robert Hart makes clear:

There are, you know, a hundred things provincials ought to do which the central offices will never order them to do. The effort at centralization is all right enough as regards great and grave international questions; but, even in them, *local* considerations are not fully weighed, and local authorities not duly considered. The Chinese idea is for the locality to *initiate*, and for the central authorities to (1st) wink at, (2nd) tacitly permit, (3rd) openly allow, (4th) officially recognize, and (5th) crystallize.[18]

The emperor's mandate, and the mandate of each lower official as well, was to preserve societal order for the general good. The localities had no rights

[18] Private letter from Robert Hart to Hosea Ballou Morse, dated August 3, 1971. Morse, *The International Relations of the Chinese Empire* (n.p., 1910), Vol 1, p. 6n.

of challenge, so disorder would be suppressed and punished. But it was a sign of incorrect leadership if disorder emerged.[19]

Mao Zedong's rural revolution reversed the center-local relation, but only temporarily. By mobilizing the peasantry in the countryside Mao built a new political force that overwhelmed the weak central state of the Guomindang, and established a party-state that was unusually strong because of its roots in rural revolution. However, Mao did not empower either the people or the localities to limit or challenge the new state, and so the new state could use its mobilizational power to be vastly more intrusive than previous Chinese states, though for mass revolutionary purposes.

The domestic pattern of center-local relations is reflected in foreign policy in a tendency to expect acknowledgment of China's pre-eminent status from regional neighbors, but not, as was the European pattern, to force a colonial restructuring and internal transformation in order to serve the metropolitan power. The emperor, as the Son of Heaven in "All under Heaven" [tianxia 天下, thiên hạ], expected deference because he was responsible for universal order, not because of conquest. Indeed, perhaps the greatest reason for the persistence of the China-centric order in East Asia was that it imposed little burden on its members. If in the Chinese village "heaven is high and the Emperor far away," how much farther away was the Emperor from the galaxy of peripheral states?

The Current Pattern of Centricity

The contemporary importance of centricity, and the problems with applying Western notions of nation-state sovereignty, can be illustrated by Figure 2.3. There are numerous artificial aspects of this representation, and I have purposely put Japan in the "south" to emphasize the schematic character of this drawing and have left out most other neighboring countries so as not to obscure the general point. The sizes and relationships are an amalgam of demographics, economics, and politics, as well as my lack of artistic talent.

The innermost square is the central leadership in Beijing, and indeed it would be more accurate to have a number of converging circles of central

---

[19] To quote from the *Book of History* (Shu jing),

"If the Sovereign err repeatedly,
Should dissatisfaction be waited for until it appears?
Before it is seen it should be guarded against.
In my dealing with the millions of the people
I should feel as much anxiety as if I were driving six horses with rotten reins.
The ruler of men –
How should he be but reverent of his duties?

From the "Documents of Xia: Songs of the Five Sons" in Clae Waltham, *Shu Ching* (Chicago: Henry Regnery, 1971), p. 58.

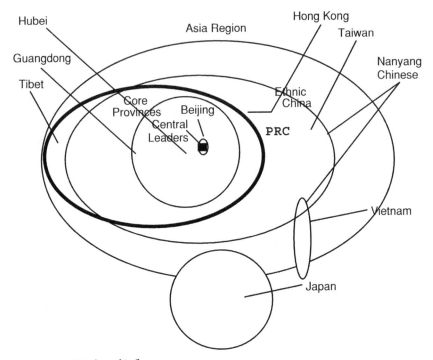

FIGURE 2.3. Circles of influence

leadership from the Central Committee to the current Paramount Leader. Although its effect diminishes throughout the circles, there is only one center.

Beijing City is the second major circle, because it is the theater of central politics, and not merely the seat of the central leadership. The events of spring 1989 showed clearly that even unofficial China took its cues from what was happening in Beijing.[20]

The third level is the Han core of China, the major provinces. This core has its places that are more central or more peripheral. Clearly, for instance, the southern province of Guangdong is part of this core, but it is considerably less central than Shanghai or Tianjin on the central coast, and Guangdong has benefited from special "peripheral" policies in the 1980s, as well as from its border with Hong Kong.

The fourth level, indicated by the darker circle, is that of the national sovereignty of the People's Republic of China. One might think that this would be a very definite area, with full rights of sovereignty on the inside and none without, and to a large extent it is. But consider the complications

---

[20] This is clear throughout the reports on provincial activities in May–June 1989 in Chan and Unger, *Popular Protests in China*.

of the sovereignty circle for China. First, Tibet has a government in exile that is recognized by no state, but the United States and Taiwan supported insurgency movements there until the early 1970s (though Taiwan did not support Tibetan independence), and many governments have received the Dalai Lama and have voiced official sympathy and concern for Tibetans. Such concerns are irritating to China, and it protests, usually ineffectually, the receptions of the Dalai Lama, but the continuous assertion of national sovereignty is made in the context of a probing international interest in the self-determination of Tibet.

Second, Hong Kong reverted to Chinese sovereignty in 1997, but it certainly did not become a homogenous part of a homogenous China, but rather the Hong Kong Special Autonomous Region. What might look like an abrupt Sinification of Hong Kong from a sovereignty point of view has in fact been a gradual process of the Hong Kong-ization of Guangdong Province.[21] China has encouraged the shading of Guangdong's economic and societal realities into Hong Kong's colors through its special policies toward Guangdong since 1980 and its creation of the Shenzhen Special Economic Zone in 1981.

Third, Taiwan is formally acknowledged by one and (almost) all to be part of China, but each side's miminum conditions for merger appear to exclude the other. From 1949 until the 1980s the situation could be considered one of frustrated sovereignty, but the actual relationship between China and Taiwan has become much more interesting and complicated over the last twenty years. China's policy of peaceful reunification put forward in 1981 under the formula of "one country, two systems" was a considerable unilateral compromise of its sovereignty claim, and even though it was rejected by Taiwan, it has increasingly undermined Taiwan's isolation from China. Despite initial governmental opposition and continuing governmental reluctance, the economy of Taiwan has become intimately tied to the economy of China.[22] But at the same time China is more constrained in its possible sanctions toward Taiwan. The former "yes or no" question of reunification seems to have become a more complicated one of where Taiwan fits in a more general Chinese socio-economy that is centered on China but not under its direct control. The bilateral cross-Strait relationship is made even more complex by the intimate but ambiguous involvement of the United States.

The fifth level of influence is that of ethnic China, which does not include all of the People's Republic of China (PRC) (the most notable exception is Tibet) but does include Hong Kong, Taiwan, and the ethnic and cultural

---

[21] See Ming Chan, "All in the Family: The Hong Kong-Guangdong Link in Historical Perspective," in Kwok and So, eds., *The Hong Kong-Guangdong Link* (Armonk: M. E. Sharpe, 1995), pp. 31–64, and Victor Sit, "Industrial Transformation of Hong Kong," in Kwok and So, pp. 163–86.

[22] The course of this development is well described by Tse-kang Leng, *The Taiwan-China Connection: Democracy and Development across the Taiwan Straits* (Boulder: Westview Press, 1996).

network of ethnic Chinese that is resident primarily in Southeast Asia. Clearly this is an important domain of commonality and influence, but in terms of political influence it is far weaker than the inner circles. Each of these groups either has its own circle of political control (e.g., Singapore) or is a part of a national, non-Chinese state. If the economic power of this sphere is assessed, it is immense, comparable in many respects to the power of Japan. However, there is only private and small-scale coordination in this sphere. It is led by neither Beijing nor Taiwan, nor could it be. Its networks are by no means insignificant, but they are not political. Moreover, they tend to be peripheral connections without a center in any particular location.[23]

The last level of influence is the Asian region. Here we certainly cannot speak of Chinese control. Indeed, the paradox exists that as China's power increases, it might cause anxiety rather than compliance among its neighbors.[24] A strong China may be counter-influential, depending on how it behaves. On another dimension, China is a potential producer and consumer of such magnitude that the regional economic plans of its neighbors would be foolish to ignore it. As China's economic gravitational pull increases, the Asian regional economy will become both more Asian and more Chinese. This will be one trend among many if the world economy also continues to expand, but if the world economy sours, the relative importance of China for Asia will increase.

Resource Sufficiency

China is fortunate to have sufficient supplies of most natural resources, both materials and energy, for its immediate and foreseeable needs. In general, the natural wealth of China is not so overwhelming that it could supply world needs or rely on the export of resources, but it is comprehensive and significant enough for China's immense population.

The fairly recent exception is petroleum. In 1985 China exported one-third of its oil production; in 1999 it imported 17 percent. By 2020 it is estimated that 60 percent of China's petroleum needs will have to be imported.[25] However, oil supplies only 22 percent of China's energy usage, and rich hydroelectric and coal resources remain to be developed.[26] For instance, in 2009 the Three Gorges Dam will be up to its full annual electrical production

---

[23] See, for instance, East Asia Analytical Unit, *Overseas Chinese Business Networks in Asia* (Canberra: Australian Department of Foreign Affairs and Trade, 1995).

[24] The situation of China's leadership in Asia is treated in more detail in Brantly Womack, "How Size Matters: The United States, China and Asymmetry," *Journal of Strategic Studies* 24:4 (December 2001).

[25] Report of the Development Research Center of the State Council, *China Daily*, December 15, 2003.

[26] Calculated from *Zhongguo Tongji Nianjian* 2000, pp. 240–1, using the factor of 1.43 to convert oil tons to standard coal equivalents.

of 84.7 billion kilowatt hours (kwh), which would be 5.7 percent of national electrical production in 2001. China's coal production in 2002 was 35 percent of the world's total, and it is already the world's second largest producer of hydroelectric energy. The International Energy Agency estimated that in 2001 China's energy production approximated that of the rest of Asia combined.[27] In the long term China's energy needs are expected to grow by more than 50 percent by 2020, but energy efficiencies are being implemented. From 1980 to 1995 the GDP quadrupled but energy use only doubled.[28] Nevertheless, China will be importing an increasing share of its oil needs, and it is diversifying its sourcing. Vietnam is now China's sixth-largest oil supplier, with 5.6 percent of the total in 2002.[29]

Although China is not radically dependent on external resources, the scale of its economy creates two structural weak points in resource sufficiency. The first is that resources are not evenly distributed within China. As a matter of domestic policy, China has to face problems of resource supply to all localities that would be matters of international trade for smaller countries. Second, as China's production expands, even a proportionally minor shortfall in available resources can have a perceptible impact on world markets. China's purchases of various raw materials, especially oil, began to have an appreciable impact on world commodity prices in 2004. Although other factors, such as the falling real value of the U.S. dollar, contributed to higher oil prices, China's demand will be an increasing pressure on world resources. Moreover, as China's buying power increases and it becomes more integrated into world markets, the incentive for importing shifts from shortage to price advantage. In 2002 China's imports of primary goods were twice the value of its exports of primary goods, and five times 1990 imports.

Historically and in the present era, China's greatest resource has been its people. In traditional China, the complementarity between population density and the labor-intensive rice cultivation that sustained it created a concentration of pre-modern civilization that was unique in its extent and in its ineluctable southward spread. Perhaps China's sufficiency of labor power precluded the development of the labor-saving power sources, machines, and organization of production that defined the industrial revolution in the West. In any case, in the current era of reform China's wealth of labor – educated, healthy, and locally organized – is its chief advantage in the world market.

---

[27] Excluding the former Soviet Union. International Energy Agency, *Key World Energy Statistics 2003* (www.iea.org/statist/key2003.pdf), p. 8.

[28] It is estimated that in 2020 China's aggregate energy use will be the same as that of the United States in 1985, or about 60 percent of U.S. usage in 2020. See National Academy of Sciences, *Cooperation in the Energy Futures of China and the United States* (Washington: National Academy of Sciences, 2000), pp. 18–20.

[29] Li Wei 李玮, "Zhongguo shiyou anquan zhong de dongnanya yinsu 中国石油安全中的东南亚因素," [The Southeast Asian Element in China's Petroleum Security], *Dongnanya zongheng* 东南亚纵横 10 (October 2003), pp. 19–23.

Complementing the presence of natural resources is the existence of a domestic economic scale that justifies their exploitation. Domestic consumption might be considered a drawback; after all, China produces more oil than Mexico but has to import to make up the difference in consumption. But the value of a commodity produced for an external market is dependent on that market. Were it not for world demand, the oil of the United Arab Emirates would be worth nothing, because there would not be sufficient local demand to justify the cost of exploitation. China's domestic market justifies any economy of scale without reference to a world market. This buffers and stabilizes the value of resources.

The significance of resource and market self-sufficiency can best be seen in contrast to the situation of other countries. To take the most obvious counterexample, Japan's shortage of vital inputs to a modern economy impelled it to become internationally oriented and is still an important parameter of its foreign policy. Market dependency can be seen in the economies of Taiwan and Singapore, which have modern economies far in excess of domestic needs. It is clear from these examples that countries can prosper in situations of resource and market dependency, but it is also clear that resource sufficiency is a basic parameter of China's external posture that distinguishes it from its Asian neighbors.

China is relatively lacking in technological and capital resources, and the internationalization of the economy has involved the large-scale import of technology and capital. But these relative deficiencies are quite different from shortages of natural resources. First, capital and technology can be accumulated domestically if necessary, though at a slower pace than outside investment and transfer would permit. By contrast, a country short of iron ore will not be able to invent it. Second, foreign investment and technology transfer must be induced; they cannot be forced. While imperial Japan could imagine that it could control its dependency on foreign raw materials by subjugating Korea, China, and the rest of Asia, China cannot coerce investment and transfer. If China had tried to seize the capital of Hong Kong, for instance, it would have traded future investment for a one-time windfall. It would have killed the goose that laid the golden egg. Technology transfer is even more sensitive to hostile or illegal contexts. Thus China's relative shortages in these areas are likely to make it more cooperative internationally rather than more aggressive.

Even China's shortage of petroleum could not be solved by aggressive actions. No neighbor that might be vulnerable to China has sufficient reserves to satisfy China's demand, and China is dependent now and for the foreseeable future on unimpeded sea access to Middle Eastern oil. China's only feasible approaches to energy security are conservation, storage, the development of non-petroleum production, and the diversification of suppliers.

The Challenge of Sustenance

In stark contrast to the sufficiency of natural resources, the size and concentration of China's population has pushed the limits of available food, space, water, and air. This is not a new phenomenon for China, but the current rate of modernization is aggravating the problem. The limits of sustainable development in China lie in the availability of renewable resources.

China's food problem is rooted in the fact that 22 percent of the world's population lives on 7 percent of the world's arable land. By comparison, the United States is a young and empty country. China reached the current American ratio of people to land in 1650; if the United States had China's current ratio, it would have a population of two billion people.

Grain production has increased along with population since 1949, and it increased dramatically from 1979 to 1984. It is unlikely that grain production will again make dramatic improvements per capita, though agricultural production has diversified, and meat and fish production have increased dramatically.[30] Nevertheless, as prosperity increases, people will eat more; they will eat meat products that require feedgrains, and they will use industrial crops that compete for arable land and – more important, in some places – available water. Meanwhile, of course, the population will increase.

The food challenge implies that food supply will remain an active and at times overriding concern of local and central governments, and it may occasionally justify strong intervention in the economy. Although grain imports provide an occasional and marginal solution, it would cause legitimate concern if China became massively dependent on foreign grain for its survival. For one thing, it would be an expensive and necessary consumption item whose cost would tend to increase, affecting the balance of trade. For another, it would imply an external dependency in a vital area, something that is not desirable in its own right, and is even less acceptable to China given its centricity and resource sufficiency. It would be a painful and worrisome exception to self-sufficiency.

As the cost of Chinese labor rises, the relative cost of food production will also rise, and it will force the government to push domestic food production upstream, against market forces, or else countenance larger and larger imports.

Food is the traditional and most obvious challenge of renewable resources, but space, air and water are also important. Improved housing in the countryside is taking cropland out of production, and yet housing is so congested, especially in cities, that further expansion is inevitable. Urbanization is experiencing its first boom since the 1950s, and it has accelerated. Two-thirds of

---

[30] G. K. Heilig, (1999): *China Food. Can China Feed Itself?* IIASA (International Institute for Applied Systems Analysis, Laxenburg (CD-ROM Vers. 1.1, 1999).

China's cities are experiencing water shortages, and in some places it is so acute that it threatens the future of the locality.[31] Desertification is estimated to have direct costs of almost U.S. $8 billion annually as well as indirect costs of $35 billion.[32] Air quality in China is terrible in urban areas. Even though remarkable improvements have been made in pollution control since 1995, the expense of these efforts diverts resources away from maximum growth and toward the more prudent target of sustainable growth.

Space, air, and water are problems that are more acute because of previous neglect, but modernization will continue to increase pressure. Modernization uses more per capita of all three, and they are limited. China cannot afford to modernize first and then worry about the environment; it does not have the room to make mistakes. But sustainable development requires central strategic control to prevail over the pursuit of marginal profit, and that is difficult.

History

At any point in time, the historical framework is a major parameter of action. To go back to our gamblers, a rich person who got wealthy through luck will probably have a different attitude toward gambling from that of a rich person whose wealth was accumulated slowly through hard work. The behavior of each state is also conditioned by its history. For instance, Japan's foreign policy in Asia operates under the ambiguous but real constraints imposed by memories of its wartime activities and of its defeat.[33] China's external posture has been similarly conditioned. Although it is impossible to go into detail here, three general eras can be described that influence, at various levels, China's present attitudes: the imperial period, modernity, and the contemporary experience of revolutionary transformation and failure.

The imperial period, from the establishment of the Chinese Empire in 211 BC to the fall of the Qing Dynasty in 1911, had tremendous internal variations. But the establishment of the empire, and its high points of glory, imposed a discourse on Chinese international relations that remained in use even when reality was quite different. In the Song dynasty, for instance, the dynasty that lost control of Vietnam, there was a strong sense of realism in the adaptation of imperial pretensions to actual realities.[34] The limits of centricity were always an active concern, even if (for obvious rhetorical reasons) they could not be discussed openly. Inside and outside its borders,

---

[31] See, for instance, *South China Morning Post*, January 23, 2001.
[32] "China Suffers Great Losses from Desertification," *People's Daily Online*, June 17, 2003.
[33] This is well described in Keiko Karube, "Japan's Desire to Be a Major Political Power and Historical Burdens," *Southeast Review of Asian Studies* 16 (1994), pp. 39–57.
[34] This is brilliantly analyzed by Wang Gungwu in "The Rhetoric of a Lesser Empire: Early Sung Relations with Its Neighbors," in Wang Gungwu, *The Chineseness of China* (Hong Kong: Oxford University Press, 1991), pp. 100–17.

China would expand its control when possible and retreat when necessary. But no new doctrine emerged of China being merely one state among many, and other cultures attracted some curiosity but little admiration.

The Chinese empire considered itself the responsible representative of a civilization that was its own, but one that was also founded on such universal principles that it could think of itself as being persuasive to anyone. Its claim to authority was not founded on a myth of conquest or theocracy, but on a myth of maintaining a natural order justified by universal principles of reasonableness. Its authority derived from its size and centrality as well as from its confirmation of local authorities and impartial regulation of disputes between states.

The challenge posed by the West from 1840 on destroyed China's traditional centric order, both domestically and internationally. Not only was China defeated by stronger outside powers, as it had been in the past, but defeat at the hands of the Japanese in 1895 demonstrated that the new civilization was learnable, and therefore that China was shackled and might drown because of its self-centeredness.

The radical rejection of the Chinese past begun by progressives at the turn of the century and brought to its extreme in the Cultural Revolution might thus appear to have ended the influence of the parameter of centricity. Few elites became so cosmopolitan so quickly as did the Chinese; within a generation of the first major translations of Western works, leading scholars such as John Dewey and Bertrand Russell were lecturing in China at the invitation of their returned doctoral students. Chinese literature was influenced by world currents; Ba Jin's famous novel *Family* (1933) described China's most basic institution as Ibsen might have, and made tradition the culprit for the travails of change.[35]

In politics, in their initial stages both the Guomindang and the Communist Party of China (CPC) depended on foreign models and advice, and the very foreignness of the models contributed to their credibility. The foreign ideas would not taint the new China with the deadly habits of old China. The CPC drew strength from the belief that it was part of a world revolution, and that its historical course had been mapped by a German scientist. Within sixty years China's self-consciousness as a civilization was turned inside out.

Despite the inversion of traditional Chinese centricity, several important continuities can be seen in modern radicalism. First, while China was no longer the center of the world, most of the radical visions remained global in their orientation.[36] The revolutionaries were cosmopolitan, but they were working for a transformed world in which China might again be pre-eminent

[35] Ba Jin was the pseudonym of Li Feigan. It combined the names of his two favorite anarchists, the first syllable of Bakunin and the last of Kropotkin.

[36] This is clear for instance in Kang Youwei's *Book of Great Harmony* [Da tong shu] and in Mao Zedong's first political essay, "The Great Union of the Popular Masses."

because of its virtue. Second, the urgency and radicalness of twentieth-century Chinese politics sprang from the total crisis within China: the collapse of traditional culture, politics, and economics. Had China prospered in its encounter with modernity, its intellectuals would have been cooler and more critical in their reception, as indeed they had been to the Jesuits a few centuries earlier. So the new models were outside China, but the fire to find them lay within. Third, the new models crashed on the rocks of Chinese reality. It proved difficult to throw books at warlords. What eventually worked for both the Nationalist Party and the Communists was a thorough adaptation of foreign models to Chinese realities. The Nationalist Party adapted to elite reality. It improved its own military strength and reached accommodations with warlords and foreign powers. Mao Zedong adapted Marxism-Leninism to the realities of the rural village and the idea of a proletarian revolution became the very different reality of a Chinese peasant revolution.

After the establishment of the People's Republic of China in 1949, centricity reemerged internationally as revolutionary centricity. China certainly was not interested in re-establishing a traditional empire – the past remained radically condemned – but China expected to be the leader of the revolutionary Third World, and it expected to be treated as an almost-equal comrade by the Soviet Union. Especially in Asia, China expected to lead, not for its own advantage, but as an implicit responsibility of revolutionary China.

Revolutionary diplomacy became even more radical in the 1960s and then collapsed in 1969–70, along with the domestic collapse of the Cultural Revolution. China took a more sober view of the world and of its relations with the superpowers, perceived that the United States was less of a threat than the Soviet Union, and replaced revolutionary diplomacy with national diplomacy during the course of the 1970s. China still claimed a leading role in the Third World and in Asia, but no longer as a beacon of revolutionary transformation. Now it was the shared problems of developing countries that provided common grounds, and the opportunities for international prestige came from the mutual acknowledgment of state visits and activities in world organizations.

China's post-revolutionary internationalism is founded therefore on an acceptance of other states and on the current array of international institutions. Moreover, its acknowledged motives of state behavior are grounded in the self-interest of states, stressing cooperation for mutual benefit. Since 1986 China has developed a multipolar theory of global international relations, and since 1995 it has become much more active in regional multilateral institutions.[37] Nevertheless, the very success of China's domestic and international pragmatism is re-creating a situation in which China's position in

[37] Brantly Womack, "Asymmetry Theory and China's Concept of Multipolarity," *Journal of Contemporary China* 13:39 (May 2004), pp. 351–66.

Asia is again becoming pre-eminent. As in the past, China is not in a position to dominate, but it is in an asymmetric relationship with each of its neighbors, with the partial exceptions, for different reasons, of Japan, Russia, and India.[38] Its position attracts regional and world attention, and its prestige depends on its external posture rather than its power. Internally as well, the economic development of China has encouraged indirect leadership and made the assertion of central control more difficult. Economically, China has expanded, and the emperor is farther away from the villages. China has not returned to a traditional centric pattern, but the basic parameters that established centricity in the first place have reasserted their influence, reshaped by the intervening traumas of modernity and revolution.

---

[38] Brantly Womack, "How Size Matters: The United States, China and Asymmetry," *Journal of Strategic Studies* 24:4 (December 2001), pp. 123–50.

3

Vietnam's Basic Parameters

To view the outside world from Hanoi, Hue, or Ho Chi Minh City is quite different from viewing it from Beijing, Chongqing, or Guangzhou. Most obviously, China is part of Vietnam's outside picture – usually and in most respects the largest single part of the picture. However, before we turn to the Sino-Vietnamese relationship we need to consider the basic parameters of Vietnam. These shape the relationship of domestic and external politics and the salience of China within Vietnamese external politics.

Since we have described Chinese politics as centric, it is quite tempting to describe Vietnamese politics as eccentric. This would be correct according to the mathematical meaning of the term. While China's politics, including its external relations, seems to revolve around itself, Vietnamese politics usually takes a more elliptical orbit. The larger focal point is Vietnam itself, but there is usually also an external point of reference that co-defines politics. Vietnam's understanding of the outside world plays a larger part in its domestic politics and self-understanding than it does for China. For traditional Vietnam, China was the primary external point of reference. For twentieth-century Vietnam, the external focus was first France and then socialist internationalism. In the twenty-first century Vietnam's external focus is more ambiguous than it has ever been before, and yet external relations are subjectively and objectively more important than they have ever been before. China is likely to play the largest single part in Vietnam's external relations, but it is by no means a dominant part. Not only is there considerable autonomy for Vietnam in its normalized relations with China, but also regional and global relations in general are more important than any single bilateral relationship.

Vietnam's major parameters are geography, a national consciousness that contains dimensions of both nationalism and cosmopolitanism, resource imbalance, the challenge of integration and diversity, and history. Some of these parameters are interrelated. Geography is the foundation of Vietnam's unique combination of nationalism and cosmopolitanism, and resource imbalance has contributed to the challenge of integration and diversity. Moreover, as with China, history is not only a parameter in its own right but it is also the record of attempts to cope with the other parameters. However, Vietnam's national consciousness was not an inevitable product of its geographical circumstances, and its resource imbalances are only one contributing factor to the policy dilemma of integration versus diversity.

Geography

One look at a map suggests that Vietnam is an unusually shaped country (Map 3.1). If we add demography to the political geography, we could argue that Vietnam is the most oddly shaped country in the world.[1] If we put this strange shape in its location, partly in intimate contact with China and partly on Southeast Asia's inner frontier between its mainland and island halves, then it is clear that internal diversity will be amplified by different exposures to external threats and opportunities.

Let us begin with the map. Vietnam is approximately as far from north to south (1,650 km) as Tianjin and Guangzhou in China, Seattle and San Diego in the United States, or Copenhagen and Naples in Europe. In the middle at its narrowest point, Vietnam is only 50 kilometers wide, the distance between Fort Worth and Dallas in the United States. It is worth noting that for most countries the notion of "narrowest point" would be rather meaningless. Vietnam borders Cambodia (1,228 km), Laos (2,130 km), and China (1,281 km), and it has a coastline of 3,444 kilometers. Vietnam's ratio of land area to perimeter is 40,[2] while for China it is 254 and for Cambodia 69. The place most distant from any perimeter – Vietnam's most "inland" place – is Vinh Yen, which is approximately 130 kilometers from Laos, Yunnan, Guangxi, and the Gulf of Tonkin.

Each end of Vietnam is defined by a major river delta, the Red River in the north and the Mekong in the south. The Red River delta has always been the historical and cultural heartland of Vietnam, while the Mekong delta was ruled first by the Hindu kingdom of Champa and then by Khmers until it was occupied by Vietnam by 1759. The Mekong enters Vietnam from Cambodia as two rivers, the Hau Giang (Bassac, "back river") and the Tien Giang (Upper Mekong, "front river"), and then quickly splits into the "nine dragons"(Cửu Long) of the delta. As the name of a part of the delta, "the Plain of Reeds" [Đồng Tháp Muoi], suggests, much of the land is low and flat and prone to flooding by the Mekong in the wet season and to salinization from the ocean in the dry season. The agricultural productivity

---

[1] Another candidate, Chile, is certainly longer, at more than 6,000 kilometers, but one-third of the population lives in the capital, Santiago, and most of the population is clustered in the middle of the country.

[2] That is, for every kilometer of border or coast there are 40 square kilometers of territory.

MAP 3.1. Vietnam

of the Mekong delta was greatly enhanced in the twentieth century by land reclamation. The Saigon River is the first river north of the Delta, and its terrain is more stable and more varied.

Weather differs greatly by location. Although snow is seen only on the mountain tops in the northwest, the winter monsoon can bring temperatures down to 10 degrees centigrade (50° F) in Hanoi, while only the availability of summer fruits such as lychees makes bearable the heat of July and August. Central and northern Vietnam are both exposed to typhoons. Meanwhile southern Vietnam basks below the typhoon belt in more moderate weather. All of Vietnam has monsoonal rain patterns, but at different times, and every place is subject to droughts and floods, but in different patterns.

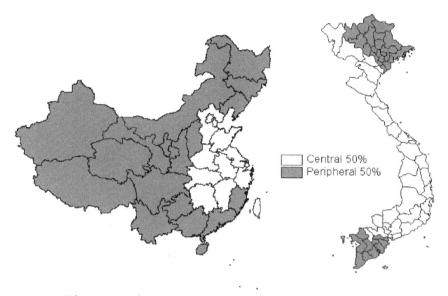

MAP 3.2. Fifty percent of population

The monsoons add a temporal flux to the spatial diversity. The monsoon is not simply a question of rainfall. The volume of water in the Mekong River changes by a factor of fifty in wet and dry seasons, flooding most of the delta from July to October. Along the coast, the prevailing winds blow from north to south in winter, and from south to north in summer. In the days of sailing ships, merchants would come down from China and Japan to ports such as Faifoo (now Hoi An), wait until the winds changed, and return home. Even now a coastal cruise is much smoother with the wind than against it. Despite the country's long coastline, the Vietnamese have not been primarily a seafaring people, except for fishing, and the expansion of Vietnamese territory and settlement has been one of entering the south overland.

The diversity of Vietnam's physical geography is in some respects amplified by its demography, while in other respects demography provides the basis for Vietnam's unity. The population is concentrated in the two major deltas. As Map 3.2 illustrates, there is nothing comparable in China to the polarization of Vietnam's population. While the bicoastal situation of the United States is more similar (and one could say that the American East Coast is its historic and cultural heartland, similar to the Red River delta), in fact the demographic bifurcation of the United States is much less extreme.

Only 23 percent of Vietnam's population is urban. While the urban population of Vietnam is not concentrated at the absolute geographical extremes of the country, Map 3.3 shows that it is concentrated in a few localities

Basic Structure

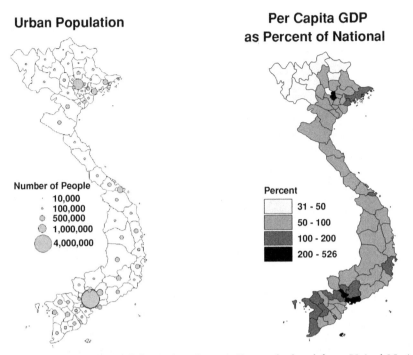

Urban Population   **Per Capita GDP**
                                         as Percent of National

Number of People
· 10,000
∘ 100,000
⊙ 500,000
◉ 1,000,000
● 4,000,000

Percent
□ 31 - 50
▨ 50 - 100
▦ 100 - 200
■ 200 - 526

MAP 3.3. Dimensions of dispersion. Source: Data calculated from United Nations Development Programme, *National Human Development Report 2001: Doi Moi and Human Development in Vietnam* (Hanoi, 2001), Statistical Appendix.

that are far apart. With 23 percent of Vietnam's urban residents, Ho Chi Minh City has a larger urban population than any of Vietnam's other seven regions, and it has over half of Vietnam's big city (over 500,000) urban residents. Hanoi has another 20 percent of the big city urbanites, so the two cities together have three-quarters of Vietnam's big city residents.

There is also a comparable disparity in the distribution of productive capacity. Ho Chi Minh City produces 20 percent of the national GDP, three times the national per capita rate. By contrast, Bac Can and Ha Giang provinces, in the Northwest on the border with China, have only one-third of the national GDP per capita. In general, as the second map in 3.3 indicates, low productive capacity is scattered throughout Vietnam, but especially in the north and in mountain areas. Because of the greater productivity of the few urban areas, most Vietnamese provinces are below the national average.

What holds Vietnam together, at least from north to south, is its ethnic homogeneity. Except for the Hoa (ethnic Chinese), who are largely urban, the 13 percent of the population that belongs to minority groups is most prevalent in mountainous areas, while the ethnic Vietnamese (Kinh) stretch from the Chinese border to the southern tip of Ca Mau in the rice-growing regions and cities.[3] There is a history of both cooperation and tension between the Vietnamese state and mountain minorities that stretches back to legendary times. However, in general local resistance is not based on separatist ethno-nationalism. There are major dialect differences among ethnic Vietnamese in northern, central, and southern Vietnam, and of course regional experiences have been quite different over the past 150 years. Nevertheless, as bitter and divisive as regional differences can be, the conflicts occur within the larger ethnic family.

First the colonial period and then wars have created a significant Vietnamese diaspora in Southeast Asia, China, France, the United States, and other places. It is estimated that there are 2.5 million overseas Vietnamese (Viet Kieu) living in ninety countries.[4] But ethnic Vietnamese abroad have not yet created a culture of permanent diaspora like that of the Nanyang (South Sea) Chinese of Southeast Asia. The idea of being Vietnamese is still closely attached to the country, regardless of the diaspora's opinion of the current regime.

The most salient fact of Vietnam's location is that it is the Southeast Asian country most exposed to heartland and maritime China. Not surprisingly, its culture, politics, and history have been more influenced by China than any other Southeast Asian country. Although the Vietnamese language is not derivative from Chinese, approximately 60 percent of Vietnamese vocabulary is borrowed from Chinese, and the proportion rises to 70 or 80 percent in the areas of politics, economics, and law.[5] To some extent Vietnam's interaction with China sets it apart from its regional neighbors. However, not only shared geography, but also similar experiences with colonialism bind Vietnam closely with Southeast Asia. With the creation of French Indochina in the 1880s Vietnam, Laos, and Cambodia were combined in one political unit, which created an ambiguity with regard to sovereignty that was not finally resolved until the 1990s. Vietnam's admission into ASEAN (the Association of Southeast Asian Nations) in 1995 was that organization's decisive step from being a Southeast Asian club of states to becoming a truly regional organization.

Vietnam's exposure to China and its regional relationships in Southeast Asia are basic facts of location that affect the entire country. However, given Vietnam's geographic dispersion, not all localities in Vietnam are affected to the same degree by external relationships. For example, Hanoi is closer to the capitals of the Chinese provinces of Yunnan, Guangxi, Hainan, Guizhou,

---

[3] See Dang Nghiem Van, Chu Thai Son, and Luu Hung, *Ethnic Minorities in Vietnam* (Hanoi: The Gioi, 2000).

[4] Vietnam News Agency, February 7, 2002.

[5] See Do Thi Thanh Huyen [杜氏清玄], "Xiandai yueyu zhong de Hanyu Jieci 现代越语中的汉语借词," [Chinese Loan Words in Modern Vietnamese], *Dongnanya Zongheng* 东南亚纵横 [Around Southeast Asia] 5 (May 2004), pp. 8–11.

Guangdong, Chongqing, and Sichuan than it is to Ho Chi Minh City, while Ho Chi Minh City is closer to six of the other nine ASEAN capitals than it is to Hanoi. It is therefore hardly surprising that Hanoi would be more concerned about China, or that Ho Chi Minh City would have strong economic links with Southeast Asia. The large Hoa population of Ho Chi Minh City is more a link to Southeast Asia than it is to China, because its ethnic Chinese are linked more closely with the Nanyang Chinese throughout the region than they are with China itself.

If we reflect on Vietnam's geographical parameter, it is clear that Vietnam is the opposite of a "melting pot" in which people of diverse backgrounds share the same locality. Instead, its unity lies primarily in its people and their feelings of community. On the one hand, the geographic dispersion and diversity implies that in everyday life Vietnamese in different places face significantly different risks and opportunities. The problem for relationships between center and locality that scale creates for China are created by dispersion for Vietnam. On the other hand, community identity means that significance of being Vietnamese is more intimate, one passed through the family and the village rather than through the marketplace. Of course, being intimate does not necessarily mean being friendly or being tolerant. Family quarrels can be the bitterest precisely because one's own identity and dignity are at risk.

Nationalism and Cosmopolitanism

We can infer from Vietnam's geography that national consciousness is peculiarly important, because it not only reflects a common ethnic and cultural background but it has to integrate a diversity of daily experience in different locations. Moreover, the degree of Vietnam's external exposure leads us to expect that relating to the outside world would play a greater role in Vietnam's idea of itself. Last, the looming presence of China and its role during the emergence of Vietnamese culture imply that relations with China would play a special role in Vietnam's sense of itself and its relationship to the world.

These factors encouraged the emergence in Vietnam of a strong national consciousness with complementary aspects of nationalism and cosmopolitanism. From the time of the Trung sisters' heroic but unsuccessful resistance to the Han dynasty in AD 44, the self-definition of Vietnam has pushed against a stronger external presence.[6] At the same time, however, Vietnam has never excluded foreign things simply because they were foreign. There is a strand of cosmopolitan opportunism in Vietnam that sees anything that is useful as

---

[6] See Sarah Womack, "The Remakings of a Legend: Women and Patriotism in the Hagiography of the Trung Sisters," *Crossroads: An Interdisciplinary Journal of Southeast Asian Studies* (Spring 1997), pp. 31–50.

good, regardless of its origins. To be Vietnamese is to resist and suffer external oppression, but it does not require abstinence from the world's good things.

The view of Vietnamese national consciousness presented here is quite different from that presented by Benedict Anderson in his influential book *Imagined Communities*.[7] Anderson presents Vietnamese nationalism as essentially a Western import facilitated by the introduction of mass communications. On the contrary, I think that the evidence is overwhelming that patriotic resistance to foreign invaders, and common suffering under the heel of the conqueror's boot, has been a constitutive part of Vietnamese identity from the beginning to the present. There was not even the lapse of a generation between the resistance to the French of the last of the patriotic mandarins and the beginnings of the modern independence movement. Clearly the transformation of Vietnam by French colonialism changed the goals and means of Vietnamese nationalism; however, it is just as clear that its claim of continuity with the past is valid.

The contrast between modern revolutionary consciousness in China and Vietnam is quite instructive. In China, the May Fourth Movement of 1919 and its flagship publication *Xin Qingnian* (New Youth) were radically critical of China's traditional culture and avidly interested in all manner of Western solutions to China's problems. Lu Xun's claim that Confucianism was cannibalism became a synecdoche for total rejection of the past. The spirit of revolution through rejection of the past continued through the Cultural Revolution, and indeed the current era of reform began with a complete rejection of the Cultural Revolution, which was its own immediate past. In Vietnam, French colonialism provided an external target for revolutionaries, and traditional resistance to China and then to France provided continuity with the past. Ho Chi Minh was attracted to Marxism-Leninism because socialist internationalism supported national liberation. In his elegant essay "Tradition and Revolution in Vietnam," Nguyen Khac Vien, a leading spokesman for North Vietnam during the American War, distances Marxism from Confucianism, but he also shows respect bordering on nostalgia for the past: "The scholars never knew what a scientist was, whereas we never knew what a worthy man was."[8]

The external orientation of Vietnam's national consciousness can also be contrasted to what might be called the mandala nationalism of Cambodia. There the traditional concept of the state and of legitimacy depended on a cosmic identity between the ruler and the gods. Angkor Wat provides a majestic example, argument, and realization of the identity between King

[7] Benedict Anderson, *Imagined Communities: Reflections on the Origin and Spread of Nationalism* (London: Verso, 1991).

[8] Nguyen Khac Vien, "Confucianism and Marxism," in Vien, *Tradition and Revolution in Vietnam* (Berkeley: Indochina Resource Center, 1974), pp. 15–74.

Suryavarman II and Vishnu.[9] Although the Khmer model of kingship derived from Hindu and Buddhist ideas that were also influential throughout Southeast Asia, the Khmer king established himself as the divine center. Angkor Wat was not a local reference to the sacred Mount Meru (now Mt. Kailash) in Tibet; it was Mount Meru's incarnation in Cambodia. Foreigners play the quite peripheral role of conquered captives, despite the fact that ongoing wars with Champa were mortal threats to the regime. The essence of Cambodia was its inside link to the heavens. It is a very long leap from Angkor Wat to the Khmer Rouge, but the notion of cleansing the Khmer of foreign influences and of getting rid of the "new people" influenced by the outside world implies the possibility of an inner, pure Cambodia that is simply unimaginable in Vietnam. Harsh policies in southern Vietnam after 1975 combined the arrogance of victory with the illusion of the superiority of socialist modernization, but there was not the radical purification of Pol Pot's "year zero," in which persons tainted by contact with the outside world were not considered part of the Cambodian people.

Confronting foreign presence involves more than the heroic resistance symbolized by the Trung sisters. It also involves maintaining inner balance while complying with oppression. The major work of Vietnamese literature, the *Tale of Kieu*, is a sensitive exploration of the dilemmas of submission to fate.[10] Although it is a romantic story of a girl torn away from true love, forced into prostitution, finally achieving reconciliation, its depiction of the agonies and quandaries of dealing with overwhelming power and its message that "a lotus can bloom in the mud" resonates with Vietnam's national situations of occupation by China, France, and the United States as well as with the personal situations of many Vietnamese.[11] Although *Kieu* does not provide a justification for collaboration, it does provide an empathic moral space for it.

As long as Vietnam is not threatened by foreign powers, it shows an impressive zest for things foreign. It is not considered un-Vietnamese to wear a beret, smoke American cigarettes, or drink Chinese beer. There is no dimension of Vietnamese life or culture that simply curls up within Vietnam and shuns the outside world. To be creative in music, art, cinema, cuisine, or literature means to be engaged in a cosmopolitan space in which anything that is useful is good. To be cosmopolitan, to learn languages, to travel, or to swim competently in world currents is not to be less Vietnamese.[12] Americans visiting Vietnam over the past twenty-five years are usually struck by the fact

[9] See Eleanor Mannikka, *Angkor Wat: Time, Space and Kingship* (Honolulu: University Press of Hawaii, 1996).

[10] Nguyen Du, *The Tale of Kieu*, tr. Huynh Sanh Thong (New Haven: Yale University Press, 1983).

[11] A touching narrative by a modern day Kieu is Le Ly Hayslip, *When Heaven and Earth Changed Places* (New York: Penguin, 1990).

[12] I suspect, for instance, that Ho Chi Minh was proud of being a sous-chef to Escoffier.

that Vietnamese do not appear resentful about the war. In my opinion, it is not because the war has been forgotten but because the American threat has passed and so the opportunities of the present are more important.

Perhaps the best example of traditional Vietnamese cosmopolitanism was the relative tolerance shown Catholic missionaries from 1550 until the early nineteenth century.[13] Like China and Japan, Vietnam welcomed early missionaries, but unlike the others there were only fitful efforts to expel them as culturally alien. Indeed, from Confucianism to Marxism, Vietnam's ideologies have all had foreign origins, and they have thrived best when they were not imposed from the outside. It is estimated that in 1660 there were 300,000 Catholics in Vietnam.[14] With the growing presence of the French in the early nineteenth century the Catholics became suspect because of their foreign connections, and a vicious cycle of persecution and French retaliation occurred. The increasing French presence had subtly transformed the Catholics from followers of an interesting and tolerated foreign ideology into the knife edge of a foreign threat. A twentieth-century twist on the story is that the Vietnamese phonetic alphabet, *quoc ngu*, was originated by the Jesuit Alexandre de Rhodes, and French colonial authorities tried to impose it to replace *nom*, the Chinese-based writing system. After some hesitation, the anti-French intellectuals and revolutionaries also started to promote *quoc ngu* as well because it aided the spread of literacy, which was one of their main practical objectives.[15] Vietnamese thus became the only major East Asian language to use a Roman alphabet.[16] Even in a time of conflict, cosmopolitan practicality prevailed over national authenticity.

In sum, it is hardly surprising that a country whose name means "South Viet" would have an orientation toward the north built into its national consciousness. Geography and history combine to make external relations of vital importance to Vietnam, and China has been and is again the most important threat and the most important model. Vietnam is pulled together as a community by external threat and by common suffering, but it shows its genius in adapting the world to its own purposes.

Resource Imbalance

Vietnam's resource situation is considerably different from that of China. On the one hand, it has a sufficient abundance of some important natural

---

[13] Joseph Nguyen Huy Lai, *La Tradition Religieuse Spirituelle Sociale au Vietnam* (Paris: Beauchene, 1981), pp. 368–460.
[14] According to a contemporary report by Alexandre de Rhodes to Pope Innocent X. In *ibid.*, p. 381.
[15] David Marr, *Vietnamese Tradition on Trial 1920–1945* (Berkeley: University of California Press, 1981), pp. 136–89.
[16] In Southeast Asia only Vietnamese, Taqalog, and Malay/Indonesian shifted to a Roman script.

resources, and it has supported its modernization efforts largely through resource export. On the other hand, the distribution of export resources is uneven, adding differences in economic geography to the physical and demographic dispersion. The north has minerals, coal, and hydroelectric power; the central highlands have a variety of commodity crops; and the south has rice, offshore oil, and the big city advantages of Ho Chi Minh City. These differences in turn create differences in opportunities and significant regional variations in income. On the other hand, Vietnam's resource situation is similar to China's in that both have large, educated, and healthy workforces and both are relatively deficient in capital and technology.

Nature and France conspired to give Vietnam an imbalance in commercial resources. Nature's contribution was the concentration of natural resources in various areas. France's contribution was that its extractive economic policy discouraged the development of an integrated modern economy in Vietnam. The natural geographical imbalance of important energy resources is rather extreme. Quang Ninh Province, one of Vietnam's sixty-one provinces, produced 95 percent of Vietnam's coal in 1997. Although coal accounts for less than 2 percent of Vietnam's exports, it is the major heating fuel of northern Vietnam. Half of Vietnam's electricity is hydroelectric, and a power line connects northern dams to southern users. On the southern end, the province of Ba Ria-Vung Tau is credited with producing 97 percent of Vietnam's crude oil. At present it is almost all exported, earning almost a quarter of Vietnam's export revenues in 2000, but a major Vietnamese refinery is expected to be in operation by 2006.

Vietnam's commercial crops also have fairly specific production locations. The Mekong delta produced more than a thousand kilograms of rice per person in 2000, two and one-half times the per capita production of the Red River delta, and accounting for 5 percent of Vietnam's total exports.[17] Dak Lak Province produces half of Vietnam's cotton and almost two-thirds of Vietnam's coffee.[18] Coffee's export share was between 4 percent and 10 percent in 1994–2000, while cotton was a significant import item. Rubber is produced mainly in the southeastern region around Ho Chi Minh City.

The colonial French contribution to Vietnam's uneven distribution of resources was their concentration on production of raw materials and discouragement of socio-economic growth and diversification. As Vietnamese Marxist authors observe, French colonial ownership (and large-scale Chinese immigration into the commercial sector) led to the emergence of a proletariat without a corresponding native bourgeoisie, or even of a "working class

---

[17] *Niên Giám Thống Kê 2001* [Viet Nam Statistical Yearbook 2001] Hanoi: Nhà Xuất Bản Thống Kê, 2002), pp. 121–2; World Bank, *Vietnam Development Report 2002* (Hanoi: *World Bank*, 2001), Statistical Appendix, Table 3–2.

[18] *Tư Liệu Kinh Tế-Xã Hội 61 Tỉnh và Thành Phố* [Socio-economic statistical data of 61 provinces and cities in Vietnam] (Hanoi: Nhà Xuất Bản Thống Kê, 1999).

aristocracy."[19] Consequently, the distribution of natural resources was not softened by reinvestment, diffusion, or urbanization. The modern economic and administrative capacities necessary to the colony were concentrated in Saigon and Cholon, its ethnic Chinese sister city. The French colonial version of "divide and rule" might be called "categorize and rule," and most of Vietnam, as well as all of Cambodia and Laos, was categorized as rural and static.

The original pattern set by extractive colonialism was not overcome by war or by socialist modernization. The fundamental effect of war was the prevention of capital formation rather than its redirection. War discouraged investment by making the future unpredictable and by disrupting economic patterns, and of course much productive capacity was directly destroyed by violence. In a sense, war leveled the economic playing field by destroying it. The emergency mentality of a wartime economy usually sets its sights no higher than the instinctive restoration of what has been destroyed. Moreover, the mentality of socialist modernization from the 1960s to the mid-1980s favored large-scale, aid-based projects that tended to create new imbalances rather than to correct old ones.[20]

The economic centrality of Ho Chi Minh City is the ultimate expression of manmade resource imbalance in Vietnam. Since 1975 the economy of Ho Chi Minh City has not been privileged. Its capacities were unrecognized and mismanaged from 1977 to 1986, and its leading role in reform has been the result of its capacity to respond to markets and to international openness rather than the result of government patronage. Nevertheless, its capacities are disproportional to the rest of the country. It produces about a quarter of the national industrial output, and about a third of centrally owned industrial output. Surprisingly, its share of foreign-invested output is smaller, around 20 percent, but if the oil-related output of Ba Ria-Vung Tau is removed, Ho Chi Minh City's share has declined from 38 percent in 1995 to 27 percent in 2000.[21] The great strength of the city is in services, where it produced one-third of the national output in 1998.[22] To the extent that market reforms encourage the most productive to become more productive, Ho Chi Minh City's unique role in the Vietnamese economy seems secure.

Map 3.4 indicates the two most important dimensions of disparity of resources. The first map shows the percentage below the poverty line, which as the legend indicates can be a considerable portion of the provincial

[19] By 1927 there were 220,000 miners and plantation workers in Vietnam. See Ngayen Khac Vien, *Vietnam: A Long History* (Hanoi: The Gioi, 1991), pp. 185–8.
[20] Adam Fforde and Stefan Vylder, *From Plan to Market: The Economic Transition in Vietnam* (Boulder: Westview Press, 1996).
[21] Calculated from *Nien Giam Thong Ke 2000*.
[22] Calculated from United Nations Development Programme, *National Human Development Report 2001: Doi Moi and Human Development in Vietnam* (Hanoi: UNDP, 2001), Statistical Appendix.

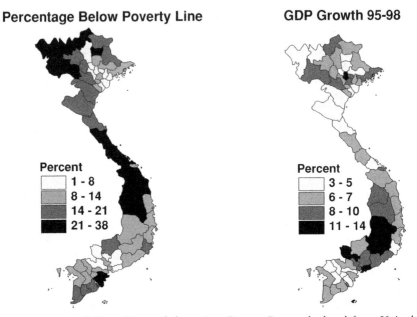

Percentage Below Poverty Line   **GDP Growth 95-98**

Percent
- ☐ 1 - 8
- ▨ 8 - 14
- ▩ 14 - 21
- ■ 21 - 38

Percent
- ☐ 3 - 5
- ▨ 6 - 7
- ▩ 8 - 10
- ■ 11 - 14

MAP 3.4. Regional disparities and dynamics. Source: Data calculated from United Nations Development Programme, *National Human Development Report 2001: Doi Moi and Human Development in Vietnam* (Hanoi, 2001), Statistical Appendix.

population. In one sense there is a certain evenness of distribution of poverty since seven of eight regions, with the exception of the Red River delta, have one or more provinces above the national average. However, some provinces are more than double the national poverty average, while Hanoi is only 10 percent of the average. Among provinces, the income of the richest 20 percent is 7.3 times the income of the poorest 20 percent, and generally provinces with greater poverty have a smaller average disparity. As one might imagine, other disparities of resources are associated with poverty. While Ho Chi Minh City has only half the national average of underweight children, the central highlands region is one-third above average. Similarly, some provinces are almost double the national average of infant mortality, while Ho Chi Minh City is only one-third of the average. But Vietnam's earlier policies of egalitarian socialist modernization deserve credit for the fact that no province is more than 10 percent above the national average on the life expectancy index, of the United Nations Development Programme (UNDP), and except for Lai Chau province in the northwest, few are more than 15 percent below average. Also, literacy is widespread, with only some of the most remote mountain and minority provinces being glaring exceptions. Meanwhile market reforms and international aid have reduced average poverty levels from 60 percent in 1990 to 29 percent in 2002, though some of the more remote locations have remained stagnant.[23] It is an impressive achievement even by global standards. The first sentence of the World Bank's *Vietnam Development Report 2004* reads, "Vietnam's achievements in terms of poverty reduction are one of the greatest success stories in economic development."[24]

The second map of average annual rates of GDP growth from 1995 to 1998 shows that variable growth rates are changing somewhat the picture of resource imbalance. It should be noted that the lowest annual growth rate among the 61 provinces is 2.9 percent, which is certainly better than stagnation or decline. Nevertheless, while not every poor province has a low growth rate, there are few provinces with a growth rate below 6 percent that are not poor. However, the most rapid growth rates are not simply those of the wealthiest units. Ho Chi Minh City's growth rate of 7.5 percent is just below the national average, and clearly the boom region of the latter 1990s was the Central Highlands. The pattern in the north is interesting, with provinces farther from Hanoi on the China border and to the south doing relatively better than the ring provinces, though Hanoi's own growth rate was an impressive 10.5 percent.

Since the discussion of resources has concentrated on disparities, we should conclude by emphasizing that some of Vietnam's most important resources are remarkably evenly distributed. It is a nation at peace, with a consistent and relatively effective national political, economic, and social order. It is capable of transferring resources among provinces and regions, and provincial revenue statistics show a considerable interprovincial transfer from rich to poor. Perhaps most important, all Vietnam has an educated, healthy population capable of responding to whatever economic opportunities present themselves.

Integration and Diversity

Every government has the problem of coordinating the invisible hand of the market with the visible thumb of government activities.[25] The Chinese solution could be caricatured as declaring everything to be unified while actually permitting a great deal of local diversity. Vietnam does not have that luxury. Its center is less central, and its localities are more diverse. The crucial policy dilemma for Vietnam is to maintain national integration without stifling local initiative and to encourage local initiative without

---

[23] United Nations Development Program, *Vietnam Development Goals: Closing the Millenium Gaps 2003* (http://www.un.org.vn/undocs/mdg03/mdg03e.pdf).

[24] World Bank, *Vietnam Development Report 2004* (Hanoi: Vietnam Development Information Center, 2004).

[25] The classic analysis is Charles Lindblom, *Politics and Markets* (New York: Basic Books, 1977).

creating irreconcilable disparities. If it errs in the direction of too much integration, as it did from 1976 to 1986, it runs the risk of weakening the nation and alienating the people. If it errs in the direction of too little integration, it runs the risk of destructive confrontations among local interests. The dilemma has roots in the past but it is just as important in the present and future.

The problem of integration and diversity has many facets, but perhaps the most obvious one is that of balancing national unity and regional differences. On the one hand, opportunities tend to be localized, and given the physical, demographic, and economic differences among northern, central, and southern parts, opportunities can be dramatically different by region. Part of the center's responsibility is not only to allow local initiative, but to facilitate and encourage it. On the other hand, the national interest is not simply the sum of local interests. Vietnam as a whole might require the regional redistribution of resources, the restriction of some types of activities, or a foreign policy that is inconvenient for a locality. For instance, a border area has an interest in maximizing trade. If trade damages national production, however, the center may want to restrict it. The restriction of trade will be unwelcome in the border area, since the production occurs elsewhere, but from the point of view of the country as a whole the restriction might be necessary.[26] However, the center is not always able to enforce policies against local interests, and imposed policies can produce unintended negative consequences. Smuggling increases when border trade is restricted. More important, the national government was capable of restricting the existing economy of Ho Chi Minh City in the late 1970s, but it was not capable of creating a viable socialist economy there.[27]

A matter that is related to but distinct from center-region relationship is the dilemma of encouraging the productivity of the rich while ensuring that the basic needs of the poor are met and that they have a chance to participate in the market economy. This not only requires measures that take from the rich and give to the poor. It also requires taking from the market economy in order to preserve and develop social and economic infrastructure that benefits all citizens. However, given Vietnam's general poverty and inadequate infrastructure, this may be too heavy a burden for its productive forces to bear. The rich are more efficient reinvestors of capital, and economic growth is based to a large extent on reinvestment.[28]

---

[26] Brantly Womack, "China's Border Trade and Its Relationship to the National Political Economy," *The American Asian Review* 19:2 (Summer 2001), pp. 31–48.

[27] William Turley and Brantly Womack, "Asian Socialism's Open Doors: Guangzhou and Ho Chi Minh City," *China Journal* 40 (July 1998), pp. 95–120.

[28] This is the socialist version of the dilemma between growth and distribution described by Samuel Huntington and Joan Nelson in *No Easy Choice: Political Participation in Developing Countries* (Cambridge: Harvard University Press, 1976).

The overseas Vietnamese (Viet Kieu) pose a policy dilemma that is unique to post-war Vietnam. Not only are the Viet Kieu deeply concerned about the welfare of their friends and relatives remaining in Vietnam, but they are also concerned about Vietnam's welfare as a whole. The Viet Kieu have made major contributions to the development of the private economy, and they are a significant influence on the foreign policies of their host countries. However, most Viet Kieu are overseas because of political differences with the current regime. Although for many the differences are now a matter of history, by and large there is still a political alienation between Viet Kieu abroad and the regime. Not only is there vociferous criticism of the regime overseas, but there are also occasional efforts at subversion within Vietnam. So the government must balance a welcoming and tolerant policy toward the Viet Kieu in general with a concern for subversive activities. It is easiest to err on the side of too much suspicion, given the general political differences between the regime and the Viet Kieu, but this further alienates the Viet Kieu and their relatives and costs Vietnam valuable support.

Last, political reform involves not only various improvements in the mechanisms of national politics but also the encouragement of local involvement in the political process.[29] To the extent that local involvement implies the articulation of local issues, the diversity of local situations becomes part of the fabric of politics. To the extent that local issues touch upon policies requiring redistribution of resources, then one locality's gain is another's loss. Political reform can therefore be expected to generate local political voices that are in conflict with one another and with current national policy, and this is already evident in the National Assembly. The current constitution swings the balance of national and local political interests rather heavily in favor of the nation, but if political reform went so far as to permit the formation of various political parties, it is hard to imagine that some of them would not aim at primarily regional constituencies.

History

History, like culture, is a parameter that is so pervasive that it can become an all-encompassing vortex of explanation. The present can be so closely linked to its past that it seems inevitable, even though the future, which is just a moment away, may come as a surprise. The specific contribution of a historical parameter, however, is not to explain everything, but to give a sense of the rhythm and dynamic that the past imparts to the present. In the case of both China and Vietnam, the amplitude of recent historical variation has been enormous, and it forms the lively memories of the present and to some extent its personality. But the role and content of history for

---

[29] See Ben Kerkvliet, "Authorities and the People," in Hy Van Luong, ed., *Postwar Vietnam: Dynamics of a Transforming Society* (New York: Rowman and Littlefield, 2003).

China and Vietnam are quite different. For China, the internal memories of empire, of revolution, and of post-revolutionary excesses set the stage for the current prolonged era of reform. China remained central to its own historical dynamic even though revolution in China demanded the radical rejection of China's past.

For Vietnam, the most important contributor to the flux of politics in the modern era has been the sorrow of war, followed by the disillusionment of peace.[30] In contrast to China's centricity, modern Vietnamese history has been shaped in essential interaction with external forces, and especially with destructive ones. Although that era is now past and Vietnam, like China, is now in the midst of an era of peaceful reform, the historical trauma of war still shapes the emotions of peace. Here we will discuss very briefly the forced subjugation and transformation of Vietnam by the French and the Americans and the tension between heroic community and pragmatic collaboration before passing on to the illusions of victory in the late 1970s and finally disillusionment of the reform era. Needless to say, a few paragraphs on such important topics cannot do them justice. However, perhaps they can impart some sense of the historical momentum borne by Vietnam's present.

The trauma of French subjugation from 1850 to 1900 was particularly extreme for Vietnam because, unlike Laos and Cambodia, the Nguyen dynasty had adapted Western weaponry with alacrity, defeated the Tay Son rebellion, and was expanding at the expense of its neighbors.[31] France stopped Vietnam in its tracks and replaced the distant order of the Chinese empire with the intrusive presence of colonists, missionaries, and soldiers. Moreover, the French could afford to be destructive in their conquest of northern and central Vietnam because their foothold was in the south and they were expecting to move beyond Vietnam to the interior of China.

But the greatest violence done to Vietnam by France was not conquest in the nineteenth century but the transformation of Vietnamese society in the first half of the twentieth century. The "mission civilisatrice" not only humiliated and sidelined traditional structures of authority; it subordinated them to the colonial regime. Village leadership that had served as the hedge between the court and the village now became the fingernails of Paris. The economy was also de-localized. Communitarian, subsistence farming was replaced by landlords who could force their tenants to yield commodity crops. Vietnamese rice entered the world market and Vietnam became

---

[30] "The Sorrow of War" is the title of Bao Ninh's well-known novel, which itself is the most radical expression of the disillusionment of peace. Indeed, the sorrow of war, according to him, was "the sorrow of having survived." Bao Ninh, *The Sorrow of War* [Than phan cua tinh yeu], tr. Phan Thanh Hao (New York: Pantheon, 1993), p. 192.

[31] On the transfer of military technology before French colonialism see Frédéric Mantienne, "Military Technology Transfers from Europe to Lower Mainland Southeast Asia (c. 16–19th centuries)," paper presented at the Annual Meeting of the Association for Asian Studies, Washington, DC, April 2002.

France's most profitable colony, but the rice was taken out of the bowls of the peasantry.

The most tragic result of France's transformation of Vietnam was the Tonkin famine of 1943–45. The externally oriented structure of rice production was made to serve the increasing needs of the Japanese army, depleting grain stores at a time of natural disasters and causing an estimated one million people in northern Vietnam to die of famine. The famine was one of the roots of revolution in Vietnam not only because of the alienation it caused between the colonial regime and the people but also because the Viet Minh's efforts to control famine in late 1945 helped establish the revolutionaries as a regime of the people.[32]

The American subjugation of Vietnam was not as obvious as French colonialism, but the destructive and transformative effects of American power were even more acute. Ostensibly the United States became involved in Vietnam in support of an independent government in the south established as a result of the Geneva Accords in 1954. However, in fact the threat of American intervention was the primary reason for the division of Vietnam,[33] and the global American goal of containing communism meant that the United States would only support a regime that served its purpose.

Again, as in the case of the French in the mid-nineteenth century, the intervention of a strong foreign power stopped a dynamic Vietnam, though not as completely as before. Without the American threat looming over the Geneva Conference, Vietnam would have been reunified under a government poor in resources but rich in popular support. Instead, one of the most physically destructive military campaigns in world history was waged. The fact that the United States was not in Vietnam to make a profit but in order to prevent the spread of communism meant more destruction rather than less, because the United States did not feel constrained to conserve resources or to preserve the socio-economic fabric of either northern or southern Vietnam. The efforts were in vain, but not without effect. Northern cities were depopulated in response to urban bombing, while people in the countryside in the south fled to the cities to escape free fire zones. Vietnam had to become intensely militarized in order to rise to the challenge of American intervention. The damage that China did to itself through the leftist policies of the Great Leap Forward and the Cultural Revolution cannot compare to the damage inflicted on Vietnam from the outside during the same period.

Besides the destruction caused by war, the American transformation of Vietnam involved the creation of a regime in southern Vietnam juxtaposed

---

[32] See Nguyen Khac Vien, *Vietnam*, p. 242.
[33] Zhou Enlai was convinced that the United States would intervene in Vietnam if Ho Chi Minh did not agree to a temporary division of the country, and he convinced Ho of this (quite credible) estimate. See Chen Jian, *Mao's China and the Cold War* (Chapel Hill: University of North Carolina Press, 2001), pp. 138–44.

to a regime in the north that considered itself the frustrated liberator of Vietnam twice over – first with the declaration of Vietnamese independence in September 1945 and then with the defeat of the French. In any case, however, the persistence and scale of American involvement created a life-situation in the south that was radically different from that in the north, and thus a generation in each that was out of touch with the other, regardless of politics or ethnicity. As the war progressed, not only did life further divide the perspectives of north and south, but the south became a more passive partner in the national mission of reunification. As we have seen earlier in this chapter, the geography of Vietnam and the distribution of its resources create natural tendencies toward regional differentiation, but the American intervention created a far more serious bifurcation.

The presence of overwhelming foreign forces confronted every Vietnamese with choices between heroic resistance and pragmatic collaboration. From a distance, these choices might appear to be dichotomous, and they might be conflated with a choice between virtue and convenience. Up close, however, they did not present a single, fateful choice between a high road and a low road, but rather a yin-yang dialectic of identity and survival. Not only did every family involve resisters and collaborators,[34] but even heroes like Ho Chi Minh compromised in order to survive,[35] while employees of foreign forces sometimes acted heroically. The heroine of the *Tale of Kieu*, the central classic of Vietnamese literature, embodies the dilemma of preserving virtue while yielding to fate.[36]

Nevertheless, the notion of a heroic community of national liberators, charged by the adrenaline of confronting a mighty foe and risking death to rescue the nation, was far more than propaganda.[37] Recent demographic research in the Red River delta shows that children of educated parents were almost twice as likely to join the army and to die in combat than children of less educated parents, in contrast to the American army in Vietnam, in which soldiers and casualties were disproportionately from lower classes.[38] By contrast, the Saigon regime lacked a sense of heroic community.

---

[34] For an excellent inter-generational glimpse of this problem see Duong Van Mai Elliott, *The Sacred Willow: Four Generations in the Life of a Vietnamese Family* (New York: Oxford University Press, 1999).

[35] For instance, Ho explained his 1946 compromises with the French with the memorable statement, "It is better to sniff French shit for a while than to eat China's for the rest of our lives." William Duiker, *Ho Chi Minh* (New York: Hyperion, 2000), p. 361.

[36] Nguyen Du, *The Tale of Kieu*, tr. Huynh Sanh Thong (New Haven: Yale University Press, 1983).

[37] Though of course it was the key theme of the propaganda of the Democratic Republic of Vietnam. See Benoît de Tréglodé, *Héros et Révolution au Viêt Nam* (Paris: L' Harmattan, 2001).

[38] Giovanna Merli, "Socioeconomic Background and War Mortality during Vietnam's Wars," *Demography* 37:1 (February 2000), pp. 1–15.

At best, Saigon saw its mission as necessary, while Hanoi saw its mission as sacred.

After the fall of Saigon in 1975 and reunification in 1976 – the end of more than a century of colonialism – Vietnamese politics was dominated by illusions of victory and fictions of community. The basic illusion was that socialist modernization could motivate the same level of enthusiastic commitment that national liberation had. As the Political Report of the Central Committee put it in December 1976,

The new socialist type of Vietnamese has striking characteristics: *collective mastery, labor zeal, socialist patriotism, and proletarian internationalism.* He is also the crystallization of what is most beautiful and noblest in the Vietnamese soul and nature, which has been forged through four thousand years of history.[39]

The north would march forward in socialist modernization begun in the 1950s and delayed by the American war, while the south would catch up with the help of its northern brethren, who were installed in leadership posts throughout the region. Meanwhile the wartime solidarity of Indochina would continue and willingly coalesce behind Vietnamese leadership. The entire socialist world would continue its full support, and Vietnam could continue to play a role in bringing the Soviet Union and China together in a common project of socialist internationalism. Even the United States would have to acknowledge defeat and pay the $4.7 billion in aid that Richard Nixon had secretly promised in 1972.[40]

Implicit in the illusions of victory were fictions of community that masked serious differences and anxieties. Yes, Vietnam was now reunified, and even southerners who had fought for Saigon were open to new horizons. But the south had its own capacities and problems, and these were ignored in the rush to remake the region in the image of the north. Le Duan was no Lincoln, binding up the wounds of war. In the region, Vietnam's insistence on the "unshakeable militant solidarity" of Indochina was taken as a threat by Cambodia. And clearly Vietnam would have to choose between the Soviet Union and China now that the necessity of military co-sponsorship was passed.

But perhaps the greatest illusion was that the sense of community created by mortal threat and sacred task could continue in the post-war era. Vietnam was not simply a community of warriors: recruitment and mortality in the Cambodian conflict reverted to the pattern of being highest among the least educated.[41] The occupation of Cambodia from 1979 to 1989 may have

---

[39] *Communist Party of Vietnam 4th National Congress Documents* (Hanoi: Foreign Languages Publishing House, 1977), p. 56. Emphasis in original.
[40] Nayan Chanda, *Brother Enemy* (New York: Macmillan, 1986), pp. 138–51.
[41] Merli, "Socioeconomic Background," p. 11.

been necessary, but it did not attract heroes. The disillusionment could be profound. As Bao Ninh puts it:

To win, martyrs had sacrificed their lives in order that others might survive. Not a new phenomenon, true. But for those still living to know that the kindest, most worthy people have all fallen away, or even been tortured, humiliated before being killed, or buried and wiped away by the machinery of war, then this beautiful landscape of calm and peace is an appalling paradox. Justice may have won, but cruelty, death, and inhuman violence have also won.[42]

By the mid-1980s the illusions of victory were being replaced by the determined pragmatism of reform (*doi moi*), and by the 1990s the success of reform policies confirmed the wisdom of the new, non-ideological commitment to economic reform and political order. The unacknowledged contradiction between the new policies and the idealism of the revolution created an unofficial community of disillusionment reflected in the bitter and critical tone of much contemporary Vietnamese literature. But the government could hardly be faulted for adjusting to a post-revolutionary reality, and their critics are not calling for a new revolution. One can regret the passing of the age of heroes without desiring a return of the challenges that called them forth. Its memory highlights the banality of normalcy without making normalcy less necessary.

The post-war realities of Vietnam were created by its vivid and stormy past. In contrast to China, which accumulated a broad-based and comprehensive socio-economy during the thirty years before reform, Vietnam began *doi moi* in 1986 with a battlefield. The primitive accumulation of resources and the reconstruction of webs of production and commerce were its first tasks. Equally difficult was the adjustment to the gray realities of post-war life. Vietnam's withdrawal from Cambodia, international openness, and normalization with China were founded on a bedrock of realism exposed by the collapse of grander visions of the future and an intimate acquaintance with the cost of conflict.

---

[42] Bao Ninh, *The Sorrow of War*, p. 193.

4

The Politics of Asymmetry

The previous two chapters have provided descriptions of the basic parameters of the politics of China and Vietnam. To complete our examination of the fundamentals underlying the relationship, we need to consider the general characteristics of asymmetric relationships, because the disparity between China and Vietnam is the most striking feature of their relationship. The purpose of this chapter is to provide an analytical framework for interpreting the relationship of China and Vietnam. After we consider the history of Sino-Vietnamese relations in Part Two, we will return to a general analysis of the variety of asymmetric relations.

China and Vietnam provide an archetypal case of asymmetry. The relationship is one of great disparities, all in China's favor, and it has been long term. Although not all asymmetric relations are between neighbors, shared borders imply a greater range of contact and therefore are usually more intense. Sino-Vietnamese relations have been through every possible variation from intimate friendship to implacable hostility, and indeed they have been through the full spectrum in the past forty years. Although the relationship has involved war on numerous occasions and the occupation of Vietnam by China, China has not been able to "solve" its differences with Vietnam by subjugating it. Whether in traditional times or in the present, China and Vietnam have usually managed their differences as autonomous but asymmetric political entities. By providing a clear bilateral case through a broad range of history and circumstance, the relationship of China and Vietnam can contribute to the understanding of asymmetry in general, and thus to the understanding of all cases in which this mode of analysis might be applied.

In this chapter we will not retrace the data on the disparity between China and Vietnam that were given in Chapter 1. Rather, we will begin by drawing a distinction between symmetry and asymmetry in international relations, and then we will analyze the politics of inattention characteristic of the larger side and the politics of overattention characteristic of the smaller side. Then we will consider the frictions and misunderstandings typical of asymmetric relationships, and the crises caused by vicious circles of misunderstandings. Hostility rarely resolves asymmetric conflicts, so the next topic is stalemate and the emergence of normalization. We will conclude with a consideration of the management of asymmetric relations. In the course of the discussion we will use China and Vietnam as examples to illustrate the model, but the primary focus here is on the model itself.

Symmetry and Asymmetry

When discussing abstractly the relationships of states, there is usually a presumption of symmetry. Symmetry does not require absolute equality, but it does imply potential reciprocity in the interaction: what A could do to B, B might likewise do to A. The basic ethical principle in such a situation should be the same for states as it is for individuals, namely, to do unto others as you would have them do unto you.[1] Moreover, understanding the other is essentially a matter of empathy, of putting oneself in the other's shoes. Since a symmetric relationship is roughly balanced, it is not misleading to interpret the other as a reflection of oneself.

However, in relationships among states there are many cases in which the disparities between the two sides are profound. Asymmetric relationships are not reciprocal. The larger side, A, can do things to the smaller, B, that B cannot do in return. Moreover, the relationship is more important to B than it is to A because B has proportionally more to gain or lose, so B will be more attentive to the relationship than A will be. If we divide the relationship, A⇔B, into its two directions, A⇨B and A⇦B, the two directions are actually quite different. Moreover, although B will be more concerned about the relationship than A, it will not necessarily interpret A's behavior correctly. In an asymmetric relationship, putting oneself in the other's shoes can be misleading.[2]

Along with the advantage in "hard power" that A enjoys comes a potential advantage in "soft power."[3] The disparity of capacities between A and B will tend to make A the center of attention, and to the extent that A can be attractive and persuasive to weaker states, it can induce cooperation rather than relying on sanctions and rewards. The traditional Chinese empire is perhaps the world's best example of international leadership sustained primarily by soft power. However, soft power is not simply a birthright of the strong. In order to be attractive, A must appeal to common values, and in

---

[1] The classic application of this logic to international relations is Immanuel Kant, *Zum ewigen Frieden* (Königsberg: Friedrich Nicolovius, 1795).

[2] Brantly Womack, "Asymmetry and Systemic Misperception: The Cases of China, Vietnam and Cambodia during the 1970s," *Journal of Strategic Studies* 26:2 (June, 2003), pp. 91–118.

[3] The term *soft power* was first used by Joseph Nye in his 1990 book, *Bound to Lead*, and further elaborated in *Soft Power: The Means to Success in World Politics* (New York: Public Affairs, 2004).

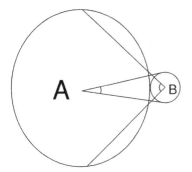

FIGURE 4.1. Asymmetric attention

order to be persuasive, A must promote common goods. Sustainable soft leadership is thus implicitly interactive.

Despite the fact that A is much more powerful than B, rarely can A simply force B to do what A wants. If A tries to dominate B, B's motive for resistance will be survival, which is likely to be stronger than A's motive for domination. Victory over B's armies does not necessarily mean that A will be able to sustain control over B's territory and people. Moreover, A has other relationships to worry about, and what it does to B will affect its relations with other states. On the other hand, B can only dream of overwhelming A. Therefore an asymmetric relation is usually not simply one of domination and submission, nor is it a situation in which a symmetric relationship is temporarily out of balance. An asymmetric relationship can be "normal."

If the collapse of an asymmetric relationship into conflict would harm the interests of both sides, then we can say that the overall relationship is managed well if the mutual interests of both sides are benefited and the peaceful relationship is sustained. From the perspective of each side, we can say that each does well if it maximizes its own interests within the constraint of achieving mutual interests and preserving the relationship. Of course, it might prove necessary to force a breakdown in the relationship in order to preserve national interests. In no international relationship is "peace at any price" the only option. Nevertheless, it is important to note that it is possible to have equilibrium in an asymmetric relationship.

However, even a "normal" asymmetric relationship is different from a symmetric one. As Figure 4.1 illustrates, A's attention to B is a much smaller percentage of A's general concerns than vice versa.[4] Even if B were the only other country in the world, A's domestic concerns would demand a greater percentage of its attention than would be true for B. Moreover, A has little

---

[4] Figure 4.1 also suggests that the effects of disparity vary inversely with distance. Although the salience of distance in political, economic, and military matters has been transformed in the last century, it is arguable nevertheless that neighboring states are likely to have more intense and diverse interactions than distant states.

to fear from B, and it has relatively little to gain. By contrast, not only does A fill a greater percentage of B's horizon, but B is less able to influence A's behavior by means of rewards or punishments. Moreover, any event in the relationship that benefits or harms both sides equally will have a greater proportional effect on B. Thus the relationship is experienced more intensely by B. Its hopes and fears regarding the relationship will be more vivid than those of A.

We can therefore expect that the normal politics of asymmetry will be quite different in A and in B. Of course, differences in perception between actors and patterns of misperception have been discussed in international relations theory, but the linkage between relative capacities and characteristic perspectives has not been explored. Robert Powell, for example, discusses "asymmetric information," but he is referring to different mixes of knowledge and ignorance among the partners in a relationship, not to the origin of the differences.[5] Similarly, Robert Jervis in his classic work treats psychological dimensions of international misperception, but these are based on individual propensities of states and their leaders, not on the structure of the relationship.[6] I am proposing a relational pattern in which disparity tends to factor a relationship into its stronger-to-weaker and weaker-to-stronger directions. The following two sections will explore the characteristic politics of each direction.

It should be noted that I do not claim that all differences of interest and attention, all misperception, or all conflict is caused by asymmetry, even among asymmetric partners. Differences of regime and ideology certainly contribute their share to international conflict, while the "Kantian variables" of liberal democratic government, international institutions, and economic interdependence do their share to mitigate hostilities.[7] However, the structural effects of asymmetry that are described here do have significant and characteristic effects that are overlooked in other theories. Moreover, the influence of asymmetry pervades even peaceful asymmetric relationships. Even if, for instance, democracies do not fight one another, the tensions caused by different exposures to the risks and benefits of a relationship will affect the behavior of large and small democracies in characteristic ways.

The Politics of Inattention

It is perhaps too harsh to call A's normal politics in an asymmetric situation "inattentive," but A will almost certainly be less attentive than B. A is likely

---

[5] Robert Powell, *In the Shadow of Power* (Princeton: Princeton University Press, 1999).
[6] Robert Jervis, *Perception and Misperception in International Politics* (Princeton: Princeton University Press, 1977).
[7] Lars-Erik Cederman, "Back to Kant," *American Political Science Review* 95:1 (March 2001), pp. 15–31.

to have a number of external concerns that are of equal or greater importance than B. As in the case of China, there might be global powers that are much stronger. If China showed the same vivid overattentiveness to the United States and the Soviet Union that Vietnam showed to China, it would necessarily reduce its attention to Vietnam. Let me emphasize that there is a difference between information and attention. China's information and expertise concerning Vietnam are excellent, but normally Vietnam is not a constant concern of the general leadership, nor of the public and the media. Moreover, the entire external world seems farther away to a larger country because domestic concerns are amplified by scale. China's centricity is an extreme example, but the same phenomenon of larger countries being more inwardly oriented can be observed elsewhere as well. If all the rest of the world seems more remote, then normal attention to smaller countries might well be even more problematic.

Of course, the question of how much attention B should receive from A is not easily answered. Almost by definition, B is not, by itself, a security threat to A, and a perception of threat is the most powerful motivator of attention, especially at the national level. If there is nothing to worry about, then only opportunities beckon. But the opportunities that B offers A are also limited, and many of them are perceived and pursued by specialized interests within A. Only in the areas bordering B are economic interests concentrated. Border areas as well as institutions profiting from (and harmed by) relations with B will push and pull on national policy, but their efforts might well be subliminal as far as national consciousness is concerned, and their effects on policy might be contradictory.

If there is not a strong pattern of national attention toward B, then A's policies specifically directed toward B are likely to be uncoordinated. For instance, the customs bureau might crack down on smuggling at the same time as a border province of A tries to deregulate cross-border trade, and the navy might do something provocative at the same time as the foreign ministry is arranging a summit meeting. The level of general leadership that would be capable of coordination would simply not be interested enough to expend the energy that thorough and sustained coordination would require. Thus, at any one time A's specific policies toward B might appear to be going in several directions.

If the perception of specific threats and opportunities from B provides only weak and scattered stimuli to A, then A's attitude toward B will be set by three general concerns. First will be A's perception of the history of the relationship and of B's attitude toward A. If B is perceived as friendly to A, then A can afford to be generous in the relationship. If B is perceived as hostile, then A can bully B and take pleasure in the damage done to B. A's attitude of friendship or hostility is often personalized as a judgment of the leader of B. Perhaps the best contemporary example of this tendency is the American policy toward Castro's Cuba in the post-Cold War era.

The second factor will be what role B is perceived to play in larger patterns of alliance and hostility. While B might not in itself be a threat to A, it might be perceived as the beachhead for some larger power. Vietnam's growing relationship with the Soviet Union in the 1970s provided the most powerful justification for China's increasing hostility. Conversely, common membership in regional and world organizations buffers the bilateral relationship between larger and smaller states.

The third factor is the consistency of "B policy" with A's general foreign policy priorities and practices. The growing inconsistency between China's hostility toward Vietnam in the 1980s and its general reform policies emphasizing peaceful economic relations was an important background factor in normalization. More important, now that China's Vietnam policy is in line with its general foreign policy, the path of least resistance will be for China to treat Vietnam as it treats other countries.

Given the importance of such framing concerns and the weakness of specific attention to B, it is hardly surprising that A's policy toward B tends to be stiffer and less responsive than vice versa. If A perceives B to be hostile, it will be difficult for B to change that perception. If A perceives B to be friendly, irritating actions by B are not likely to lead to an immediate condemnation, though A might try to push B back in the "right direction." If there is a crisis in the relationship, it is likely to be perceived by A to be a crisis caused by B's alliances rather than by B alone. Thus, even though the crisis centers on B, A is actually more concerned with regional or global strategy. There will be much talk about "the B problem," but A might be insensitive to B's actual situation, and inattentive to what B is saying or doing.

The Politics of Overattention

In an asymmetric relationship the less powerful side is vividly aware not only of the importance of the relationship, but of the fact that the other side plays the leading role. Therefore the leadership of B not only pays more attention to the bilateral diplomacy of the relationship, but it also tries to figure out what A thinks and what A is up to. In effect, B is tempted to spend more effort trying to analyze A's politics vis-à-vis B than A spends coming up with the policy, and this may lead to distortions of overattention.

The fact of vulnerability to A leads B to be sensitive to all possibilities of A's actions. It is of course important to know what A presently intends to do, but the future-oriented "what if...?" questions are also important. If A abruptly changes its attitude toward B, or if it changes its general policies in ways that affect its relationship to B, B must be prepared for the change. For example, Vietnam was affected by the Chinese Cultural Revolution in the sixties, and in the eighties by Gorbachev's new policy of peaceful cooperation in the Pacific. In its turn, China was shaken by the anti-Stalinist shift in Soviet domestic policy and international outlook under Khrushchev, even though

Stalinist policies had not been particularly favorable to China.[8] Burdened with the knowledge that their relationship with A can be upset by A's other domestic and international concerns, the leadership of B is likely to hedge against the possibility of a change for the worse. On a sunny day the leaders of B and their advisors are likely to look for clouds on the horizon, and on a cloudy day they will fear a typhoon.

It is important to note the difference in attitude toward the relationship. A compensates for its inattentiveness to B by relying on the general atmosphere of the relationship, while B will not completely trust the atmosphere of the relationship, even if it is friendly. While A can behave in a relaxed manner because it is not threatened, B is likely to be nervous and suspicious no matter how many reassurances A gives. A will probably feel that it is being generous to B, and B might well appear to be insufficiently grateful and unnecessarily suspicious. Because it feels the need to hedge against changes in A, B's posture toward A is likely to seem more cold and distant than circumstances warrant. B will resent its vulnerability to A, and since the vulnerability results from the disparity in capacities rather than A's policies, there will always be a residual resentment.[9]

In contrast to the uncoordinated picture of A's policies toward B, B's policies toward A are likely to be better coordinated at any one time because of the greater attention of central leadership. However, by the same token the leadership is likely to change policy more frequently. So A's policy toward B would present a fuzzier picture at any given time but be generally more stable, while B's policy toward A would usually be coordinated but would fluctuate over time.

The leadership of B will be tempted to buffer its direct exposure to A's superior capacities. One method is to join with A in multilateral associations and agreements. Such multilateral arrangements bind both sides and provide an indirect venue for both sides. Another method is to join with other small states in regional associations or on matters of common interest. Such associations provide a better public forum for B's concerns while at the same time they do not threaten A. The third and far more risky method is for B to ally itself with a power, C, sufficiently strong to challenge A. B might intend the relationship with C to be partial or arms-length, and in any case

---

[8] As Chen Jian points out, Khrushchev's early China policy had actually been more favorable than Stalin's, but his failure to consult with the Chinese before his denunciation of Stalin and the new political direction that this move initiated undermined China's trust in Soviet international leadership. Chen Jian, *Mao's China and the Cold War* (Chapel Hill: University of North Carolina Press, 2001), pp. 61–72.

[9] Charles Kindleberger observed that English derogatory slang toward the Dutch – "Dutch uncle (severe disciplinarian), "Dutch courage" (alcohol), "Dutch treat" (the guest pays his share) – originated in the rather brief period of Dutch naval and trade superiority in the seventeenth century. Kindleberger, *World Economic Primacy, 1500–1990* (New York: Oxford University Press, 1996), pp. 43–4.

it is unlikely over the long term that C's relationship with B will be more important than C's relationship with A. But the problem with such alliances is that from the perspective of A, they immediately create a crisis. A final method that must be mentioned is the development of nuclear weapons by B. If B has the capacity to develop and deliver nuclear weapons, their huge destructive capacity can provide an equalizing counter threat against mortal threats from A. However, assuming that A also has nuclear weapons, they can only be a threat of mutual suicide. Because they are so extreme, such threats are limited in their actual utility, but they do create a certain kind of equality.

Deference, Autonomy, and Misperception

The fundamental expectations of each side in an asymmetric relationship are different. A expects deference from B. It expects B to act in a way that respects A's greater power. This does not necessarily imply subservience (though larger powers are of course quite happy with subservience), but B must articulate and manage its disagreements with A in such a way that its defense of its own interests does not challenge the asymmetry of the relationship. If B has an inflated idea of its own strength or if B colludes with others to balance A, then B's lack of deference threatens A. On the other side, B expects A to acknowledge B's autonomy. Precisely because of A's greater power, B needs to be assured that there are boundaries A will not cross. Otherwise B feels exposed to A's whims. To the extent that B does not believe that A acknowledges its autonomy, B feels vulnerable.

Deference and autonomy are not necessarily contradictory, but they are in a delicate relationship. B can afford to be deferential only if the superiority of A's power does not threaten B's vital interests. Otherwise B should either surrender or fight. Deference requires a confidence in autonomy. Likewise, A's acknowledgment of B's autonomy is not absolute. It is an acknowledgment within the context of asymmetry. But the reciprocal expectations of deference and autonomy can become contradictory if they are presented as unilateral demands. If A demands deference, it is implicitly threatening the autonomy of B. If B demands autonomy, it is implicitly challenging the greater power of A. To demand deference is to demand submission. To demand autonomy is to assert equal power. Conflict can escalate if each side absolutizes its own demands and interprets the other's position as a denial of its basic interests.

A might attempt to force B into greater deference by using its superior force to push B or by linking an issue under dispute to unrelated matters of vital interest to B. Such bullying behavior is usually not intended by A as a general threat but as a reminder of the asymmetry of the relationship. In extreme cases, such as the defeat and removal of General Noriega of Panama by the United States military, actions that by any standard are an act of war are used to accomplish a specific purpose as if no general threat to B were intended. However, it is understandable that B's perspective would be quite different. A's pushing and inappropriate linkage exceeds the proper boundaries of negotiation, and it raises the question of how far A would go to get its way. If A appears to respect B's autonomy only when it is convenient for A to do so, this is small comfort to B.

B is usually not in a position to force A to acknowledge its autonomy, but it can behave in such a way that A might doubt that B has a realistic view of the relationship. B can try to assert substantive as well as formal equality with A in negotiations, and it can have an allergic reaction to actions by A that appear to touch on B's interests. From B's point of view, it may simply be trying to maximize its position vis-à-vis A. Better relations with A can be equated to losing nothing to A rather than cooperating in an asymmetric relationship. But from A's perspective, B's assertive and allergic behavior is not only tiresome and irritating; it also raises the question of whether B understands and accepts its place in the relationship. If B has illusions of greatness or illusions of A's hostility, it might create a security problem for A, either through B's own acts or through B's alliances with others. If B strives for autonomy without deference, then A is put in the position of granting autonomy at its own risk.

Characteristic misperceptions can result from the pushing and shoving of an asymmetric relationship. If B extrapolates from A's bullying behavior to what A could do to B, then B is likely to become paranoiac toward A. B will see each frown or push from A as a step toward war. If A extrapolates from B's assertive behavior, A will see B as an untrustworthy and ambitious viper that could ally with others and threaten A. Both these tendencies will reinforce one another. A is likely to respond to B with more pushing until A perceives a crisis. If B's affronts to A's dignity or its alliances with others provoke a crisis, there will be little that B can do to avoid conflict. Meanwhile, as A pushes harder on B to get B back in line, B's sense of vulnerability will become stronger and its defensive measures will become more desperate. Thus the misperceptions and countermoves of each side are likely to produce a vicious circle, a negative complementarity of action and reaction leading to conflict.

Stalemate and Normalization

The irony of asymmetric hostility is that precisely because of A's greater coercive capacities, B usually has a stronger sense of mortal threat. Since B cannot overrun A, A's war aims are usually limited: to force B into a position that A prefers. If military action is involved, it will usually occur on B's territory, and it might even start with the destruction of B's standing army and the occupation of its cities. But distant warfare is expensive, it is hard to keep the domestic public excited about the "little B threat," and sometimes pacification seems to drag on and on.

By contrast, B feels mortally threatened by A and therefore its war aim, while defensive, is unlimited: to preserve its identity and autonomy that are under threat by A. If fighting occurs in B, then vulnerability to A is felt by the whole community. A's defeat of B's troops can have the indirect and contrary effect of consolidating B's resistance. "Asymmetric warfare" – guerilla war, sabotage, terrorism – causes damage to A, and A's countermeasures can further isolate its pacification efforts. Meanwhile B's resistance continues because B has no alternative. A can give up and go home, but B cannot.

When each side perceives that its frustration is likely to continue indefinitely and that there is no feasible way to prevail over the opponent, then the situation of stalemate has been reached. The possibility of stalemate is usually unforeseen at the beginning of a conflict and emerges only as the initial hopes of A are frustrated and the initial fears of B remain unrealized.

Stalemate is a situation in which both sides of a hostile conflict no longer see a reasonable chance of winning.[10] Winning is the unilateral resolution of conflict. Victory, by contrast, is the defeat of the organized forces of the enemy, and, as we can see in the American involvement in Iraq, it is often not the resolution of conflict. We can distinguish between "hot" stalemate, a situation of active military confrontation, and "cold" stalemate, a situation of confrontation in which interaction is based on the zero-sum premise that "if you win, I lose." The American war in Vietnam is an example of hot stalemate, while the U.S.-Iran relationship since 1980 is one of the longer-running cases of cold stalemate.

It is especially hard for A to accept the fact of stalemate, since it is by definition the stronger side. It is threatening to A's self-image, to its reputation for competence, and to its credibility with other countries. A loses face.

Moreover, the situation of stalemate is not as obvious to A as it is to B. Perhaps the commitment of more resources or the reframing of hostilities can turn apparent stalemate into the pause before success. To use the example of the American war in Vietnam, President Lyndon Johnson responded to the frustration of stalemate by increasing troop levels, while President Richard Nixon attempted to reframe the conflict, first by expanding the theater to include Cambodia and later by attempting to cut Soviet and especially Chinese support for Vietnam. Since A by definition has many more resources than B, there is likely to be a "war party" that believes that more commitment will succeed. But in the long run the promise of "light at the end of the tunnel" can lead to disillusionment.

In the case of cold asymmetric stalemate the situation is less vivid, but the dynamics are similar. If we take the long standoff between the United States

---

[10] The English word is derived from the game of chess, and describes a situation in which no further moves are possible, but checkmate is not accomplished. Until the nineteenth century a stalemated game was credited as a victory to the weaker side; since then it has been considered a draw.

and Iran as an example, as the Reagan administration became convinced that isolating Iran would not achieve its aims, it attempted behind-the-scenes adjustments – the famous Iran-contra affair. For the past twenty years Iran has been interested in ending the conflict, but not at the price of changing its regime, and various American administrations have considered adjusting their policies but hesitated because of the domestic price of policy change.

By definition, stalemate does not end itself, so it can last a long time. When a relationship is in the phase of stalemate, psychologically the situation appears to go on forever. On the other hand, once stalemate is acknowledged, then it is admitted that nothing can be gained by the current hostility. So continuing in an acknowledged stalemate is simply a waste of time and resources. The feeling grows that something else must be tried.

Most of the options for ending stalemate are in the hands of A. Stalemate is usually more costly to B than to A, at least proportionally, so B will usually offer to negotiate long before A accepts. Although A is also frustrated by stalemate, it gains some satisfaction from the greater suffering of B and it postpones bearing the costs of losing face. In some cases the domestic political costs of losing face are greater than the chronic losses from continuing stalemate, and so it goes on. Sometimes a distracting event elsewhere can become the catalyst for A deciding to end stalemate.

A acknowledges that a situation of stalemate exists when the options of prevailing are considered unfeasible or unacceptable and the costs of maintaining stalemate become unbearable. The United States reached this point in Vietnam in 1968 after the Tet Offensive, and again in 1972 after Nixon's expansion of the war and the failure of the Christmas bombing. In the case of cold stalemate, such as the United States-Iran relations, the cost of maintaining stalemate may be so low or diffuse that A prolongs it indefinitely. In the case of United States-Cuba relations, hostility may produce a domestic clientele that is strong enough to prevent negotiations.

There are unilateral options to ending stalemate. B can accommodate gradually to a new identity as subordinate to A. A can withdraw, though the implicit admission of failure is difficult for the larger side. Either A or B can offer unilateral accommodations. For instance, A might set up a native government or offer amnesty to the resistance. B might try to demonstrate to A that it is not a threat. Such steps can be preliminary to negotiation, but they can also of themselves shift the terms of hostility.

Another possibility is negotiation. Negotiation is often difficult to initiate because it involves the implicit recognition of the other side. The protocol of negotiation (the shape of the table, or which parties are officially involved) can be seen as prejudicing the outcome. Nevertheless, if the opponent is in fact controlling assets that are capable of sustaining stalemate, then negotiation may be the best way out.

Confidence-building is a major obstacle in negotiations. Since negotiations start in a situation of hostility, the natural assumption is that a zero-sum game still exists. Each side suspects that any concession demanded by the other side is an attempt to gain a decisive advantage. In fact, negotiation is win-win in stalemate, but it is difficult to move beyond the zero-sum mentality. Ultimately the ending of the mutual frustration of hostility is more important than the details of the negotiation. Demarcation lines and cease-fires that are initially intended to be temporary can become a basis for indefinite non-hostile coexistence. Or, as in the case of the 1973 Paris Accords that ended American direct involvement in Vietnam, an unworkable agreement (the "leopard spot" truce in place) can serve as a figleaf to withdrawal. But a more appropriate result is a mutual agreement to normalize the relationship.

The moment of normalization is reached when both sides formally agree that peace is preferable to hostility. The fact of recent hostility has two contrary effects. On the one hand, both sides know the cost and futility of conflict. On the other hand, each has few positive links with a recent enemy. Each remains suspicious and vigilant. The agreement to normalize relations may produce a formal moment of normalization, the cold handshake of heads of state and the declaration of peace, but usually a long way must be traveled to reach real normalcy. The relationship has crossed a threshold from war to peace, but it has not developed the habits of peace.

The fundamental task of negotiation is the establishment, or re-establishment, of a framework of deference and autonomy. A ceases to threaten B on the assumption that B will not threaten A, and in turn that assumption is premised on B's acceptance of the asymmetric situation. In short, A requires deference from B. From B's perspective, the fact of stalemate demonstrates that A cannot force B's submission, and A must acknowledge that fact. B acknowledges A's power on the assumption that A will cease encroaching on B, and in turn that assumption is premised on A's acknowledgment of B's autonomy.

At the point of normalization, the relationship is usually cool and distant. Not only are there few points of contact between the former belligerents, but also the negotiation of new issues such as trade and borders opens areas where interests differ and both sides want to win. The weaker side will be sensitive to new vulnerabilities that emerge from peaceful relations. The stronger side may show residual resentment by being slow to treat B as a friendly state. Since the possibility of conflict is still vivid, the approach of both sides is cautious.

Gradually, however, the new opportunities provided by peace attract entrepreneurs, and as normalization continues, both sides become more confident in its permanence. But the relationship remains sensitive to hot button issues of deference and autonomy, and although neither side wants hostilities to resume, each is willing to confront the other over perceived breaches and thereby to create crises that put peaceful pursuits at risk. A backward-stepping brinkmanship is not uncommon.

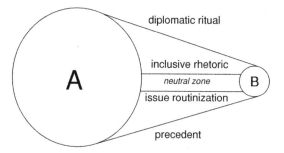

FIGURE 4.2. Factors moderating structural misperception

The transition from the process of normalization to the situation of normalcy may or may not be marked by a dramatic moment. The key characteristic of normalcy is that both sides become confident of the positive mutual benefit of peaceful relations, and they expect to be able to negotiate any disagreements within that framework. Confidence in peace grows gradually from success in normalization, and so it is not a break from the past. The difference between not-yet-normalcy and normalcy lies in sensitivity to crisis. Before normalcy, both sides are willing to openly confront the other and to appear to put peaceful ties at risk. After normalcy, both sides assume that the differences of interest can be settled within the framework of the relationship.

Normalcy is a mature stage in a bilateral asymmetric relationship because it is based on the awareness that coercion is not a feasible option. Although normalcy involves deference from B to A, it is not a relationship of domination, because the tradeoff is A's recognition of B's autonomy. Even in a normal relationship B remains vulnerable to A's greater capacities, but these vulnerabilities do not involve threats of coercion, and they can be managed by negotiation.

Managing Asymmetry

It is possible to maintain a normal asymmetric relationship, but it is not easy to do so. The natural tendency of each side to view the relationship only in its own terms is particularly dangerous, because each side is so different from the other. Nevertheless, many asymmetric relations maintain equilibrium despite the tensions and differences of interests inherent in international relations. We will first discuss the management of bilateral asymmetric relations and then the effect of multilateral contexts.

Figure 4.2 illustrates the major dimensions of managing asymmetric relations. The two basic management tasks are to neutralize possible areas of conflict by creating a neutral zone in the relationship, and to control the escalation of misunderstanding and conflict by creating a sleeve of normalcy. The neutral zone reduces the likelihood of conflict by removing potentially divisive issues from immediate political attention, and the sleeve of normalcy moderates the vicious circle of confrontation.

The first step in neutralizing areas of conflict lies in their formulation. If issues are formulated by both sides in terms of their exclusive interests, then by definition a victory of one side will mean a defeat of the other. If an issue is formulated in terms of common interests (with different points of view on each side), then it is legitimate for both to participate in negotiating or managing the problem. For instance, each side is usually interested in border control for very different reasons. What is harmful to one side is likely to be less harmful to the other. Smuggling and drugs harm the target country more than the transit country. However, both countries have an interest in effective state control at the border, and each country has problems of smuggling, even if the specific issues are different. So if the problem is formulated in terms of common interests, then the two states are more likely to work side by side. If the problem is formulated as one state's protest against another state's indolence, then the two states are more likely to confront each other face to face.

The second method of neutralizing issues is to create joint commissions of experts to handle common problems. Topics such as trade, transportation, border demarcation and regulation, use of common rivers, and so forth will constantly engender new and unforeseen problems, but their management can be institutionalized and routinized. This method has many advantages. First, it means that when problems arise they are referred to joint committees of specialists rather than immediately becoming political issues. Second, the experts are more likely to apply common international standards to the resolution of disputes and hence defuse conflict by supplying a general point of reference. Third, committees and commissions can make such potentially hot issues as boundary questions cold and tedious by means of endless meetings. Of course, even if topics are turned over to expert commissions, there is always the chance that the issues can be seized and politicized by one side or the other, or that commission recommendations would be rejected. But even in such cases of failed routinization the burden of proof would be on the disruptive party, and perhaps this would be a moderating influence on its behavior or a divisive factor in its domestic politics.

Although routinization can neutralize many issues, the normalcy of an asymmetric relation depends on the confidence of both sides that whatever issues emerge, eventually a solution acceptable to both sides will be found. To put it another way, as a problem emerges and escalates, neither side should extrapolate a worst case scenario and begin the vicious circle of bullying and paranoia that could lead to a breakdown in the relationship.

There are basically two kinds of reassurances of normalcy in an asymmetric relationship. First, diplomatic ritual pays homage to the importance of the relationship for both sides and the importance of shared interests. When one chief of state visits another, the major contribution of the occasion is not the questions that are decided at the "summit," but rather the symbolism of normalcy and mutual respect. Ritual can be thought of as an outer sleeve to the relationship that, when strong, can keep the tensions of the relations within the bounds of normalcy. Ritual is reinforced by exchanges at lower levels and by the establishment of regular visits of state. The high-level visits between China and Vietnam each year since 1991 are an excellent example of diplomatic ritual and its utility.

The second kind of external sleeve to a normal asymmetric relationship is simply precedent, its own history. Commonsense expectations are set by what is familiar and what has happened before. If a relationship has been normal, those who think a current crisis will lead to war or that the other side has dark and hostile intentions will be taking an extraordinary position. Even if they present a logical argument, people will be slow to accept their conclusions because they are inconvenient and against common sense. Probably the strongest pillar of any established asymmetric relationship is simply the fact that it is established.

By the same token, the most dangerous time for an asymmetric relationship is when a fundamentally new situation presents itself. The post–Cold War world has presented a number of such situations, but perhaps the most complex has been the series of crises in the Balkans. Most conflicts have been between asymmetric states that, with the disintegration of Yugoslavia, have no existing, mutually acceptable pattern for their relationship. Hence it is hardly surprising that bullying and paranoia have run rampant, and the situation has been further complicated by foreign intervention. In the case of China and Vietnam, the reunification of Vietnam and the liberation of Indochina created very different notions of the new order in China and Vietnam, and the absence of a pattern for the relationship contributed to its decline into war.

The pattern of managing asymmetric relations that we have discussed so far has been one that is operative directly between the two countries involved, but bilateral relations – and especially asymmetric bilateral relations – are also affected by multilateral relationships, arrangements, and institutions. First, it should be noted that the four factors that moderate the bilateral relationship are reflected at the multilateral level as well. There are multilateral diplomatic rituals such as Asia-Pacific Economic Cooperation (APEC) and ASEAN meetings; there are regional commonsense expectations of continuity; there are multilateral commissions on common problems (and ultimately such global institutions as the IMF and World Bank); and inclusive rhetoric and problem formulation can easily have a multilateral audience. Issue neutralization and the establishment of sleeves of normalcy at the multilateral level amplify the effect of all associated bilateral assurances.

Second, membership of one or both parties in regional organizations buffers some dimensions of the relationship. This is especially important for the smaller party, because in certain face-to-face situations there will be other interested faces not very far away and watching closely. Third, the fact that each party in a bilateral relationship must also have a regional and global foreign policy means that the calculation of the appropriate bilateral posture will be influenced by concerns of general consistency. It is quite possible for a country to be inconsistent in its foreign policy, but this can hardly be considered a virtue, and the inconsistency will probably exert a gentle pressure on the exceptional policy.

Last, the manifold interconnections among countries that can be called globalization means that no relationship can be simply bilateral. Bilateral interactions will be judged according to world standards of economic regimes, security regimes, human rights, and other concerns, and although such concerns are rarely backed by force, they affect the myriad of independent judgments that determine the external environment of a state and therefore increasingly its domestic environment. If investors and tourists stop coming, if trade dries up, if other, unrelated countries feel threatened or outraged by a particular action, then what is intended as a bilateral action can have consequences that extend well beyond and then rebound on the parties involved. Globalization has not only integrated the world's economies; it has turned the lights on for the world's politics.

This first part of the book has dealt with the components of the Sino-Vietnamese relationship – China, Vietnam, and asymmetry – rather than with the relationship itself. In presenting these general topics we outlined Chinese and Vietnamese external relations in their most general parameters, and we have discussed asymmetry in terms that should fit all asymmetric relationships, not just the one between China and Vietnam. Perhaps this has been frustrating for readers who are primarily interested in the facts of the relationship, or more likely they have simply skipped ahead to the next chapter. For the more patient readers, I hope that a foundation has been laid for understanding the structure of the relationship and its place in the lives of both countries, so that the facts of the next part will become facts that are located geographically within the parameters of China and Vietnam and that are situated analytically within the model of asymmetric relations.

PART TWO

THE RELATIONAL DYNAMIC

5

From the Beginnings to Vietnamese Independence

The history of relations between China and Vietnam is a major focus of this study. Our research concerns the interactive changes in China and Vietnam over the course of their development, and history is the record of these changes. However, the perspective taken is not that of a historian. Rather than presenting a narrative of the relationship, we shall look in the historical record for its structure. The task here is not history but the utilization of history as part of an attempt to understand comprehensively the pattern of an asymmetric relationship.

Chinese and Vietnamese authors are often concerned with the origins of their present polity – "How did we get here?" For Chinese studies, Vietnam plays a marginal role if it is noticed at all. For Vietnam, China is the foil for the development of Vietnamese nationhood. What will be stressed in this chapter is that in the beginning both polities were in a state of flux, and their interactions helped shape domestic developments and each polity's notion of itself. This is more obvious in the case of Vietnam, but Vietnam has also been an important influence on the course of China's development. For the sake of convenience, "Vietnam" and "the Vietnamese" shall be used to denote the current territory of Vietnam and its residents, and the same will be done with "China" and "the Chinese," as well as present-day provinces such as Guangxi. But it will soon become clear that a major thesis of this chapter is that neither "China" nor "Vietnam" was always the same reality in the past as that today.

Before China and Vietnam: Pre-imperial Relationships

The history of China is usually told from the perspective of its taproot in northern China. The taproot is very deep: none of the Chinese tales of origin mention people coming from elsewhere. But it is located in the north along the Yellow River, a long way from Vietnam. However, southern kingdoms originally not considered Chinese such as Chu on the Yangtze River and the

Yue people scattered from Shanghai down the coast vigorously interacted with northern neighbors, and a sinitic realm – connected by warfare and commerce rather than unified by politics – did stretch to Vietnam during the first millennium BC. The "Hundred Yue," of whom the Lac Viet [Luo Yue 雒 越] in Vietnam were a tenuous part, were related to the Yue kingdom centered in Zhejiang that was defeated by Chu in 333 BC.

The replacement of the Shang dynasty by the Zhou dynasty in 1100 BC[1] can be considered the beginning of Chinese political identity. The Zhou did not claim to be innovators, and they respected the rites of the Shang, but from the beginning they emphasized that their claim to rule was based on the mandate of heaven lost by the last Shang king because of misrule. The classic statement of the mandate of heaven by King Wu, the conqueror of Shang, is important both for its moral content and for its inclusive centricity:

I...am about to administer a great correction to Shang. Shou, the present king of Shang, is without principle, cruel and destructive to the creatures of heaven, injurious and tyrannical to the multitudes of the people. . . . Having obtained the help of virtuous men, [I] presume reverently to comply with the mandate of heaven and make an end of his disorderly ways. Our flowery and great land, and the tribes of the south and north, equally follow and consent with me.[2]

The principle of virtuous rule articulated here became fundamental to the Chinese elite's self-understanding of authority, both domestic and external. The importance of maintaining the welfare of the people did not imply democracy, but it did place a high value on general prosperity and the preemption of popular unrest. Moreover, the mandate of heaven put the Chinese state in a unique relationship to heaven. As Herlee Creel put it, "Henceforward China was a state – and, since it ideally embraced 'all under Heaven,' the only state – created by, and maintained under the direct supervision of, the highest deity, Heaven."[3] There were of course other peoples, the barbarians, but there was not and could not be another moral center (Table 5.1).

The China of the Western Zhou dynasty was roughly twice the area of contemporary Vietnam, only a small part of what became the sinitic realm

---

[1] Traditionally the beginning of the Zhou dynasty was marked at 1122 BC, but more recent estimates put it as late as 1020. However, we do know for certain, from a bronze inscription at the time, that the Shang capital was conquered in the morning. See Wen Fong, ed., *The Great Bronze Age of China* (New York: Knopf for the Metropolitan Museum of Art, 1980), pp. xv, 203.

[2] Translation based on Clae Waltham, *Shu Ching: Book of History* (Chicago: Regnery, 1977), pp. 122–3. The historicity of the early use of the mandate of heaven is confirmed by the text of a bronze inscription written a few years after the event. The bronze was discovered in 1963. See Fong, *The Great Bronze Age of China*, p. 204.

[3] Herrlee Creel, *The Origins of Statecraft in China* (Chicago: University of Chicago Press, 1970), vol. 1, p. 93.

TABLE 5.1. *Chinese and Vietnamese pre-unification history*

China	Vietnam
Xia dynasty c. 2205–c. 1766	
2000 BC	
	legendary Van Lang, 2879–258 BC
first bronzes	
Shang dynasty c. 1766–1122	
1500	
Zhou dynasty c. 1122–256	
Western Zhou c. 1122–771 1000	
	Dong Son c. 650 BC–100
Spring and Autumn 770–476	
500	
Warring States 475–221	
Chu conquest of Yue 333	Au Lac c. 220–180
Qin dynasty 221–206	part of Nan Yue 180–111
Han AD 202–20	Defeat of Nan Yue 111
AD 0	
Defeat of the Trung sisters by Ma Yuan AD 43	

of pre-imperial China.[4] And the Zhou people themselves had only recently settled down; the grandfather of King Wu had been a barbarian. Although China asserted a moral and civilizational superiority, the civilizing mission of the Zhou and its successor states was one of example and education rather than conquest. As the Zhou descended into feudalism in the Spring and Autumn period and then into anarchy in the Warring States period, the example became a memory, but education spread broadly.

The fantastic bronzes, musical instruments, and lacquers of the non-Chinese state of Chu from the early Warring States period (400 BC)[5] are sufficient proof that, beyond the northern taproot, other groups contributed to the common cultural fund of China and also maintained local identities. Like the three centuries of the Hellenistic era in the eastern Mediterranean from the death of Alexander the Great in 323 to the Roman conquest, the cultural realm of pre-imperial China was characterized by cultural interaction

---

[4] Creel estimates the size of Western Zhou territory at 282,000 square miles, or 730,000 square kilometers, roughly the size of Texas. *Ibid.*, p. 101.

[5] The major Chu excavation is the Zeng Hou Yi tomb near Suizhou City, on display at the Hubei Provincial Museum in Wuhan. It includes a sixty-five-piece set of bronze bells, many complex and bizarre bronze vessels, and an extensive collection of lacquer objects ranging from coffins to utensils. See Hubei Provincial Museum, eds., *Zeng Hou Yi mu wenwu zhenshang* [Appreciating the Cultural Relics of the Zeng Hou Yi Tomb] (Wuhan: Hubei Fine Arts Publishing House, 1995).

and mutual learning despite political and military discord.[6] Especially in the era preceding the unification of China in 221 BC, China was not a state, but rather an *oecumene*, an "inhabited area" of cultural interaction and convergence. As Herrlee Creel says, "Quite clearly it was the confluence of numerous traditions, and the opportunity that this provided for cross-fertilization and selection, that made Chinese culture great."[7]

Despite the chaos of the half-millennium of the Spring and Autumn and Warring States eras and the lack of an effective central government, it should not be thought that Chinese culture remained embryonic. This was the golden age of classical Chinese thought, the age of Confucius and Mencius, of Lao Zi and Zhuang Zi, of Lord Shang and Han Fei Zi. While it is not surprising that the Chinese military classics could take shape in such an era, it is strange that the writers whose works would form the moral and intellectual pillars of the dynasties of imperial China would themselves be living in turbulence and advising local rulers in situations of regional anarchy. The Warring States era lived up to its name, with more than a million trained and armed soldiers among the major states and as many as 360,000 involved in a single battle.[8]

Of the non-Chinese groups participating in the pre-imperial Chinese *oecumene*, the Yue are of greatest interest to us. As the "Viet" in "Vietnam" and the southernmost sinitic area, they would of course attract our attention, but they have a more intimate relevance for our study throughout this chapter. In the pre-imperial period there was little distinction between the Yue in Guangxi and in Vietnam; the kingdom of Au Lac, claimed by Vietnam, was founded by a Yue king based in Guangxi. Less than fifty years after its founding, Au Lac was consolidated into the "empire" of Nan Yue, ruled from Guangzhou. This conquest too was traditionally accepted by Vietnamese historians as a legitimate change of rule.[9] The conquest of Nan Yue by General Lu Bode in 111 BC resulted in the peaceful transfer of both Guangxi and northern Vietnam to Han China.

The pathbreaking and remarkably comprehensive research of Jeffrey Barlow enables us to integrate the story of the Guangxi Yue into our account of

---

[6] The classic work on the Hellenistic era is M. I. Rostovtseff, *The Social and Economic History of the Hellenistic World* (Oxford: Oxford University Press, 1941).

[7] Herrlee Creel, *The Origins of Statecraft in China*, vol. 1, p. 227.

[8] Sun Pin, *Military Methods*, tr. Ralph Sawyer (Boulder: Westview, 1995), "Historical Introduction," p. 29. By contrast, Alexander's expeditionary force against the Persian Empire was comprised of 30,000 infantry and 5,000 cavalry. The Persians, at three times Alexander's strength, were approximately equal to the state of Chu, which had the sixth-largest military in China. See Seton Lloyd, *Ancient Turkey* (Berkeley: University of California Press, 1989), p. 136.

[9] There is an old legend of the defeat of the Au Lac king by the Nan Yue king, which alleged trickery on the part of Nan Yue but nevertheless treated the transfer as legitimate. See Keith Taylor, *The Birth of Vietnam* (Berkeley: University of California Press, 1983), p. 25.

relations between China and Vietnam.[10] As the name "Hundred Yue " suggests, the Yue were disparate and scattered, and Barlow concentrates on the southern Yue who reached from Guangdong through Guangxi to Vietnam. The Neolithic remains in Guangxi point to a culture quite similar to that of Vietnam in its early origins (30,000 BC), burial patterns, and rice cultivation, though perhaps not as advanced as either Vietnam or the coastal Yue in Zhejiang.[11] By the time of the Qin invasion in 219 BC, the Guangxi Yue had developed from a shaman culture to one of military lords, though the major unit was still tribal. The Yue had participated as mercenaries in the conflicts of the Warring States, and they were able to frustrate the Qin armies, totaling 500,000 men, that were sent against them. According to Charles Hucker, even after the official pacification of Nan Yue in 210 "the Qin commanderies and counties on the south coast, nominally incorporating territories as distant as the Hanoi region of Vietnam, were little more than isolated outposts; the southern peoples were by no means assimilated or firmly controlled".[12] Several decades later, the editor of the *Han History* summarized the experience as follows:

I have heard that Yue has no cities nor walled places; they live among the streams and valleys, in the midst of the bamboo. They are good at fighting on water, skilled at using boats; their land is deep and there are many dangerous waters. Chinese people do not know of this dangerous situation and enter their territory; (there) one hundred (Chinese) cannot fight against one (Yue). If you occupy their lands, you cannot establish commanderies and counties. If you attack, you cannot obtain it by violence.[13]

The description is not only evocative of China's future problems with Vietnam, but it also expresses the situation common in asymmetric relations in which the stronger side finds it difficult to sustain pacification despite military superiority.

The increasing militarization of the Yue led to the rise of a new king in the region of Guangxi, An Duong. He defeated the local lords in the Red River area and established the kingdom of Au Lac, which included most of Guangxi and northern Vietnam. An Duong built a major citadel, Co Loa, in the vicinity of Hanoi, and several thousand bronze arrowheads have been found there.

---

[10] Professor Barlow's e-book is available in an Internet format. Jeffrey Barlow, *The Zhuang: A Longitudinal Study of Their History and Their Culture* http://mcel.pacificu.edu/as/resources/zhuang/.

[11] Barlow, *The Zhuang*, ch. 1: "Origins of the Zhuang: The Bai Yue." Unfortunately the e-book format of Barlow's book does not permit page number citation, but chapters and their subdivisions can be located easily from the table of contents.

[12] Charles O. Hucker, *China's Imperial Past* (Stanford: Stanford University Press, 1975), p. 45.

[13] *Han Shu* 64:2778. As quoted in Barlow, *The Zhuang*, ch. 3: "The Qin Invasion of the Lingnan."

The attempt to conquer the Yue lands was one of the last campaigns of Qin Shi Huangdi, the first emperor of Qin. Indeed, he died on his way back from a triumphal visit to the conquered capital in 210 BC, the thirty-seventh years of his reign as Qin king and the eleventh year of his rule as emperor of China. Almost immediately the empire began to collapse under his son, and the viciousness and lawlessness of the ensuing chaos surpassed even the excesses of the Warring States period.[14] It was mercifully brief, however. The Qin dynasty collapsed in 206, and Liu Bang initiated the Han dynasty four years later in 202 BC. The Han lasted for the next 400 years. For the first sixty years, Liu (now Han Gaozu) and his successors were preoccupied with reuniting under a more moderate rule the territory previously conquered by Qin.

In the unconsolidated territories of Yue, a Qin official named Zhao Tuo used the opportunity of chaos to create an independent kingdom of his own called Nan Yue (Southern Yue). Nan Yue was in a tenuous relationship of subordinate autonomy with the new Han dynasty. Zhao had been recognized as king of Nan Yue by the Han in 196 BC, but in 185 he took the title of Emperor of Nan Yue and seized territory from Han. In turn, An Duong in the kingdom of Au Lac was in a similar situation of subordinate autonomy to Nan Yue. In 180 BC, when relations with Han were stabilized, Zhao Tuo defeated An Duong and annexed Au Lac.[15] What eventually became northern Vietnam was divided into two prefectures of Nan Yue, Jiaozhi [交趾Giao Chi] and Jiuzhen (九真 Cuu Chan). Finally the Han dynasty sent five armies against Nan Yue and defeated and annexed it in 111 BC. The Han general, Lu Bode, marched to Jiaozhi and Jiuzhen, received the surrender of the Nan Yue prefects, and then reappointed them as Han prefects. Nan Yue was renamed the circuit of Jiaozhi and divided into seven prefectures, three of which – Jiaozhi prefecture, Jiuzhen, and Rinan – were located in Vietnam. Thus the official entry of the territory of Vietnam into the Chinese empire was contingent on the defeat of the larger unit of Nan Yue and was relatively peaceful.

Vietnam's history before China's annexation in 111 BC is a tangled mass of archeology, legend, and assertions of independence that appears to be intimidating even to professional historians.[16] It is clear, as Nguyen Khac Vien points out, that Vietnam had different ethnic roots from northern China and autonomous cultural roots in the Stone Age and Bronze Age (the Dong Son culture of the Red River delta), although Barlow's research demonstrates that the clear distinction between Vietnamese culture and the classical culture of north China does not exist between Vietnam and the

---

[14] For the gory details see Szuma Chien (Sima Qian), tr. Yang Hsien-yi and Gladys Yang, *Records of the Historian* (Beijing: Commercial Press, 1974), especially pp. 185–450.

[15] See Taylor, *Birth of Vietnam*, pp. 23–7.

[16] A good case study of the confusion is presented by Taylor in *ibid.*, Appendix C, pp. 309–11.

Yue.[17] Politically, however, it is not clear that the ancestors of Vietnam had much more in common than disorganized localism, or that their localism distinguished them from their nearest Yue neighbors across the (future) border.

In Vietnamese legend and traditional history, the Hung kings of Van Lang are proposed as the founding dynasty, dating from 2879 BC (making Vietnam older than China) until An Duong used his magic crossbow to defeat the last Hong king in 258 BC. Despite the impressive cultural relics from Vietnam's bronze age, however, there is little evidence of a regional political identity corresponding to Van Lang. Moreover, An Duong clearly conquered the region by force (his magic crossbow), and yet he is accepted as the legitimate founder (and sole king) of a Vietnamese dynasty, which itself straddled the future border. Legend also treats Zhao Tuo (Trieu Da), the ethnic Chinese former Qin official who was ruler of Nan Yue, as the founder of a new Vietnamese dynasty, the Trieu.[18] As we will see in the next chapter, the celebrated thirteenth-century Vietnamese historian Le Van Huu considered Zhao Tuo the first Vietnamese emperor.[19] It is interesting, however, that Nguyen Khac Vien in his careful and comprehensive history of Vietnam devotes three pages to the sixty years of Au Lac and only a half sentence to the eighty years of Nan Yue.[20] The ruins of An Duong's citadel of Co Loa, the most impressive ruins of ancient Vietnam, are certainly part of the reason, but the writer of a Vietnamese national history must be diffident about an event like Zhao Tuo's defeat of Au Lac and his subordination of Vietnam to a larger empire headquartered in Guangdong.

Clearly the reason that Vietnam's entry into the Han empire was peaceful was that the transition demanded little change at the time. Not only were the Nan Yue officials left in place, but the Han initially continued the practice established by Au Lac and Nan Yue of relying on local leaders. However, the dynasty took its civilizing mission seriously, and gradually it centralized its administrative structure and imposed greater economic and cultural demands. A model example of a Han official would be Ren Yan, appointed prefect of Jiuzhen in AD 25. According to his official biography, he introduced draft animals and iron plows, sorted all the adult men and women into monogamous relations, and then returned north.[21] Although Ren may not have accomplished as much as he claimed, his activities

---

[17] Nguyen Khac Vien, *Vietnam: A Long History* (Hanoi: The Gioi Publishers, 1993), p. 19.

[18] The kings of the Trieu dynasty are listed in Nguyen Ngoc Huy and Ta Van Tai, *The Le Code: Law in Traditional Vietnam* (Athens: Ohio University Press, 1987), vol. 3, pp. 52–4.

[19] See O. W. Wolters, "Historians and Emperors in Vietnam and China: Comments Arising Out of Le van Huu's History, Presented to the Tran Court in 1272," in Anthony Reid and David Marr, eds., *Perceptions of the Past in Southeast Asia* (Singapore: Heineman Educational Books (Asia), 1979), pp. 69–90.

[20] Vien, *Vietnam: A Long History*, pp. 20, 16–18.

[21] See Taylor, *Birth of Vietnam*, pp. 34–36.

illustrate the Han interest in settled agriculture and in patriarchal Chinese values.

Not all officials were models. Su Ting, who became prefect of Jiaozhi in AD 29, was considered greedy and inept in both Chinese and Vietnamese accounts, and his misrule led to the famous uprising led by the Trung sisters in AD 40–43. The rebellion, which spread to the Yue prefecture in Guangxi, was suppressed by an army collected from all the southern commanderies and led by General Ma Yuan. The Trung sisters thus initiated the Vietnamese tradition of heroic resistance to China, and they have been part of the core national memory of Vietnam ever since.[22]

The defeat of the Trung sisters was the fourth and final stage in the incorporation of Vietnam into the Chinese empire. The conquest by An Duong had tied Vietnam's fate to the southern Yue, and the annexation of Au Lac into Nan Yue had made Vietnamese territory the southern part of a state centered to the north. The defeat of Nan Yue by the Han in 111 BC marked the official entry of the territory into China, but it was not until the accumulated pressures of Chinese presence provoked a popular rebellion led by the local elite that China's control was tested by the people of the region. The fact that the rebellion occurred did not bode well for the consolidation of Chinese rule in the long run. The act of rebellion went some distance toward defining the people of Vietnam. However, the fact that the rebellion was successfully suppressed established the reality of Chinese control. As long as China was strong enough to suppress rebellions it would remain in control of the territory of Vietnam.

Recall that at this point what we have been calling "Vietnam" was not yet Vietnam even geographically. Our attention has been concentrated on the northern part of Vietnam and especially the Red River delta area in the vicinity of Hanoi. Further south there was another Bronze Age culture, the Sa Huynh culture, related to but distinct from the Dong Son culture. In central and southern Vietnam, the original Malayo-Polynesian cultural roots were influenced by Southeast Asian trade with India, and eventually the Hindu state of Champa defined the frontier of Chinese influence and became a major challenge to the sinicized Vietnamese. Just as China's cultural roots were originally located in a small part of its contemporary territory, Vietnam's were originally located in the Red River delta. Moreover, Vietnam's eventual territorial expansion was not preceded by a Vietnamese *oecumene*, but was based rather on the defeat of competing states that were quite different culturally.

The pre-imperial relations of China and Vietnam are most interesting because they occurred in an era when China was not yet China and Vietnam

---

[22] For accounts of the later permutations of the story see Taylor, *ibid.*, Appendix H, pp. 334–9; also Sarah Womack, "The Remakings of a Legend: Women and Patriotism in the Hagiography of the Trung Sisters," *Crossroads* (Spring 1997), pp. 31–50.

was not yet Vietnam. Vietnam was at the far southern edge of the sinitic *oecumene* of the Warring States period, affected more by the indirect pressures of war and conquest on the Yue than by direct influence. These pressures were sufficient to bring Vietnam into the Yue and then into the Han orbit, but they were not sufficient to overcome the sense of locality and cultural autonomy of Vietnam's substantial population. The assimilation forced by Ma Yuan's defeat of the Trung sisters appeared to define a Chinese frontier across the middle of what is now Vietnam, but at the same time, in contrast to the earlier victories of An Duong and Zhao Tuo, it eventually defined Chinese control as illegitimate in the memories of the Vietnamese people.

The relationship of China and Vietnam at this time can be described as one of amorphous asymmetry. Even though the units are not self-defined, the fate of each and its relationship to the other are affected by the difference in scale. The territory and people that became China were focused on problems of disorder within their own realm. While each kingdom in the Warring States period had to worry about its neighbors, as a whole the problems of the realm that became China were internal rather than external. Ambitions for domination, desires for security, and visions of peace all combined to push toward centralization. Like the birth of a galaxy, the gravitational pressure of a great realm of discord eventually produced a nucleus of central power.

Vietnam's location on a double periphery – the periphery of the southern Yue periphery of the Sinitic realm – allowed it to develop its own cultural and demographic substance in the relative peace of small-scale, tribal organization. No larger Vietnamese self-consciousness was necessary because there was no counter-identity of China present at the time. The best proof of Vietnam's cultural autonomy is not the imaginary early dynasties contrived by patriotic historians in the fourteenth century, but rather the plain fact that Vietnam was there when China arrived.

However, Vietnam was vulnerable to the increasing wealth, power, and conflict produced by the emergence of China. The participation of the northern Yue in the sinitic conflicts and later the involvement of Yue mercenaries created a diffusion from the north toward the south of the use of iron and the most modern weaponry. In part, the diffusion contributed to the dogged resistance of the southern Yue to Qin unification, and to the formation and relative success of the Nan Yue kingdom. But the spread of the inventions, techniques, and concerns spawned by the ancient world's most competitive environment put the autonomy of the Vietnamese region at a fatal disadvantage. As the struggles of the era increased the scale of political organization, Vietnam was incorporated first into An Duong's kingdom and then into Zhao Tuo's Nan Yue.

Amorphous asymmetry is situational rather than conscious, but it is real nevertheless. The society of Vietnam was not destroyed by its subordination to northern neighbors; on the contrary, its series of incorporations play an interesting, ambivalent role in its later national consciousness. However, it was put at a structural disadvantage. Without effective resistance it was made part of larger entities the center of whose interests and concerns were increasingly remote, and yet whose power was increasingly intrusive. Such circumstances make resistance inevitable and lead to the emergence of a defensive consciousness.

Vietnam as Part of China

Because of the revolt of the Trung sisters and its suppression by Ma Yuan, the asymmetric relationship between China and Vietnam was no longer amorphous. But the defensive consciousness stimulated by the Trung sisters was not that of one state juxtaposed to another, but that of a part of a state – a locality – juxtaposed to the central government. I call this internal asymmetry. It is important to note that – despite Vietnam's eventual independence – the tension between part and center in internal asymmetry does not necessarily spring from the part's suppressed desire for independence but from the inevitable differences of perspective and interests between the part and the whole, and between local elites and central leadership. Because Vietnam was China's most distant and most self-conscious part, the tensions of internal asymmetry were especially acute, and they developed into a desire for independence.

The Chinese empire emerged as the resolution of seven hundred years of mortal struggle within the sinitic *oecumene*, and thus it began with a remarkably clear idea of the requirements of an extended empire. Nevertheless, there were important developments in China's idea of itself during the thousand years that Vietnam was a part of China, and Vietnam's eventual independence in the Song dynasty was a product of those developments (Table 5.2).

The term *the Chinese empire* can be taken in two senses. First, it can refer to China itself during the period from the founding of the Qin Dynasty in 221 BC to the fall of the Qing Dynasty in 1911. Second, it can be used in an extended sense to refer to the various countries of Asia that sent emissaries to the Chinese imperial court and participated in the tribute system, which involved periodic exchanges of gifts and the bestowal of seals of office by the Chinese emperor. For Vietnam, the only part of China to become an autonomous state recognized by China itself, the difference is vast, and Vietnam began to make the transition between the two meanings in 968. As an imperial power relating to other recognized governments China was patriarchal but mild, as we shall discuss in the next section on "unequal empires." But as a central government relating to its parts, China has insisted on the absolute prerogative of the center since the first day of Qin Shi Huangdi's government in 221 BC.

What did it mean for Vietnam to be part of China? We will take three approaches to answer this question. The first addresses the question of the

TABLE 5.2. *Vietnam as part of China chronology*

China	Vietnam
	AD 0
	Defeat of the Trung sisters by Ma Yang AD 43
	Han 206 BC–AD 220
Wang Mang 9–23	
	Later (Eastern) Han 25–220
	Cham kingdom of Lin-yi established 192 near Hue
	Three Kingdoms 220–80
	Wu (Nanjing) 220–280
	Era of North-South division 316–589
	500
	Liang (Nanjing) 502–57
	Ly Bi rebellion 546–48
	Chen (Nanjing) 557–89
	Sui Dynasty 581–618
	Tang Dynasty 618–907
	Protectorate of Annam 679–866
	Five Dynasties 907–60
	Southern Han or Yue (Guangzhou) 907–71
	battle of Bach Dang River 938
	Ngo Quyen founds independent government 939
Song Dynasty 960–1279	
	Dinh Bo Linh proclaims Empire of Dai Co Viet 968
	Linh recognized by Song as Military Governor 971
	Le Huan defeats first Song invasion 981
	1000
Northern Song (Kaifeng) 960–1127	Ly Dynasty 1009–1225
	Nong Zhigao rebellion, 1041–55
	Song-Dai Viet treaty 1078
Southern Song (Hangzhou) 1127–1279	

political structure of China and the relationship between the center and localities. The second approach considers how China was affected by having Vietnam as its southernmost territory. The last approach considers the effect of being part of China on what became Vietnam.

As the Grand Historian Sima Qian vividly describes the new emperor's first counsels in 221 BC, Qin Shi Huangdi was on the verge of following the normal practice of installing his sons as feudal rulers of far-flung parts of his newly conquered territories when Li Si, his chief justice, pointed out that they would eventually struggle with one another, and the empire would fall apart. Thereupon Emperor Qin set up the world's first centrally controlled bureaucratic state, with a governor, an army commander, and an inspector for each of the thirty-six new provinces.[23]

The political scientist Lin Shangli describes six dimensions of central control of localities in traditional China.[24] First, the Emperor alone rules. Imperial autocracy means that localities cannot challenge the center, and within the center the emperor was the ultimate authority. Although China was divided into localities, there was no devolution of power, much less charters or constitutions stipulating the rights of localities. Autocratic centralization reached its apex in the Song dynasty. Second, laws and regulations had to be unified. The legal code of the Qin was the first national code of laws in East Asia, and it stipulated that laws were determined by the center and administered by localities. Third, personnel was controlled by the center. Central control was enhanced by not appointing officials to their native places (the rule of avoidance) and by circulation of officials. As we shall discuss below, the Tang dynasty developed a system for allowing and utilizing local leadership in non-Han areas. But this was also a matter of central policy, not an embryonic federalism.

Fourth, the center controlled finances. Tax returns were centralized, and the center appreciated the importance of an adequate economic base. As we shall see, the prosperity of Vietnam (and the rest of China) was encouraged under the Han dynasty in order to make the state rich and powerful. Fifth, inspection was strengthened. The system of separate central organs for inspection and control of local officials began in the Qin dynasty and was perfected in the Tang. Sixth, military power was centralized. The First Emperor confiscated all private weapons and drafted more than one-third of suitable males for military service. The Song dynasty switched to a hired army, again to enhance control.

These six dimensions of central control are testimony to the iron commitment of the Chinese emperor to autocratic government, but they also suggest that control in such an extended traditional polity was a constant problem.

---

[23] Szuma Chien, *Records of the Historian*, pp. 166–8.

[24] Lin Shangli林尚立, *Guonei zhengfu jian guanxi*国内政府间关系 [Domestic Intergovernmental Relationships] (Hangzhou: Zhejiang renmin chubanshe, 1998), pp. 265–71.

Indeed, as the discussion of centricity in Chapter 2 suggested, although the hard lines of authority were gathered in the capital, lower levels were always seeking and finding opportunities to pursue their own interests and to shield their activities from the view of the center. To paraphrase Han Fei Zi, the center and localities fought a hundred battles a day, and at the end of the day the center was in charge, but the field belonged to the localities. Being already a settled population at the far fringe of China, Vietnam was less successfully homogenized and controlled.

Besides the daily differences between center and localities, the general effectiveness of central leadership underwent ebbs and flows. When there was tension at court or division in the empire, localities would seize the opportunity to ignore central directives or even to declare independence, as we have already seen with the kingdom of Nan Yue. The periphery was particularly prone to rebellion. Generally, however, the social integration of China as well as the strength of the center eventually prevailed over the divisive opportunism of local leaders. Vietnam was the exception, because the strength of its local identity was eventually great enough to prevail over a distant center. As Keith Taylor puts it, "Han immigrants were more effectively 'Vietnamized' than Vietnamese were sinicized."[25] But Vietnam's numerous failed uprisings during its millennium of being a part of China were similar to – and sometimes a part of – a general pattern of local countermoves against weakened centers.

What did Vietnam mean to China before Vietnam's independence? First, it was a part of China and thus subject to the controls mentioned above. Hence its visible history is one of good and bad officials and their activities, and of unrest dealt with. From the perspective of China as a whole, Vietnam was not the conscious target of central policy but simply one among many places where the general history of China unfolded. For instance, the misrule in Vietnam that instigated the rebellion of the Trung sisters could be seen as yet another example of the ill effects of the usurper Wang Mang, who disrupted central politics from AD 9 to 23, and General Ma Yuan is remembered as one of the three great generals who restored civil as well as political order throughout the empire. For the officials themselves, to be sent as far away from the center as Vietnam was a punishment rather than an honor, but fortunately for Vietnam it was not always the unworthy who were exiled.[26]

Second, Vietnam was a significant but not major part of China. According to the Han census of AD 2, China had a total population of 60 million, while the territory that is now northern Vietnam had a population of 1.4 million, roughly 2.3 percent of China's total and less than half its current ratio.[27] This is not surprising since there was a general demographic shift

[25] Keith Taylor, *Birth of Vietnam*, p. 53.
[26] For examples see *ibid.*, pp. 183–7.
[27] See Taylor's careful discussions of Vietnam's population in *ibid.*, passim.

from north to south from Han to Tang, and even in the Tang the population ratio of north to south was 2:1.[28] Vietnam's peculiarity, as Keith Taylor demonstrates, was that the Red River delta was by far the most populous area in the Guangdong/Guangxi/Vietnam area in the Han, with about 78 percent of the region's population.[29] By the time of the Tang, the population of Guangdong and Guangxi had increased enormously, but it is important to note that Vietnam was not only China's most southern part; it was also a well-settled and populated part rather than a frontier of diminishing interest and utility.

Third, Vietnam was unruly but not threatening. Unlike the unrest of the Xiongnu and other nomadic groups in the north, the uprisings in the south, including Vietnam, threatened only to dismember the Empire, not to defeat it. As Owen Lattimore argued in his classic *Inner Asian Frontiers of China*, the grasslands of the steppes created a natural limit to the expansion of Chinese settled agriculture and a natural base for nomadic cavalry.[30] By contrast, Chinese farmers could seep south over the centuries and gradually transform the socio-political landscape.[31] Unrest in the south was a symptom of central weakness rather than the cause of the disease. Conversely, it was a task of any new, strong dynasty to confirm control over the south, and Vietnam was the farthest significant target of that ambition.

Fourth, possession of Vietnam made China a part of Southeast Asia. Contrary to Keith Taylor, I do not believe that this was the motive behind China's annexation of the territory, since Vietnam was already a part of Nan Yue.[32] Moreover, China did not use Vietnam as a stepping stone to further expansion. China's national perspective was an inland, northern one in which Vietnam was a fringe reality. Nevertheless, controlling Vietnam made China a neighbor to Champa and eventually to Angkor, and thus closer to regional developments.

For modern Vietnam, the period of being part of China is a dim one, located between original autonomy and eventual independence, and lit intermittently by the heroic fires of local resistance. But such a "dark ages" view slights not only the material accomplishments of the era but also the fundamental reshaping of Vietnam and the Vietnamese that took place during the

---

[28] Charles Hucker, *China's Imperial Past* (Stanford: Stanford University Press, 1975), p. 172.

[29] Taylor, *Birth of Vietnam*, p. 55.

[30] Owen Lattimore, *Inner Asian Frontiers of China* (Hong Kong: Oxford University Press, 1988, originally American Geographic Society, 1940).

[31] C. P. Fitzgerald, *The Southern Expansion of the Chinese People* (New York: Praeger, 1972).

[32] Taylor claims that "the Chinese could not control the economy of the South China Sea and secure unrestricted access to the southern trade routes unless they ruled the Vietnamese, who demographically dominated the region" (*ibid.*, pp. 54–5). However, it is unnecessary to add this motive for Ma Yuan's presence, since Vietnam had already entered the Han peacefully with the fall of Nan Yue and it would have been a dangerous embarrassment not to regain control of territory in revolt.

millennium. Vietnam entered the era as the southernmost of the Yue, closely related and lately subservient to their northern kinsmen. Vietnam exited as the Empire of Dai Viet, a counter-China, an organized, ambitious, multi-ethnic state, while its kinsmen to the north in Guangxi Province became the Zhuang, China's largest ethnic minority.

The process of mitosis between the Yue of Guangxi and the Yue of Vietnam is one of the most important and fateful socio-political developments of the era. Thanks to the research of Keith Taylor on Vietnam in this era and that of Jeffrey Barlow on the proto-Zhuang, it is possible to venture some observations on this development.

Clearly one reason that Vietnam became independent in contrast to the Yue area of what is now Guangdong and Guangxi (called "Lingnan" because it is south of the Ling mountains, and also the "Two Guangs" for obvious reasons) was that Vietnam was more distant from the center. After all, the kingdom of Lin Yi, which was farther down the coast in central Vietnam and eventually became Champa, declared its independence in 192 and managed to survive subsequent occupations by China. Although Lin Yi was founded by a rebellious local official from Chinese Vietnam, the new state soon developed an Indianized culture rather than a sinitic one.[33] And in Yunnan, Lingnan's western frontier, the kingdom of Nan Zhao was a major threat to Lingnan and to Vietnam during the Tang dynasty. While it is possible to imagine Lingnan being a part of a larger rebellious area (and this happened with the formation of the Nan Han dynasty – first called the Nan Yue dynasty – in Guangzhou in 907–971), it would be difficult for Lingnan to rebel while more distant localities remained loyal.

Nevertheless, why did the border end up where it did? The most basic reason is geo-politics. The Vietnamese were already the major population of the Red River delta when China arrived, and despite the economic, political, and social transformations of the ensuing millennium, they could maintain their cohesiveness and absorb immigrants rather than being dissolved into a larger political community. By contrast, Lingnan experienced massive migrations, and the potentially rebellious native population was based in isolated mountain valleys where cooperation was difficult. By the time of the Tang (618–907), Lingnan was treated as a part of "normal China," though with a greater number of special ethnic districts than Vietnam had, while Vietnam became a border protectorate, that of the "Pacified South" (Annan).[34] The mountainous frontier between the Red River valley and Lingnan became the border, not because it was the edge of Vietnamese ethnic presence (the local

---

[33] See G. Coedes, *The Indianized States of Southeast Asia*, ed. Walter Vella, tr. Susan Cowing (Honolulu: East-West Center Press, 1968), pp. 42–4.

[34] Other protectorates included the "Pacified West" in the Tarim Basin, the "Pacified North" in Mongolia, and the "Pacified East" on the Korean border. See Taylor, *Birth of Vietnam*, p. 171.

population of the border region was and is largely composed of transborder minorities), but because the mountains were a natural line of defense.

The major attempt at Zhuang independence, the rebellion of Nong Zhigao (Nung Tri Cao) in 1049–53, proved the importance of geopolitics and its sociological corollaries.[35] The rebellion was centered in the mountainous northern bulge of Vietnam and was initially directed against the Vietnamese. Vietnam's independence had created a new force pressuring the Zhuang from the south, and the tightening of local controls in the Song dynasty cornered the Zhuang. Nong was unsuccessful with his own forces against Vietnam, and then unsuccessful in enticing the Chinese officials at Nanning into a joint operation against Vietnam. So he attacked China. He was initially quite successful, taking Nanning and Wuzhou and laying siege to Guangzhou. He planned to establish a new state of Nan Yue there, but the siege failed and Song forces collaborated with other Zhuang clans to defeat Nong. Vietnam offered troops to relieve the siege, but their offer was declined by the Song court. After Nong Zhigao, subsequent Zhuang uprisings did not aspire beyond controlling their own localities.

Nong Zhigao's rebellion is more similar to the revolt of the Trung sisters one thousand years earlier than to the founding of Dai Viet in 968. It sprang from the rejection by an indigenous elite of outside intrusion rather than from the growing strength of an emerging political center. The difference between Nong and the Trung sisters is that the Zhuang elite was fractured in their mountain valleys, and Nong lacked the internal cohesiveness necessary for a defensive war. Nong had to expand his territory to include Guangzhou because the source of his troubles was China itself, not its presence on his doorstep. But this fact made his attempt an internal rebellion rather than an independence movement, and the odds were against him. The failure of the Zhuang to establish independence did not mean that they were weak or without influence in China. The reputation of the Zhuang for ferocity and martial talent remains to this day. The mutiny that eventually ended the Tang dynasty started in Guilin, then capital of Guangxi, and the Zhuang were involved in the Taiping Rebellion from its beginnings in Guangxi in 1850. On a more positive note, the old Yue capital Guangzhou is not doing badly as part of China in the reform era, and, after a slow start, the same can be said for Guangxi Province.

Ultimately, China's success at retaining Guangdong and Guangxi and failure at retaining Vietnam opens an important window on the major political miracle of traditional China, namely, its relative geographic stability despite extended distances, poor communications, and numerous periods of chaos and disunity. Vietnam demonstrated that China could lose an edge piece. Why didn't China simply continue to unravel?

---

[35] This discussion relies on Barlow, *The Zhuang*, ch. 9.

Clearly half the answer is the structure of central authority established at the beginning by Qin Shi Huangdi. Rational, bureaucratic centralization pre-empted the development of new regional elites outside patterns of central control. Even when central power broke down, the parts would use their regionally based power to contend for the center. But the other half of the answer, in my opinion, lies in the policies of handling local elites that were perfected in the Tang dynasty. In practice during the Han, and by policy in the Sui and Tang, compliant local elites in ethnically non-Han areas were often acknowledged and left in place by central officials. In the Tang, the policy was articulated as *ji mi* (loose reins), and it permitted even hereditary appointment of local leaders in designated *ji mi* districts and military that were locally raised and commanded (*tu bing*).[36] In the Protectorate of Annan, many of the top officials were second-generation southerners, in violation of the rule of avoidance in the Chinese bureaucracy.

There appear to have been three major effects in Vietnam of the policies of accommodating elites. The first was that it allowed central officials to sidestep confrontations and to present themselves as allies rather than challengers of the local order. As a result, many Tang officials are remembered positively in Vietnamese folklore, and in general the later reputation of the Tang in Vietnam was better than one might expect from the last and most dynamic era of Chinese rule.[37] Second, the legitimation and reinforcement of local elites created the foundation for an emerging Vietnamese national elite. The most obvious case is the Khuc family, who ruled Vietnam for the first half of the tenth century.[38] Third, the collusion of elites enabled a distance to develop between ordinary people and the elite. Taylor records that in 687 a peasant rebellion occurred, probably in resistance to increasing taxes, but in any case not led by the local elite. It is a reminder that one should not assume that the interests of the people and of even its local elite are identical.

The same *ji mi* policies in Lingnan did not produce the same outcome. There the Zhuang and Yao minorities were not physically or politically united, and the *ji mi* policies could entice the collaboration of individual leaders. Moreover, officials could use Zhuang *tu bing* against other rebellious minorities and against the Vietnamese. Nong Zhigao's rebellion was fatally undercut by the collaboration with the Chinese of other Zhuang leaders, and ultimately this collaboration was made possible by central policies that co-opted local elites rather than alienating and cornering them. Had the Tang mercilessly enforced central control in the south, it might have delayed

---

[36] See *ibid.*, ch. 6.

[37] Possibly the best example would be Gao Bian (Cao Bien), a Tang general who led an army into Vietnam, but was incorporated into Vietnamese folklore as a king and sorcerer. See Keith Taylor, "Kao Pien/Cao Bien and the Vicissitudes of Being Remembered in Vietnam," paper presented at the Annual meeting of the Association for Asian Studies, 1997.

[38] See Taylor, *Birth of Vietnam*, pp. 259–63.

Vietnamese independence, but at the cost of creating the potential for new Vietnams further inland.

The transformation of life and society in Vietnam during the first millennium AD provided the basis upon which an independent Vietnam could be built. With the Han began the iron age in Vietnam. Farming shifted from mobile slash-and-burn techniques to hydraulic works and wing plows as part of the Han's "civilizing mission." Although Vietnam was best known to the center as a supplier of exotic products such as pearls and ivory, the transformation of its agriculture permitted a change in the scale and structure of society. With an economic structure cognate to the settled Han areas to the north, the Red River valley could develop a sense of itself as a sub-center with its own periphery of minorities. Although the Vietnamese [*jing, kinh*] and the mountain-dwelling Muong, Tay, Nong, Zhuang, and so forth were all Yue cousins,[39] the Vietnamese managed to become a settled agricultural population with towns and extended territories, like the Chinese on a smaller scale but – unlike the immigrants to Lingnan – maintaining a non-Chinese local identity.

Buddhism transformed the spiritual and political life of Vietnam.[40] Similar to the economic transformation, Buddhism was an influence that passed through China (and was and remains different from Buddhism in the rest of Southeast Asia), but it was reshaped in doctrinal content. More important, as Buddhism became rooted in the people, it became rooted in a different people, and so it reflected local spirituality. With independence, Buddhism rather than Confucianism supplied the dominant intellectual paradigm for Vietnamese politics from the tenth to the fourteenth centuries. Ultimately the conflict between Buddhism and imperial Confucianism that developed in China in the Tang also developed in Vietnam, but the conflict was delayed by five centuries and reshaped because Vietnamese Confucianism took much longer to unfold.

Meanwhile, Vietnam's regional neighborhood was also undergoing transformation. The original Austronesian populations of the coast were being crowded by additional migrations from mainland and island Southeast Asia, and both directions bore the influence of Hindu culture. On the immediate southern border, the centerpoint of the Cham kingdom of Champa (Lin Yi) gradually moved further down the coast toward Nha Trang, closer to the Hindu kingdom of Funan in the Mekong delta. The Protectorate of Annan had to cope with invasions from Champa, but there were also very profitable Chinese expeditions in 446 and 605 that sacked the Lin Yi capital and carried back booty. As an independent state Vietnam eagerly shouldered the mandate of southern expansion.

---

[39] This is well argued in Barlow, ch. 7.
[40] Keith Taylor provides a careful analysis of the formation of Vietnamese Buddhism. See Taylor, *Birth of Vietnam*, passim.

It is not coincidental that the founding of Dai Viet coincides with the founding of the Song dynasty. The most immediate reason for the coincidence was that Song's march southward threatened the autonomy that Vietnam had enjoyed since the decay of the Tang. The major military accomplishment of Dinh Bo Linh [Ding Buling丁部 领], the first Emperor of Dai Viet, was the defeat of local rivals. He never fought the Song or its regional predecessor, the Nan Han. However, the facts that Dinh had consolidated local control, that Nan Han had been defeated by Dinh's predecessor in the battle of Bach Dang River in 938, and that Vietnam was difficult terrain for Chinese armies constrained the Song to accept offers of tribute from Dinh and to recognize him as "King of Giaozhi" and his son as military governor in 975. He declared himself emperor of Dai Co Viet [大瞿 越] in 966, and inaugurated his reign period of Thai Binh [太平] in 970.

The relatively peaceful beginning of Vietnamese independence was rooted in a profound difference of perspective between Dinh and the Song court. Officially, Dinh was only requesting acknowledgement of his rule of a part of China [neifu内附], not of an independent kingdom. And as James Anderson argues, "the revival of Giao Chi as a subordinate frontier region was most certainly the Song's ultimate plan."[41] Clearly, however, the purpose of Dinh's deference was to have his autonomy acknowledged by the Song. The best evidence is the behavior of Champa, which itself requested *neifu* status, even though it had never been part of China, and began to send generous annual tribute missions to the court at Kaifeng.[42] Meanwhile, Vietnam invaded Champa and sent Cham captives to Kaifeng as tribute. The court returned the captives to Champa, thus displaying its distance from the actions of its troublesome non-subordinate. The Song attempted and failed to regain control of Vietnam by invading in 981, and again in 1077, after Vietnam had invaded, seized, and sacked Nanning in 1076. The current border between China and Vietnam was set after the second failure.

The Song dynasty was noted for a realistic foreign policy and a disciplined domestic order. Vietnam benefited from Song's realism. The titles granted to Dinh Bo Linh were not those of Emperor and King, but they did suggest an ambiguous recognition of political autonomy rather than merely the status of local officials within China. Song did not invade until the murder of Dinh and his son offered the formal and practical occasion, and then it discovered that rather than splitting the local elite into pro-Song and anti-Song factions, the invasion united everyone behind the Dai Viet army and its commander. It did not invade again until the troubles with Nong Zhigao raised the questions of border control to crisis levels.

---

[41] James Anderson, "From Tribute to Trade: Examining a Pivotal Period in Middle Period Sino-Vietnamese Relations," paper presented at the Annual Meeting of the Southeast Conference of the Association for Asian Studies, 2003.

[42] *Ibid.*

Meanwhile, the Song's attention to domestic order continued to transform Lingnan into more integrated parts of China.[43] Although the *ji mi* policies were continued, greater Han migration and the founding of Confucian academies changed the cultural focus of Lingnan. Moreover, the Song introduced new techniques in rice agriculture, and Guangxi became a center of sugar and silk production. As Jeffrey Barlow concludes, "In the Song, Han Chinese impact upon the Zhuang was much deeper than in any previous period."[44] Not only did the Song recognize an autonomous state to the south and eventually delineate the border between China and Vietnam, but its very successes in continuing to transform Lingnan widened the societal gulf between Vietnam and its neighbor. After the Song, Vietnam could only have returned to Chinese control as a colony, never as a part of China.

Asymmetry before Independence

One claim of this book is that the relationship between China and Vietnam covers the entire spectrum of possible asymmetric relations, and the two eras covered in this chapter provide the best evidence for this claim. Even before the formation of China and Vietnam as political entities, let alone as autonomous states, the difference of scale between them structured an interactive pattern of amorphous asymmetry. Before Vietnam's resistance to China in AD 44, the pattern cannot yet be called a relationship because it did not involve the juxtaposition of two self-conscious entities. Nevertheless the ascription of asymmetry is not simply an anticipation of later events, even if later developments are the source of our interest.

The centric concerns of the sinitic *oecumene* were clearly a function of its scale, as was the magnitude of the effects of the Qin solution. The fate of Vietnam on the periphery of China was an effect of scale in two senses. First, Vietnam lacked the massiveness that might enable it to remain indifferent to developments in China. As the more northerly Yue were affected by and became involved in the *oecumene*, they brought a vortex to Vietnam's border that Vietnam could not resist. On the other hand, although Vietnam became a part of China, it did not simply dissolve into it. Vietnam had enough demographic and cultural substance and geographic distance to remain a place where a distinct identity could form.

A counter-factual reversing of the hypothesis can test the salience of amorphous asymmetry. Let us imagine that China and Vietnam have the same disparity in scale, but that Vietnam undergoes the Chinese experience of cultural unification in 1100 BC followed by 500 years of chaotic competition and then imperial unification. Meanwhile China is culturally advanced but

---

[43] See Barlow, *The Zhuang*, ch 9.
[44] *Ibid.*

politically not yet organized. One could imagine that Vietnam could sweep parts of southern China into its vortex, but even if Vietnam managed to conquer all China, the Chinese equivalent of the uprising of the Trung sisters – in this case, the Zhong sisters? – would be a formidable event for the extended Vietnamese empire. Vietnam could become a part of China for a thousand years, but the reverse is hard to imagine. Size does not imply superiority, but it does make a difference.

Although Vietnam did not become a single entity within China until the formation of the Protectorate of Annan in the Tang, the internal asymmetry of part versus whole is clearer than the amorphous asymmetry of the earlier era.

The revolt of the Trung sisters and its failure were equally significant for the emergence of a Vietnamese identity. The revolt established a locus of national consciousness. Although at the time Vietnam may have desired only to be left alone, the idea of a communal self, if only as a rejection of a larger whole, was a necessary bridge between autonomy and independence. The failure of the revolt was important because the civilizational content of Vietnam was transformed by its union with China. Although Vietnam was not simply a miniature China in 968, it was even further from being simply a branch of the Yue. In calling itself an empire, Dai Viet was proclaiming both its independence from China and its acceptance of a common universe of discourse that would not have been intelligible to the Trung sisters.

Having Vietnam as a part of China was a claim that China ultimately could not sustain. In the following chapter we will deal with China's long process of coming to terms with an independent Vietnam, a process that began in 968 but was not completed until the defeat of the Ming occupation in 1427. However, there are implicit lessons for China in the emergence of an independent Vietnam and the successful retention of the Lingnan provinces of Guangdong and Guangxi.

Most basically, we can argue that China's overall policy of national integration was as successful as it could have been. Although Vietnamese independence could be blamed on the "loose reins" of the Tang, those same loose reins permitted the integration of Lingnan. It may be possible and necessary to defeat challengers in battle, but to maintain a political union by force is to nourish the self-consciousness of alienation in the locality and to encourage the desire for independence. Over time, the centrifugal force of the part will find its opportunity to cut loose from the whole. Like Zeno's paradox, any force applied to maintain domination generates additional resolution to resist, and so there is no amount of force that solves once and for all the problem of resistance.[45] The overall correctness of China's policy of inclusive

---

[45] The Greek philosopher and mathematician Zeno posed the following paradox. If the fleet-footed Achilles were having a race with a tortoise and gave the tortoise a head start, Achilles

hierarchy is proven by the endurance of China as an extended empire, and Vietnam's independence can be taken as the exception that proves the rule.

could not catch up with the tortoise despite his speed. The reason would be that it would take Achilles a certain amount of time to reach the tortoise, but in that amount of time the tortoise would also have moved further. So Achilles could get closer and closer to the tortoise but could never pass him. Zeno used the paradox to prove the unreality of the visual world and the reality of numbers. Here, of course, the analogy breaks down.

6

Unequal Empires

With the declaration of the Empire of Dai Co Viet by Dinh Bo Linh (Dinh Tien Hoang) in 968, and especially with the Song Dynasty's recognition of Dinh as King of Giaozhi in 975, contact between China and Vietnam entered the realm of international relations.

But relations between China and Vietnam over the next thousand years do not fit the stereotypes of contemporary thinking about international relations.[1] Nations are often imagined to be sovereign units confronting one another like knights on a field of battle. First, they are assumed to be unitary actors, usually personified by the leader or the capital city – "Beijing thinks this . . . Hanoi does that." Second, the internal structure, identity, and values of each presumably are not influenced by the others. Like balls colliding on a pool table, states remain unaffected by the other states they strike, except that their trajectory will change and they may be destroyed by the collision. Third, it is axiomatic that states will contend for power, because if one state is clearly stronger than another, it will dominate the weaker one. If a state is vulnerable to a stronger adversary, it will either collude with other states in order to balance the adversary's advantage, or it will submit.

Each of these three expectations is well grounded in the essential characteristics of sovereignty as it has been understood in the West since Machiavelli. The minimum condition for the existence of a state is that it controls territory. This implies a monopoly or at least recognized superiority of the central military power, and this in turn implies an ultimate decision maker. If the state is to be the ultimate decision maker in domestic affairs, it must not only be stronger than other internal forces but it must also be capable of maintaining its boundaries against external forces. A state that is stronger than other internal forces but unable to resist the interference of an external force is not really a sovereign state but rather a subordinate of the more

---

[1] The major exceptions to this generalization would be the constructivists and the English school.

powerful state. Last, there is no world policeman to enforce international order, so a state must look after itself and protect its own interests. To the extent that its interests are competitive with a more powerful state it will either collude to form an alliance capable of withstanding the larger state or it will lose. Security is assumed to be the ultimately competitive interest, if you have a larger gun than I do, you become more secure because I become more vulnerable to you. Therefore the scramble for security is essentially a struggle for domination.[2]

The relationship between China and Vietnam that we are about to analyze presents a fundamentally different picture of international relations. First, while there might be an ultimate decision maker in a state, the relationship of that decision maker to the polity can vary enormously. Was China, for instance, a succession of dynasties, or did its unity persist over time? The attempt of the Ming occupation of Vietnam was based on the former view; its failure confirmed the latter. Likewise, the basic characteristics of Vietnam's idea of itself evolved over time.

Second, China and Vietnam were fundamental influences on one another's development even after Vietnam achieved independence. This is more obvious in the case of Vietnam, but it is true for China as well. The defeats of the Yuan armies by the Vietnamese contributed to the frustration, disorientation, and eventual decay of Mongol rule, while the Yuan demands for submission required the Vietnamese to reach beyond their agreements with the Song in order to establish their national identity. The Mongols pushed aside the agreements with the Song, saying in effect, "Those were with the Song, whom we defeated. We are the Yuan." Vietnam was driven to develop the answer, "You are China, we are Vietnam, and we have always been so."

Third, Vietnam considered itself the equal of China only in its right to autonomy, never in the relationship itself. But deference to China was not the same as submission. Meanwhile, China learned that Vietnam, although never a threat, was impractical to subdue. Thus China and Vietnam developed a mature asymmetric relationship in the context of their unequal empires. The arrival of France in the nineteenth century upset the relationship and destroyed both the Vietnamese and the Chinese imperial systems.

The chapter begins with the formation and confirmation of the asymmetrical relationship between China and Vietnam from the establishment of Dai Co Viet in 968 (called Dai Viet after 1054) to the consequences of the defeat of the Ming occupation in the fifteenth century. During this time Vietnam underwent profound changes, and its relationship with China was both a stimulus and a consequence of these changes. Initially it was the

---

[2] The logic of this position is best developed by Kenneth Waltz in *Theory of International Politics* (New York: McGraw Hill, 1979) and more recently by John Mearsheimer, *The Tragedy of Great Power Politics* (New York: Norton, 2001).

non-Chineseness of Vietnam and its peripheral location that led to the declaration of independence, and thus there was a relaxation of the cultural controls of the sinitic realm while military prowess remained important. In dealing with the demands and major military incursions of the Yuan in the late thirteenth century Vietnam was challenged to define itself and to develop a bond between the aristocracy and the people strong enough to withstand the onslaughts of a much more powerful foe. The historian Le Van Huu played a key political and cultural role in articulating an autonomous identity for Vietnam.

For China as well, the transition from Song to Yuan to Ming was an exploration of national identity. The Song was careful about controlling its territory, which required it to be prudent in assessing the limits of its capabilities. For the Song, the conservation of central power was the highest priority. In total contrast, the Mongols succeeded in establishing the largest empire in world history by relying on an overwhelming margin of power at the periphery. They despised the Song (and in general the sedentary Chinese) for their caution, and they certainly felt no obligation to respect the Song's concessions to its neighbors. The pursuit of the margin of power eventually led to defeats on the periphery and to a decay of order at the center. The Ming began as a Chinese rebellion against Mongol rule, but its notions of China's horizons were tantalized by Mongol conquests, and it began its diplomacy in a mood of triumphalism quite different from the caution of the Song.

The twenty years of Ming occupation of Vietnam marked a turning point for both China and Vietnam. For China, the defeat brought the horizons of ambition back to the established boundaries of China. Although the subsequent Qing dynasty brought additional territories from the nomadic periphery into China and it occasionally involved itself in internal struggles in Vietnam, it did not consider Vietnam a lost province to be regained. Five hundred years later the lesson of the Ming defeat echoed when Jiang Jieshi (Chiang Kaishek) declined Franklin Roosevelt's offer to take control of Vietnam.[3] For Vietnam, the struggle against China required the mobilization of the population in protracted war against the invader, and decisive victory put the founder of the Le dynasty at a historic cusp at which he could define both the significance of the victory and the new direction Vietnam

---

[3] President Roosevelt dispatched Vice President Wallace to make the offer of Indochina and Hong Kong to Jiang: "He [FDR] told me [Wallace] to inform Chiang that he proposed to see that both Hong Kong and Indo-China would be returned to China, and that he wanted to see a strong, truly democratic government in China, willing and anxious to live at peace with its neighbors." Henry Wallace, *Toward World Peace* (New York: Reynal and Hitchcock, 1948), p. 97. Bernard Fall confirmed the story (and Jiang's declining of the offer) with Wallace. See Bernard Fall, *The Two Vietnams: A Political and Military Analysis* (New York: Praeger, 1967), pp. 53; 453n.

should take. Fortunately he had at his side the remarkable creative intellect of Nguyen Trai.

At the beginning and at the end of the period we are about to discuss, China and Vietnam faced each other as independent states with unequal power. But during the five centuries from the Song to the Ming defeat, the meaning of sovereignty had been transformed in a process of interaction that tested the significance of unequal power and eventually confirmed an asymmetric relationship as normal.

Establishing Autonomy and Deference: Song to Ming

The Song dynasty was realistic in the most appropriate sense of the word. It took reality seriously. And the reality it faced was one in which the center's effective control of its territory had to be increased, but also central resources had to be conserved for use against the Khitans and nomadic challenges in the north and west. As a memorial from 988 formulated the general strategy:

> If they [the enemy] come, be fully prepared to resist them; if they depart, resist the temptation to pursue them.[4]

From the beginning of the dynasty Vietnam was considered beyond the pale of controllable territory and thus its independence was acknowledged, especially after the failed invasion of 980–81. This did not imply peaceful coexistence, because independence created the problem of new boundaries and also Vietnam became the alien power closest to China's southern gate. But the major trouble for the Song lay elsewhere, and trouble with nomadic powers pushed the Song out of the north of China in 1127 (Table 6.1).

Independence did not solve all of Vietnam's problems. When it had been the southernmost part of China, Vietnam had had to cope with maintaining the coastal frontier against the Chams and the upland frontier against various migrating groups in the mountains, but it did have the support of a mighty hinterland. Independent Vietnam was generally more powerful than Champa and eventually occupied Champa's territory in central Vietnam in 1471, but Champa was close enough in capacity to be a challenger. There was frequent warfare between the two, and sometimes Champa held the upper hand. From 1360 to 1390 Champa invaded Vietnam often and twice occupied Hanoi.[5] Champa was in turn threatened on its southern flank, especially after Cambodia absorbed the Mekong delta kingdom of Funan in 600, but Champa had long-established relationships with its former neighbor China,

---

4 Zhang Ji, quoted in Wang Gungwu, "The Rhetoric of a Lesser Empire," in Morris Rossabi, ed., *China among Equals* (Berkeley: University of California Press, 1983), p. 53.
5 G. Coedès, *The Indianized States of Southeast Asia*, ed. Walter Vella, tr. Susan Cowing (Honolulu: East West Center, 1968), pp. 237–8.

TABLE 6.1. *From Vietnamese independence to the Ming occupation*

	Dinh Bo Linh proclaims Empire of Dai Co Viet 968
Dinh recognized by Song as Military Governor 971	
Le Huan defeats first Song invasion 981	
1000	
Northern Song (Kaifeng) 960–1127	Ly Dynasty 1009–1225
Southern Song (Hangzhou) 1127–1279	Temple of Literature 1070
Yuan (Mongol) 1206–1368	
1206 established as a state	Tran Dynasty 1225–1400
1271 proclaimed a dynasty	Le Van Huu's history 1272
1279 defeated Song	1st Mongol incursion 1257
1260–94 Yuan Shizu (Kublai Khan)	2nd incursion 1285
1274, 1281 unsuccessful attacks on Japan	3rd incursion 1287–88
1300	
Ming 1368–1644	decline of Tran 1368–1400
Ming Taizu (Hongwu)1368–99	
1400	
Ming Chengzu (Yunglo) 1403–24	Ho Dynasty 1400–07
Ming occupation of Vietnam 1407–27	
Capital moved to Beijing 1421	Le Dynasty 1428–1788
Admiral Zheng He's naval voyages 1405–33	Le Thai To 1428–33
Ming Yingzong captured by Mongols 1449	Le Thanh Tong 1460–97
	Destruction of Champa 1471

and it could call on China in its disputes with independent Vietnam. Vietnam sent 45 of the Song Dynasty's total of 302 tribute missions; Champa sent 56.[6] The most important effect of independence on Vietnam was domestic. Because of their military prowess Vietnamese now ruled Vietnam.[7] Vietnam was never tempted to adopt the more sacral notions of power of its Indianized

---

[6] Chen Yonghua 陈永华, "Liang Song shiqi Qhong Guo yu Dongnanya de Maoyi 两宋时期中国与东南亚的贸易," [Trade between China and Southeast Asia during the North and South Song Dynasties], *Dongnanya Zongheng* 东南亚纵横 [Around Southeast Asia] 5 (May 2004), pp. 16–19.

[7] "Vietnamese" in the broadest possible sense of not being Chinese officials. The Tran dynasty descended from Chinese fishermen.

neighbors to the south,[8] but Buddhism rather than Confucianism provided the initial paradigm of rule.[9] Independence, however, was the final stage of a localization of real power that had been evolving over the previous century, and, perhaps inevitably, the process did not produce a small model of Tang Confucianism but rather a more confused and power-oriented mélange of military notables. Although the Temple of Literature was established in the 1070s and the two centuries of the Ly dynasty provided some stability, the literati were individual servants of the king rather than members of a powerful Confucian bureaucracy.[10] The ruling class was a feudal landed nobility whose privileges were usually based on military service, and Vietnamese Buddhism was shaped into a holistic spiritual and political ideology during the Ly.[11] There was attention to the economy, exemplified by major hydraulics projects and expansion of handicrafts, shipbuilding, and commerce.[12] In short, Vietnam was no longer required to be like China, so it relaxed into the conveniences of local interests and arrangements.

The eminent historian Wang Gungwu observed that the Song gave up the attempt to re-establish the glories of the Tang after their first thirty years of rule, though they retained the comforting rhetoric of tribute and hierarchy. But, as Wang observes, "When all you could do was to try to hold the line, there was obviously no Chinese world order."[13] The Song held the line, or actually a series of receding lines, for another three centuries, and its longevity is testimony to the wisdom of sustained prudence. And for the first time since the Chinese Empire was founded by Qin Shi Huangdi, Vietnam was on the other side of the line.

The contrast between the Song and the great Khans of the Mongols could hardly have been greater. Genghis Khan created a world order several times larger than China, and he did so not by establishing a central power, but by pushing at the margins of his realm with constantly moving, overwhelming force. China was valued for its wealth and despised for its weakness; officials of the Yuan dynasty continued to use the Mongolian language and imported many foreigners, such as Marco Polo, into their administration. The very name of the dynasty, "Yuan," was derived from the *Yi Jing* (Book of Changes) "qian yuan," meaning "the original creative force." The name was picked in order to break with the tradition of Chinese dynasties from

---

[8] O. W. Wolters, "Assertions of Well-Being in Fourteenth-Century Vietnam: Part I," *Journal of Southeast Asian Studies* 10 (September 1979), pp. 435–50, especially p. 441.

[9] See John Whitmore, "Chu Văn An and the Rise of 'Antiquity' in Fourteenth-Century Đài Viêt," *The Vietnam Review* 1 (1996), pp. 50–61.

[10] *Ibid.*, pp. 435–6.

[11] Cuong Tu Nguyen, "Rethinking Vietnamese Buddhist History," in Keith Taylor and John Whitmore, eds., *Essays into Vietnamese Pasts* (Ithaca: The Southeast Asia Program, Cornell University), pp. 81–115.

[12] Nguyen Khac Vien, *Vietnam: A Long History* (Hanoi: The Gioi, 1993), pp. 33–4.

[13] Wang Gungwu, "The Rhetoric of a Lesser Empire," p. 62.

the Qin on and to refer back to the legendary sage-kings.[14] Under these circumstances it is hardly surprising that the Yuan did not feel itself bound by
the concessions of the Song in its dealings with Vietnam. Indeed, the Mongols did not demand Vietnam's submission because it had once been a part
of China but because Vietnam, like the rest of the world, was weaker than
itself. The Yuan also annexed Yunnan and attempted to invade Champa,
Java, and Japan, places that had never been part of China. Everywhere the
China of the Yuan demanded submission, and it welcomed war.

The Mongols first invaded Vietnam in 1257 as part of a southern offensive
against the Song. They occupied and destroyed Hanoi (Thang Long), but
then withdrew. After the defeat of the Song in 1279, the Yuan decided to
install a member of the Vietnamese mission to Beijing as king, and sent him
back to Hanoi with an escort of a thousand soldiers. The escort was defeated
and the pretender captured. In 1283 a large army was landed in Champa,
and in 1284 an army of 500,000 crossed the northern border under Kublai
Khan's son Toghan. In a series of battles the Mongols were defeated, and
Kublai gave up plans for another invasion of Japan in order to prepare for
revenge against Vietnam.[15] In late 1287 Toghan again crossed the frontier
with 300,000 troops in coordination with a fleet of 500 ships. The fleet was
destroyed in one of Vietnam's famous river battles by General Tran Hung
Dao, and Toghan retreated. Kublai died in the midst of plans for a fourth
invasion, and his successor Timur abandoned the project.

Vietnam's military resistance was accompanied by diplomatic deference,
though not to the satisfaction of the Yuan. The Tran ruler in Hanoi, Thanh
Tong, treated Mongol envoys as if he were ruler of an independent kingdom
(which, of course, he was), and Kublai sent a threatening message in 1270.
The Vietnamese response avoided claiming independence and said merely
that the treatment of the envoys was simply in accord with the customs of
the country.[16] The rejection of the Mongol-appointed king in 1279 confirmed
Kublai's suspicions of Vietnamese insubordination, and thus the scene was
set for the second and third invasions. Upon the defeat of the third invasion,
Vietnam sent a mission to China offering tribute, and the captured generals
and officers were returned the following year.

These confrontations with the Mongols cover a period of intense crisis for
Vietnam, and the crisis required a fundamental rethinking of Vietnam's identity. Besides Vietnam's need to survive massive invasions, Kublai's demands
for submission required the Vietnamese court to face the questions of the

[14] John Langlois, "Introduction," in John Langlois, ed., *China under Mongol Rule* (Princeton:
Princeton University Press, 1981), pp. 3–4.
[15] Nguyen Khac Vien, *Vietnam: A Long History*, pp. 42–6. See also Coedès, *The Indianized
States*, pp. 192–3.
[16] W. O. Wolters, "Historians and Emperors in Vietnam and China," in Anthony Reid and
David Marr, eds., *Perceptions of the Past in Southeast Asia* (Singapore: Heinemann, 1979),
pp. 69–70.

grounds for Vietnamese autonomy and of the proper relationship of Vietnam to China. Both of these questions pointed at a deeper one of Vietnamese identity. There was no answer at hand, and so the court demanded that Le Van Huu write a history of Vietnam, and that he should start with the Nan Yue kingdom of Zhao Tuo (Trieu Da, 207–111 BC), crossing from there on the stepping stones of various uprisings against Chinese rule to the Dinh dynasty of 968.

Le Van Huu's history had a fundamentally different purpose from the dynastic histories of China and Korea, which were written to establish an orthodox Confucian account of the preceding dynasty.[17] His writing was defined by the contemporary political task of establishing the historical grounds of Vietnam's autonomy from China. His task was not to argue that Vietnam had in fact been independent from China for 300 years or to claim that autonomy was better than subservience to China – these were obvious to his audience. Rather, his task was to establish a record of autonomy from China. Without such a record, autonomy gained under the Song was up for renegotiation with the Yuan and other succeeding dynasties. The point of Huu's history was that Vietnamese independence did not depend on Song recognition, but rather that Vietnam had been independent from of old, and the Song merely recognized the fact. Thus Huu's history – and succeeding Vietnamese histories, including Nguyen Khac Vien's – has a subtext of nationalist polemic. As the contemporary historian Nguyen The Anh puts it eloquently:

The intention was to demonstrate that the founders of Van Lang, the ancestors of the Vietnamese kingdom, were the Vietnamese equivalent of Huang-di [the Yellow Emperor], and their cultural innovations were comparable to those of the latter. ... the concern was to affirm the equality of North and South, according to the political and cultural criteria already used by China to proclaim its superiority over other peoples.[18]

To the Confucian burden of holding the past up to the standards of ethical judgment was added the nationalist political burden of proving Vietnam's autonomy.

Huu did not shirk his Confucian duties of historical criticism. Although he appreciated the military prowess of the Ly dynasty, in general he did not consider them exemplary rulers.[19] The Ly dynasty (1009–1225) was the immediate predecessor of the Tran that Huu served, and thus they were the

---

[17] See *ibid.* for a somewhat different discussion of this point.
[18] Nguyen The Anh, "La frontière sino-vietnamienne du xie au xviie siècle," in n. a., *Les frontières du Vietnam: histoire des frontiers de la pénninsule indochinoise* (Paris: L'Harmattan, 1989), p. 66.
[19] See O. W. Wolters, "Le Van Huu's Treatment of Ly Than Ton's Reign (1127–1137)," in C. D. Cowan and O. W. Wolters, eds., *Southeast Asian History and Historiography* (Ithaca: Cornell University Press, 1976), pp. 203–26.

end of his history. The Ly dynasty was weakened, especially in matters of succession, by its departures from Chinese imperial practices. Only two of the eight Ly rulers were mature men at the time of their accession, and the appointment of heirs involved a free-for-all struggle of counselors and the many empresses and their progeny. The Tran had in fact come to power by insinuating themselves into the Ly court, but once in power they had adopted a policy of naming the new emperor early while the power still remained with the "Senior Emperor" (tai shang huangdi) until his death. In this matter, therefore, Huu is confirming the wisdom of his Tran patrons. However, the domestic import of his history was a call to use the Chinese model to strengthen the institutions of imperial rule. Huu's reliance on the Chinese model of governance does not contradict his argument for Vietnam's autonomy, but it does demonstrate that the intellectual horizons of Vietnam remained within the Chinese sphere. Vietnam's new identity, articulated under the pressure of Mongol demands for submission, both pushed against China in assertions of autonomy and leaned on China as a model of governance. This pattern held for the next 700 years, until France replaced China as Vietnam's greatest threat and model.

Vietnamese intellectuals of the next century developed both strands of Huu's history.[20] On the one hand, they extended the roots of Vietnamese autonomy back to the Hung kings of Van Lang and praised the martial spirit of the northern border area. By creating the Hung dynasty (2879–258 BC) Huu's successors declared Vietnam's independence from even China's sage rulers and gave Vietnam a period of majestic autonomy comparable to that of China's Golden Age. An Duong, the Yue conqueror of Vietnam from Guangxi, became the founder of the Thuc, the second dynasty. Then came the Trieu of Zhao Tuo, the northerner who founded Nan Yue in Guangdong. The elaboration of historical independence was complete.

But more pressing to the intellectuals in the fourteenth century was the obvious decline of the Tran and the increasing aggressiveness of Champa. China had ceased to be an active threat because of the internal problems of the Yuan. But Vietnam itself was falling apart under the late Tran, and the literati ascribed this to departures from the sinitic virtues of Vietnam's newfound golden age. There is criticism of the influence of Buddhism, of the weakness of the civil bureaucracy and the outrages of court favorites, and of the increasing gulf between the aristocratic landed oligarchy and the people. Eventually the Tran was replaced by one of its ministers, Ho Quy Ly (originally Le Quy Ly), and he attempted radical reforms. Inspired by the claims of Vietnamese historians concerning the ancient origins of Vietnam and by the example set by the Mongols in naming their dynasty "Yuan," Ho renamed Dai Viet "Dai Yu," after the second Sage Emperor, and made his

---

[20] See O. W. Wolters, "Assertions of Well-Being in Fourteenth-Century Vietnam: Part I," and "Part II," *Journal of Southeast Asian Studies* 11 (March 1980), pp. 74–90.

son emperor.[21] Ho's power base was in Thanh Hoa, south of the Red River delta, and his program of land redistribution threatened the gentry of the delta.[22] But Ho's establishment of his own dynasty in 1400 also provided the pretext for the Ming invasion of Vietnam in 1407.

For China, the rise of the Ming dynasty meant the restoration of Chinese control of China. Zhu Yuanzhang (Ming Taizu) was the first commoner on the throne since Liu Bei founded the Han, and nationalism and populism were two pillars of his rise to power. But how far did China extend? In the northwest, the answer was still framed in terms of the power of the Mongols, whose central Asian empire persisted another century. But in the south the answer was less clear. Should the Ming accept the self-limited China of the Song, or should it explore new horizons? It was, after all, a more vigorous dynasty in a stronger position.

Southeast Asia presented two major opportunities for the Ming. One was the development of maritime China. China's naval exploits reached their height with Admiral Zheng He's voyages as far as Africa, but the Ming mentality was decidedly land-bound, and Zheng's explorations were discontinued in 1433, never to be resumed.[23] The other opportunity was Vietnam. The Ming had the military strength to return Vietnam to its status as a province of China, and the overthrow of the Tran dynasty by Ho Quy Ly provided the occasion.

The following description by a modern Chinese scholar gives a Chinese version of the Ming occupation:

The Emperor Ming Chengzu [Yongle], angered at Annan's Le Quy Ly father and son [Ho Quy Ly and Ho Han Thuong] because he usurped power, killed officials and envoys and was utterly despotic, ordered General Zhang Fu to lead the army to punish the tyrant and comfort the people. Within eight months he restored order to the country...and captured the two Les. Because Annan was from ancient times Chinese territory and the Tran lineage had been destroyed by Ho so that there was no successor, the populace requested again to be included among the provinces of China, as the stories from the Han and Tang described. The emperor approved their request, and changed the false name of "Yu Kingdom" to Jiaozhi, and established the three offices of general administration, justice and military affairs. Thereupon the southern lands that had been lost for more than 400 years, and in olden times had been prosperous, were regained, and several million Annan brethren, happy and enthusiastic, returned to the bosom of their ancestral country. For this accomplishment Zhang Fu was made a duke, an honor greater than

---

[21] Alexander Woodside, "Early Ming Expansionism (1406–1427): China's Abortive Conquest of Vietnam," *Papers on China* 17:4 (1963), p. 7.

[22] Ho established an alternative capital in Thanh Hoa called the Tay Do (the Western Capital, though it was due south of Hanoi).

[23] Wang Gungwu, *The Chinese Overseas* (Cambridge, MA: Harvard University Press, 2000), pp. 19–23.

that given to General Ma Fubo [Ma Yuan, who put down the revolt of the Trung sisters].[24]

As one might expect, Vietnamese historians have a different view of the Ming occupation. According to Nguyen Khac Vien:

Towards the end of the 14th century a great crisis shook the country. The Ming court, then reigning in China, took advantage of this to invade Dai Viet and impose on it a form of direct rule which was to last for twenty years (1407–1427). However, the invaders encountered stiff resistance right from the beginning, and national independence was eventually wrested back in 1427 by Le Loi, the founder of the Le dynasty.[25]

Although these two views of the occupation are clearly incompatible, neither is simply false. The eminent Vietnamese historian Le Thanh Khoi admits that the Ho dynasty's radical reforms were so unpopular that the Ming pretext of restoring the Tran was quite successful in placating opposition.[26] Indeed, a recent prize-winning Vietnamese historical novel entitled *Ho Quy Li* paints a complex picture of a figure somewhat like the *Three Kingdoms* villain Cao Cao, who combined great ability with ruthless ambition.[27] After Ho had ambushed the bodyguard of 5,000 troops sent with the Tran pretender and killed him, General Zhang Fu came with armies of more than 215,000 troops, a force as large as the contemporaneous Ming expeditions against the Mongols.[28] Once the Red River delta was under control, Zhang Fu gathered all of the remnants of the Tran court and received their petition to return Vietnam to its status as a Chinese province. Because Chinese culture had begun again in the previous century to provide the backbone of Vietnamese intellectual life, Vietnamese scholars and artisans were quickly integrated into imperial service. For example, the Vietnamese architect Nguyen An (Ruan An) played a key role in designing the new Ming capital in Beijing.[29]

---

[24] Zhang Xiumin 张秀民, "Ming dai jiaozhi ren zai Zhongguo neidi zhi gongxian 明代交趾人在中国内地之贡献" [The contributions of people from Jiaozhi inside China during the Ming dynasty], in Zhang Xiumin, *Zhong Yue guanxi lunwen ji* 中越关系史论文集 [Collected essays on Sino-Vietnamese relations] (Taipei: Wen Shi Zhe, 1992), p. 45. This essay was written in 1947. My thanks to Chen Jian for his assistance with the translation. It should be noted that contemporary mainland scholarship takes a more objective viewpoint. The entries for Le Loi (Li Li 黎利) and Le Thanh Tong (Li Sicheng 黎思诚) in the Chinese encyclopedia *Ci Hai* 辞海 (Shanghai, 1999) are quite laudatory. See vol 3, pp. 4984, 4986.

[25] Nguyen Khac Vien, *Vietnam: A Long History*, p. 64.

[26] Le Thanh Khoi, *Le Vietnam* (Paris: Editions de Minuit, 1955), pp. 203–5.

[27] The novel by Nguyen Xuan Khanh (Hanoi: Vietnam Women's Press, 2001) is the subject of a lengthy review by Lin Ziping 林子苹 in *Dongnanya Zongheng* 东南亚纵横 [Around Southeast Asia] 5 (May 2003), pp. 25–9.

[28] Woodside, "Early Ming Expansionism," pp. 11.

[29] My thanks to Huang Yunsheng for information concerning Nguyen An.

On the other side of the coin, General Zhang Fu's initial efforts to welcome Vietnam back into the mainstream of the empire were quickly superseded by the sort of neglect, incompetence, and rapacity typical in peripheral areas of a large empire. While Zhang Fu was one of the Ming's leading generals, his civilian counterpart and successor, Huang Fu, had problematic relations with the Chinese court. Alexander Woodside mentions that sons of army officers who failed their military examinations were banished to Vietnam. In 1420 a regional inspector reported that most of the Chinese officials in Vietnam were inept and untrained southerners who had failed higher examinations.[30] Clearly Vietnam was not a plum location: it was dangerous, pestilential, and full of barbarians. With an incompetent administration and continuing unrest, the Vietnamese economy could not support the army, and rice for the army had to be brought in from China. Meanwhile more entrepreneurial Chinese, such as the eunuch Ma Chi, were scouring the country for gold, gems, and pearls.

When the Ming intention of annexing Vietnam became clear, a series of rebellions ensued led by Tran pretenders. From 1418 a superb guerila leader, Le Loi, began to emerge, and he started to be successful in his resistance against the Chinese in 1424–27. Le Loi was from Thanh Hoa, a province south of the Red River delta that was the former stronghold of Ho Quy Ly, and most of his generals and advisors were also Thanh Hoa men. The shining exception was his advisor and spokesman Nguyen Trai, who was from the delta. Complementary to Le Loi's reliance on the people for military support, Nguyen Trai fashioned the claims of Vietnam to autonomy that had been formulated in the previous century against the Mongols into a ringing patriotic message.

The costs and trend of the war in Vietnam gave rise to a peace faction in Beijing that included the new emperor, who came to the throne in 1425.[31] After Le Loi's victories in 1426 against both the occupying army and the forces sent to relieve it, the decision was made to recognize a Tran restoration in Vietnam (ostensibly the initial objective of Ming involvement). The defeated soldiers, all 86,000 of them, were evacuated to China in 1427–28, along with several thousand horses. Vietnam resumed tributary relations. After a decent interval Le Loi deposed the Tran place-holder, sent an expiatory effigy to Beijing, and was invested as the ruler of Dai Viet.

These events were of course profoundly significant for Vietnam, as we shall discuss at the beginning of the next section. However, there is too little appreciation of how important the withdrawal from Vietnam was for China's history and idea of itself. The Ming dynasty had to defend itself in the north. While it was self-confident enough to move its capital to Beijing, it also restored the Great Wall, launched a series of expeditions against the Mongols, and, two centuries later, lost to the Manchus. The south was the

---

[30] Woodside, "Early Ming Expansionism," p. 16–17.
[31] *Ibid.*, pp. 30–2.

direction of opportunity. Vietnam's past as a part of China created an entry for territorial expansion that was complemented by maritime exploits. But Vietnam's defeat of China's re-annexation turned the tide of the Ming from expansion to retrenchment. By doing so, it set China's boundary in the south at the Southern Gate between Vietnam's Lang Son and China's Pingxiang.[32] Although China remained suzerain of Vietnam and occasionally interfered in its politics, it no longer aspired to its territory. As far as maritime commerce and Southeast Asia are concerned, China's great turn inward had begun, to be broken only by British gunboats in 1840.

The circumstances of the Ming frustration in Vietnam were essential to the historic effect. First, China decided for itself not to persist; there was no mortal threat from Vietnam, but simply disillusionment with re-annexation, the cost of war, and the defeat of forces already committed. As a Chinese decision rather than an external imposition, it expressed an internal realignment of national horizons. Second, Vietnam prevailed against the Ming at the peak of China's strength. Future Chinese leaders could not tell themselves that Vietnam had emerged at an ebb tide and could be rejoined to a stronger China. Third, just as the Tran had been careful not to offend the Mongols, Le Loi refrained from vengeful and insulting behavior in his moment of triumph. Had he massacred the captured troops or demanded recognition as an equal from China, China would have felt honor-bound to treat Vietnam as an enemy. As it was, the diplomatic basis for unequal empires was confirmed, with China dwelling on the "unequal" and Vietnam emphasizing "empire."

Unequal Empires, 1427–1858

For the next 400 years the Sino-Vietnamese relationship was usually routinized into tributary exchange, and it became less a matter of concern for either side than it had been for the previous 1,500 years. Freed from the fear of China, Vietnam copied more closely the Chinese model of domestic governance. It also expanded its domain and regional influence, successes that encouraged regional separatism. Ultimately internal disunity and decay brought about a failed Chinese invasion and afterward a second attempt at applying a Chinese model, both of which were pale reflections of fifteenth-century originals. Meanwhile, as China accustomed itself to being the middle kingdom among other kingdoms that were inferior but not subordinate, Southeast Asia became less interesting. In a situation of bounded superiority it was natural that China turned inward.

---

[32] According to the historical marker at the gate, some claim that the gate was first established in the Han dynasty while others claim it was established in the early Ming. Certainly its function as one of the nine gates marking the boundaries of China dates from the Ming. It has been "Youyi Guan" (Friendship Gate) since 1965.

The great English historian Arnold Toynbee observed that nations and civilizations are defined not only by population and territory but by the challenges they face.[33] As we have described, Vietnam's identity was shaped by earlier challenges, but it was confirmed by the Ming occupation. The occupation tried to return Vietnam to a Chinese womb from which it had long ago emerged politically and from which it had emerged intellectually in the previous century under the threat of the Mongols. Vietnam had the cultural good fortune to be blessed at this crucial time with a remarkable intellect, Nguyen Trai. Trai articulated not only the popular struggle with the Ming, but most memorably the significance of victory (Table 6.2).

In his "Binh Ngo Dai Cao" (Ping Wu dagao – Proclamation of victory over Wu [China]), Nguyen Trai flourishes the claim of historical equality with China that was articulated by the fourteenth-century historians.[34] But, fresh from defeating an occupation by means of guerilla warfare, Trai emphasizes the people – their sufferings and their support for resistance. The strength and greatness of Le Loi was grounded in his concern for the people, and thus he prevailed over the forces of the Ming. In the voice of Le Loi he says,

> Around our standard on a fragile bamboo pole
> I mustered forces from a scattered populace.
> As they drank my wine so I drank their water
>   And we became like son and father,
> Soldiers of one heart.[35]

Until this time Vietnamese government had been aristocratic and its pride had been in the martial ardor and skill of its generals. The Confucian intellectuals of the previous century had emphasized the virtue of the ruler, but they lacked the Mencian notion of *minben*, the people as the root of the state. With Trai, the idea of Vietnamese national identity finally reached the ground of the people.

Trai's populist idealism did not lead immediately to a refounding of Vietnam on a new, broad base. He himself was executed in 1442, along with his father's, mother's and wife's clans, as part of the palace intrigues after the death of Le Loi.[36] Despite Trai's fine words, in fact the army had been led

---

[33] Arnold Toynbee, "Introduction," *A Study of History* (Oxford: Oxford University Press, 1947).

[34] The Proclamation is translated in full in Nguyen Khac Vien, *Vietnam: A Long History*, pp. 81–6, and in Truong Buu Lam, *Patterns of Vietnamese Response to Foreign Intervention: 1858–1900* (New Haven: Yale University Southeast Asia Studies Monograph Series No. 11, 1967), pp. 54–62. See also the careful textual study by Stephen O'Harrow, "Nguyen Trai's *Binh Ngo Dai Cao* of 1428: The development of a Vietnamese national identity," *Southeast Asian Studies* 10:1 (March 1979), pp. 157–74.

[35] Quoted from O'Harrow, *ibid.*, p. 173.

[36] John Whitmore, *The Development of Le Government in 15th Century Vietnam* (Ph.D. dissertation, Cornell University, 1968), p. 36.

TABLE 6.2. *Ming occupation to French arrival*

1400	
Ming Chengzu (Yunglo) 1403–24	Ho Dynasty 1400–07
Ming occupation of Vietnam	
1407–27	
Capital moved to Beijing 1421	Le Dynasty 1428–1788
Admiral Zheng He's naval voyages	Le Thai To 1428–33
1405–33	
Ming Yingzong captured by	Le Thanh Tong 1460–97
Mongols 1449	
	Annexation of northern Champa
	1471
1500	
	Mac dynasty 1527–92
China defends Korea against	
Hideyoshi 1590s	
1600	
	Trinh lords in north, 1570–1786
Ming dynasty defeated by peasants,	Nguyen lords in center-south,
replaced by Qing (Manchu)	1600–1777
dynasty, 1644	
Southern resistance to Qing	
continues to 1662	
	Completion of Champa
	annexation (Binh Thuan) 1693
	Annexation of Saigon 1691
1700	
Kangxi (Shengzi) 1661–1722	
Qianlong (Gaozong) 1735–96	Tayson revolt 1771–88
Expedition to Burma 1765–69	
Chinese expedition to support the	
Le 1788–89	
Lord Macartney mission to China	Tayson dynasty 1788–1802
1793	
White Lotus rebellion 1793–1804	Completion of Mekong annexation
	1790
1800	
	Nguyen dynasty 1802–1945
	Emperor Gia Long 1802–19
	Emperor Minh Mang 1820–40
First Opium War 1839–42	Attempted annexation of
	Cambodia 1834
Taiping Rebellion 1850–65	
	Evacuation of Phnom Penh 1841
	French attack Danang 1858

by the generals from Thanh Hoa, and as in the past they became the power behind the court after the death of the founder. Trai, one of the few members of the inner circle not from Thanh Hoa, thus became a target. Free from the threat of China, the victors began to enjoy the spoils.

Fortunately for Vietnam's political future, an emperor emerged with the skill to deal with the Thanh Hoa courtiers and the imagination to refound the government on Chinese bureaucratic principles. Le Thanh Ton, who ruled from 1460 to 1497, managed for the first time in the history of independent Vietnam to establish the scholar-bureaucracy as the core of central administration. Thanh Ton encouraged debate and even criticism of himself, and he set about to institute a full-fledged governmental structure staffed by persons selected on merit.[37] He established Confucian temples of literature in all provinces, to compete with the popularity of Buddhism. In the economy, he encouraged agriculture by reforming the system of communal lands, establishing in every province offices to encourage farming and to inspect the dikes, and he established military-agricultural colonies. He ordered the first census and mapping of independent Vietnam. He also perfected a comprehensive legal code, the Le Code, that began to be compiled after the Ming invasion.[38] Greater Confucian efficiency was not without its side effects. Three hundred twenty-three people were executed in 1463 as opposed to only forty-two in the lax days of 1448, mourning rites were enforced with stiff penalties, and resident barbarians were required to adopt Vietnamese names and ways.[39] In general, however, Thanh Ton's reign earned its reputation as the apogee of traditional Vietnamese government.

It is ironic that Emperor Le Thanh Ton's Confucian zeal for reforming and restructuring Vietnam is perhaps most reminiscent of the best of the Han administrators sent in after the victory of Ma Yuan over the Trung sisters. But, as John Whitmore points out in his careful study of the early Le dynasty, Thanh Ton applied the Chinese model for precisely the same reasons that the Chinese had orginally developed it. The Chinese court innovated and refined its institutions and ideology to face the challenge of preserving central order for the common good. Thanh Ton faced the same problem, and China provided an agenda of "best practices." Chinese "best practices" included practical investigation of national conditions and attention both to innovative and to critical memorials from officials. As a result, Thanh Ton's application of the Confucian model was a creative one, well adapted to Vietnamese conditions. It is particularly evident in the Le Code that Thanh Ton's earlier reforms of the legal system gave him a good idea of what laws would be appropriate, and thus the Code is thoroughly Vietnamese in its

[37] *Ibid.*, especially pp. 139–41.
[38] Also called the Hong Duc Code, a misnomer since it was initiated before the Hong Duc (Le Thanh Ton) reign period, 1470–97.
[39] *Ibid.*, pp. 160, 163, 216.

content.[40] Thanh Ton's further sinification of Vietnam was thus similar to the later adoption and adaptation of Marxism by both China and Vietnam. It was not imposed from the outside, but rather became attractive as a paradigm because of domestic problems, and it wasn't blindly applied, but rather developed in a dialectic with local conditions.

It should be emphasized that Thanh Ton's sinification was premised on Vietnam's independence from China. If China were still an active threat, then Vietnam's political task would have been military cohesion (behind the Thanh Hoa generals), and its intellectual task would have been one of differentiation from China, as it had been against the Mongols. But the Tran intellectuals and Nguyen Trai had accomplished the task of differentiation, and Le Loi had confirmed Vietnam's independence. Therefore Thanh Ton could face the no less daunting problem of how best to rule. And for that, a distant – but clearly successful – China provided useful lessons.

The withdrawal of the Ming acknowledged and confirmed the existence of an autonomous Vietnamese space, but what were its boundaries? The general location of the boundary was not an issue. Although the specification of a continuous border was not complete until the Sino-French surveys of 1889–94, the main outlines and key points (usually fortified outposts) emerged from the administrative demarcations of the Han, and many of the disputes over border location from the fifteenth to the nineteenth century were handled by negotiation.[41]

There were, however, two serious problems associated with the border. First, most of the border area was in fact a mountainous frontier straddled by minorities. Besides the Zhuang and their associated groups, the Miao (Hmong) and Yao moved into the high mountain areas of Vietnam and Laos by the end of the nineteenth century. Both ethnic Chinese and ethnic Vietnamese were, in effect, sojourners on the frontier. As late as 1908 ethnic Vietnamese were estimated to be only 2 percent of the population of the mountainous region, with 75 percent belonging to Tay groups.[42] In times of famine and revolution, ethnic Vietnamese retreated from the mountainous margin of wet-rice cultivation and their upland fields reverted to minority control.[43] On the other side of the coin, mineral resources on the frontier and the lack of central control attracted Chinese miners, remnants of defeated armies, and bandits. One Vietnamese mine employed between

[40] *Ibid.*, pp. 153–4; Le Thanh Khoi, pp. 225–6.

[41] See Philippe Langlet, "La frontière sino-Vietnamienne du xviiie xixe siècle," in *Les frontières du Vietnam*, pp. 70–9.

[42] Colonel Edouard J. J. Diguet, *Les Montangards du Tonkin* (Paris: A. Challomel, 1908). As referred to in Yumio Sakurai, "Peasant Drain and Abandoned Villages in the Red RiverDelta between 1750 and 1850," in Anthony Reid, ed., *The Last Stand of Asian Autonomies* (New York: St. Martins, 1997), note 5, p. 152.

[43] Sakurai, "Peasant Drain," p. 145.

20,000 and 30,000 Chinese miners in the mid-eighteenth century.[44] Meanwhile the border populations pursued local opportunities without regard to national sovereignty, and given the greater dynamic of the Chinese socio-economy after the fifteenth century, this led to a Chinese seepage into the frontier. As Philippe Langlet puts it, "Despite the appearance of good rapport between the two states and a quasi-official partition, in reality the Sino-Vietnamese frontier was a formal line of defense that was rather ineffective against Chinese infiltration."[45]

The second border problem was the difference between Chinese and Vietnamese views of what the border meant. For Vietnam, it was the perimeter of its sacred "mountains and rivers," Vietnamese since the beginning of civilization and won from China by the blood of martyrs. As we shall see shortly, Vietnam had a more flexible notion of its southern and western boundaries, but the difference between itself and China was what defined Vietnam. For China, the boundary marked a concession of autonomy to an inferior state. It was a serious concession. Not only did China negotiate border disputes with Vietnam, but on several occasions it declined opportunities to split Vietnam that were presented by the petitions of separatist groups for legitimation.[46] Moreover, the pressure of Chinese on the border was driven by local opportunities rather than masterminded by Beijing. Nevertheless, respect for the border was at China's discretion. It could pursue local rebels and bandits across the border, preferably in coordination with Vietnam. It could defend militarily the legitimate claimant to the throne, as it did in 1788 when it sent a force of 15,000 to help restore the Le dynasty and defeat the Tay Son uprising. Needless to say, Nguyen Hue of the Tay Son viewed the invitation to the Chinese by the Le as a national betrayal, and his defeat of the Qing occupation of Hanoi is considered one of the great moments in Vietnamese history.

It is hardly unique to China and Vietnam that the stronger side is less concerned about the border than the weaker side. More unusual was the international framework of unequal but autonomous relations embodied in the Chinese tribute system, in which Vietnam and Korea were the two most constant participants. The tribute system formalized not only an asymmetry of power but an asymmetry of roles. China was the legitimizing patriarch, while tributary states were inferior. Not only did independent Vietnam from its beginnings publicly accept its status as a vassal, but it sent its most prominent scholars as emissaries on tribute missions. Why did Vietnam accept the subordinate status implied by seeking legitimation from Beijing for each new ruler and sending periodic missions of tribute?

---

[44] Alexander Woodside, "The Relationship between Political Theory and Economic Growth in Vietnam, 1750–1840," in Anthony Reid, ed., *The Last Stand of Asian Autonomies*, p. 259.
[45] Philippe Langlet, "La frontière sino-Vietnamienne," p. 76.
[46] *Ibid.*, pp. 70–1.

First, Vietnam's deference to China in offering tribute was reciprocated by China's official acknowledgment of Vietnamese autonomy. Considering that China was always Vietnam's greatest potential threat, China's recognition of the Vietnamese court as the legitimate rulers of the country was invaluable. While it might appear degrading that the Chinese emperor was able to reject the name "Nam Viet" proposed by Gia Long in 1803 and instead bestow the name "Viet Nam," it was nevertheless an acknowledgment of Vietnam's right to exist.[47] In contrast to the colonialism of Western imperialism, China acted as the passive guarantor of a matrix of unequal but autonomous relationships rather than as an active metropolitan power. To go to Beijing was more reassuring than to have Paris come to you.

Second, China provided a model of external relations as well as of internal governance. As Alexander Woodside has detailed in his classic *Vietnam and the Chinese Model*, vis-à-vis its other neighbors Vietnam considered itself in turn to be the model of civilization and the center of a galaxy of lesser powers. Clearly the Nguyen dynasty of the early nineteenth century exceeded earlier precedents in claiming Burma, France, and England among its thirteen vassals[48] and in setting up nine urns to represent the nine sections of the world at its new palace in Hue.[49] But it could be argued that from the time of Thanh Ton, if not earlier, the paradigm of international relations set by China and accepted by Vietnam pre-empted a more appropriate model of relations with neighbors of comparable capabilities and different cultures. Vietnam's claim to centricity, which could only really shape its relations with Champa, Cambodia, and Laos, was more evangelical than natural. The reality of Southeast Asia was more equal and interactive than Vietnam's sinitic lens would admit. In this respect Vietnam would have been better off without a Chinese model.

Third, Chinese legitimation was a factor in domestic power struggles in Vietnam, though not a controlling one. It was important to every new ruler – even to recent victors over the Chinese like Le Loi or Nguyen Hue – to secure recognition from Beijing. Of course, the other side of the coin was that it was important for China to be shrewd in designating a ruler who would not embarrass Beijing by being deposed. "Normalization" of the relationship, putting it back in the familiar ritualistic grooves of deference and recognition, ended the risks and inconveniences of an undefined situation. In extreme cases the legitimized ruler could ask for help from Beijing in retaining his

---

[47] Alexander Woodside, *Vietnam and the Chinese Model: A Comparative Study of Vietnamese and Chinese Government in the First Half of the Nineteenth Century* (Cambridge, MA: Harvard University Press, 1971), p. 103.

[48] *Ibid*, p. 237.

[49] Alexander Woodside, "The Relationship between Political Theory and Economic Growth in Vietnam, 1750–1840," p. 248.

throne, but the invasion of 1788 demonstrated the risks of such an option for each party.

Truong Buu Lam's very careful study of the Qing invasion of 1788 can be used as the exception to the normal pattern of Sino-Vietnamese relations that proves the stability of its underlying framework.[50] Lam argues convincingly that while the local leader in Guangdong was trying to utilize an opportunity to win military glory by restoring the Le dynasty, the court in Beijing was more hesitant about intervention and more concerned about its moral obligations to the Le dynasty than about gaining either glory or territory. After the Chinese army occupied Hanoi it became clear that there was little merit in the Le court, and before the defeat by Nguyen Hue the court had already ordered withdrawal from Vietnam. Nguyen Hue, upon crowning himself Quang Trung, sent a double in his place to receive investiture and thereafter maintained annual tribute missions to Beijing. His double was allotted a place of honor at the eightieth birthday celebrations of Emperor Qianlong.

The matrix of inequality embodied in the role asymmetry of the tribute system provided a robust and useful framework for negotiating the necessarily unequal relations between China and Vietnam. It provided a routinization of mutual assurances, and when it failed, as in 1407 or 1788, it was to the interests of both sides to restore it. Nevertheless, it did not solve the problem of inequality, it merely provided a framework for managing it. China was still tempted to trespass, and Vietnam still pretended to equality. Vietnamese emperors tried to evade the dilemma of being supreme at home but subordinate in Beijing. Before the Ming invasion, the Tran ruse of appointing a child as emperor and letting the "senior emperor" continue to rule not only solved succession problems but it also meant that officially it was the child who dealt with Beijing. Moreover, beginning in the Tran dynasty Vietnamese emperors used false names in their diplomatic correspondence with China.[51] Nguyen Hue's utilization of a double to receive investiture in Beijing was a mark of prudence on his part that also avoided the humiliation implicit in acting as a courtier. In Beijing and toward Beijing, Vietnam was a vassal, but away from Beijing and to itself, Vietnam was China's equal. The ultimate fantasy of equality was a notation in an official history made by Emperor Tu Duc in the mid-nineteenth century regarding Zhao Tuo's kingdom of Nan Yue:

In general, one could say that, before and after [Nan Yue], we lost more than half of our territory to the gain of the Chinese. It is unfortunate that, although in the course

[50] Truong Buu Lam, "Intervention versus Tribute in Sino-Vietnamese Relations, 1788–1790," in John K. Fairbank, ed., *The Chinese World Order* (Cambridge, MA: Harvard University Press, 1968), pp. 165–79.

[51] Nguyen The Anh, "Attraction and Repulsion as the Two Contrasting Aspects of the Relations between China and Vietnam," *China and Southeast Asia: Historical Interactions. An International Symposium.* University of Hong Kong, July 2001.

of successive regimes there was no shortage of enlightened sovereigns and wise and talented subjects, not an inch of territory was reconquered. It is truly deplorable! But one can see that the recovery of lost territory was already arduous in the past, and not merely a problem in the present.[52]

Here, by a curious transformation, Tu Duc, who was afraid to fight the French, uses the fantasy of Nan Yue as a frustrated greater Vietnam to justify his own failures in defending Vietnamese territory.

The stabilization of relations with China had a profound effect on Vietnam's regional situation and, ultimately, on Vietnam's domestic politics. For the first 500 years of independence, China was the dominant concern, while regional difficulties, especially with Champa, were occasionally acute. With the northern border secure, Vietnam spent the next 500 years expanding down the coast, destroying Champa, and eventually occupying the Mekong delta. Expansion added central and southern Vietnam, creating a demographic outlet for what gradually became northern Vietnam, diversifying Vietnam's international contacts and creating the base for prolonged regional factionalism.

Although it had managed to occupy Hanoi twice during the fourteenth century, Champa's doom was triply sealed in the following century. First and most obviously, the defeat of the Ming in 1427 ended Vietnam's two-front dilemma. Second, Thanh Ton's neo-Confucian policies led to a remarkable increase in population and economy. The population tripled between 1417 and 1539.[53] Thus the relationship with Champa was transformed from a competitive one to an asymmetrical one. Last, in the course of civilizing themselves, the Vietnamese created a greater distance between themselves and "barbarians" like the Chams. Originally Champa had been founded by Vietnamese officials whose court eventually became Indianized, and Vietnam's wars with Champa had involved large-scale raids but not much territorial fluctuation. Beginning with Thanh Ton, Vietnam began to expand into barbarian territory in the *nam tien* (southern push), and Champa was destroyed. In 1471 its capital Vijaya fell, 60,000 people were killed, and 30,000 were taken prisoner.[54] Later the Mekong delta was taken over from the Khmers, and in the nineteenth century, as the French threat loomed over its own head, Vietnam occupied Cambodia. Vietnam had its own *mission civilisatrice*.

---

[52] Quoted in Nguyen The Anh, "La frontière sino-vietnamienne du xie au xviie siècle," p. 66.
[53] Li Tana, *The "Inner Region": A Social and Economic History of Nguyen Vietnam in the 17th and 18th Centuries* (Ph.D. dissertation, Australian National University, 1992), quoted in John Whitmore, "Literati Culture in Dai Viet, 1430–1840," *Modern Asian Studies* 31:3 (1997), p. 669.
[54] Coedès, *The Indianized States*, p. 239.

As Vietnam expanded, it became a more interactive part of what Woodside has called a "globalized" Southeast Asia.[55] The best example was the trading city of Hoi An (also called Faifoo), founded in 1613–21. Peopled by merchants from Japan, China, Portugal, and elsewhere, it became important not only because of trade but also for introducing Portuguese cannon making and Japanese weaponry and martial techniques. Christianity was introduced to Vietnam through Hoi An, in part by Japanese refugees from persecution.[56] Hoi An's prominence declined as further southward progress was made over the following century, but that progress into the Mekong region opened up new vistas of interaction with Cambodia, Thailand, and with Chinese refugees who had settled near Saigon after the fall of the Ming dynasty in 1644. Thus the external horizons, cultural influences, and ethnic composition of the new areas in the center and south became vastly more heterogeneous.

By tripling Vietnam's length, the *nam tien* created new arenas for regionally based factionalism. While the new territories quickly became part of a Vietnamese *oecumene*, they were under the control of the Nguyen lords of the south rather than the Mac or later the Trinh in Hanoi. Contrary to what many theories of "divide and rule" would predict, China did not encourage separatism but rather refused the requests of the Mac remnant to recognize a separate kingdom in the northern mountains and of the Nguyen lords to recognize a southern kingdom. Vietnam was eventually unified by the Tay Son brothers in 1789, with the crowning achievement of the unification being the defeat of the Chinese attempt to reinstall the Le king. By 1802 the last remaining Nguyen returned to defeat the Tay Son and establish a new capital of unified Vietnam in Hue.

The Nguyen dynasty of the early nineteenth century was famously Confucian, but the differences between its Chinese model and that of Thanh Ton 350 years earlier marked Vietnam's habituation into a more stable but still unequal relationship. First, Confucianism had soaked more deeply into the fabric of Vietnamese life and thought. It was by no means the only influence, but rebels as well as scholars worked in its arena of discourse.[57] Second, the

---

55 To quote Woodside, "'globalization' here becomes a shorthand term for the constant modification of local political communities' evolution through the progressive intensification of the transactional webs which shape their relations with world circulatory systems for goods, people, capital, information and ideas." Alexander Woodside, "The Relationship between Political Theory and Economic Growth in Vietnam, 1750–1840," p. 247.

56 Nguyen Van Hua, *Hoi An* (Danang: Nha Xuat Ban Da Nang, 1999). Today Hoi An is a UNESCO World Heritage Site because of its variety of merchant housing dating from the seventeenth century.

57 Alexander Woodside, "Conceptions of Change and of Human Responsibility for Change in Late Traditional Vietnam," in David Wyatt and Alexander Woodside, eds., *Moral Order and the Question of Change: Essays on Southeast Asian Thought* (New Haven: Yale University Southeast Asian Studies, 1982), pp. 104–50.

Nguyen preferred the cosmological fatalism of the Han philosopher Dong Zhongshu (179–104 BC) to the more active sense of personal responsibility of the Song and Ming neo-Confucians who inspired Thanh Ton. Dong's approach may have been more compatible with non-Chinese influences on the Nguyen;[58] in any case, cosmological Confucianism was more compatible with the dynasty's all-consuming interest in stability. Third, the Nguyen court was critical of contemporary Qing China for being an alien, corrupt dynasty, and it considered itself closer to the Confucian ideal. Five hundred years of unequal autonomy had allowed sinitic influence to become more pervasive while China itself became less of a vivid looming presence.

The Chinese Empire as an International Political Order

With Vietnamese independence the relationship of China and Vietnam entered the realm of international relations, but it entered by a different gate than that used by the modern Western international system. The major events in the Sino-Vietnamese relationship were instances of acknowledged loss of control by China but continued deference by Vietnam. The Song recognition of Dinh Bo Linh in 971 and the Ming retreat in 1427 did not contest who was the more powerful country, nor did they define equal sovereignties. They founded an asymmetric relationship based explicitly on China's superiority, but one that nevertheless provided Vietnam with the assurance of autonomy.

In the same thousand years a very different pattern was unfolding in the West. As waves of armed migrations began to settle down and Roman Christianity prevailed, a tension emerged between the universal claims of the Church and the congealing temporal power of local rulers. The suicidal wars of religion were ended with the acknowledgment of the equal autonomy of sovereign states in the Peace of Westphalia in 1648, which led in turn to balancing of powers (and frequent wars to re-balance powers) thereafter. The notion of an anarchy of powers that were equal in the sense that each could mortally threaten the other, and whose pecking orders were established by victory, fit the Western experience, but not the Asian.

Nevertheless, there are fundamental values and concerns embodied in the tribute system that are universal. Security is not the only value in international relations, but it is the most basic. China achieved security by surrounding itself with deferential states, and the reward of deference was recognition of autonomy. One could view the resulting international order as primarily a

---

[58] This is the argument of Nola Cooke, "The Myth of Restoration: Dang-trong Influences on the Spiritual Life of the Early Nguyen dynasty (1802–1847)," in Anthony Reid, ed., *The Last Stand of Asian Autonomies*, pp. 269–98. Dong would certainly support a greater interest in astrology.

moral order, since it meant that China controlled its own exercise of power.[59] But morality was based on realism. China had experienced the limits of its power, not by being defeated by a greater power but by having its available resources exhausted by a smaller one.

Likewise, Vietnam's security was enhanced by the tribute system. Being a tributary did not mean being a slave state vulnerable to China's whims, rather, it guaranteed that China's actions toward Vietnam would begin with the premise of the legitimacy of Vietnamese rule. The premise was not ironclad – the overthrow of the Tran created the occasion for Ming intervention, and the overthrow of the Le brought in the Qing army – but it meant that in a normal year, in a normal decade, or in a normal generation, China could be counted on not to use its preponderance of capacity against Vietnam.

There were other advantages of the system besides security. In the case of border troubles or boundary disputes, there was a forum in Beijing that was removed from the immediate interests of the border region. The court in Beijing would have to balance the distant and partial interests of its own border regions with the inconvenience of possible international conflict. In a broader context of interaction, China and Vietnam were not the same size, but they had similar political, economic, and social problems and could learn from one another's experiences. In trade, the exotic goods of Vietnam were attractive to China, and the high manufactures and cultural products of China were valued in Vietnam.

The tribute system was thus well constructed for the mutual but asymmetric concerns of disparate states. Its fatal, unmodern flaw was its patriarchal assumption that China was superior and Vietnam inferior. The smugness of Chinese superiority made the expression of deference degrading, and thus it contributed to a gulf in Vietnam's behavior between public deference in Beijing and private thoughts in Hanoi. From China's perspective, Vietnam could become more civilized by more closely approximating China – and in fact it was considered one of the most civilized barbarian countries – but it would always remain an inferior. China saw itself not as a negotiator in dealing with Vietnam, but as a condescending dispenser of righteousness and mercy to a distant petitioner, with of course a prudent sidelong glance at reality.

Although the role asymmetry of the tribute system came about by a very different process from Western international relations, it is structurally and logically similar to feudal relationships, and hence the feudal terminology of *suzerain, vassal,* and *tribute* seems appropriate. The king required fealty of the landed nobility and presence at court, but their patents of nobility granted

---

[59] In contemporary terminology China "limited the returns on power," something characteristic of constitutional orders. See John Ikenberry, *After Victory* (Princeton: Princeton University Press, 2001), pp. 3–49.

them autonomy in their domains. The major differences between, say, the French king and the Chinese emperor would be that China was dealing with states outside of and much smaller than its own territory. Therefore there was more of a confidence of centricity in China, less of a context of collective struggle between the vassals and the center, and less of a need on the part of the center to integrate the vassals into more active service to the center. At least in Southeast Asia – and in part due to Vietnam's defeat of the Ming – China was content to be surrounded by distant deference. The goal was to sustain hegemony at minimal cost rather than to maximize the gain of the center.

Traditional China's patriarchal sense of superiority was quite different from Western colonialism's enforcement of submission. Western imperialism was built on a steep slope of coercion, but its internal architecture became increasingly based on formal principles of equality. The structural inequality of colonial arrangements was dissonant with domestic politics and it had to be justified with arguments ranging from sixteenth-century Spain's contention that Indians did not have souls to the nineteenth-century's "white man's burden" and *mission civilisatrice*. Eventually, independence movements could argue within this framework for equality rather than simply for convergence.

7

The Brotherhood of Oppression

1840–1950

Until the nineteenth century, the relationship between China and Vietnam was largely unaffected by third-party relationships, and it was managed within a common cultural framework. The greater firepower of Western imperialism and its interest in transformative domination destroyed the traditional context of the relationship. Asymmetry and its effects did not disappear. Both China and Vietnam were clearly in asymmetric relations with the West, and the military and cultural disjunction reduced the relationship to a physical collision of unequal capacities. China and Vietnam related to Western imperialism as the earth might relate to the impact of a large asteroid. The Western impact was a different kind of shock for China than it was for Vietnam, because for the first time in China's civilizational memory it was not the center of its world. From its experiences with nomadic groups, China was accustomed to occasional relative weakness, but it was not accustomed to relative insignificance. For Vietnam, the traditions of patriotic resistance to the Chinese could be re-targeted toward France, as could opportunistic habits of learning from and collaborating with the powerful.

Distracted from their mutual differences and sharing similar burdens of oppression, China and Vietnam moved from a face-to-face relationship to a shoulder-to-shoulder one. For the first time Vietnam faced an international challenge more important than China, and for the first time China had to face a world that laughed at its presumptions of centricity. Vietnam's experience of colonialism was not the same as China's experience of total crisis and internal collapse, and Vietnam's sense of national injustice was different from China's sense of humiliation. Nevertheless, China and Vietnam were never closer than in the fraternity of this era of suffering. Although the disparities between them remained, and their brotherhood was that of elder and younger brother, a mutual empathy was grounded in the common fate of being weak and vulnerable in the modern world.

From broadly similar problems rose broadly similar solutions. Out of a cacophony of adaptations, solutions, and collaborations, communist parties arose in both countries and eventually provided the sole credible leadership for national revolution. Communist ideology played an important role in success. It provided an articulate critique of oppression, a larger community of socialist internationalism, and a disciplined, revolutionary party. More important, however, both communist parties learned from their mistakes. Under the leadership of Mao Zedong, the Chinese Communist Party turned to rural revolution after the failure of urban-based collaboration with the Guomindang in 1927. Under the leadership of Ho Chi Minh, the Indochinese Communist Party learned lessons from unsuccessful uprisings in 1930–31 and founded the Viet Minh in 1941 to lead a protracted struggle from a rural foundation. The common pattern of rural revolution was based as much on parallel situations as it was on interaction between the two parties.

Because the relationship between China and Vietnam was tangential to the major challenge of each country, it was less tense and defensive on the Vietnamese side and less haughty on the Chinese side than it had been in the past. As China ceased to be the major challenge for Vietnam, it also ceased to be its major model. Meanwhile China began to see itself as a wronged and humiliated nation rather than as the apex of culture and virtue, thereby placing itself in the brotherhood of the oppressed. The collaboration of the communist parties was still asymmetric, but the effects of asymmetry were buffered by socialist internationalism and the shared problems of rural revolution.

The pattern of asymmetry introduced by this era into Sino-Vietnamese relations is one of distracted asymmetry. The basic condition of asymmetry between China and Vietnam did not change, but the perceptions in the bilateral relationship of risk and opportunity were massively affected by the context of other concerns, both international and domestic. The role asymmetry of the previous era had been built on the presumption of China's international centrality, and that presumption no longer held. Indeed, traditional role asymmetry would never be restored, because the emerging new identities of China and Vietnam would be constructed from modern components as well as traditional ones, and the new relationship, however important, would be managed in a diverse and complex international context.

This chapter will begin with the challenge posed to the Chinese and Vietnamese empires by Western imperialism in the nineteenth century, and then proceed to a brief consideration of the transformations of both societies in the twentieth century. Then the emergence and collaboration of successful revolutionary movements will be discussed. The chapter will conclude with a reflection on disjunctive and distracted asymmetries.

The Western Collision, 1840–1900

The purpose of this section is not to give a complete narrative of the impact of Western imperialism on China and Vietnam, especially since this is one

TABLE 7.1. *China, Vietnam, and the West*

Macartney Mission 1793	Rescue of Nguyen Anh (Gia Long) by Pigneau 1777
1800	
First Opium War 1839–42	Occupation of Danang 1858
Taiping Rebellion 1850–65	French occupation of three provinces in Cochinchina 1862
1858 Tianjin Treaty recognizes Western governments as equals	Occupation of all Cochinchina 1867
Anglo-French sacking of Beijing 1861	Dupuis occupies Hanoi 1872
Sino-French War 1883–85	
2nd Treaty of Tianjin 1885	
Sino-Japanese War 1895	1897 establishment of Indochinese Union
Marking the Sino-Vietnamese border 1887–96	
Boxer Rebellion 1900	Paul Doumer 1896–1902

of the most popular topics of historical analysis for both countries. Instead, the purpose here is to contrast the disjunctive asymmetry between Western imperialism and both China and Vietnam with the previous system of China-centered role asymmetry and to note its impact on Sino-Vietnamese relations (see Table 7.1).

The success of Western imperialism in destroying traditional governments and implementing direct colonial rule is perhaps the greatest challenge so far to the underlying assumptions of asymmetry theory described in Chapter 4. The two basic premises of asymmetry theory are that, first, disparity creates significant differences in attention, but that, second, because of the difficulties in subjugating the weaker side, asymmetric relationships are usually negotiated rather than forced. If these two conditions hold, then asymmetry can be treated as a "normal" condition, and the management of asymmetry merits study.

However, nineteenth-century Western imperialism appears to violate the second premise. Power prevailed, and negotiation appeared to have no more significance than the rattle of pebbles on a beach as a wave subsides. In East Asia, China's international regime based on role asymmetry was replaced by one based on subjugation. Vietnam was restructured as three of the five parts of French Indochina,[1] while China began a descent into total chaos in which the only secure spaces within its own territory were the privileged

---

[1] Tonkin (north), Annam (center), and Cochinchina (south), together with Laos and Cambodia.

zones of the foreigners. Not only did the stronger dominate the weaker, but the governments of the weaker were destroyed.

The problem of imperial subjugation can be divided into two questions. First, why were China and Vietnam unable to resist European aggression? Vietnam had defeated a Chinese army in 1789, and yet could only slow down the French advance from the occupation of Danang (Tourane) in 1858 to the consolidation of French Indochina in 1897. For China, the process of defeat was longer and more humiliating. The Opium War of 1839–42 began the chain of successful Western challenges to the Qing.[2] By 1860 the foreign community in Shanghai had decided that it would rather deal with a weak empire than the Taiping rebels, and so it raised the "Ever Victorious Army" to join in defense.[3] In 1895 China was defeated by a modernized Japan, and after the Boxer Rebellion of 1900 even the Empress Dowager threw in the towel and began to westernize the dynasty.

Second, how thoroughly did power prevail? Clearly traditional states collapsed, and, in the case of Vietnam, the court in Hue lost its power to the colonial government, an administrative organ of Paris. But to what extent was the imperialist project shaped by the limits of its power? By the necessity of indigenous collaboration? By security concerns against resistance? Ultimately – in less than one-tenth of the life span of Vietnam as a part of China – French colonialism failed in Vietnam, and for its part China stood up on legs much sturdier than in the past. If power simply prevails, how could this happen?

The answer to the first question concerning the reasons for imperial victory must begin with the sudden appearance of overwhelming military superiority. Like the large asteroid that wiped out the dinosaurs, modern naval power confronted China and Vietnam with a terrifying force coming from an unexpected direction. Very abruptly the sea changed from being a Great Wall of water to being a highway for well-armed foreigners. Second, the governments of China and Vietnam had become too successful as traditional governments. China had built a comfortable regional nest of centricity and its chief security concerns were internal. Vietnam was less secure, but the new dynasty was adroit in using foreigners in its internal conflicts. Rather than being in a position to mobilize new popular resources against the external threat, both governments were further undermined and weakened by the domestic effects of foreign pressure. In Vietnam, Emperor Tu Duc chose to fight peasant rebellion in the north and to make concessions to the French.[4] In China the results of the Opium War directly contributed

---

[2] A thorough and vivid account of the process is provided by Hosea Ballou Morse, *The International Relations of the Chinese Empire*, 3 vol. (London: Longmans Green, 1910–1918).

[3] See Richard J. Smith, *Mercenaries and Mandarins: The Ever-Victorious Army in Nineteenth Century China* (Millwood: KTO Press, 1978).

[4] As Truong Buu Lam demonstrates, the resistance to the French in the north was initially loyal to the dynasty and then became disillusioned with the inactivity of the Hue court. See

to the rise of the Taiping Rebellion, which in turn led to the emergence of local armies that were the ancestors of the warlords fifty years later.[5] Last, the cultural disjunction between the West and China and Vietnam facilitated conflict, inhibited negotiation, and encouraged breaches of trust. There was a "clash of civilizations," though not for the reason given by Samuel Huntington.[6] Huntington argues that civilizations form such basic patterns of value and thought that they cannot understand one another. But especially the Vietnamese court was quite familiar with the French and with Catholicism. The threat posed by France to the entire structure of rule and way of life in Vietnam led to increasing resistance and more extreme measures against missionaries. Meanwhile the cultural arrogance of the "white man's burden" and the *mission civilisatrice* provided ideological cover for pushing the advantages of power as far as they could go. As Prince Gorchakov, the Russian Foreign Minister, put it to his ambassadors in 1864:

The United States in America, France in Algeria, Holland in her colonies, England in India – all have been irresistibly forced, less by ambition than by imperious necessity, into this onward movement where the greatest difficulty is to know where to stop.[7]

The second question is how thoroughly did Western power prevail? Control cannot simply be judged by who wins. The important questions remain of what can the winner actually accomplish, is collaboration with indigenous forces necessary, and how long can domination be sustained. These questions have received too little attention in the histories of both China and Vietnam.

It is obvious in the detailed histories of imperialist ventures that the project of subjugation is shaped and reshaped not only by the opportunity provided by victory but also by the resources at hand. Behind the military presence lurk the problems of the scale of pacification and occupation, of interest and support by the home government, and of competition and cooperation with other imperialist powers. In the case of China, the foreseeable scale of occupation made even its defenseless, warlord-riven hulk too much to digest for any single imperialist power. To take a specific illustration, the British decision in 1898 to lease 952 square kilometers adjacent to Hong Kong (known subsequently as the New Territories) rather than to seize them had nothing to do with respect for the Qing. Rather, Britain did not want to license the

Truong Buu Lam, *Patterns of Vietnamese Response to Foreign Intervention, 1858–1900* (Yale University Southeast Asia Studies, Monograph Series No. 11, 1967).

5 Philip Kuhn, *Rebellion and Its Enemies in Late Imperial China* (Cambridge, MA: Harvard University Press, 1970).

6 Samuel Huntington, *The Clash of Civilizations and the Remaking of World Order* (New York: Simon and Schuster, 1996).

7 Quoted in Adam Watson, *The Limits of Independence: Relations between States in the Modern World* (London: Routledge, 1997), pp. 50–1.

seizure of other territories by other imperialists.[8] Since possession of all of China was impossible, access to all of China was the next best goal, and that was formulated in the Open Door policy. The following year China was forced to grant a ninety-nine-year lease to France of 842 square kilometers at Zhanjiang in Guangdong (then known as Fort Bayard or Kwang-chau-wan), and France controlled the area until the Japanese occupied it in 1943. In the case of Vietnam, the French had been decisively victorious by 1883, but their first attempt to create an Indochinese Union in 1887 foundered on the resistance of the navy and of the French *colons* in Cochinchina.[9] Only when former Finance Minister Paul Doumer took over in 1896 was it possible for the governor-general to prevail, and the *colons* remained to the end a strong counterforce to the attempt to manage French Indochina as a unified colony. Meanwhile, the imperialist presence in both China and Vietnam was complicated by wars at home, competitive grabs for territorial advantage, and occasional alliances.

Just as important as the physical limits of power were those imposed by the necessity of collaboration. In Vietnam, collaboration began at the beginning.[10] The first seizure of Hanoi was carried out by a party of 25 Europeans and 150 Chinese and Filipinos led by a French smuggler living in Wuhan.[11] But even before the shelling of Danang there were Vietnamese who desired cooperation with France in order to pursue their own projects of change. In the 1860s the Catholic official Nguyen Truong To argued for a modernization of the educational system as well as for collaboration with and concessions to France:

> At the present time, in our country, the students learn Chinese characters and many forms of poetry.... [But] in this world our country is, after all, an independent country. It is not a Chinese colony. Within our borders, we have problems of organization and the maintenance of order, problems that we ought to think of in the present, for the future.[12]

Just as Vietnamese could sincerely believe in Catholicism, they could believe that the future path of their country lay in a more westerly direction. After the establishment of the colony, collaboration occurred because it was the only career available or because the function in question was necessary in any

---

[8] See Jung-fang Tsai, *Hong Kong in Chinese History: Community and Social Unrest in the British Colony, 1842–1913* (New York: Columbia University Press, 1993); Geoffrey Robley Sayer, *Hong Kong 1862–1919* (Hong Kong: Hong Kong University Press, 1975).

[9] See Joseph Buttinger, *Vietnam: A Political History* (New York: Praeger, 1968), pp. 55–116.

[10] I concentrate on Vietnamese collaboration because the lines of authority were clearer and so collaboration was better defined.

[11] Buttinger, *Vietnam*, p. 94; also D. G. E. Hall, *A History of Southeast Asia*, 4th ed. (New York: St. Martin's, 1981), p. 697.

[12] Nguyen Truong To, "Memorial on Eight Reforms Urgently Needed (1868)," in Truong Buu Lam, *Patterns of Vietnamese Response*, pp. 92–3.

case.[13] The choice to collaborate involved submission to the French order, but in fact France itself could not reach every nook and cranny of the colony, and the collaborators could mix personal agendas with regime support. Pham Quynh, a cultural collaborator so notorious that he was one of the first people executed when the Viet Minh seized power in August 1945, used the French support for his magazine to pursue his goal of reforming and establishing a Vietnamese national identity.[14] The colony could not have functioned without indigenous military, police, professionals, and officials, and therefore the colonial project was shaped by its collaborationist incorporation.

Last, a regime of external domination is inevitably caught in a dilemma of permission and repression vis-à-vis the population. Permissiveness reduces the incentive to rebel but allows formation of an oppositional community; repression addresses the risk of opposition but increases popular alienation from the regime. As we shall see shortly, once a revolutionary base is established, both phases of the dilemma can be used to further liberation.

Had China been successful against the British in the Opium War or against the joint Anglo-French expedition of 1858–61, then perhaps Vietnam might have turned to China earlier for assistance against the French. As it happened, it was not until the 1880s, after France had consolidated its control in the south and was pursuing the total subjugation of Vietnam, that China protested France's violation of its imperial rights and Vietnam requested protection. A complex struggle ensued in which Chinese troops defeated the French twice near Langson, but French naval attacks on Fujian and Taiwan led to China's surrendering of all claims to Vietnam. With the Treaty of Tianjin (Tientsin) of 1885, China relinquished two millennia of claims to Vietnam. In conjunction with other treaties and conventions signed by China in 1876–1885, the external dimension of the Chinese empire was terminated. But Vietnam did not gain thereby. When border stones were set in 1896, the languages on the markers were Chinese and French.[15]

Fates Compared: China's Total Crisis versus Colonialism in Vietnam, 1900–1950

Although the traditional societies of both China and Vietnam were fatally undermined by Western imperialism and neither was to achieve effective

---

[13] For examples see Duong Van Mai Elliott, *The Sacred Willow: Four Generations in the Life of a Vietnamese Family* (New York: Oxford University Press, 1999).

[14] Sarah Womack, *Colonialism and the Collaborationist Agenda: Pham Quynh, Print Culture, and the Politics of Persuasion in Colonial Vietnam* (Ph.D. dissertation, University of Michigan, 2003).

[15] For a detailed discussion of boundary setting, see M. Ch. Fourniau, "La fixation de la frontière sino-vietnamienne 1885–1896," in *Etudes indochinoise: Frontières et contacts dan la Peninsule Indochinoise* (Provence: Institut d'histoire des pays d'outre-mer, *Études et documents no. 13*, 1981), pp. 114–42.

TABLE 7.2. *Chaos and colonialism*

China	Vietnam
Last imperial examination 1908	Paul Doumer, Governor-General 1896–1902
Qing Dynasty falls 1911	Last imperial examinations, 1915 (Tonkin), 1918 (Annam)
Warlord era, 1915–27	Japanese presence 1940–45
Northern Expedition 1927	French removed by Japan March 9, 1945
Japan occupies Manchuria 1931	
Anti-Japanese War 1937–45	Japanese surrender August 10, 1945
Civil war 1945–49	Emperor Bao Dai abdicates to Viet Minh August 28, 1945
Founding of People's Republic of China October 1, 1949	
	French return September 1945– March 46
	Geneva Conference 1954

self-government until the second half of the twentieth century, there were fundamental differences between the dissolution of political and social order in China and Vietnam's transformation into a profitable colony. Nevertheless, the same kind of rural revolution eventually prevailed in both countries.

Because of the chaos in China and colonialism in Vietnam, the Sino-Vietnamese relationship of this era can certainly be called "distracted asymmetry." The relationship did not disappear and it did not become symmetric, but for the first time ever China was not Vietnam's most important relationship, and China's internal problems made even neighbors seem farther away. On the other hand, since both were now victims of more powerful external forces a new dimension of fraternal suffering was added.

It is difficult to overestimate China's situation of total crisis[16] in the first half of the twentieth century. China's share in the world's GDP dropped from one-third in 1820 to less than a tenth in 1913, and further to only 5 percent in 1952.[17] China's per capita GDP fell from nine-tenths of the world average to one-third in 1913 and less than one-fourth in 1952. Of course, part

---

[16] I borrow this term from Tang Tsou, who used it as the key to understanding Chinese political developments in the twentieth century. See Tang Tsou, "Reflections on the Formation and Foundations of the Communist Party-State in China," in Tang Tsou, *The Cultural Revolution and Post-Mao Reforms: A Historical Perspective* (Chicago: University of Chicago Press, 1986), pp. 259–334.

[17] It was back up to 11 percent in 1995. See Angus Maddison, *Chinese Economic Performance in the Long Run* (Paris: Development Centre Studies, OECD, 1998), p. 56.

of the problem was the industrial revolution in Europe. British per capita industrial production in 1750 was only 10 percent of what it became in 1900. But China was not simply left behind by modernization; its existing economy collapsed. In 1750 China's per capita industrial production was 8 percent of Britain's in 1900, and in 1913 it was only 3 percent.[18] In 1860 China was second only to Britain in total manufacturing output; by 1913 it had slipped to seventh place.[19]

The collapse of traditional institutions put Chinese intellectuals in a harsh dilemma. If they themselves did not reject their own past root and branch and copy Western sources of wealth and power, then the racist and social Darwinist theories concerning their innate inferiority were correct.[20] For the first time China cut itself off from its past and learned from foreign models about the future. Just as the French Revolution had cut across European historical consciousness like a knife, severing a once living fabric of cultural continuity into "the present age" and the "old regime," the radical response to the Western challenge suddenly made China's traditions mere history. As President Yuan Shikai, himself a dark symbol of the times, noted in 1915 as the warlord era was beginning:

The Confucian colleges are crumbling amongst thorns and thistles; their drums and gongs are thrown aside, amid rank grass and weeds. Thus the reverence paid for thousands of years to Confucius has declined, and none seeks to repair it.[21]

From 1898 to 1927 China experienced a remarkable era of compressed intellectual modernization.[22] In 1898 very few Western books were translated into Chinese and few Chinese could read Western languages, but by 1919 Bertrand Russell and John Dewey were visiting their returned Ph.D. students, lecturing to large audiences, and having their talks appear in the next day's newspapers. Politically the May 4th Movement of 1919, popular demonstrations against the Versailles Treaty, created the basis of modern political parties. With the founding of the Chinese Communist Party in 1921 and the reorganization of the Guomindang in 1924, large-scale organized parties became the leading edge of Chinese politics.

[18] P. Bairoch, "International Industrialization Levels from 1750 to 1980," *Journal of European Economic History* 11:2 (Fall 1982), pp. 269–334, p. 281.
[19] *Ibid.*, p. 284.
[20] The thinker and journalist Liu Renhang published in 1926 a list several pages long of the differences between Chinese and Westerners that needed to be combined in a future utopia. See Wolfgang Bauer, *China und die Hoffnung auf Glück* (Munich: Carl Hanser Verlag, 1971), pp. 454–63.
[21] Quoted in Joseph Levenson, *Liang Ch'i-ch'ao and the Mind of Modern China* (Berkeley: University of California Press, 1959), p. 193.
[22] The term "compressed intellectual modernization" is from Brantly Womack, "The Phases of Chinese Modernization," in Steve Chin, ed., *Modernization in China* (Hong Kong: Hong Kong University Press, 1979), pp. 1–15.

But the very radicalism and foreignness of the various Western models advocated – from the YMCA and literacy to nationalism and communism – created a crisis of inappropriateness for China's actual conditions. China's actual conditions continued to decline with the fall of the dynasty in 1911 and the rise of warlordism after 1915. The solutions offered were cosmopolitan and urban, while the nine-tenths of China in the villages became more fragmented and desperate. The Guomindang's reunification of China in 1927 instituted a weak authoritarian government dependent on former warlords for local order and too unsure of its hold on power to mobilize the population against Japanese incursions, which began with the occupation of Manchuria in 1931.

Vietnam was literally marginal to the crisis in China. Sun Yatsen garnered support there for his anti-Manchu activities, and several of his early uprisings against the Qing were launched in towns close to the Vietnamese border. Although the French reluctantly gave up their ambition of using Vietnam to force a back door to China through Yunnan, they did become the major foreign influence in Yunnan, Guangxi, and southern Guangdong. Using 80,000 Chinese and Vietnamese laborers, 25,000 of whom died, they built a railroad from Haiphong through Hanoi to Kunming in 1910, racing the Canton-Kowloon railway the British were building.[23] Catholic churches sprouted up on the China side of the border, and the most impressive buildings in Chinese border towns like Hekou in Yunnan Province were the offices of French officials. France ran Zhanjiang (Fort Bayard) in Guangdong, on the far side of Hainan Island from Vietnam, but failed to develop it into a significant colony.

Vietnam's colonial experience was no less traumatic than China's, but it was vastly different. In contrast to China's economic decline Vietnam grew into France's most profitable colony, making most of its money from the export of rice. In the 1930s Vietnam became the world's third-largest rice exporter, after Burma and Thailand.[24] However, the replacement of subsistence farming in autonomous villages with commercial estates and plantations left most Vietnamese with less food and less security than they had before. The integration of Vietnam into the world economy made Vietnam vulnerable to the worldwide economic depression of the early 1930s. But the most fatal effect of economic transformation occurred when Japan's rice requisitions, French control over production, and natural conditions produced a famine in 1943–45 that claimed one to two million lives out of a population of almost ten million.[25] The hardest hit provinces lost over half their

---

[23] Buttinger, *Vietnam*, p. 115.
[24] *Ibid.*, 164.
[25] See Nguyen The Anh, "Japanese Food Policies and the 1945 Great Famine in Indochina," in Paul Kratoska, ed., *Food Supplies and the Japanese Occupation in Southeast Asia* (New York: St. Martin's Press, 1998), pp. 208–26.

population.[26] In percentage terms the starvation rate was three times higher than that experienced in China's Great Leap Forward. To put it in American perspective, a tidal wave that would destroy the entire populations of West Coast states of California, Oregon, and Washington would be comparable in proportional magnitude.[27] For most Red River villages, the loss of population from the 1945 famine was much worse than the combined casualties in the subsequent wars against the French and the Americans.[28] Although the Vietnamese socio-economy under the French was better organized than China's total chaos, Vietnam's distress was at times more acute.

Although French occupation certainly produced crises both cultural and personal for Vietnamese, it led to a reaffirmation of the continuity of Vietnam's national identity rather than to a radical rejection of the past.[29] The fact that the last of the mandarin resisters to French colonization could join hands with the first pioneers of national liberation created a physical link. Ho Chi Minh's father was a scholar and court official with ties to the anti-French resistance.[30] China played an ironic role in the continuity because the traditions of heroic resistance against China could be refocused on the new threat of France. Similarly, though less heroically, practices of collaboration and submission resonated with previous situations of subordination. China itself became neither threat nor model, but the transposition of traditional attitudes from China to France was a central thread of Vietnam's intellectual reorientation.

Colonial politics in Vietnam reflected the vast spectrum of French politics with the addition of Asian influences. Ho Chi Minh became a founding member of the French Communist Party in 1920 before journeying on to Moscow and then coming to China in 1924 as part of Mikhail Borodin's entourage.[31] Japan's success against the Russians in 1905 and its rapid rise as an Asian power attracted Vietnamese admirers, and the Guomindang's reunification of China in 1927 spawned a sister party in Vietnam. By 1930 there were three groups in Vietnam calling themselves communist, much to the disgust of the Comintern, which backed Ho's efforts at consolidation. Within the French administration of Vietnam the major tensions did not come from Vietnamese

---

[26] In Nam Dinh Province, 646,147 died of a population of 1,259,734. *Ibid.*, p. 217.

[27] These estimates are based on a 15 percent population loss, the average of the upper and lower estimates of famine deaths in Tonkin. The Great Leap Forward comparison is based on the often-quoted estimate of 30 million deaths.

[28] Motoo Furuta, "A Survey of Village Conditions during the 1945 Famine in Vietnam," in Paul Kratoska, *Food Supplies*, pp. 227–38, p. 237.

[29] The emphasis on historical continuity continues in contemporary Vietnamese historiography. See John Whitmore, "Communism and History in Vietnam," in William Turley, ed., *Vietnamese Communism in Comparative Perspective* (Boulder: Westview, 1980), pp. 11–44.

[30] William Duiker, *Ho Chi Minh* (New York: Hyperion, 2000), pp. 14–45.

[31] For details on the Borodin mission see Zhihong Chen, *Die China-Mission Michail Borodins bis zum Tod Sun Yatsens* (Münster: Lit Verlag, 2000).

parties but rather from the hostility between the conservative *colons* of the south and the governors-general from Paul Doumer onward who promoted, usually with little success, plans that were more dynamic and occasionally more progressive.[32]

A common thread among the various Vietnamese currents was the importance of education. Vietnam had been a fairly literate society before the French, but colonization destroyed traditional schools and was extremely slow in setting up new ones.[33] The *colons* considered native education the wellspring of revolution, sensing that only an ignorant and isolated population would long bear their domination. By the same token, even the most conservative of Vietnamese reformers assumed that education was essential to national salvation.[34] The question was whether the core of education was moral, modern, or revolutionary.

By 1900 both China and Vietnam were irreversibly part of the modern world. China's traditional centric order, which like a bowl had concentrated attention on the center, had been turned upside down, so that attention now flowed to the farthest reaches of new horizons. Vietnam had a greater continuity with its past, but it was a continuity that demanded reeducation and resistance. Both countries were still overwhelmingly rural and at the limits of their endurance.

Revolutionary Comradeship

In retrospect, certainly the most important dimension of Sino-Vietnamese similarity, contact, and cooperation during the first half of the twentieth century was between the Chinese Communist Party (CCP), founded in Shanghai in 1921, and the Indochinese Communist Party (ICP), founded in Hong Kong in 1930.[35] Both parties were inspired by the success of the Russian revolution, influenced by direct contact with European communist parties, especially the French Communist Party, and were assisted by the Communist International (Comintern). But their most significant common ground lay in the challenge of protracted revolution in overwhelmingly rural environments, and in facing this challenge the CCP and the ICP grew to be more similar to one another than to any other communist party.

---

[32] A critical overview is provided by Buttinger, *Vietnam*, pp. 101–47.

[33] David Marr estimates that 25 percent of the pre-colonial population had basic literacy, whereas only 5 percent were literate in any language by the 1920s. In 1929 only 121 Vietnamese were enrolled in public secondary schools. See David Marr, *Vietnamese Tradition on Trial 1920–1945* (Berkeley: University of California Press, 1981), esp. pp. 15–54, 136–89.

[34] Sarah Womack, *Colonialism and the Collaborationist Agenda.*

[35] It was founded as the Vietnamese Communist Party in February 1930 and renamed the Indochinese Communist Party at the insistence of the Comintern in December. It renamed itself the Indochinese Marxist Study Society in November 1945, the Vietnam Workers Party in 1951, and finally the Communist Party of Vietnam in 1976.

For both China and Vietnam, the fundamental attraction of communism was the combination of its demonstrated success in the Russian revolution, its critique of imperialism, and its commitment to world revolution. Underlying all three of these was a commitment to a mass-based political community, but a community that required a dedicated and tightly organized revolutionary leadership. Having never been simply a nation among other nations, Chinese were particularly excited about a cosmopolitan revolution that would dissolve narrow nationalisms. The idea of leaping from the troubled world of imperialist oppression to a world beyond boundaries was already outlined in Kang Youwei's *Book of Great Harmony* [Da tong shu 大同书] and in Mao Zedong's pre-Marxist writings.[36] By contrast, national liberation from France was Vietnam's great concern. For Ho Chi Minh the Leninist critique of imperialism as a distorted relationship among nations was more important than the critique of nationhood per se.[37] For Mao "national liberation" meant a transformation of China in a world context beyond nationhood; for Ho it had the more practical focus of the restoration of Vietnam as an autonomous political community. Although these aims were not in conflict, they do show that even shared revolutionary visions remain located in national realities.

On the more practical side of being communist parties, the CCP and the ICP shared a commitment to socialist internationalism, party discipline, class struggle, and united front. Socialist internationalism involved membership in the Comintern (which was the third "Socialist International," after the one founded by Marx in 1864 and the "Second International" founded in 1889, condemned by Lenin as revisionist), which in turn involved Soviet leadership, advice, and aid as well as more equally fraternal relations with other communist parties. Party discipline implied democratic centralism – concentrated and unquestioned leadership in a context of intimate comradeship. Class struggle provided both an ideological template for analyzing current politics and mass-based positioning of the party's own agenda. The tactic of "united front" provided a means of working toward common objectives with non-communist groups and individuals. United front tactics allowed the party to concentrate on proximate political objectives. In a united front, the party could mobilize all social forces that shared a concrete objective (such as fighting the Japanese or opposing the French), neutralizing elements that remained uncommitted and isolating the enemy.

---

[36] For Kang, see Wolfgang Bauer, *China*, pp. 412–51; for Mao, see Brantly Womack, *The Foundations of Mao Zedong's Political Thought, 1917–1935* (Honolulu: University Press of Hawaii, 1982).

[37] Ho was inspired to become a Marxist upon reading Lenin's "Theses on the National and Colonial Questions" in *l'Humanité* when he was in Paris. See William Duiker, "Vietnamese Revolutionary Doctrine in Comparative Perspective," in Turley, *Vietnamese Communism*, p. 46.

The individuality of the CCP and the ICP developed as they adapted an essentially urban revolutionary outlook to their rural environments in response to their own failures.[38] Failures were inevitable. Revolutionary ideologies are by nature optimistic and the people they attract are risk takers. Moreover, the Bolsheviks had succeeded as an urban, proletarian party utilizing national crises, thus setting the expected pattern. The CCP failed as an urban revolutionary party in 1927, when it was cast aside by the victorious GMD at the conclusion of the Northern Expedition and lost 90 percent of its membership. The ICP failed to overthrow French colonialism by insurrection in 1930–31 and suffered brutal repression thereafter. Although the ICP supported rural insurrections, these were part of an urban-centered strategy of creating crises for the colonial regime. These were massive disasters, and they could have spelled the ends of both parties as serious participants in politics.

Survival required a solution to the failure of urban communist parties, and Mao Zedong gradually pieced together a strategy of rural revolution in 1927–34 and then made his thought the guiding line of the CCP when he took charge in 1935–37. Rather than exploit rural unrest to destabilize the cities,[39] Mao built rural revolutionary bases far from the cities, defended them with guerilla warfare, and expanded them to eventually surround the cities. In a country that was 90 percent rural, revolutionary victory was to be concluded in the cities, but it would be won in the rural areas.

The key to rural revolutionary success was the mobilized support of the peasantry. Although the party remained in charge, mass-regarding policies had to be developed that stimulated peasant support and involvement in the politics, economy, and military activities of the base area. Land reform and the overthrow of the village class structure were key policies, but they were by no means simple to implement. The party's need for popular support – the only resource it had against a more powerful enemy – created a quasi-democratic system, a governing structure that was responsive to popular opinion and needs and yet managed by an authoritarian party.[40] Not only did the party as a whole need the people's support, but each local leader

---

[38] This is discussed by Pierre Brocheux, "Vietnamese Communism and the Peasants," in Turley, *Vietnamese Communism*, pp. 75–90.

[39] As Zhang Xiuhua argues, even after the failure of urban insurrection the party looked for rural areas that could support new urban insurrections. Indeed, it was only after the failure of the assault on Changsha in 1930 that Mao himself confirmed his commitment to a rural revolutionary strategy. See Zhang Xiuhua, "Changqi hunxiao di jige zhongyao guannian – nongcun geju, junshi da benying he nongcun geming genjudi di guanxi zhi wo guan" [Several important concepts that have been confused for a long time – My opinion about rural separatist rule, military strongholds and revolutionary rural bases], *Lishi Jikan* [Collected Papers of History Studies] 2002:3, no. 88 (July 2002), pp. 28–31.

[40] This idea is developed more fully in Brantly Womack, "The Party and the People: Revolutionary and Post-Revolutionary Politics in China and Vietnam," *World Politics* 39:4 (July 1986), pp. 479–507.

could maximize his or her personal chances of survival and victory only by maximizing local support. Once popular support was mobilized, government repression would only increase revolutionary solidarity.

The success of the Chinese revolution in 1949 had at its core the creation of a new political-military force from a mobilized peasantry, aided by a united front with a broad range of groups disillusioned by the Guomindang. In contrast to the Bolshevik revolution of 1917, the CCP did not seize state power and then fight a civil war, but rather fought and won a civil war in the teeth of the Republic of China and its foreign support. Rather than utilizing urban insurrection and national crisis, the CCP built a counter-state in the countryside that by 1949 simply overwhelmed the opposition. At the time of victory the CCP had 23 years of base area experience and 4.5 million members, as many members as the Communist Party of the Soviet Union at that time. Economic recovery was rapid. Within three years pre-revolutionary production had been surpassed, despite war in Korea. China had indeed stood up, and it was a different China from before.

In Vietnam, the ICP was both more and less successful than the CCP, and it used a different mix of the same basic strategies. After organizing the united front organization of the Viet Minh in 1941, the ICP led the most determined resistance to Japanese and French control of Vietnam and developed a network throughout the country. In 1945 the combination of the Japanese seizing control of Vietnam from the French, the severe famine, and the surrender of Japan in August created the opportunity for Ho Chi Minh to declare Vietnam an independent Democratic Republic of Vietnam (DRV), four years before the success of the Chinese revolution.[41] The opportunity for state leadership was fleeting. The UN mandated the acceptance of the Japanese surrender and the maintenance of order to the GMD in the north and the British in the south. The British occupation forces favored the re-establishment of French colonialism, and the Guomindang forces encouraged a mixed leadership.[42] When the French returned in 1945–46 the Viet Minh were driven underground and to remote base areas on the Chinese border. The DRV was not recognized by any government until China's recognition in January 1950. But the Declaration of Independence in September 1945 had established Ho Chi Minh as the leader of Vietnam's independence movement against the French,[43] and the struggle in the countryside could continue.

Because the target of the ICP was a foreign colonial order, united front activities could play a larger role than in China. During the Anti-Japanese

---

[41] The magisterial book on the crucial year of 1945 is David Marr, *Vietnam 1945: The Quest for Power* (Berkeley: University of California Press, 1995).

[42] King Chen, *Vietnam and China 1938–1954* (Princeton: Princeton University Press, 1969).

[43] The breadth of Ho's appeal as an independence leader can be gauged by the autobiography of a South Vietnamese general. See Tran Van Don, *Our Endless War* (San Rafael: Presidio Press, 1978).

War the CCP could unite with all patriotic forces and subordinate class struggle to national unity, but before and afterward the target was the Guomindang regime. In Vietnam the basic components of rural revolution – land reform and mass mobilization in the villages – were essential parts of the Viet Minh program, but the prominent role of the Viet Minh (and later of the National Liberation Front) is evidence of the central role of national unity in Vietnamese national liberation.

Ho Chi Minh did not concentrate on national liberation because he was a more extreme or inflexible nationalist than Mao Zedong. Far from it. In 1945–46 he was willing to go to great lengths to make compromises with the French, and to claim to Americans that he really was not a communist, and to offer Cam Ranh Bay to the Americans as a naval base.[44] He was not willing to ask (Guomindang) China's help against the French, saying, "It is better to sniff French shit for a while than to eat China's for the rest of our lives."[45] Independence was Ho's highest political objective, but the path to independence was expected to be long and twisted.

We have analyzed the common situations of China and Vietnam before considering the contacts between them, but certainly contacts were important. Vietnamese reformers and revolutionaries were woven into Chinese political activities from the beginning. Before the 1920s the language fluency of the Vietnamese elite and the fact that China was facing similar problems led to a great interest in intellectual currents to the north. In 1913 the conservative Francophone Nguyen Van Vinh criticized the famous nationalist Phan Boi Chau for getting all of his ideas of the West via China. According to Vinh,

It is hard enough to select primary French concepts that are digestible to the Annamites, but if one picks up these things via Chinese books and Chinese characters, with pieces carved off the top and the bottom and strange ingredients added here and there, then it is not just a matter of indigestion or choking, but of being poisoned.[46]

Not only Western ideas but Chinese modes of coping with the West were of interest to Vietnam. The idea of preserving a national essence while copying foreign things for their utility [*thê-dụng; ti-yong* 体用], which Zhang Zhidong had articulated in 1898, was still popular in Vietnam in the 1930s, long after it had gone out of fashion in China.[47]

Perhaps the golden age of direct revolutionary contact between China and Vietnam was the First United Front between the Guomindang and the Chinese Communist Party in 1924–27. At that time Chinese revolutionaries were united behind Sun Yatsen and both felt sympathy for Vietnam. When

[44] Duiker, *Ho Chi Minh*, pp. 390–1.
[45] Paul Mus, *Viet-nam: Sociologie d'un guerre* (1952), quoted in Duiker, *Ho Chi Minh* p. 361.
[46] Quoted in David Marr, *Vietnamese Tradition on Trial*, pp. 151–2.
[47] *Ibid.*, p. 113.

in 1924 a Vietnamese revolutionary died trying to assassinate the governor-general of Indochina during a visit to Guangzhou, Sun Yatsen had him buried with honors in the cemetery for Chinese revolutionary martyrs.[48] There were Vietnamese cadets at the Whampoa Military Academy in Guangzhou in the 1920s, and according to Buttinger at least 250 Vietnamese communists were trained in China before the founding of the ICP in 1930.[49] Ho Chi Minh himself ran a training institute in Guangzhou in the 1920s, which featured guest lectures by Zhou Enlai, Liu Shaoqi, and Peng Pai, and during the Second United Front in the late 1930s he participated in an institute in Hunan set up by the Chinese Communist Party's Eighth Route Army to train Guomindang officers in guerilla warfare.[50]

Relations between the GMD and Vietnamese revolutionary groups became quite complex in the 1940s. On the one hand, the GMD opposed French colonialism and even more so Japanese occupation, so there was a common ground between them and even the ICP. On the other hand, the GMD was anti-communist, and so it enthusiastically supported non-communist Vietnamese nationalists and was suspicious of Ho and his colleagues. Ho's personal experience with the GMD is illustrative of the ambivalence. In August 1942 he was arrested and imprisoned for more than a year in conditions that ruined his health, and immediately thereafter he was selected by the commander of Guangxi to organize Vietnamese nationalists in preparation for an anti-Japanese Indochina campaign. After the surrender of Japan, the GMD became the occupying force of northern Vietnam, and the ambivalence continued. In contrast to the British in the south the GMD did not attempt to re-install the French and it negotiated with Ho's newly established government, but it strongly favored non-communists and plundered the country. In March 1946 it permitted the French to return in exchange for the French giving up their imperialist privileges in China, including their lease of Zhanjiang.[51] When the French re-occupied the north, the Viet Minh base areas on the Chinese border developed understandings and trade routes with the local Guomindang power holders in the area before the arrival of the People's Liberation Army (PLA) at the end of 1949.[52]

The relationship between the ICP and the CCP was friendly from the beginning, but it underwent important developments. The ICP shifted from a Soviet model of revolution in the 1930s to a Chinese model in the 1940s. Despite the difference in relative weighting of tactics between the CCP and the ICP, by the time of the anti-French war in 1946, the successes of China

[48] Five Cantonese businessmen died in the explosion, but not the governor-general. Duiker, *Ho Chi Minh*, pp. 117–8.
[49] Buttinger, *Vietnam*, p. 178.
[50] Duiker, *Ho Chi Minh*, pp. 236–7.
[51] Buttinger, *Vietnam*, pp. 238–9.
[52] See Christopher Goscha, "The Borders of the DRV's Early Trade with the Chinese during the War against the French (1945–1950)," *Asian Survey* 40:6 (December), pp. 986–1008.

in its rural revolution and the cogent writings of Mao Zedong explaining
his strategy had become the proximate model for Vietnamese communism.
General Secretary of the ICP Truong Chinh, whose *nom de guerre* meant
"Long March," borrowed freely from Mao's ideas. Perhaps the best state-
ment of the ICP's attitude toward the Chinese revolution was given by Ho Chi
Minh in his Political Report to the Second National Congress of the Vietnam
Workers Party:

Marx, Engels, Lenin and Stalin are the common masters of the world revolution.
Comrade Mao Zedong has skillfully sinicized the doctrines of Marx, Engels, Lenin
and Stalin, applied them in the most judicious way to the Chinese situation, and thus
has led the Chinese revolution to total victory. By reason of its geographic, historical,
economic and cultural conditions, the Chinese revolution exercises a considerable
influence on the Vietnamese revolution. The Vietnamese revolution must learn and
has learned a great deal from the experience of the Chinese revolution.[53]

As Ho's carefully worded statement suggests, it was the general similarity
of situation rather than direct advice and assistance that made the Chinese
revolution important for Vietnam, especially before 1950. In contrast to
Korea, which shared a border with Northeast China, an area of early communist victories in the Chinese civil war, there were only isolated pockets
of CCP activities in south China until the arrival of the People's Liberation
Army in late 1949. Moreover, due in part to Japanese encouragement of emigration to Manchukuo during the 1930s, there were hundreds of thousands
of ethnic Koreans resident in China who could form an ethnic link between
the two revolutions. In 1949 the PLA sent between 30,000 and 40,000 ethnic
Korean troops back to Korea, greatly strengthening Kim Il Song's military
capacity.[54] By contrast, there are no significant numbers of ethnic Vietnamese
in China, and while some of the ethnic Chinese in Vietnam supported the
Viet Minh, they did so primarily through Southeast Asian channels and
networks.

Considering the shadow that China had cast over Vietnam for the previous two millennia, the relationship from 1885 to 1950 was mild indeed.
Although the disparity remained – China did not shrink nor did Vietnam
grow – Western domination and revolutionary activities so distracted the
bilateral asymmetry that the fraternal tie of common oppression governed
the relationship. As Ho Chi Minh claimed, the shared situation dictated
political commonalities. The Chinese revolution eventually became a model
for Vietnam not because of China's scale and power but because of China's
success. Presumably if Vietnam had been successful with rural revolution
before China then China would have copied Vietnam. The utilization of

---

[53] Quoted in Brocheux, "Vietnamese Communism," p. 75. This paragraph is missing from the
version of the report in the 1977 *Selected Works of Ho Chi Minh*, pp. 101–29.
[54] Chen Jian, *China's Road to the Korean War* (New York: Columbia University Press, 1994),
p. 110.

the Chinese revolutionary model does resonate with Thanh Ton's utilization of the neo-Confucian model of governance in the sixteenth century, since both Ho and Thanh Ton were adapting successful Chinese institutions and approaches to similar Vietnamese circumstances. But the presence of the French and the more general revolutionary context of communism provided a different external context.

Asymmetry Distressed

In this chapter we have discussed two modalities of asymmetry – disjunctive asymmetry and distracted asymmetry – that were new to the Sino-Vietnamese relationship but are not uncommon in international relations. Before moving on to the next phase it may be worthwhile to reflect on the general character of these two situations.

Disjunctive asymmetry as experienced by Vietnam vis-à-vis France and by China vis-à-vis the West contained two elements: military superiority that was qualitatively overwhelming and a deep cultural disjunction. Although these two elements often occur together, they can be analyzed separately.

Military disjunction can be viewed as an extreme form of asymmetry. When the disparity in military capacity is so extreme that not only can the stronger defeat the weaker with no difficulty, but the weaker is destroyed beyond the capacity of significant resistance, then the stronger side will not be forced to negotiate with the weaker side. Victory can be complete.

However, as Machiavelli points out at the beginning of *The Prince*, governing an occupied territory is difficult even when no organized opposition exists. In our cases, the imperialist powers wisely decided not to try to govern China beyond their urban zones of safety, and France had to rely increasingly on collaboration by individual Vietnamese in order to staff its colony. Moreover, victory is achieved against a government, not a people, and new, more powerful forms of resistance may emerge. Victory may be complete, but occupation remains a process of implicit negotiation.

Cultural disjunction, the second element, refers to a difference in values, systems, and expectations so vast that negotiation is impossible because its pre-condition of credible communication does not exist. Cultural disjunction is not a form of asymmetry because cultures cannot be placed on a scale of disparate capabilities, but the disjunction can certainly be a significant difference. In our cases, negotiations were assumed by all sides merely to be agreements required by the duress of circumstances rather than components of a stable, mutually beneficial arrangement. Under these circumstances the strong and the weak are driven to test continually the limits of their respective power.

Cultural disjunction destroys negotiation not because of some absolute mutual unintelligibility but because there is no accepted common ground that can provide a framework for a negotiated asymmetry. Recalling the framework for managing asymmetric relations put forward in Chapter 4, there is no sleeve of mutual diplomatic acknowledgment and there is no common sense of an established, non-pathological relationship. The stronger will bump against the weaker until exhaustion produces a truce in place that becomes useful to both sides. Even so, however, a truce of this sort is constructed over a cultural fault line. For instance, the decision in 1482 by Ferdinand of Aragon and Isabella of Castile to launch the *reconquista* against the Moors pushed aside centuries of mutual understandings and trade between Christians and Muslims in central Spain. A situation of cease-fire may be the beginning of a more robust relationship, but by itself it is vulnerable to any perceived shift of advantage that might induce one or the other side to try again.

Distracted asymmetry might be said to occur whenever the two sides of a specific asymmetric relationship are preoccupied with a more important relationship. In our cases, both China and Vietnam had to deal with Western imperialism, Vietnam in the more concrete form of French colonialism. If China had been distracted by the Mongols and Vietnam by the French, it would have produced the same effect of lessening the attention to the relationship, but it would not have produced a common fraternity of suffering. Distracted asymmetry should be distinguished from more complex situations of asymmetry such as triangular relationships. In a case such as that among the United States, China, and Taiwan, the three bilateral relations of the triangle each influence one another, so that any one relationship does not necessarily become any less important, but it does exist in a more complicated environment.

Perhaps one could find relationships of distracted asymmetry in Latin America, since all countries in the region have the major concern of their relationship to the United States. The relationship between Mexico and Cuba, for instance, might not be as fraternal if they did not have the same neighbor to the north. More generally, regional relationships below the level of "great power" relationships are usually moderated by the existence of larger concerns, even if the bilateral relationship is quite asymmetric.

8

Lips and Teeth

1950–1975

With the establishment of the People's Republic of China on October 1, 1949, and the arrival of the People's Liberation Army at the Vietnam border in December, a new era began of intense and intimate cooperation between China and Vietnam. Party-to-party relations between the Vietnam Workers Party (VWP)[1] and the Chinese Communist Party formed the core of the relationship, while state-to-state relations between the People's Republic of China and the Democratic Republic of Vietnam, established in January 1950, provided the public form.[2]

Of course, the situations of China and Vietnam over the next twenty-five years were quite different. China had finished its civil war in 1949 and had stabilized by 1952. Its major troubles of the period were largely self-imposed: the Great Leap Forward of 1958–60 and the Cultural Revolution of 1966–69. Only after Mao Zedong's death in 1976 could China begin to change its leftist policies. By contrast, the Democratic Republic of Vietnam in 1950 was still waging a desperate war with French colonial forces. Over the next four years, with Chinese help, it grew into a major and finally a victorious challenge to colonialism, and then became the government of northern Vietnam. In the 1960s the effort to reunify Vietnam began again, and in 1965–73 American direct intervention greatly increased the costs and risks of the war effort. Although Vietnam had declared independence in 1946, it was not until the defeat of the Saigon regime in 1975 that it was in a situation of unified national autonomy comparable to that of China in 1949.

Because the Vietnamese revolution remained incomplete from 1950 to 1975, revolutionary comradeship required that the CCP provide every

---

[1] The Indochinese Communist Party renamed itself the Indochinese Marxist Study Society in November 1945, the Vietnam Workers Partyin 1951, and finally the Communist Party of Vietnam in 1976.

[2] As of 2004, China still considered the party relationship primary.

possible assistance to the VWP. The comradely relationship was often said to be "as close as lips and teeth" [*chun chi xiangyi* 唇齿相依 *gắn bó như môi với răng* – more literally, "as interdependent as lips and teeth"]. Although even without Chinese help the Vietnamese would certainly have persisted and eventually would have prevailed in their quest for independence, the course taken by the VWP from 1950 on and the resources available were shaped by Chinese assistance. Although the VWP was by no means subordinate to the CCP, it leaned heavily on Chinese support, and there was no alternative comparable to Chinese support. China supplied necessities of life as well as the means of struggle. If Vietnam had alienated China, the VWP would have suffered a setback comparable to the American entry into the war. Underlying revolutionary comradeship, therefore, was dependent asymmetry.

Although China was not dependent on Vietnam, its aid to Vietnam was its most important sustained foreign policy commitment from 1952 to 1975, and the survival and success of the VWP was crucial to China. First, Vietnam's struggle and success validated the significance of the Chinese revolution by extending its methods beyond China's borders. Aiding Vietnam promoted a socialist internationalism that was implicitly China-centered. Second, the struggle with the United States that had begun in Korea could be continued in Vietnam without risking China's own security. Although many analysts exaggerate China's fear of the United States and underestimate China's self-confidence, the fact remains that, confident or not, China perceived the United States as its primary threat until 1969, and therefore offering full support for someone else's war against the United States made sense. Third, support for Vietnam had domestic resonance. Especially in 1965 mobilization for Vietnam and against America played a role in stirring a general sense of crisis and danger that was useful for Mao's domestic agenda in the Cultural Revolution.

These three factors are not equal in importance. The domestic political utility of support for Vietnam varied considerably over a quarter-century, and yet support remained relatively constant. Likewise, the perception of the United States as the principal enemy changed in 1969, and yet China resolutely refused to bargain with the United States concerning China's support for Vietnam during the Kissinger and Nixon visits of 1971–72. Most basic was China's interest in the success of a fraternal party, one that would both validate the world significance of the Chinese revolution and extend China's influence. Vietnam's victory in 1975 did not mean to China what it meant to Vietnam, but each considered it its own triumph.

There were two major phases in the Sino-Vietnamese relationship during this period. In the first, 1950 to 1965, the momentum of common suffering and Vietnam's obvious need for China's aid and advice created a remarkable intimacy in the relationship. In the second, 1965–75, China's leftward plunge created a distance between China and Vietnam despite continuing aid. Vietnam began to receive aid from the Soviet Union as well, and in 1972 Nixon's visit began a new era in U.S.-China relations. While none of these developments led to a break in the alliance, the differences in perspective that they laid bare produced a cooling of the original intimacy. In 1950 there were no clear differences of interests between China and Vietnam; by 1967 the differences began to emerge, and by 1974 they were clear.

The chapter is divided into three parts. The first two analyze the two phases, and the last considers dependent asymmetry more generally by contrasting the Chinese relationship with the Democratic Republic of Vietnam in North Vietnam and the American relationship with the Republic of Vietnam in South Vietnam.

Intimate Comradeship, 1950–1965

In 1950 the communist parties of both China and Vietnam were experienced in rural revolution, opposed imperialism, and supported the socialist camp. As the Chinese scholar Guo Ming has pointed out, they shared a similar situation, similar ideology, and a long comradeship in struggle.[3] The major difference between them was that the CCP had just succeeded in its revolution. By contrast, the VWP had survived and expanded since being driven out of the cities by France in 1946, but it did not control significant territory. Even though its command base was and had always been in the vicinity of the Chinese border, the French controlled all the major and minor border strong points. When Ho Chi Minh walked to China in January 1950, it took him seventeen days to cross the border.

The visit was definitely worth the effort. On January 14, just before crossing the Chinese border, Ho announced that "the DRV is willing to establish diplomatic relations with any country on the basis of equality and mutual respect for sovereignty and territory and to work together to preserve world peace and democracy."[4] Both the location and the wording of the announcement are evidence of Ho's concern about preserving Vietnam's autonomy and international options in the face of China's looming embrace. On January 18, 1950, China became the first country to establish diplomatic relations with Vietnam, an action that delayed China's establishment of relations with France until 1964. At the formal banquet Liu Shaoqi suggested to the Soviet ambassador that Ho be invited to continue on to Moscow.[5]

China's recognition of the Democratic Republic of Vietnam and full diplomatic support were of crucial importance to Vietnam. As Christopher

---

[3] Guo Ming 郭明, ed., *Zhong Yue guanxi yanbian sishi nian* 中越关系演变40年 [The 40-year Evolution of Sino-Vietnamese Relations] (Nanning: Guangxi Renmin Chubanshe, 1992), pp. 18–19.

[4] *Ibid.*, p. 22.

[5] William Duiker, *Ho Chi Minh* (New York: Hyperion, 2000), p. 420.

TABLE 8.1. *Lips and teeth*

China	Vietnam
	Declaration of Vietnamese independence,
Founding of PRC October 1, 1949	September 2, 1945
	Establishment of PRC-DRV relations
	January 18, 1950
	Fall of Dien Bien Phu May 7, 1954
	Geneva Conference on Indochina
	May 8–July 21, 1954
Bandung Conference 1955	U.S. support for Diem begins 1955
Great Leap Forward 1958–61	NLF formed; war in South 1960
Open anti-Soviet polemic 1962	Gulf of Tonkin Incident August 2, 1954
	American War in Vietnam, 1964–73

Goscha puts it, "It was thanks to the support of the CCP and its leaders that Vietnam under the leadership of the ICP was able to enter officially the communist community under the direction of the Communist Party of the Soviet Union. The way to Moscow passed through the CCP."[6]

Goscha provides a detailed and convincing narration of Soviet disinterest in Vietnam from 1945 to 1950.[7] Not only did Stalin not respond to Ho's requests to bring Indochina before the United Nations, but at the same time that Stalin was ignoring Vietnam he was energetically supporting Indonesian independence, even though Indonesia had suppressed its communist party. Goscha argues that in his efforts to appear acceptably non-communist to the West, Ho alienated potential Soviet support. Perhaps more important, Stalin had a low opinion of Ho's chances and in any case valued more highly his relations with the French. Thus, as the Vietnamese plaintively observed in 1947, "At the moment, Vietnam is alone in its struggle."[8]

It might appear that China's embrace and the acceptance of the DRV into the communist community was a mixed blessing diplomatically, but the fact of communist victory in China had already ended American ambivalence in supporting the French. In May 1949 U.S. Secretary of State Dean Acheson had given instructions to provide economic and military support to the Bao

---

[6] Christopher Goscha, "La survie diplomatique du Parti Communiste Indochinois et l'importance de la Chine communiste (1945–1950)," p. 1.

[7] *Ibid.*

[8] Quoted in *ibid.*, p. 11.

Dai government instituted by France.[9] Had China adopted Stalin's attitude of preferring relations with France and of cool distance toward communist parties not under its control, the DRV would have been caught between the Scylla of increased anti-communist cohesion among its enemies and the Charybdis of actual disinterest on the part of China and the Soviet Union. As it was, public support by China and then by the Soviet Union made the DRV unequivocally a part of the communist world, and this final alignment made the aid supplied by China even more urgent and important.

What significance did support for fellow revolutionaries in Vietnam have for China? China's foreign policy entered an exciting but uncharted new era on October 1, 1949, and support for Vietnam played a uniquely important role in China's new international self-consciousness. First, China was proud of its rural revolutionary success, and support for Vietnam was a means of generalizing the significance of the Chinese revolution. As Liu Shaoqi, Mao's second-in-command and the central leader designated to handle cooperation with Vietnam, put it to Luo Guibo, the first CCP liaison representative, "it is the duty of those countries that have achieved the victory of their own revolution to support peoples who are still conducting the just struggle for liberation."[10] Second, support for Vietnam provided a comfortable point of certainty in the otherwise complex questions of how to cope with imperial and republican traditions and to relate to the socialist bloc. Support for Vietnam did not raise the delicate questions that policy toward Hong Kong, Mongolia, or Korea did, or later that the 1956 uprisings in Poland and Hungary posed. China was quite self-confident in 1949, but its new identity was embryonic. Supporting a fraternal communist party's national liberation movement in a former part of the Chinese empire resonated with all levels of China's identity, old and new. Last, China's military and political security would be enhanced by supporting the VWP. If Ho prevailed, a friendly neighbor would replace the last colonial regime on China's border. As long as Ho continued fighting, anti-communist forces would be distracted from tightening the noose around China itself. However, if Ho lost, then a situation would be created like that in Korea in 1950, when a triumphant and anti-communist foreign army arrived on China's border.

In its support for the VWP China did not displace Vietnamese leadership and control (unlike the American relationship to the Saigon regime in the 1960s), but it did provide unstinting aid and advice to every aspect of the

---

[9] *History of the Indochina Incident, 1940–1954* (Washington: Historical Division, Joint Secretariat, Joint Chiefs of Staff, originally prepared February 1955, 2nd ed. 1971, declassified edition 1981), p. 135.

[10] Quoted in Chen Jian, "China and the First Indochina War, 1950–1954," *China Quarterly* 133 (June 1993), p. 87.

Vietnamese revolution.[11] China's most capable generals provided military advice and training, and China's top leadership was intimately involved in discussions of strategy. Behind the battlefield, ideological training, government reorganization, and economic development were important areas of Chinese involvement. As far as cost was concerned, Liu Shaoqi said:

If the Vietnamese do not have or lack materials to exchange, those goods can be viewed as military aid for the time being. In the future when mutual trade is possible and when the Vietnamese can offer materials, [we] will ask them to pay for some of our goods. At present since they are unable to pay, we will not mention it. We should now focus our attention on how to help them defeat imperialism effectively and should relegate other issues to a secondary place.[12]

The comradely intimacy of the relationship can be illustrated by the first major military campaign of the Viet Minh, the campaign in the second half of 1950 to gain control of the China-Vietnam border.[13] General Chen Geng became the senior military advisor to the newly renamed People's Army of Vietnam (PAVN) in the summer of 1950, and his instructions from Liu Shaoqi were to develop a comprehensive strategic plan on the basis of actual conditions, including aid and training. Chen found a military force that was primarily engaged in small-scale hit-and-run attacks against French outposts and therefore had weak command structure and discipline. Chen gave a four-hour lecture to PAVN commanders about their deficiencies, which, as Chen remembers it, the Vietnamese – including General Vo Nguyen Giap, commander of PAVN – found very educational.[14] Chen designed a plan for attacking the small French outpost at Dong Khe, because this was a mission within the PAVN's capacities and it would create further opportunities to attack relief columns. Although the attack did not go quite as planned, the campaign was successful and the French abandoned their border outposts in October 1950. At the invitation of Ho Chi Minh, Chen addressed a PAVN review conference for four days, pointing out the strengths and weaknesses of the operations and commenting on the general strategic picture. As Chen noted in his diary, General Giap observed that "the victory shows that Mao's military thought was very applicable to Vietnam."[15] Shortly afterward Chen was transferred to become the deputy commander of the Chinese People's Volunteers in Korea.

---

[11] Details of the aid can be found in Guo Ming, *Zhong Yue guanxi*; Qiang Zhai, *China and the Vietnam Wars, 1950–1975* (University of North Carolina Press, 2000); Chen Jian, "China and the First Indochina War," pp. 85–110.

[12] Liu Shaoqi, May 19, 1950, as quoted by Qiang Zhai, *China and the Vietnam Wars*, p. 19.

[13] This description relies on Qiang Zhai's research in *ibid.*, pp. 26–33.

[14] Chen Geng's diary as quoted in *ibid.*, p. 29.

[15] *Ibid.*, p. 33.

Clearly the assistance of the CCP created, as the distinguished historian Chen Jian put it, a "golden opportunity" for the VWP.[16] The advice from experienced Chinese comrades was probably as valuable as the material assistance because the material assistance made possible a new and unfamiliar level of aggressive and sustained warfare. Before the border campaign China delivered 14,000 rifles, 1,700 machine guns, 150 cannons, and 2,800 tons of grain from April to September 1950, despite the beginning of the Korean War in June.[17] There were problems of absorbing so much good fortune into the personnel, habits, and strategies of the PAVN. From 1950 to the victory at Dien Bien Phu in 1954, intensive Chinese aid and advice made possible the new forward strategy of the PAVN.

Despite the importance of Chinese aid and gratitude for China's generosity, however, it is easy to imagine that Vietnamese, and especially the leadership of the VWP, would be anxious about their intimate dependence on China and also would be resentful of the superior attitudes of Chinese advisors. Although at this point the interests of China and Vietnam were parallel, the disparity in their roles would create warmth, if not heat. After all, Vietnam had already been fighting the French for four years without Chinese assistance, and the newly arrived advisors seemed to have little appreciation for their earlier efforts and experience.[18] By 1949 the Viet Minh already controlled most of the countryside of Vietnam and over half the population.[19] Hence it is not surprising that General Giap launched the campaign subsequent to the border campaign against the recommendations of his new advisors, or that Mao Zedong found it necessary on several occasions to remind his team to "avoid imposing their own opinions on Vietnamese comrades."[20] On the Chinese side, there were concerns that on the one hand the Vietnamese were expecting the new weapons to win the war for them, and on the other that the Vietnamese were neglecting equipment and supplies that represented a considerable sacrifice for China, which was fighting a costly war thousands of miles away.

While the differences between China and Vietnam during the First Indochina War could be dismissed as no more than partners rubbing shoulders in a joint enterprise, the process of settling the war's outcome at the Geneva Conference in 1954 brought latent differences in priorities closer to the surface. China and Vietnam shared the same goals in the peace negotiations, and their intimate cooperation continued and increased in the post-war interim. However, China's main goal was the defeat of imperialist

[16] Chen Jian, "China and the First Indochina War," p. 86.
[17] *Ibid.*, p. 93.
[18] For example, although the Vietnamese were unable to attack Dong Khoi before Chinese assistance arrived, the outpost was already isolated and from January 1949 its supplies had to be delivered by air. See *History of the Indochina Incident*, p. 142.
[19] *Ibid.*, p. 128.
[20] As quoted in Chen Jian, "China and the First Indochina War," p. 106.

encirclement, while Vietnam's was national liberation.[21] A peaceful settlement that removed the French and did not bring in the Americans satisfied China's primary concern. National liberation, however, is not accomplished by halves. Anything less than total victory could not be the end of the struggle for Vietnam.

Besides the difference in priorities, the Geneva Conference had a difference in function for China and Vietnam. For China, participation in the conference marked the confirmation of its status as a major state and the resolution, at least for the time being, of the two major conflicts on its borders. Together with the Asian African Conference in Bandung in 1955, where China was one of the five sponsoring countries,[22] the Geneva Conference marked the general acceptance of China as a state, though a revolutionary one, and in response China offered the Five Principles of Peaceful Coexistence [23] as the basis for state-to-state relations and suggested that nations with different political systems could still cooperate. By contrast, for Vietnam the conference was the culmination of a century of resistance to colonialism and eight years of military struggle with France. Vietnam desperately wanted its struggle to be over, and the Geneva Conference was the best chance for achieving national liberation and reunification. Although Ho Chi Minh had demonstrated his willingness to compromise in 1946, his position on the ground was incomparably stronger in 1954.

Both China and Vietnam desired Vietnamese reunification, but Vietnam wanted it more. Therefore the prospect of an unsuccessful conference and of American intervention in Vietnam was more daunting to China than it was to Vietnam. China (and the Soviet Union) counseled the VWP to accept the temporary demarcation line and to await the promised elections in 1956. Ultimately Vietnam accepted the suggestion. American intervention was certainly a major concern for the VWP. Despite the victory at Dien Bien Phu and the evident exhaustion of the French, the Viet Minh were not quite at the gates of Hanoi, much less Saigon. When Zhou Enlai asked

---

[21] A detailed account of the Geneva negotiations is given by Li Jiazhong, China's former ambassador to Vietnam, in "Yuan Yue Kang Fa he 1954 nian Rineiwa Huiyi 援越抗法和谈1954年日哪瓦会议" [The 1954 Geneva Convention and Aid Vietnam Oppose France], *Dongnanya Zongheng* 东南亚纵横 [Around Southeast Asia] 2004:6 (June), pp. 1–6.

[22] For the speeches delivered at the conference, see *Africa-Asia Speaks from Bandung* (Jakarta: Indonesian Ministry of Foreign Affairs, 1955).

[23] Mutual respect for one another's territorial integrity and sovereignty; mutual nonaggression; mutual noninterference in one another's internal affairs; equality and mutual benefit; and peaceful coexistence. These were first formulated in December 1953 in the preface of a letter of agreement with India concerning trade and communications with Tibet, and then became a major part of Zhou Enlai's diplomacy in the runup to the Bandung Conference in April 1955. They were applied to the socialist world in November 1956 after the disturbances in Poland and Hungary. See Pei Jianzhang, ed., *Zhong Hua Renmin Gonghe Guo Waijiao shi 1949–1956* [History of the foreign relations of the PRC 1949–1956] (Beijing: Shijie Zhishi Chubanshe, 1994), pp. 5–8.

the Vietnamese leaders in July 1954 how long it would take to defeat the French without American intervention, General Giap estimated two to three years while Ho estimated three to five.[24] With American intervention, it was possible that the eight-year war might only be half over. This scenario was unpleasant enough for the Vietnamese leadership, but it was unacceptable to China.[25] Moreover, to incur American involvement by acting against China's advice was to risk being isolated against a formidable enemy. Ho's agreement to the Geneva Accords preserved the continuity of his relationship to China, but the rocks of real differences of interests were visible beneath the surface.

Another important development at the Geneva Conference was China's discovery of Laos and Cambodia. Until Geneva, China's contact and involvement with Indochina had been exclusively through the VWP in support of rural revolution. But at Geneva it was confronted by hostile criticisms by the royalist delegations from Laos and Cambodia, and after looking into their claims Zhou Enlai had to agree that they were nationalist governments seeking independence even though they were not revolutionary.[26] Strategically it was important to respect the autonomy of Laos and Cambodia because most of the governments of Southeast Asia were anxious about communism and they needed reassurance. Vietnam was reluctant to de-emphasize the communist parties in Laos and Cambodia that it had sponsored, and it considered Indochina an integrated revolutionary battlefield. The notion of an "Indochina Federation" put forward by Pham Van Dong was criticized by Zhou and was withdrawn.[27]

With the division of Vietnam and the final establishment of the DRV as a state with territory, China's assistance continued unabated, but it shifted from revolutionary aid to socialist transformation. China was aware of Vietnam's historical issues with the Chinese presence – Zhou Enlai visited a temple dedicated to the Trung sisters – and it was self-conscious in its criticism of big country chauvinism. Nevertheless, as is common among big countries helping smaller ones, China's idea of what was good for Vietnam was essentially an extrapolation of its own experience.

The character of China's development aid to Vietnam from 1954 can be compared to Soviet aid to China in 1950–60. Like Soviet aid, it proceeded from the assumption that development was socialist transformation,

[24] Qiang Zhai, *China and the Vietnam Wars*, p. 58–59.
[25] Qu Xing 曲星, "Zhong Yue zai Yinzhi zhanzheng wenti de zhanlue yizhi yu celue chayi 中越在印支战争问题的战略．致与策略差异" [The strategic unity and tactical differences of China and Vietnam regarding the Indochina war], *Guoji Luntan* 国际论坛 [International Forum] 2:3 (June 2000), pp. 42–50.
[26] The Geneva Convention was the beginning of a long special relationship between China and Cambodia. See Sophie Richardson, *China, Cambodia, and the Five Principles of Peaceful Coexistence: Principles and Foreign Policy* (Ph.D. dissertation, University of Virginia, 2004).
[27] Qiang Zhai, *China and the Vietnam Wars*, p. 61.

essentially a political process with economic prerequisites. The core role and mission of the Stalinist developmental state was accepted by all communist states in the 1950s. The economic prerequisites included the development of heavy industry, state control of the marketing and distribution of essential goods such as food, and the socialization of agriculture.

But China and Vietnam had more in common than did the Soviet Union and China, and Vietnam's economic situation was more primitive and precarious than China's. First, in contrast to the frosty negotiations between Mao Zedong and Stalin in 1950 regarding Soviet aid, Sino-Vietnamese relations were warm and intimate. Chinese aid was less oriented toward key projects and was more multi-dimensional and flexible. Second, because the revolutionary experiences had been so similar, both China and Vietnam began with the presumption that China's post-revolutionary experience, though only a few years old, could be applied directly to Vietnam. By contrast, China was unimpressed with Soviet failures in agriculture and united front work, and so it never copied the Soviet model in these areas. China's big disasters – the Great Leap Forward and the Cultural Revolution – were entirely of its own making. Vietnam accepted the fundamental Chinese premise of development through popular mobilization, but the harshness of Chinese emphasis on class struggle did not fit the Vietnamese situation. Thus the most traumatic political failure of the DRV in the 1950s was a China-inspired and advised land reform, which Ho Chi Minh later moderated and criticized. A moderate land reform policy had been part of Viet Minh rural revolution from the beginning, but under Chinese guidance a radical, class-based campaign was launched in 1954, and it led to considerable conflict and confusion.[28] The disruption led to a Rectification of Errors campaign in 1955–56 that had the lasting effect of neutralizing pre-revolutionary class labels, in contrast to China's bitter experience with class labels and class struggle from 1949 to 1979. The experience with land reform created enough distance from the Chinese model so that the Great Leap Forward's main effect in Vietnam was the relatively benign one of mobilization for irrigation construction. Nevertheless, given the relatively low growth in food production in 1957–60 compared to irrigation and industrialization, it is clear that Vietnam, like China, traded rural productivity for its ambitions of mobilized modernization.[29]

The third major difference from the experience of Soviet aid to China was that, beginning in 1954 and intensifying in 1965 with American bombing, Chinese aid had to be more oriented toward emergencies. As Adam Fforde and Suzanne Paine describe it, Vietnam had an "aggravated shortage

---

[28] See Ed Moise, *Land Reform in China and North Vietnam* (Berkeley: University of California Press, 1983).
[29] Growth in grain production from 1957 to 1960 was less than 1 percent. Calculated from Vien, *Vietnam: A Long History*, p. 298.

economy."[30] Even foreign-assisted industrialization projects competed with basic needs, and state resources became assets in the hard scrabble for survival. In 1954 war had disrupted agricultural production, and the DRV lost the expertise of the departing French and the massive rice transfers from the south. A million people were threatened with starvation.[31] Even as the economy stabilized, the structural difficulty of lacking the food resources of the south and the growing problem of American support for Ngo Dinh Diem in Saigon meant that development had to be more concerned with the urgencies of the present than with future transformations. While both China and the DRV would have preferred to postpone war in the south, the aggressiveness of the Diem regime against all real and imagined opposition required the return to war.

Unlike the Soviet Union, which shocked Vietnam in 1957 with a proposal to admit both Vietnams into the United Nations,[32] China consistently supported Vietnamese reunification. But China considered reunification a protracted struggle, and it was considerably less eager to return to military options than was the VWP leadership in Hanoi, which in turn was not as desperate as the remaining cadres in the south. Le Duan, a southerner, emerged as the spokesman for the urgency of military action in the south, and he became acting general secretary of the VWP in 1957 and was elected first secretary in 1960. But even Le Duan was cautious in the beginning. It was the desperate situation of the south that led the VWP's Fifteenth Plenum in 1959 to approve violent struggle. When armed resistance was finally permitted, the political vacuum in the countryside created by the Diem regime made it quite successful and this in turn drew the United States into increased military support for Diem. By 1963 Diem's failure to stem the tide of rural insurgency led to an American-supported coup and his replacement by a succession of military governments. Finally, by 1964 the United States decided that the containment of communism demanded direct and massive American military involvement.

The emergence of the Sino-Soviet split in 1960–63 put Vietnam in a quandary that was complex and acutely uncomfortable. At the most basic level, socialist internationalism as Ho Chi Minh understood it required the unity of the socialist camp and support for its frontline state. China's denunciation of Khrushchev as a revisionist could not lead to a reform of the Soviet Union, but only to a division of the socialist camp. On the other hand, Khrushchev's policies of peaceful coexistence and his preference for peaceful reunification in Vietnam were unrealistic and unhelpful as far as Vietnam

---

[30] Adam Fforde and Suzanne Paine, *The Limits of National Liberation* (New York: Croom Helm, 1986), especially pp. 55–74.
[31] Guo Ming, *Zhong Yue guanxi*, p. 62.
[32] The Soviet Union later withdrew its proposal, but they continued to argue for peaceful reunification in Vietnam. See William Duiker, *Ho Chi Minh*, p. 500.

was concerned. By contrast, China supported reunification and understood that in the long run it would not be peaceful. Moreover, as military conflict increased in the south in the early sixties China increased its military aid. However, the Soviet Union was considerably richer than China and it had considerably more clout with the United States and in diplomatic circles more generally. To side with China decisively and publicly would be to cut off the possibility of Soviet aid in the future.

Hence the Vietnamese position on the Sino-Soviet split before the Cultural Revolution was one of official neutrality but with much greater sympathy for China. In 1963 protegées of Vo Nguyen Giap were purged by a secret Politburo tribunal established to remove pro-Soviet revisionists.[33] The draft resolution of the Ninth Plenum in December 1963 included a direct attack on Khrushchev, but it was removed before publication at the request of Le Duan.[34] After the Gulf of Tonkin incident in August 1964 Mao Zedong personally assured Ho of Chinese support and recommended an aggressive strategy. Meanwhile the Soviet Union continued its appeal for peaceful reunification. However, with the intervention of the United States the "Vietnam War" became a global issue and the Soviet Union reconsidered its position in the light of both the Cold War and its rivalry with China.

Although the reasons for the Sino-Soviet split did not involve Vietnam, it is worthwhile to reflect on the role of Vietnam in China's leftism. Khrushchev aimed at securing a global condominium with the United States both in order to avoid nuclear war and because it anchored Soviet authority within its own realm of the communist world. His position was, as the Chinese claimed, revisionist, because it replaced revolutionary strategy with a cautious encouragement of improvements within the existing international framework. By contrast, China's success gave Mao Zedong confidence in the transformative potential of revolution, and he was famously unconcerned with the threat of nuclear war. Vietnam was less important as an ideological ally than as the best and closest living example of the ongoing processes of world revolution. From 1960, Mao's aggressiveness, optimism, and commitment to Vietnam were not only a continuation of a familiar relationship but also the most prominent international instance of newly radicalized commitment to continuing revolution.

If in 1965 China had disappeared, suddenly and completely, Vietnam might well have been the country most distraught by its disappearance. First, the suspicion would loom large that God was an American. Certainly if America had been granted a wish in 1965 to have one state disappear, China would have been high on the list, and possibly in the number one position. Second, and not unrelated to the first, Vietnam might infer that it might be the next country to disappear. It would be – and would see itself as – the

[33] *Ibid.*, p. 538.
[34] *Ibid.*, p. 537.

country most similar to China in politics and objectives. Third, even if Vietnam's atheism held firm, it would have lost its most loyal, steadfast and generous supporter. Aside from the dire implications that this would have for its future struggles for reunification, it would mourn the passing of a revolutionary brother.

As this fantasy implies, the relationship between China and Vietnam from 1950 to 1965 was closer and was perceived to be more mutually beneficial than the relationships that either had with any other country. There were real differences of interest and perception, but these remained unarticulated in the service of larger common purposes. China's caution at the Geneva Conference stemmed from considerations that were also important to Vietnam, and Ho Chi Minh and the VWP Politburo could be persuaded to accept its advice. Vietnam could operate within a relationship of dependent asymmetry with China in the confidence that although China had its own perspective and was not always correct, its aims were parallel to Vietnam's.

Clenched Teeth, 1965–1975

From 1965 to 1975 China remained the most important source of foreign aid and support for the Democratic Republic of Vietnam in its continuing struggles with the United States and the Saigon regime. Despite the chaotic political situation caused by the Cultural Revolution in 1966–69 and a chronic shortage of food and industrial goods throughout the period, China continued its massive aid program. It also consistently and steadfastly resisted American enticements in 1971–72 to distance itself from Vietnam, and even increased its military aid after Nixon's visit in 1972. Chinese aid and support was essential to the course that Vietnam's war took to victory in 1975. The basic strength of the national liberation movement in Vietnam was in the villages rather than in foreign aid,[35] but without China's help the path to victory would have been significantly longer and more difficult.

Despite the continuing mutual commitment to the relationship, profound tensions accumulated and antipathies stirred under the surface of official harmony. The fundamental problem was related to the American entry into the war, but initially it did not spring from a difference in policy toward the Americans. Rather, the American entry created a distance between the war that Vietnam was fighting and the war that China was supporting.

From 1950 to 1965, China's support for Vietnam was fraternal and instinctual, an extension of its own revolutionary experience to a familiar neighbor. The American entry into the war not only raised the stakes of China's support, a challenge that China was quite happy to meet, but it elevated the conflict itself from being an important local one to being the central battleground between international revolution and its foes. As Zhou

---

[35] See Jeffrey Race, *War Comes to Long An* (Berkeley: University of California Press, 1972).

TABLE 8.2. *Clenched teeth*

China	Vietnam
	American war 1964–73
Cultural Revolution 1966–69	Tet Offensive 1968
Kissinger visits Beijing 1971	Ho Chi Minh dies September 3, 1969
PRC enters UN 1971	
Shanghai Communiqué 1972	Paris Peace Accords January 1973
South Vietnam incorporates Spratly Islands 1973	
China occupies Paracel Islands 1974	
	Fall of Saigon April 30, 1975
Mao dies September 9, 1976	Vietnam reunified January 1976
Gang of Four arrested October 6, 1976	

Enlai put it in 1966, "Vietnam is the great standard-bearer representing the world's revolutionary peoples."[36] From the Korean War, China knew the costs of engaging the United States, and it took steps to clearly signal to the United States its intentions in supporting Vietnam and to minimize the chance of an unnecessary confrontation.[37] Nevertheless, an American invasion of Vietnam was taken as a real possibility, and China prepared to fight. The Chinese population was mobilized in massive demonstrations of support, industry was moved away from vulnerable coastal locations to a "third front," and the completion of transportation links to Yunnan and Guangxi were given highest priority.[38] On the eve of the Cultural Revolution, the public mind of China was fixated on Vietnam and the threat of American imperialism.[39]

The American challenge in Vietnam became for China the international equivalent of its domestic class struggle. It combined the committed belief in revolutionary transformation (Vietnam will win!) with the urgency of danger (the Americans are at the gate!). For Mao Zedong, opposing the Americans in Vietnam and initiating the Cultural Revolution were the external and

---

[36] Zhou Enlai to Le Duan, March 23, 1966, in Odd Arne Westad, Chen Jian, Stein Tonnesson, Nguyen Vu Tung, and James G. Hershberg, eds., *77 Conversations between Chinese and Foreign Leaders on the Wars in Indochina, 1964–1977* (Washington: Woodrow Wilson Center, Cold War International History Project Working Paper no. 22, May 1998), p. 93.

[37] In this respect both countries learned a lesson from Korea. See John Stoessinger, *Nations in Darkness*, 2nd ed. (New York: Random House, 1975), pp. 72–85.

[38] See Chen Jian, "China's Involvement in the Vietnam War, 1964–1969," *China Quarterly* 142 (June 1995), pp. 359–71.

[39] See the personal account by Chen Jian, "Personal-Historical Puzzles about China and the Vietnam War," in *77 Conversations*, pp. 21–33. See also Giovanni Blumer, *Die chinesische Kulturrevolution* (Frankfurt: Europäische Verlagsanstalt, 1968).

domestic dimensions of the same revolutionary commitment. Although Mao criticized Red Guards who crossed into Vietnam because they "do not know what an international border means," he himself would occasionally lapse into talking about "our troops in the South" when talking to Vietnamese leaders.[40] By elevating Vietnam to such high importance and embracing it so tightly, China lost touch with the realities of Vietnam's situation and the limits of Vietnam's own ambitions.

There is no question of the extent of China's support for Vietnam in its war against the United States. China figured the total cost of its support for Vietnam at twenty billion dollars, and it sent 320,000 military-related personnel in 1965–69, primarily for transportation construction and repair and manning antiaircraft batteries. According to Chinese calculations its troops accounted for 38 percent of American air losses over Vietnam, and China suffered casualties of 1,100 killed and 4,200 wounded.[41] China's general support of the basic economy was just as important as military aid. Overall China provided 5 million tons of food, the equivalent of Vietnam's total food production for one year. In 1966 China provided 500,000 tons of food, 10 percent of Vietnamese production that year.[42] Adam Fforde and Suzanne Paine estimate that by the mid-1970s Vietnam was dependent on external sources (mainly Chinese and Soviet aid) for 10 to 15 percent of its food supply.[43] Because of the difference in scale the aid was proportionally less costly to China than it was helpful to Vietnam, but it was not an insignificant burden. China's willingness to assist Vietnam was expressed in 1965 by Liu Shaoqi in a very generous offer that was sensitive to Vietnam's requirements for autonomy:

It is our policy that we will do our best to support you. We will offer whatever you are in need of and we are in a position to offer. . . . If you do not invite us we will not come, and if you invite one unit of our troops, we will send that unit to you. The initiative will be completely yours.[44]

By 1966 the strain of sustained generosity – and of sustained gratitude – was beginning to show. The offer of maximum help on Vietnam's terms was twisted into the petulant complaint that if Vietnam had reservations or objections to Chinese presence, then all the Chinese could simply come home.

A second friction from the Chinese perspective was Vietnamese handling of military strategy and especially of negotiations with the Americans. In

---

[40] Mao Zedong to Pham Van Dong, April 10, 1967; Mao to Dong, November 17, 1968, in Westad, *77 Conversations*, pp. 104, 142.
[41] Guo Ming, *Zhong Yue guanxi*, pp. 69–71.
[42] The 1966 figure is from Pham Van Dong to Mao Zedong, April 17, 1967, in Westad, *77 Conversations*, p. 105. The percentage total is calculated from food production data translated in Fforde and Paine, *Limits*, p. 194.
[43] *Ibid.*, p. 69.
[44] Liu Shaoqi to Le Duan, April 8, 1965, in Westad, *77 Conversations*, p. 85.

1954 China had counseled compromise at the Geneva Conference, but by 1968 Zhou Enlai was strongly criticizing Vietnam's initial attempts to start peace talks with Lyndon Johnson.[45] Moreover, China was critical of the Tet Offensive of 1968. Both initiatives were also controversial within the Vietnamese leadership, and the outcomes of each did not invalidate China's concerns. Even though China's attitude toward negotiation was influenced by leftism, the major difference between policy disagreements in the 1950s and the 1960s was that the decisions were no longer made collaboratively. Instead Vietnam made major decisions and reported them to China, and China criticized the decisions, sometimes vehemently, without the expectation that the Chinese viewpoint would prevail.

By far the most important difficulty in the China ⇒ Vietnam direction of the relationship was that Vietnam would not repudiate the Soviet Union. As the conflict in Vietnam became globalized the Soviet Union provided greatly increased support, including sophisticated surface-to-air missiles that China could not supply. In 1965, Zhou Enlai told Pham Van Dong that Vietnam should refuse Soviet aid.[46] According to Zhou the reasons the Soviets wanted to aid Vietnam were, first, to isolate China, second, to improve Soviet-U.S. relations, and last to engage in subversive activities against China and possibly against Vietnam.[47] As these reasons suggest, China's major problem with Soviet aid was the effect of Soviet involvement in Vietnam on China's struggle with the Soviet Union. As Zhou put it in 1967, "So, we hold that the closer to victory your struggle is, the fiercer our struggle with the Soviet Union will be."[48] China did reluctantly accommodate itself to Soviet involvement and provided rail transport to Vietnam for Soviet goods, but it never accepted the notion of Vietnam-Soviet friendship.

As one would predict from asymmetry theory, Vietnam's view of the relationship with China was fundamentally different from China's view. To begin with the problem of Soviet aid, from Vietnam's perspective it was acceptable because it was premised on socialist internationalism, the same premise as Chinese aid. It did not indicate leaning to the Soviet side in the Sino-Soviet dispute or a tolerance of revisionism. From Vietnam's perspective the Sino-Soviet split was most regrettable, and even when it sided with China before 1965 it did not encourage international divisiveness. China's reluctance to cooperate with the Soviet Union in aiding Vietnam clearly made China the offender in terms of socialist internationalism.

---

[45] At one point Zhou even suggests that Martin Luther King, Jr., was assassinated because of Vietnam's announcement of negotiations. Zhou Enlai to Pham Van Dong, April 13, 1968, in *ibid.*, p. 124.

[46] Zhou Enlai to Pham Van Dong, October 9, 1965, in Westad, *77 Conversations*, pp. 89–90.

[47] Zhou Enlai to Ho Chi Minh, November 8, 1965, in *ibid.*, p. 90.

[48] Zhou Enlai, April 11, 1967, in *ibid.*, p. 107.

The fundamental reason for Vietnam's alienation from China in the 1960s was that China's leftism, expressed especially in the Cultural Revolution, showed that China was unreliable as a model and as an intimate friend. When Ho Chi Minh looked out over hundreds of thousands of Chinese gathered in his honor at Tiananmen in July 1966, he probably found it less reassuring than his hosts had hoped. He had just sent a message to the Vietnamese people that coined his most famous slogan, "Nothing is more precious than independence and freedom."[49] The crowd mobilized to greet him was certainly evidence of Chinese support for the war against America but not necessarily support for Vietnamese "independence and freedom." Moreover, many of his Chinese colleagues on the reviewing stand were on the edge of personal disaster. Within months Liu Shaoqi, the person who had managed China's aid to Vietnam during the war with the French, had been vilified as "the chief Party person in power going the capitalist road," and his wife, Wang Guangmei, was accused of being an American spy.[50] If Mao could betray his closest comrades, how safe were his closest international friends?

From 1966 to 1969 the Cultural Revolution convulsed Chinese society, and Vietnam had a front row seat for observing the chaos in Guangxi Province. Guangxi had lost 2 percent of its population during the Great Leap Forward, and starvation there must have already been a lesson to Vietnam. In the Cultural Revolution Guangxi was especially hard hit, in part because of the militarization of the province due to its being the "great rear area" for Vietnam. Guns were more plentiful there than in most of China, and the provincial leadership under General Wei Guoqing was brutal in suppressing the Red Guards. Estimates of deaths in the province range from an official 83,000 to 300,000, and there were lurid stories of cannibalism.[51] Moreover, the atrocities of the Cultural Revolution lasted longer in Guangxi. In the town of Qinzhou during a 1970 campaign there were 239 attempted suicides, of which 188 were successful. The leftist leadership even used the slogan of "a new comprehensive Great Leap Forward" to describe their construction program in 1969.[52] Unlike onlookers in more remote locations, Vietnam was face to face with the contradiction between

---

[49] Ho Chi Minh, "Appeal to Compatriots and Fighters throughout the Country," in *Ho Chi Minh Selected Writings* (Hanoi: Foreign Languages Publishing House, 1977), pp. 307–10, here p. 308.

[50] Kang Sheng repeated the accusation against Wang to Pham Van Dong on April 29, 1968, as part of a long and chilling expose of the crimes of major leaders, in Westad, 77 *Conversations*, p. 133. For Liu Shaoqi see Lowell Dittmer, *Liu Shao-ch'i and the Chinese Cultural Revolution: The Politics of Mass Criticism* (Berkeley: University of California Press, 1974).

[51] For the official death estimate see *Dangdai Zhongguo de Guangxi* 当代中国的广西 [Contemporary China's Guangxi] (Beijing: Dangdai Zhongguo Chubanshe, 1992), vol 1, pp. 125–34; for cannibalism see Zheng Yi, *Scarlet Memorial: Tales of Cannibalism in Guangxi*, tr. T. P. Sym (Boulder: Westview, 1996).

[52] *Dangdai Guangxi*, vol. 1, p. 138.

the slogans of the Cultural Revolution and the reality. It is hardly surprising that in 1966 Vietnam blocked subscriptions to *Renmin Ribao* (*People's Daily*) by its Chinese residents.[53]

But Vietnam needed China's support and thus it could not articulate its concerns about China's domestic and international politics. Indeed, the leadership conversations could become quite surreal, as in this exchange between Le Duan and Mao in 1970:

Le Duan: We Vietnamese people keep Chairman Mao's great goodness always in our mind.... Why dare we fight a prolonged war? This is mainly because we have been dependent on Chairman Mao's works.

Mao Zedong: This is not necessarily true.

Duan: Of course this is true. We also need to apply [Chairman Mao's teaching] to Vietnam's practical situation.

Mao: You have your own creations. How can you say that you don't have your own creations and experience? ... [54]

Undoubtedly this text was provided by Chinese archivists to discredit the notoriously anti-Chinese Duan, but it is also a reminder that from 1966 to 1976 the only person in China not required to worship Mao Zedong was Mao himself.

With the unadmitted failure of the Cultural Revolution and a concomitant downgrading of expectations regarding imminent world revolution, China's foreign policy shifted from revolutionary transformation to revolutionary pragmatism. China did not give up its self-identification as the world's revolutionary model, but from 1971 it assumed that world revolution was not around the corner.[55] Moreover, with the impending defeat of the United States in Vietnam, China saw the Soviet Union as the major threat to its security.

Although China continued its aid to Vietnam until the defeat of the Saigon regime in 1975, its new pragmatism contributed to further alienation. Most obviously, the visits of Henry Kissinger and Richard Nixon to China in 1971–72 raised questions about China's support for Vietnam. Second, with the removal of the American threat, China's own interests in the war diverged even more sharply from those of Vietnam. Last, differences over territorial claims began to emerge.

The story of the rapprochement between the United States and China is well known, and in both countries it is usually viewed in terms of global politics and the "strategic triangle" of the two with the Soviet Union. However, a major motivation for Nixon to rethink his China policy was the necessity of extricating the United States from Vietnam, and he hoped to induce China

---

[53] Guo Ming, *Zhong Yue guanxi*, p. 99.
[54] Mao Zedong and Le Duan, May 11, 1970, in Westad, *77 Conversations*, p. 165.
[55] See Chen Jian, *Mao's China*, especially p. 244.

to cease or reduce its support for Vietnam. In the short term, his efforts were a failure. As Mao said after Kissinger's secret visit, "We are not in a hurry on the Taiwan issue because there is no fighting there. But there is a war in Vietnam and people are being killed there. We should not invite Nixon to come just for our own interests."[56] Immediately after Kissinger's visit, Zhou Enlai visited Hanoi to discuss the meeting and China's stand. In the Shanghai Communiqué of February 1972 China stated its position in ringing terms:

Wherever there is oppression, there is resistance. Countries want independence, nations want liberation and the people want revolution – this has become the irresistible trend of history. All nations, big or small, should be equal: big nations should not bully the small and strong nations should not bully the weak. China will never be a superpower and it opposes hegemony and power politics of any kind. The Chinese side stated that it firmly supports the struggles of all the oppressed people and nations for freedom and liberation and that the people of all countries have the right to choose their social systems according their own wishes and the right to safeguard the independence, sovereignty and territorial integrity of their own countries and oppose foreign aggression, interference, control and subversion. All foreign troops should be withdrawn to their own countries. The Chinese side expressed its firm support to the peoples of Viet Nam, Laos and Cambodia in their efforts for the attainment of their goal and its firm support to the seven-point proposal of the Provisional Revolutionary Government of the Republic of South Viet Nam and the elaboration of February this year on the two key problems in the proposal, and to the Joint Declaration of the Summit Conference of the Indochinese Peoples.[57]

China actually increased its military aid to Vietnam in the spring of 1972. Nevertheless, the rapprochement with the United States was seen as a "stab in the back"[58] by Vietnamese leaders, and they held China responsible for the renewed ferocity of American attacks in 1972.[59]

Regardless of China's refusal to negotiate its support for Vietnam with the United States, the confident prospect of U.S.-China normalization fundamentally affected China's sense of threat from the south. For two decades the prospect and then the reality of American presence in Vietnam had created a common defensive interest for China and Vietnam. While China's continued support for Vietnam from 1972 to the end of the war in 1975 and reunification in 1976 demonstrated China's deeper commitment to revolutionary

[56] *Ibid.*, p. 267.
[57] *Joint Communiqué of the United States of America and the People's Republic of China* (Shanghai Communiqué), February 28, 1972. www.china.org.cn/english/china-us/26012.htm.
[58] The phrase was used by Le Duc Tho in the 1980s. William Duiker, *China and Vietnam: The Roots of Conflict* (Indochina Research Monograph no. 1. Berkeley: Institute of East Asian Studies, 1986), pp. 59–60.
[59] It should be noted that Vietnam did not engage in official criticism at the time, though there were oblique signs of dissatisfaction. See Kay Möller, *China und das wiedervereinte Vietnam* (Bochum: Studienverlag Brockmeyer, 1984), pp. 240–52.

solidarity and to continuity in foreign policy, the cause for its heightened attention had passed. China was still Vietnam's great rear area, but China was no longer concerned about becoming a frontline state if Vietnam lost. In effect, although China continued to support Vietnam, its own Vietnam war was over.

In China's estimation the military power and ambition of the United States had been blunted and broken in Vietnam, and this left the "social imperialism" of the Soviet Union as the greatest threat to the world's peoples. The invasion of Czechoslovakia in 1968 and the clash between Chinese and Soviet troops on the border island of Chenbao in 1969 showed the danger that the Soviet Union posed even to communist countries. While the American bombings of 1972 demonstrated that Vietnam still needed Soviet aid, it was only this necessity, from China's perspective, that justified continued relations between Vietnam and the Soviet Union.

The last issue to emerge in the early 1970s, conflicting territorial claims, developed into the official casus belli of the Sino-Vietnamese war of 1979. As earlier chapters have made clear, the general configuration of the land border was set in the Song dynasty, and the detailed demarcation of the border was carried out by a joint Chinese and French effort in 1887–95. In November 1957 the Central Committee of the VWP proposed to maintain the status quo border of the colonial period. It was agreed after negotiations that the border would not be changed unilaterally and the status quo would be respected, but that both parties reserved the right to reconsider the border in the future.[60] The agreement embedded a difference between the two sides. Until 1974 differences and border problems were suppressed, but then hundreds of violations began to be reported by both sides, jumping from 300 cases in 1974 to 1800 cases in 1976.[61] Vietnam began to make claims beyond the Sino-French agreements to more favorable "historical" borders.[62] No large amounts of territory were involved, but the differences were acute.

Territorial disputes concerning offshore islands also became acute in the 1970s, mostly because of the prospects for offshore oil. The two major reef and island groups are the Paracels, equidistant from China's Hainan Island and central Vietnam, and the Spratlys, halfway between southern Vietnam and southern Philippines. Neither group is part of the continental shelf; both have miserable weather (ten typhoons per year), dangerous navigation, little dry land or fresh water, and insignificant surface resources.[63]

---

[60] Antoine Dauphin, "La frontière sino-vietnamienne de 1895–1896 à nos jours," in *Les Frontières du Vietnam* (Paris: Éditions L'Harmattan, 1989), pp. 104–18, here p. 111.
[61] *Ibid.*, p. 113.
[62] Henry Kenney, *Shadow of the Dragon* (Washington: Brassey's, 2002), p. 53.
[63] In the first part of the twentieth century Japanese entrepreneurs mined guano on the islands, but the phospate reserves are estimated at less than ten million tons.

According to Pierre-Bernard Lafont, there are historical traces of Chinese and Vietnamese official interest in the islands, but no conclusive territorial claims before the eighteenth century, and afterward records of conflicting claims but not of the resolution of conflicts.[64] French presence reinforced the original Vietnamese claims, but not without continuing protests from Republican China. A French proposal to submit claims to arbitration in 1937 was rejected by China. Ironically, the strength of the Chinese claim to the islands depends rather more on the activity of Taiwan since 1945, though both the Republic of China and the People's Republic of China have steadfastly maintained their (common) claim. Taiwan occupied the largest island in the Spratlys in 1945–49, returned in 1956, and since then has been in continuous occupation. Meanwhile, China secured acceptance by the DRV of its claims to the islands on several occasions in the 1950s and 60s, the most important being Pham Van Dong's note of acceptance of China's sovereignty claims on September 14, 1958.[65] For its part, the Republic of Vietnam in Saigon announced the incorporation of the Paracels into Quang Nam Province in 1961.

From 1968 the Economic Commission for Asia and the Far East (ESCAP)[66] began issuing optimistic geological reports concerning offshore oil on the continental shelf of Asia from Vietnam to Taiwan.[67] The Saigon government and the Philippines began granting exploration licenses in July 1973, and Saigon announced the annexation of ten Spratly islands into Phuoc Tuy Province in September.[68] In January 1974 a series of incidents in the Paracels led to a defeat of the Saigon forces by China and Chinese occupation. In response, the Saigon government occupied six of the Spratlys, and the DRV continued occupation from April 1975.

The DRV did not publicly claim the islands until December 30, 1978, after the open rupture with China but shortly before the beginning of armed conflict. However, its silence did not imply disinterest. It was a measure of Vietnam's inability to articulate national interests in contradiction to China while it was dependent on China's support. The general struggle for independence

[64] Pierre-Bernard Lafont, "Les archipels Paracel et Spratly: Un conflit de frontières en Mer de Chine méridionale," in *Les Frontières du Vietnam* (Paris: Éditions L'Harmattan, 1989), pp. 244–62; here pp. 246–9. By contrast, the claims of the Philippines to the Spratlys do not begin until 1956 with the alleged discovery of them by a Filipino fisherman, Tomas Cloma. Ferdinand Marcos's formal statement of the Philippine claim in 1971 was based on the Spratlys being *res nullius* and therefore open to occupation.

[65] The original is reproduced in Guo Ming, ed., *Zhong Yue guanxi*, frontmatter. See also *ibid.*, pp. 251–2.

[66] A United Nations organ founded in Shanghai in 1947, renamed United Nations Economic and Social Commission for Asia and the Pacific (UNESCAP) in 1974. Its membership became the basis for the creation of the Asian Development Bank (ADB) in 1965.

[67] See Lee Lai-to, "The People's Republic of China and the South China Sea" (Singapore: Department of Political Science, University of Singapore, Occasional Paper no. 31, 1977), pp. 6–7.

[68] *Ibid.*, p. 11.

required a dependence on China, and thus differences with China were left unarticulated, only to emerge after the main task was accomplished.

If China had disappeared suddenly and completely in April 1975, at the moment of victory, Vietnam might well have imagined that God was Vietnamese. While Chinese assistance had been just as essential in the previous decade as it had been before 1965, a serious alienation had developed. Vietnam no longer identified its regime goals with China. The Cultural Revolution had been a sobering spectacle for China's closest neighbor, and it had been a demonstration of China's capacity to change its politics suddenly and without regard to Vietnam's interests. Meanwhile, God had already smiled upon Vietnam with the removal of the American combat forces in 1973 and then had assisted the unexpectedly easy overthrow of the Thieu regime in 1975. Vietnam was now united and strong, and it no longer needed to be subservient to China in return for aid. Vietnam would not wish China's destruction, but it could now thrive without China's continued existence. Moreover, with the end of colonialism and the removal of the French and then the Americans, Vietnam was now back in the familiar situation of being more vulnerable to China than to any other country. The removal of China might seem a cruel and ungrateful act by a Vietnamese god, but perhaps he would simply be looking ahead.

Dependent Asymmetry and the Two Vietnams

"Dependent asymmetry" has been used in this chapter to describe the relationship between China and Vietnam because Vietnam had no alternative to compliance with China if it wanted to avoid a retrogression of its liberation struggle to the primitive resources and conditions of unassisted rural revolution. It would not be too much of an exaggeration to say that any non-Chinese gun or bullet had to be taken from the enemy. Moreover, North Vietnam's food resources were deficient for its population, and only China could supply the rice imports that earlier had been shipped up from the Mekong delta. Vietnam needed China.

However, China did not take over decision making in Vietnam, nor did it sanction Vietnam for not following its advice. The VWP remained in charge. Liu Shaoqi's statement, quoted earlier, that "if we are not invited, we will not come. . . . the initiative is yours,"[69] was an important principle of Chinese policy. Vietnam remained deferential and grateful to China, but doing so was Vietnam's decision.

North Vietnam thus had a self-constrained autonomy in its relationship to China. By contrast, the governments in the south were constrained by their patrons, and thus they lacked autonomy. This was most obvious with the government of Bao Dai that the French set up as a rather transparent

---

[69] Liu Shaoqi to Le Duan, April 8, 1965, in Westad, *77 Conversations*, p. 85.

attempt at indirect colonialism. It was also true of the sequence of southern leaderships that the United States supported after 1954. Ngo Dinh Diem, president of the Republic of Vietnam (South Vietnam) from 1954 to his assassination in 1963, was quite aware that he operated within the parameters of American strategic interests. If he could not contain communism, he would be removed. And he was. His successors were not permitted to consider a "third way" of compromising with the North. As the American presence increased in the 1960s, the South Vietnamese were reduced to a supporting military role and a supplicant political role. Not only were decisions made in Washington more important than decisions made in Saigon, but the aid provided specifically to Saigon was contingent on subservience. The government of South Vietnam was reduced to being a spectator of its own defense, and eventually of its own demise.[70] Not only did Henry Kissinger negotiate directly with the North Vietnamese in Paris, but he hardly bothered to keep the South Vietnamese delegation informed of his actions. The United States was never happy with the performance of the South Vietnamese political or military leadership, but it never allowed them significant autonomy. In the words of Frances Fitzgerald's classic, *Fire in the Lake*, they could only be "bad puppets."[71]

The difference between the two relationships is best illustrated by the course of the relationships. As China and Vietnam grew apart politically, Vietnam ceased to consult China before making major decisions and also made decisions against China's advice. Nevertheless, aid continued and official solidarity continued. By contrast, South Vietnamese regimes became increasingly more compliant to American preferences. The most notable disagreement between Saigon and Washington was President Thieu's rejection in November 1972 of the provisional peace agreement that had permitted Kissinger to say in October, "Peace is at hand." Clearly this objection was useful to the Nixon administration, and after the Christmas bombing of the North, Thieu accepted essentially the same agreement. Even after the American military departure, the Thieu government could not have acted outside the parameters of American interests in containing communism without threatening the lifeline of American economic aid. And in any case, by the time Thieu emerged as leader, the government of South Vietnam had already become an appendage of the American presence.

In short, precisely because the Democratic Republic of Vietnam and the Vietnam Workers Party did not permit themselves to become a compliant appendage of "world communism" or of "Chinese communism," they maintained the autonomy and the legitimacy necessary to lead a difficult struggle for national liberation. By contrast, the regime in Saigon, despite its

---

70 Bui Diem with David Chanoff, *In the Jaws of History* (Boston: Houghton Mifflin Company, 1987).
71 Frances Fitzgerald, *Fire in the Lake* (Boston: Little, Brown, 1972).

parliamentary institutions and its post-colonial status, could never develop autonomy or legitimacy because it was forced to remain a creature of American policy. For North Vietnam, the dependency of "dependent asymmetry" was an internal constraint. For South Vietnam, dependency was an external constraint. In the former, autonomy was compressed and frustrated. In the latter, autonomy was impossible.

9

Illusions of Victory

1975–1991

American attention toward Vietnam faded rapidly after the withdrawal of American combat troops in early 1973, and therefore Americans generally do not have a sufficient appreciation for the significance of Vietnam's victory in 1975 and the subsequent reunification of the country. A deeper reason might be that no country likes to dwell on situations that demonstrate the limits of its power. Although America became obsessed with its own traumatic experience of defeat in Vietnam, it was far less interested in the implications of Vietnam's victory. Indeed, in America the word *Vietnam* referred to the American war there, not to the country. Vietnam itself had slid out of the frame of American attention already in 1973, and tortured replays of the war experience in such movies as *The Deer Hunter* (1978) and *Rambo* (1982) took its place and its name.

For the rest of the world, Vietnam's victory was a remarkable accomplishment. From a global perspective, it demonstrated the limits of American power and was a vindication of the critical distance from American engagement that most of the world had maintained. Indeed, until the end of the Cold War and the success of the Persian Gulf War, anxieties persisted even within the United States concerning America's global leadership.[1]

The Soviet Union was quite aware that it did not control Vietnam, but on the chessboard of bipolar politics Vietnam was the most significant "win" since Cuba, and Soviet aid and support over the previous ten years had been crucial. Moreover, Vietnam remained high on the Soviet agenda because of its ambiguous position in the Sino-Soviet rivalry. Thus it is not surprising that the Soviets remained active supporters even after the congratulatory handshakes.

From the perspective of Southeast Asia, Vietnam's victory ended the colonial era and the commanding presence of Western powers in the region. The

---

[1] See Joseph Nye, *Bound to Lead: The Changing Nature of American Power* (New York: Basic Books, 1990), for a reflection and attempted refutation of these concerns.

novelty was not altogether pleasant, since most of the governments in the region were fragile and some faced their own communist-related insurgencies. Moreover, the United States had been the defining international presence in the region since 1954, and its rapid change from being an intimidating, single-minded intervener to being a profoundly uninterested bystander created a hole in regional power relations that many feared was a vacuum. Nevertheless, the region was willing to consider the realignments necessary to accommodate the new governments of Vietnam, Cambodia, and Laos.

For China, the extreme urgency of the war in Vietnam that had begun with American involvement had subsided with Nixon's visit to China in 1972 and the Paris Peace Accords in January 1973. Nevertheless, victory was the culmination of twenty-five years of wholehearted support for the Democratic Republic of Vietnam, and it ended the uncertainty of having a war raging in a neighboring country. During the war Vietnam had expressed its gratitude for Chinese friendship and aid, and after victory Vietnam presumably would remain grateful and deferential. However, the fact of Soviet assistance to Vietnam was troubling. Even though China had reluctantly accepted the necessity of Soviet assistance during the war, the only flaw in an otherwise perfectly satisfactory development was the continuing friendship between Vietnam and the Soviet Union.

On a more practical note, China was not a rich country and its emergency wartime aid to Vietnam caused deprivation at home. Now that the emergency was over, China could hope to reduce its aid to more reasonable levels. The measure of China's generosity shifted from "whatever is necessary" to "whatever could be spared." Meanwhile, China's internal and external environments were in flux. By the middle 1970s China's leadership politics had been introverted by the struggle between the leftists of Mao Zedong's inner court and the returning party pragmatists led by Deng Xiaoping. In foreign relations, the new pragmatism of the 1970s was transforming China's diplomatic horizons. By the end of 1978 China had established diplomatic relations with 116 states.[2] Alliance against Soviet hegemonism remained an organizing principle, but this now required the wooing of right-wing politicians like Franz Josef Strauss of Bavaria rather than the formation of leftist splinter groups. For Chinese foreign policy, Vietnam's victory was more the end of a successful historical episode than a future promise or threat.

For Vietnam, victory was sweet indeed. One hundred years of subjection, of heroic resistance mixed with unheroic accommodation, and of national division were over. Forty years of guerilla war were over. The twenty-year-old

---

[2] Chen Zhongyuan, Wang Yuxiang and Li Zhenghua, eds., *1976–1981 Zhongguo* [China 1976–1981] (Beijing: Zhongyang Wenxian Chubanshe, 1998), p. 145. Vietnam plays a very small part in this book's review of China's foreign affairs.

Saigon regime was defeated, despite its American backing. Moreover, Vietnam had played a leading role in the Cambodian and Lao revolutions, and expected their cooperation and deference. Most important, Vietnam was now truly independent. It had defeated its enemies, and it was no longer under the duress of war when dealing with its friends. It was the world's hero of 1975, and it expected to be as successful and respected in peace as it was at war.

For all concerned, then, victory had created a completely novel context. No one knew quite what to expect, but China and especially Vietnam had high expectations. They were not mutually hostile, zero-sum expectations, but Vietnam's role in China's illusion of victory was that of a grateful and deferential client, willing to throw off its relation with the Soviet Union and less demanding of aid. In Vietnam's illusions of victory, China would be impressed by Vietnam's victory and become a respectful socialist internationalist. China would realize that it had a major, autonomous power to its south, one that would pursue an independent foreign policy and consolidate its own sphere of influence in Indochina. With victory, the Vietnamese leadership wanted to resume the socialist transformation of the north and require the southern economy to reorganize and catch up. The ambitious goals of the Fourth Party Congress in December 1976 were premised on the continuation of aid from the Soviet Union and China, as well as on Nixon's 1972 promise of reparations.

As we have noted on several occasions, the most dangerous time for asymmetric relations is when they must be constructed in a novel situation. Far from being an exception to this rule, China and Vietnam from 1975 to 1979 provide an archetypal case of systemic misperception.[3] The first part of this chapter will describe the process of interaction that by 1979 produced an apparently unavoidable but winless war. China's insensitivity and Vietnam's over-sensitivity interacted in a negative complementarity of misperception, a process that can be seen in the four major issues of the war: the Soviet-Vietnam alliance, Cambodia, Vietnam's treatment of its ethnic Chinese residents, and territorial issues.

In the second part of the chapter, the ensuing twelve years of Sino-Vietnamese hostility are analyzed. From 1979 to 1985, both sides came to know the limits of their respective power. Vietnam thought that it could present the region and the world with the *fait accompli* of its control of Indochina, and China and Southeast Asia would quickly adjust, as they had to Vietnam's victory in 1975. China thought that the "lesson" of its invasion of 1979 could be supplemented with international isolation and criticism, and perhaps a second lesson, and thus Vietnam could be bled dry until it was forced to capitulate.

---

[3] See Brantly Womack, "Asymmetry and Systemic Misperception: The Cases of China, Vietnam and Cambodia during the 1970s," *Journal of Strategic Studies* 26:2 (June 2003), pp. 91–118.

By 1985 a stalemate was in place. Vietnam was indisputably in control of Indochina, but China and ASEAN had formed an entente against Vietnam. The entente could not force the end of Vietnam's occupation of Cambodia, but for its part Vietnam could not force its way out of regional and international isolation.[4] Vietnam attempted to break the stalemate by announcing a unilateral withdrawal of its forces by 1990, and Prince Norodom Sihanouk's courageous response to this offer eventually led to the disintegration of regional isolation. China ended its opposition only after seeing clearly that it would itself become isolated if it continued to support the Khmer Rouge and to oppose a settlement. By 1991 a Cambodian agreement was in place, Vietnam was behaving more deferentially toward China, and normalization could take place.

The final section of the chapter explores the life cycle of systemic misperceptions as illustrated by this dark period in Sino-Vietnamese relations. The downward swing of the cycle is governed by the negative complementarity of misperceptions in a context that is not controlled by the commonsense expectations of an established relationship. Bottom is reached with stalemate. The larger power is unwilling to commit additional resources to support its frustrated but limited objectives, and the smaller power realizes that its long-term future requires some sort of accommodation with the larger power. But the larger power is more complacent with stalemate than the smaller power, because the smaller power suffers more from it. Eventually, however, the lack of continuing justification for hostility undermines the larger power's malevolence, and normalization occurs. Normalization under such conditions is more stable than the lack of affection between the two sides might suggest, because both sides have been sobered by the disillusioning and costly experience of hostility.

Illusions of Victory, 1975–1979

In 1975 both China and Vietnam expected to adjust their relationship, both sides were suspicious of what the other might do, but neither expected that the other would become a serious security problem.

If we recall from Chapter 4 the four factors that moderate misperception in asymmetric relationships, trouble could be predicted. The context of the "outer sleeve" of diplomatic ritual and historical common sense was changed completely by victory, and the enforced intimacy of wartime had suppressed rather than neutralized concrete problems in the relationship.

Diplomatic ritual had been driven by wartime needs and the global setting of Vietnam's struggle against the United States; now the topic for summitry

---

[4] Brantly Womack, "Stalemate in Indochina: The Case for Demilitarization," *World Policy Journal* 4:4 (Fall 1987), 675–93.

TABLE 9.1. *Illusions of victory*

China	Vietnam
	Fall of Saigon April 30, 1975
Le Duan's stormy Beijing visit September 1975	
	4th Party Congress December 1976
No new aid from China February 1977	
	Vietnam attacks Cambodian border December 1977
Public dispute begins over ethnic Chinese in Vietnam May 1978	
Deng returns to power 1978	Vietnam joins council for Mutual Economic Assistance (COMECON) June 28, 1978
China normalizes with United States December 1978	Vietnam's treaty with Soviet Union November 1978
	Vietnam invades Cambodia December 25, 1978
Deng visits United States January 1979	Phnom Penh falls January 7, 1979
China invades Vietnam February 17–March 16, 1979	
	Soviets arrive Cam Ranh Bay March 27, 1979

was aid, and that would be a sore subject. As Mao Zedong told Le Duan in 1975,

Today you are not the poorest under heaven. We are the poorest. We have a population of 800 million.[5]

Beyond congratulations over victory, there was no outer sleeve of common ground for the relationship that would permit both countries to affirm benevolent intentions toward the other while not sacrificing concrete negotiating positions.

Historical precedent, the lower part of the outer sleeve, was also problematic. Clearly, the establishment of an independent Vietnam in the modern era marked a new stage in the relationship. There were historical referents, but there was little historical inertia of common expectations. And the historical referents were different. China dwelt on the recent history of its generosity to

[5] Mao Zedong to Le Duan, September 24, 1975, in Odd Arne Westad, Chen Jian, Stein Tonnesson, Nguyen Vu Tung, and James G. Hershberg, eds., *77 Conversations between Chinese and Foreign Leaders on the Wars in Indochina, 1964–1977* (Washington: Woodrow Wilson Center, Cold War International History Project Working Paper no. 22, May 1998), p. 195.

Vietnam and overlooked the long past of its encroachments on Vietnamese autonomy. As relations began to cool in 1975 Deng Xiaoping sharply criticized historical references in Vietnamese media to Chinese incursions in the Vietnamese press and the "threat from the north."[6] But a leader in Hanoi could not walk outside without being reminded by some location or monument of heroic resistance to China, and he or she could not look at a map of Vietnam without being reminded that China was still there, only a hundred miles away. Since both China and Vietnam expected a new chapter in their relationship rather than merely a new paragraph, both – and especially Vietnam – looked at the whole course of history for inspiration. Instead of supplying a common sense framework for a normal relationship, history amplified the misinterpretation of the present.

There was little to neutralize issues of conflict. Inclusive rhetoric could not neutralize issues, because China's rhetoric of anti-(Soviet) hegemonism clashed with Vietnam's rhetoric of socialist internationalism. One could not sing the other's song without surrendering.[7] There were few mechanisms of conflict management in place because the wartime relationship had not been constructed on a state-to-state basis; between "lips and teeth" no mechanisms were necessary. Moreover, although aid had created a considerable amount of contact between Chinese and Vietnamese, there was little commercial trade, and there were no groups on either side of the border with an institutionalized material interest in peaceful relations.[8]

Although the various issues in the relationship each had its own rhythm, they all fit into a general pattern of deterioration. The first phase, from victory over the Thieu regime in April 1975 to Party General Secretary Le Duan's visit to Beijing in September 1975, might be called the honeymoon. While not very romantic, it combined the inertia of revolutionary solidarity with the desire of both China and Vietnam to woo the other into post-war cooperation on its own terms. A dramatic end to this phase was provided by Le Duan's stormy visit to Beijing and in particular his early departure and failure to host the customary return banquet. Although in retrospect the outlines of incompatible agendas were clear, there were still forces in the leadership of both sides that preferred accommodation. China agreed to new aid programs, although they were not as generous as the Vietnamese requested.

In the second phase, hardening of opposition from October 1975 to May 1978, the leadership on both sides became more univocal, and China's sanctions against Vietnamese impertinence thinned out the veneer of official

---

[6] "Deng Xiaoping and Le Duan, 29 September 1975" *77 Conversations*, p. 195.
[7] This was painfully evident already in September 1975, at an exchange of toasts between Deng Xiaoping and Le Duan. See Kay Möller, *China und das wiedervereinte Vietnam* (Bochum: Studienverlag Brockmeyer, 1984), pp. 277–83.
[8] Brantly Womack, "Sino-Vietnamese Border Trade: The Edge of Normalization," *Asian Survey* 34:6 (June 1994), pp. 495–512.

solidarity. China rejected new requests for aid and lagged in the implementation of existing agreements. Meanwhile Vietnam removed from its leadership
all ethnic Chinese, those who were sympathetic to China, and even members
of border-area ethnic minorities. Finally, in May 1978 China went public in
its criticism of Vietnamese expulsion of ethnic Chinese, marking the period
of open criticism that lasted until war in February 1979. Vietnam joined
the Soviet-led Council for Mutual Economic Assistance (COMECON) in
June 1978 and signed a treaty of friendship and cooperation with the Soviet
Union in November. In December it invaded Cambodia and quickly pushed
the Khmer Rouge to the Thai frontier. China responded with the invasion
and destruction of Vietnam's northern provinces in February–March 1979.
After the brief but bloody border war, officially a war to defend the border
but unofficially an effort to teach Vietnam a "lesson,"[9] there was a cold war
from 1979 until official normalization in November 1991.

The four explicit issues that culminated in China's invasion of Vietnam
were the Vietnamese alliance with the Soviet Union, Vietnam's invasion of
Cambodia in December 1978, Vietnam's mistreatment and expulsion of
ethnic Chinese, and territorial disputes. Underlying these issues were economic crises in both countries that were linked to the failure of the socialist
model of economic development. Economic crisis created a sense of domestic emergency in both countries that greatly affected international options.[10]
On the background of political transformation and economic crisis, each
of the explicit issues played its own role in the conflict. The invasion and
occupation of Cambodia provided China's primary diplomatic rationale for
its invasion of Vietnam and subsequent hostility. The treatment of ethnic
Chinese was the focus of a spectacular public relations battle in 1978. Border disputes provided a formal excuse for a limited armed intervention.
But the most important issue was Vietnam's relationship with the Soviet
Union.[11]

The unfolding of the Soviet issue strengthened the hawks on both sides
and eventually provided a level of crisis sufficient to justify a major hostility, but it was an issue grounded in misperception and ending in futility.
China perceived Vietnam's unwillingness to join its opposition to the Soviet
Union as an indication of hostility, whereas in fact continued cooperation
with both China and the Soviet Union was Vietnam's most reasonable course
of action. If, as China claimed,[12] the withdrawal of the United States left a

---

[9] The *lesson* terminology was used informally by China even during preparations for the
    invasion. See Nayan Chanda, *Brother Enemy: The War after the War* (New York: Macmillan,
    1986), p. 323.
[10] For Vietnam, see Alexander Woodside, "Nationalism and Poverty in the Breakdown of
    Sino-Vietnamese Relations," *Pacific Affairs* 52:3 (Autumn 1979), pp. 381–409.
[11] This is well argued by Robert Ross in *The IndochinaTangle* (New York: Columbia University
    Press, 1988) and confirmed by numerous interviews in China.
[12] *Ibid.*, pp. 28–30.

vacuum in Southeast Asia, few countries would have a greater interest in keeping a major power from monopolizing the area than Vietnam. But only China was positioned to dominate Vietnam against its will; the Soviet Union (or the United States) would have to be invited in. Chinese sanctions were therefore predictably counter-productive. Rather than indicate the negative consequences of a Soviet alliance, they demonstrated the reality of a Chinese threat. Moreover, there were many indications that Vietnam was unwilling to deepen its relationship with the Soviet Union to the point of alliance.[13] Not only did it resist Soviet pressure to join COMECON until the summer of 1978, but until the summer of 1977 Vietnam was as difficult and rude in its diplomacy toward the Soviets as it was toward the Chinese.[14] Vietnam also engaged in multi-faceted efforts to establish relations with its regional neighbors, international financial institutions, and the United States, though these efforts were hampered by its revolutionary rhetoric, its commitment to a command economy, and its unwillingness (until 1978) to give up on its expectation of $4 billion in reparations promised in the Paris Peace Agreement by the United States. By 1978 Vietnam felt cornered by China's hostility and the inability of its domestic economy to survive unassisted. If Vietnam were "Asia's Cuba," as Deng Xiaoping put it, then it was because China presented itself as Vietnam's United States. On March 27, 1979, a Soviet naval contingent dropped anchor in Cam Ranh Bay, and by 1985 Cam Ranh had developed into the largest offshore Soviet naval facility.[15]

Vietnam's perception of China's anti-Soviet concerns was equally flawed, but in the opposite direction. In contrast to China's overly global interpretation of Vietnam, Vietnam's interpretation of China was overly local. Vietnam interpreted China's anti-Soviet pressures as a deliberate attempt to isolate and dominate Vietnam. In the most extreme statement of Vietnam's position, a long internal speech given by Le Duan in the first half of 1979, he claimed that Mao had wanted to take over all of Southeast Asia in order to settle excess Chinese there.[16] But it should have been clear that China's stance toward Vietnam was derivative from its global policy.

To put it bluntly, from 1975 to 1978 Vietnam was not that important to China. The domestic transition from Mao and the Gang of Four to Hua Guofeng and Deng Xiaoping filled the agenda. Initially China encouraged the United States to restore economic relations with Vietnam[17] and called

---

[13] See Gerhard Will, *Vietnam 1975–1979: Von Krieg zu Krieg* (Hamburg: Mitteilungen des Instituts für Asienkunde, 1987), pp. 67–8.

[14] Chanda recounts a memorable instance in *Brother Enemy*, pp. 170–1, and mentions many other direct and oblique expressions of Vietnamese autonomy vis-à-vis the Soviets.

[15] *Ibid.*, p. 398.

[16] Stein Tonnesson and Chris Goscha, *Le Duan and the Break with China*, Dossier No. 3 (Washington: Cold War International History Project, Woodrow Wilson International Center for Scholars, 2001), http://cwihp.si.edu/tonviet.htm.

[17] Ross, *The Indochina Tangle*, p. 15.

for peaceful negotiations between Vietnam and the Khmer Rouge,[18] both measures aimed at relieving Vietnam's "vacuum" by diversifying its alternatives and reducing isolation. Moreover, since Vietnam increasingly acted as if China were already hostile, it underestimated the severity of China's action when it did finally cross the threshold of hostility. After China turned the corner in late 1977 from being friendly but increasingly irritated to being hostile, it began to supply maximum aid to the Khmer Rouge, and in 1979 as it ended its military "lesson" it destroyed the northern border areas of Vietnam. Throughout the 1980s, forging and maintaining a regional and global alliance against Vietnam was one of China's major foreign policy goals. Had Vietnam been able to stay on the cold side of friendship with China, its next decade would not have been as dark.

Although Vietnam's leaning to the Soviet side was the most important cause of Sino-Vietnamese hostility, Vietnam's invasion of Cambodia on December 25, 1978, provided the occasion for armed conflict, and Vietnam's subsequent occupation of Cambodia became the main object of China's pressure on Vietnam during the following decade of hostility.

From China's perspective, Vietnam's pressure on Cambodia was simply a matter of Vietnamese expansionism egged on by the Soviet Union.[19] From Vietnam's perspective, they were dealing with a viscerally anti-Vietnamese clique (Pol Pot's Khmer Rouge) that had shown its unwillingness to cooperate with Vietnam before 1975 and by 1978 had allied itself with China and was receiving Chinese military assistance as fast as it could be delivered.[20] Although there are grounds for both interpretations, a strong case could be made that Cambodia's relationship to Vietnam was an asymmetric relationship parallel to Vietnam's relationship to China.[21]

The Khmer Rouge viewed the Paris Peace Agreement of January 1973 as a deliberate betrayal of Cambodia by Vietnam. Although the Vietnamese made every effort to persuade the Khmer Rouge to participate and like themselves to accept a compromise solution, the fact was that after Vietnam's separate peace, the United States engaged in the most intensive bombing of Cambodia. As Khieu Samphan summarized the situation to Sihanouk in 1973, "Hanoi

---

[18] Qiang Zhai, *China and the Vietnam Wars, 1950–1975* (Chapel Hill: University of North Carolina Press, 2000), p. 212.

[19] See for instance *Zhonghua Renmin Gonghe Guo duiwai guanxi shi (chu chao), di si zhang: Zhong Mei guanxi kaishi zhengchanghua zhi Sulian junshi ruqin Afuhan di duiwai guanxi* [1972/2 zhi 1979/12]中华人民共和国对外关系史(初抄): 中美关系开始正常化止苏联入侵阿富汗的对外关系 [History of external relations of the PRC (first draft): ch.4, from the beginning of Sino-American normalization to the Soviet military invasion of Afghanistan (February 1972 to December 1979)] (n.p., n.d. – an internal graduate-level text from the mid-1980s), pp. 48–113.

[20] For pre-1975 problems, see Luu Van Loi, *Fifty Years of Vietnamese Diplomacy* (Hanoi: The Gioi Publishers, 2000), pp. 2069.

[21] A more detailed analysis of the asymmetric relationship between Vietnam and Cambodia is presented in Womack, "Asymmetry and Systemic Misperception."

has dropped us."[22] It was a sentiment very close to the "stab in the back" the Vietnamese had felt from China only a year earlier at the time of the Shanghai Communiqué.

At the deepest level, Vietnam and Cambodia became alienated because Vietnam viewed Cambodia as part of a larger struggle centered on Vietnam, while the Khmer Rouge desperately sought an autonomous identity. Consider the following statement by Nguyen Khac Vien:

> Their [the Khmer Rouge] greatest error was to regard Cambodia as if it was in a vacuum – isolated in its own territory. Had Ho Chi Minh thought like this, we would never have united with the Laotian and Kampuchean resistance forces in the struggle against the French colonialists and the Japanese militarists.[23]

To Vietnam, Cambodia was frustratingly localistic in its concerns. But Cambodia did not have Vietnam's option of leading a regional struggle. It had only the option of being a subordinate part of such an enterprise, with every edge of its identity available for trespass by Vietnam in the name of the common goal.

There were three major causes of the Vietnamese invasion of Cambodia in December 1978. Historically the first were armed border incidents that began in the first month after victory and escalated in 1978. Since Cambodia claimed most of South Vietnam as its rightful territory, the incidents were not limited attempts to occupy disputed land, but rather terrorist raids meant to frighten ethnic Vietnamese.[24] Vietnam did not publicize the attacks, unlike Thailand which documented and publicized similar assaults by the Khmer Rouge. However, Vietnam eventually launched a large-scale counterattack in December 1977, after which Democratic Kampuchea severed relations, began public denunciations of Vietnam, improved relations with Thailand, and stepped up the execution of Khmer Rouge on the eastern front who were now tainted by their defeat. Border raids became more severe in 1978, and the official reason for launching the December 1978 campaign was to defend the border, though the campaign ended on the other side of Cambodia at the Thai border.

Another justification for the war that was more important after the fact was genocide. It was, of course, convenient for Vietnam to emphasize the crimes of the Khmer Rouge government since they legitimized both the invasion and the new government that Vietnam installed in Phnom Penh, and one can easily imagine that it must have been a shocking experience to be the first outsiders to view the enormity of Khmer Rouge mass murders.

---

[22] William Shawcross, *Sideshow: Kissinger, Nixon and the Destruction of Cambodia* (New York: Simon and Schuster, 1979), p. 281.

[23] Quoted in Wilfred Burchett, *The China – Cambodia – Vietnam Triangle* (Chicago, IL: Vanguard Books, 1981), p. 55.

[24] See Chanda, *Brother Enemy*, pp. 192–5, for an account of a border raid and the Vietnamese suppression of information.

The final and most important motive for Vietnam's invasion was Cambodia's alliance with China. The first airplane to land in Phnom Penh after the Khmer Rouge victory was Chinese, and from the start the Chinese aid program to Cambodia increased while aid to Vietnam dwindled. For its part, Cambodia adopted Beijing's anti-hegemony rhetoric in August 1975 and was effusive in its praise for Mao, while Vietnam signed large, long-term aid contracts with the Soviet Union in October 1975. Somewhat to Pol Pot's surprise the China-Cambodian relationship survived the death of Mao in September 1976 and the fall of the Gang of Four. Nevertheless, until mid-1977 China was still offering its services as arbiter of an Indochina summit, and Vietnam's "Cambodia lesson" of December 1977 was aimed at border raids rather than at Cambodia's foreign relations. But the rough reception that Pham Van Dong received in Beijing in June 1977 was, in retrospect, a turning point. Afterward Vietnam prepared for a China-Cambodian alliance by concluding a treaty of friendship with Laos, which Pol Pot in turn saw as the first step in an enforced Indochina Federation.

By 1978 the die was cast. China's Central Committee decided in December 1977 to "give energetic support to Cambodia . . . we did our best in all aspects, except for sending our own soldiers there." And in fact more than 1,500 advisors were sent, along with complete equipment for three divisions as well as food, medicine, and ammunition for 100,000 troops.[25] Vietnam began preparing a Cambodian government in exile that it could put into place. Pol Pot stepped up the executions of East Zone cadres and normalized relations with Thailand to create a rear supply area.

On December 25, 1978, Vietnam began its invasion of Cambodia. Phnom Penh fell on January 7, two days after Pol Pot had told Sihanouk that the Khmer Rouge would wipe out the Vietnamese.[26] The control of the rest of Cambodia's major towns took only two more weeks. The Khmer government that Vietnam had formed a few weeks before the invasion[27] established the People's Republic of Kampuchea on January 10, and signed a twenty-five-year friendship treaty with Vietnam on February 18. Meanwhile, on January 14 Chinese Politburo member Geng Biao and Vice Foreign Minister Han Nianlong held a secret meeting at Utapao Airbase in Thailand with Thai Premier Kriangsak and made arrangements for Thai-Chinese cooperation in supporting the Khmer Rouge along the border of Cambodia and Thailand.[28]

The third major issue in the deterioration of Sino-Vietnamese relations was Vietnam's mistreatment and finally expulsion of large numbers of its

[25] "Keng Piao's [Geng Biao's] Report of the Situation of the Indochinese Peninsula," delivered January 16, 1979, for high-level internal circulation. *Issues and Studies* (January 1981), pp. 78–96; here pp. 85, 90. I have confirmed the authenticity of this document.

[26] Chanda, *Brother Enemy*, p. 344.

[27] *Ibid.*, pp. 338–41.

[28] *Ibid.*, pp. 348–9.

ethnic Chinese (*Hoa*) residents.[29] The situation of the Hoa in Vietnam was complex, and quite different in north and south. On the one hand, in the 1950s Cholon ("big market"), the Chinese quarter of Saigon, was the second largest ethnic Chinese city outside of China (after Singapore). Chinese controlled most of the wholesale trade and nearly 90 percent of the non-European capital. In the north there was a smaller Chinese population, mainly laborers and fishermen. Governments in both north and south moved to control ethnic Chinese in the 1950s, though the north was of course circumspect in its efforts.[30]

Startled, perhaps, by the numbers of Chinese in the streets of Saigon waving Mao posters as the PAVN forces entered the city in April 1975, the government began to suppress Chinese publications in both north and south. In August the Hanoi newspaper *Xin Yue Hua Bao*新越华报 [New Vietnam Chinese Newspaper] was shut down; in autumn 1976 all Chinese-language newspapers and schools in the South were shut down.[31] The major problem in the South, however, was economic rather than political. From the Fourth Party Congress in December 1976 Le Duan decided to push the South to "catch up" with the North in socialist transformation, and the Hoa were the main organizers and beneficiaries of the old economic order.[32] Hoa in the South were thus pressured from two directions. On the one hand they comprised most of the bourgeoisie of Vietnam, and they stood in the way of socialism. On the other, they were an alien community and a possible "fifth column" for China.

In late 1977 the economic situation in the South failed to respond to Hanoi's directives and relations with China worsened, and on March 23, 1978, an ad hoc paramilitary force moved into Cholon and other Chinese districts throughout the country, ransacking and confiscating retail businesses and outlawing private wholesale businesses.[33] Many fled.[34] The number of "boat people" from Vietnam received in other Southeast Asian countries

[29] See Pao-min Chang, *Beijing, Hanoi and the Overseas Chinese* (Berkeley: Center for Chinese Studies, China Research Monograph no. 24, 1982).

[30] See Ramses Amer, "The Chinese Minority in Vietnam since 1975" [*Ilmu masyarakat: terbitan Persatuan Sains Sosial Malaysia* Sociology: Proceedings of the Malaysian Social Science Association] 22 (1992), pp. 1–39; E. S. Ungar, "The Struggle over the Chinese Community in Vietnam, 1946–1988," *Pacific Affairs* 60:4 (Winter, 1987–88), pp. 596–614.

[31] Li Gu李谷, *Cong en'en yuanyuan dao pingdeng huli: Shiji zhi jiao di Zhong Yue guanxi yanjiu*从恩恩怨怨到平等互利:实际之交的中越关系研究 [From graciousness and resentment to equality and mutual benefit: research on Sino-Vietnamese relations at century's end] (Hong Kong: Honglan Chuban Gongsi, 2001), p. 47; Chang, *Beijing, Hanoi and the Overseas Chinese*, p. 17.

[32] The situation is most eloquently described in Woodside, "Nationalism and Poverty."

[33] Chang, *Beijing, Hanoi and the Overseas Chinese*, p. 27.

[34] Amer estimates the total number leaving Vietnam up to the end of September 1979 at almost 600,000, of which the Hoa were approximately 450,000. Amer, "Chinese Minority," pp. 24–5.

doubled to 5,000 in April 1978 and then redoubled in October. Meanwhile, almost the entire ethnic Chinese communities of Hanoi, Haiphong, and Quang Ninh Province were forced across the Chinese border, more than 160,000 persons.[35]

Meanwhile, in 1977 China had begun to adopt a more friendly attitude toward overseas Chinese in order to attract patriotic investment.[36] The Vietnamese mistreatment and expulsion of ethnic Chinese was the first test of China's newfound solicitude as well as a tremendous refugee problem for China. Thus the first public airing of differences between China and Vietnam was occasioned by Vietnam's mistreatment of the Hoa. The public polemic began in May 1978 and provided the occasion for the suspension of Chinese aid projects in Vietnam in order to "divert funds and materials in order to make working and living arrangements for the Chinese expelled."[37] In June, a much-publicized effort to send ships to Haiphong and Ho Chi Minh City to pick up refugees foundered because of a series of disagreements concerning concrete arrangements. In June China ordered the closure of Vietnamese consulates in China in retaliation for Vietnamese obstruction of its consular functions, and on July 12 it closed the border. The three decades of people-to-people relationships between China and Vietnam were over.

The public war of words – accusations, proposals, and counter-proposals – between China and Vietnam concerning the ethnic Chinese was a classic case of divisive rhetoric.[38] Each statement was a verbal cannon shot designed to do damage to the case of the other side and to yield nothing of one's own. Rather than neutralizing an issue as inclusive rhetoric might do, divisive rhetoric absolutizes each side's commitment to an interpretation of the issue that excludes the other side's perspective and interests. If either side attempted serious negotiations it would appear to be admitting fault and surrendering to the other side. When democratic states engage in bouts of exclusive rhetoric, the leadership can be suspected of "grandstanding" for a domestic audience. It is interesting that in this case the leaders of neither China nor Vietnam were particularly bound by domestic public opinion. Here the interaction between states seems quite similar to a shouting match between individuals who have become extremely frustrated with each other for a variety of reasons and are triggered by an event to express themselves and their frustration rather than to resolve the problem at hand.

By mid-1979 the "Orderly Departure Program (ODP)" administered by the United Nations became the chief mechanism of emigration from Vietnam,

---

[35] *Ibid.*, pp. 14–15.

[36] The relationship between the ethnic Chinese of Southeast Asia (the "Nanyang" [Southern Ocean] Chinese) and the People's Republic of China is too complex to discuss here, but suffice it to say that the Cultural Revolution profoundly disturbed and alienated the relationship.

[37] New China News Agency (Xinhua) May 30, 1978, quoted in Chang, *Beijing, Hanoi and the Overseas Chinese*, p. 37. The final directive suspending all aid was issued on July 3.

[38] The dispute is best narrated by Chang in *Beijing, Hanoi and the Overseas Chinese*.

usually to camps in Southeast Asia. Until 1984 ethnic Chinese accounted for more than 70 percent of ODP participants; between 1984 and 1991 the share declined to 20 percent.[39] In 1994 the United Nations ended automatic asylum for Vietnamese emigrants, and the primary regional concern in the 1990s was repatriation of refugees and the closure of camps. In Vietnam, Hoa policy fluctuated from 1979 and 1986 between continued control and grudging permissiveness, and then the reform policies of *doi moi* (renovation) beginning in 1986 allowed a revival of the private economy and hence some degree of restoration of the Hoa role in the South.

With the closing of the border, there was a subtle shift of attention away from the Hoa and toward the physical confrontation of two sovereignties. A number of violent incidents occurred as Vietnamese guards tried to push the people who had gathered along the border through the Chinese guard-posts. Border clashes rose from a total of 1,625 reported by both sides in 1977 to 2,175 reported by Vietnam and 1,108 reported by China in 1978.[40] In fact, the border was more a venue for confrontation than a matter of serious dispute, but the fact of confrontation made every disputed hectare a potential war zone because each side would feel obligated not to yield it to the other. Although neither side denied the sovereignty of the other, the precise boundary became the venue and symbol of irreconcilable differences because it was at the border that the two sides must meet, and they disagreed on where it was. Hence, although the issue of the ethnic Chinese provided the emotional heat for conflict, the Vietnamese invasion of Cambodia on December 26, 1978, provided the occasion, and the growing relationship between Vietnam and the Soviet Union provided China's main motive, the official reason given for China's invasion of Vietnam on February 17, 1979, was "a counterattack in defense of our [China's] frontiers."[41]

Writing only a few months after the Chinese invasion, Alexander Woodside begins an article that is still the most insightful analysis of the breakdown in relations between China and Vietnam with the following statement:

In their relations with each other since the second Indochina War ended in 1975, both China and Vietnam have suffered complete foreign policy disasters. Neither country can gain from the recent crisis in Sino-Vietnamese relations. Vietnam in particular, even with the most lavish self-interested Soviet aid, quite lacks the means to sustain a long-term enmity with China and to industrialize itself successfully at the same time. Since neither side can gain, it is obvious that each side has made catastrophic miscalculations about the other.[42]

[39] Amer, "Chinese Minority," p. 29.
[40] Antoine Dauphin, "La frontière sino-vietnamienne de 1895–1896 à nos jours," in *Les Frontières du Vietnam* (Paris: Éditions L'Harmattan, 1989), pp. 104–18, here p. 113.
[41] *Beijing Review* 8 (February 23, 1979), pp. 8–11.
[42] Woodside, "Nationalism and Poverty," p. 381.

Woodside goes on to predict that the Vietnamese occupation of Cambodia would be unsustainable in the long term, and that the Soviet-Vietnamese relationship would prove more tenuous than either China or Vietnam expected. It was too obvious for Woodside to mention that the idea of China bullying Vietnam back into line by teaching it a "lesson" was fatuous. In effect, at a time when the hostile propaganda of both sides was at its height, Woodside evaluated the conflict in terms of a remarkably accurate estimate of consequences that would play themselves out over the next twelve years.

Hostile Isolation, 1979–1990

On February 17, 1979, a rather peculiar war began. China massed 300,000 troops on the border, and as many as a thousand airplanes and a thousand tanks, as well as 1,500 pieces of artillery.[43] The 80,000 troops that China actually committed were met by 75,000–100,000 Vietnamese militia and troops, and casualties are estimated at 25,000 Chinese and 20,000 Vietnamese dead.[44] China entered Vietnam at twenty-six points along the entire border and captured the provincial capitals of five of the six border provinces.[45]

Nevertheless, it was a limited action. Neither side used air power, and China announced its withdrawal within hours of attaining its last and most important objective, the occupation of Langson, on March 5, and the withdrawal was completed by March 16. Vietnam committed a few regular army units to the defense of Lang Son, but the brunt of the fighting was a "people's war" by local forces. Vietnam was not on the edge of defeat, nor was its army seriously damaged. Had China gone beyond Lang Son or used air power, its losses would have been considerably greater, victory uncertain, and occupation impossible (Table 9.2).[46]

The invasion fit into an overall pattern of limited but determined opposition to Vietnam that set China's policy until 1990–91. It reflected not simply a disagreement with Vietnam, but a root-and-branch rejection of the Vietnamese regime, including calls for a "second revolution" and support for

---

[43] Harlan Jencks, "China's 'Punitive' War on Vietnam: A Military Assessment," *Asian Survey* 19:8 (August 1979), pp. 801–5.

[44] The figures are not official, and there are significant differences between Chinese and Vietnamese estimates. However, there were high and roughly comparable losses on both sides. See Henry Kenny, "Vietnamese Perceptions of the 1979 War with China," in Mark Ryan, David Finkelstein, and Michael McDevitt, eds., *Chinese Warfighting: The PLA Experience since 1949* (Armonk: M. E. Sharpe, 2003), pp. 217–40.

[45] The capital of Quang Ninh Province, Hon Gai, is quite far from the border, and an attack would have involved a direct threat to Haiphong and the Red River delta.

[46] See Kenny, "Vietnamese Perceptions." Besides the obvious military difficulties of occupying Vietnam, such an occupation would have nullified China's principal international justification for the war, namely, Vietnam's occupation of Cambodia.

TABLE 9.2. *Stalemate*

China	Vietnam
China invades Vietnam February 17–March 16, 1979	
	Coalition Government of Dem Kampuchea formed June 22, 1982 Withdrawal from Cambodia by 1990 announced August 1985
Occupation of Lao Shan 1984	
Hu Yaobang removed January 1987	6th Party Congress 1986
Sihanouk meets with Hun Sen December 7, 1987	
Jakarta Informal Meetings start July 1988	
Naval battle in Spratlys March 1988	
Sino-Vietnamese vice minister talks begin January 1989	
Tiananmen June 4, 1989	Pullout from Cambodia September 1989
Secret summit meeting Chengdu September 1990	
Qian Qichen attends ASEAN meeting 1991	7th Party Congress May 1991
Normalization announced November 1991	

insurgents. Internationally, China used its position in the UN to criticize Vietnam's refugee creation and its occupation of Cambodia, and it joined with the United States to preserve the Khmer Rouge's UN seat.[47] Common opposition to Vietnam continued to provide a bond in the U.S.-China relationship throughout the 1980s, though China was much more vocal on the issue. There was a subtle but important shift in the role of Vietnam in Sino-Soviet relations during the 1980s. In response to a 1982 initiative by Leonid Brezhnev to improve relations, China specified three obstacles to normalization, the first of which was Soviet support for Vietnamese occupation of Cambodia.[48] However, apparently China became less worried about the Soviet-Vietnamese alliance per se. In 1985 Deng Xiaoping indicated that China had no objections to the Soviet base in Cam Ranh Bay as long as

[47] The first vote of the UN Credentials Committee was September 19, 1979. After the Coalition Government of Democratic Kampuchea(CGDK) was set up on June 22, 1982, the UN seat was awarded to the CGDK, which included both Sihanouk and the Khmer Rouge.
[48] Qian Qichen 钱其琛, *Waijiao shi ji* 外交十记 [Ten stories of a diplomat], (Beijing: Shijie zhishi Chubanshe, 2004), pp. 1–40.

Vietnam withdrew from Cambodia.[49] In Southeast Asia, China continued to strengthen its military relationship with Thailand and to join with ASEAN in opposition to Vietnam's occupation of Cambodia.

Meanwhile, China opened the "Deng Xiaoping Trail" to support Khmer Rouge camps on Thailand's border with Cambodia and to support guerilla operations inside the country.[50] Whenever Vietnam attacked the camps, China would increase its own military activity on the Vietnam border. Deng Xiaoping was personally involved in derailing Sihanouk's attempt to defect to the United States in January 1979 and later pushed him to join an anti-Vietnam coalition.[51] China was closely involved in establishing the Coalition Government of Democratic Kampuchea (CGDK) in 1982, which combined the Khmer Rouge, Sihanouk, and supporters of the Lon Nol regime in a diplomatic front in which each party had a veto over initiatives and which was dedicated to opposition to the Vietnam-installed People's Republic of Kampuchea (PRK) government. When ASEAN diplomats tried to remove some of the more notorious Khmer Rouge from the CGDK in 1984, Deng's response was, "I don't understand why some people want to remove Pol Pot. It is true that he made some mistakes in the past but now he is leading the fight against the Vietnamese aggressors."[52]

Given the hostile situation, China's direct relations with Vietnam were limited. China proposed negotiations on February 17, 1979, the day of the invasion, but the proposal noted that "past negotiations have all failed because of the lack of good faith on the Vietnamese side."[53] Both sides used the negotiations that were held from April 1979 to March 1980 as platforms for their polemics. High-level talks were not resumed until 1989. On the border, China responded promptly to Vietnam's incursions into Thailand from 1980 to 1985 with military actions. In 1984 a major action was launched to seize and hold Lao Shan, on the Yunnan-Vietnam border near Malipo. China linked the resumption of relations to a Vietnamese withdrawal from Cambodia,[54] but in fact the isolation of Vietnam was a more important policy objective. As Deng Xiaoping told Japanese Prime Minister Masayoshi Ohira in late 1979, "It is wise for China to force the Vietnamese to stay in Kampuchea because that way they will suffer more and more and will not be able to extend their hand to Thailand, Malaysia and Singapore."[55]

---

[49] Chanda, *Brother Enemy*, p. 400.

[50] *Ibid.*, p. 381. According to a personal communication from a senior Thai general, the Thai army did not act as an intermediary between China and the Khmer Rouge.

[51] See *ibid.*, pp. 363–9, for the very interesting story of the defection.

[52] *Ibid.*, p. 394.

[53] "Authorized Statement by Xinhua News Agency," *Beijing Review* 1979:8 (February 23, 1979), pp. 8–9.

[54] See the "8 Point Proposal" contained in "Speech by Han Nianlong, Head of Chinese Government Delegation," *Beijing Review* 18 (May 4, 1979), pp. 10–17, esp. p. 16.

[55] Chanda, *Brother Enemy*, p. 379.

As this comment suggests, by 1979 China's various specific issues that had led to the breaking of relations had streamed together into a general hostility toward Vietnam. The issues that once caused the hostility became subtly transformed into policies derivative from hostility. The point was no longer simply to get Vietnam out of Cambodia but to "bleed Vietnam white" in Cambodia. By 1982 the Vietnamese alliance with the Soviet Union was no longer a threat. Soviet aid to Vietnam was simply an obstacle to better Sino-Soviet relations, which in any case evolved toward normalcy from 1982 to 1989, before the Vietnamese withdrawal. Although China joined the chorus of international condemnation of Vietnam concerning refugees, after 1978 it was careful not to claim a special responsibility for the ethnic Chinese among them.[56] And although China demanded a return to the original Sino-French border at the time of the invasion,[57] it seized and occupied Vietnamese territory at Lao Shan in 1984. Moreover, while China improved its relations with ASEAN (and especially with Thailand) in the early 1980s by making common cause in opposing Vietnamese expansionism, China's support for the Khmer Rouge was always a strain on the relationship, and by 1988 the rigidity of its anti-Vietnam attitude was beginning to cause serious tensions in its regional relations with Southeast Asia.

In contrast to China's complacent hostility throughout the 1980s, Vietnam's policies underwent major changes. Three phases can be distinguished. In the first, 1979–85, Vietnam concentrated on consolidating its control over Indochina. In the second, from 1985 to 1989, Vietnam pursued a two-track policy of promising to withdraw from Cambodia but at the same time reserving its option of re-occupation if its security demanded it. In the third phase, 1989–91, international openness took a decisive priority over maintaining control in Cambodia, and normalization of relations with China became a top priority.

From 1979 to mid-1985, Vietnam conducted a series of dry season offensives against Khmer Rouge enclaves, culminating in the 1984–85 offensive that removed the last of the major Khmer Rouge strongpoints within Cambodia.[58] It also crossed the Thai border in pursuit of the Khmer Rouge and continued to generate refugees, both Vietnamese and Cambodian. It reciprocated China's harsh condemnations, criticizing China and particularly Deng Xiaoping for "betraying Marxism-Leninism."[59] Although national security was the major justification for seeking control of Indochina, there was a

---

[56] For a careful analysis of the legal issues involved and the transformation of the Chinese position, see Hungdah Chiu, "China's Legal Position on Protecting Chinese Residents in Vietnam," *The American Journal of International Law* 74:3 (July 1980), pp. 685–9.

[57] This was one of China's "8 Points" in March 1978. See "Speech by Han Nianlong," p. 17.

[58] The Cambodian dry season is from November to April, though it lasts only three months in the Cardamom Mountains, a major Khmer Rouge area.

[59] See for instance "Vietnam Comments on 'People's Daily' Article on Marxism," *BBC Summary of World Broadcasts*, December 14, 1984.

strong undercurrent of regional hegemonism. Vietnam had ignored over-
tures from Sihanouk in late 1979.[60] As General Le Duc Anh put it in January
1985:

> Experience over more than half a century on the Indochinese peninsula shows that
> to the Japanese fascists, French colonialists, and U.S. imperialists as well as to the
> Chinese expansionists and hegemonists at present, Indochina has always remained a
> target of aggression and a unified battleground in their plots of aggression. Dividing
> one country from another and using one country as a springboard from which to
> annex another and then to annex all the three countries became the law for all wars
> of aggression by outside forces against the Indochinese peninsula. In their plots to
> annex Indochina and to expand into Southeast Asia, the Beijing reactionaries cannot
> help but follow this law.
>
> Consequently, if in the past the path to liberation for the peoples of Vietnam,
> Laos and Cambodia was the path of alliance to fight side by side against a common
> enemy, so now their path of national construction and defense must also be that of
> special solidarity and strategic and close combat alliance among the three countries
> and three nations in line with a common plan for strategic coordination.[61]

But Vietnam was in no position to enjoy its consolidation of Indochina in
1985. Its economy was in dire straits and it had isolated itself from almost
all countries outside the Soviet bloc, including Indochina's neighbors on all
sides. Moreover, the Soviet Union was getting more restive concerning the
Vietnamese presence in Cambodia and the cost of supporting Vietnam. Thus
Vietnam's occupation of Cambodia stood in the way of developing other
strategic options.

The second phase of Vietnamese policy began with the following promise
made at the Eleventh Meeting of the Indochina Foreign Ministers Conference
in Phnom Penh on August 16, 1985:

> Vietnamese volunteer forces will conclude their total withdrawal [from Cambo-
> dia] by 1990. In case these withdrawals are taken advantage of to undermine the peace
> and security of Kampuchea, the governments of the People's Republic of Kampuchea
> and the Socialist Republic of Vietnam will consult each other and take appropriate
> measures.[62]

Considering that the previous policy was that Vietnam "will consider the
withdrawal of Vietnamese troops when the threat from China no longer

---

[60] Chanda, *Brother Enemy*, p. 385.
[61] Senior General Le Duc Anh, "The VPA and Its Lofty International Duty in Friendly Cam-
    bodia," Part 2, *Foreign Broadcast Information Service*, East Asia, January 4, 1985, p. K6.
[62] *Communiqué of the Eleventh Conference of the Foreign Ministers of Kampuchea, Laos
    and Vietnam, issued at Phnom Penh on 16 August 1985*. Included in *Documents on the
    Kampuchean Problem, 1979–1985* (Bangkok: Ministry of Foreign Affairs, n.d.), pp. 188–9.

exists,"[63] the promise of a unilateral withdrawal by 1990 was a major change in Vietnam's policy, even though it was conditioned by an "escape clause" concerning security. When Foreign Minister Nguyen Co Thach met with foreign delegations he began to emphasize that "the train would leave the station" by 1990, and any negotiations for a coalition government would have to be launched before then.[64]

The primary target of the change in Cambodia policy was Southeast Asia and the United States rather than China. Not only was China perceived to be more uncompromising and hostile, but some Vietnamese leaders such as Thach would not have wanted a rapprochement with China unless it were balanced by better relations with other states as well. The leadership became aware of the economic importance of better regional and global relations from 1984, and in May 1988, under pressure from Thach, the Politburo decided to make joining the world economy a top priority.[65] Since the official position of the United States[66] and of ASEAN was that achieving normal relations was contingent solely on withdrawal from Cambodia, Vietnam could hope that its offer would provide some openings for its diplomacy regardless of China's attitude.

Unfortunately for Vietnam (and for Cambodia), the Cambodian stalemate had become well entrenched by 1985. Inside Cambodia, Vietnam was in charge. Outside, the United States, China, and ASEAN had a common cause for the first time, and fears of an expansionist Vietnam had eased. The anti-Vietnam entente refused to negotiate with the Vietnam-supported People's Republic of Kampuchea, and Vietnam and the PRK refused to consider the participation of the Khmer Rouge. Vietnam's announcement of a unilateral withdrawal was first ignored, and then derided as insincere.[67] However, on May 7, 1987, Prince Sihanouk announced that he was taking a one-year leave of absence from the presidency of the CGDK, ostensibly because of a Khmer Rouge attack on his forces. The leave of absence freed Sihanouk from the veto of Khmer Rouge, and on December 7, 1987, he held a historic first meeting with Prime Minister Hun Sen of the PRK.

Three observations should be made about Sihanouk's initiative. First, without his action, there would probably not have been an agreement on a coalition government. By 1989 the PRK was strong enough to sustain

---

[63] Indochina Foreign Ministers Conference, Ho Chi Minh City, January 28, 1981. In *Documents on the Kampuchean Problem*, pp. 2, 152.

[64] Personal experience, 1985–89.

[65] Gareth Porter, "The Transformation of Vietnam's World View," *Contemporary Southeast Asia* 12:1 (June 1990), pp. 1–19.

[66] The question of remains of soldiers missing in action (MIAs), was officially considered a humanitarian rather than a diplomatic concern by the United States until 1989.

[67] A rather thorough chronology of the Cambodian war prepared by the Associated Press in 1990 omits the 1985 offer of unilateral withdrawal, as did most press accounts in the 1980s. Associated Press, "A Chronology of the Cambodian War," September 10, 1990.

itself with only indirect military help from Vietnam, and it would have had little reason to compromise its power in a coalition.[68] Second, Sihanouk's action was a move of high courage and patriotism at considerable risk to himself. By meeting with Hun Sen he put one foot into a moving boat, with no certainty that it would not overturn. Had he not acted he could still have lived a comfortable life as a victim of Vietnamese aggression. Third, China deserves credit for not preventing or punishing Sihanouk's move. Clearly it was in contradiction to Chinese policy of support for the CGDK and for the Khmer Rouge in particular, but China's personal relationship with Sihanouk and respect for his autonomy of action overrode such concerns.[69] Sihanouk continued to travel to Beijing, and he was not publicly criticized for his initiative.

After initial hostility and cynicism, Sihanouk's action occasioned a general rethinking of stalemate in Southeast Asia. In July 1988 the first Jakarta Informal Meeting (JIM) was held, a format that allowed heads of all four Cambodian factions to meet. Although the negotiations (and Sihanouk's own position) seesawed up and down throughout 1988 and 1989, and ultimately a UN-brokered solution prevailed in 1991, the atmosphere in 1988 regarding Cambodia had shifted from stalemate to endgame. In 1989 Prime Minister Chatichai of Thailand initiated political and economic exchanges with the PRK, and China was clearly irritated with his plan to turn Indochina "from a battlefield into a marketplace."[70]

By 1989, Vietnam's two-track policy of breaking the stalemate and yet maintaining control in Cambodia had become a one-track policy. Although Vietnam continued to defend its interests and influence in Cambodia, it traded its option of control for international normalization and economic construction. In April 1989 Vietnam publicly announced that it would with-draw the remainder of its troops from Cambodia by the end of September. This stimulated an international conference in Paris in July, but the conference foundered on the inclusion of the Khmer Rouge in a coalition government. After numerous meetings under various auspices, a second Paris conference reached a compromise acceptable to all parties for a UN-supervised transitional government and election, and on November 14, 1991, Sihanouk returned to Phnom Penh as head of the Supreme National Council after thirteen years of exile.

---

[68] I was told by a Thai senior general that by 1987 the PRK military had displaced the Vietnamese in the front lines against the Khmer Rouge, and in any case military actions were at a low level.

[69] Sihanouk himself said that the Chinese were unhappy with his action and they hoped the talks would fail. *Le Monde*, February 10, 1988.

[70] Charles McGregor, "China, Vietnam, and the Cambodian Conflict: Beijing's End Game Strategy," *Asian Survey* 30:3 (March 1990), pp. 266–83, esp. pp. 274–6.

In conjunction with the withdrawal from Cambodia, Vietnam energetically pursued better relations with both China and the United States. The results were initially disappointing with China, and they remained disappointing with the United States as American interest shifted from Cambodia to the interminable process of locating the remains of American servicemen still classified as missing in action (MIA). In December 1988 China answered Vietnam's third request for a meeting of foreign ministers by proposing a vice ministerial meeting in Beijing in January 1989.[71] Although the tone of the meeting was polite, China insisted on settling the Cambodia issue before normalization could be discussed, and it insisted that the Khmer Rouge participate in any coalition government.

Although high-level relations remained blocked until 1989, there had been gradual improvements in the relationship since 1985. The first informal meeting of retired officials took place in Beijing in April 1985,[72] and later that year Li Xiannian congratulated Vietnam on its National Day and a Vietnamese delegation attended the Guangzhou Trade Fair. But China rejected Vietnamese proposals for official talks, claiming that the promise to withdraw troops "did not merit attention,"[73] and heavy fighting continued at the border into 1987, especially at Laoshan.[74] By December, however, an agreement on avoiding border conflict had been reached, and border trade, which Vietnam had condemned as "psychological warfare" in 1985–87,[75] reappeared in 1988 and was gaining momentum by 1989.[76]

Normalization required more than the cessation of direct hostilities and resumption of trade. A major obstacle continued to be sovereignty disputes. The most spectacular of these was a naval confrontation in the Spratly Islands in March 1988 in which two Vietnamese ships were sunk and seventy sailors lost their lives.[77] There were also diplomatic confrontations. Vietnamese Foreign Minister Nguyen Co Thach met with Chinese Vice Foreign Minister Liu Shuqing during the unsuccessful Paris conference of July 1989 and adamantly presented Vietnam's position. Thach repeated his aggressive

---

[71] The details of this meeting are given in Li Jiazhong, "Zhong Yue guanxi zhengchanghua qianye di liang guo fu wai zhang cuoshang" [Negotiation between vice foreign ministers on the eve of Sino-Vietnamese normalization], *Dongnanya Zongheng* [Around Southeast Asia] 4 (April 2003), pp. 36–9. Li Jiazhong was present at the meeting and later served as China's ambassador to Vietnam from 1995 to 2001.

[72] The retired officials were Phan Anh from Vietnam and Li Qiang from China. *Ming Bao*, May 1, 1985.

[73] See *Japan Times*, August 22, 1985; *South China Morning Post*, September 12, 1985.

[74] *Japan Times*, January 9, 1987.

[75] *South China Morning Post*, October 18, 1985; April 16, 1986; *Wen Hui Bao*, April 24, 1986; *Christian Science Monitor*, June 9, 1988.

[76] Brantly Womack, "Sino-Vietnamese Border Trade: The Edge of Normalization," *Asian Survey* 34:6 (June 1994), pp. 495–512.

[77] Henry Kenny, *Shadow of the Dragon* (Washington: Brassey's, 2002), pp. 66–7.

posture in a meeting with Vice Foreign Minister Xu Duxin during the latter's visit to Hanoi in June 1990, earning Thach personal criticisms in the Chinese media.[78]

China's insistence on Khmer Rouge participation in a coalition government in Cambodia was supported by the United States until July 18, 1990, when Secretary of State James Baker announced that the United States would seek contacts with Hanoi to reach a Cambodian settlement and would no longer support the three-party coalition containing the Khmer Rouge in the UN. The American action left China as the only supporter of the Khmer Rouge, and this led China to a serious reconsideration of its position for the first time since 1979. Arrangements were made for a secret summit meeting in Chengdu, Sichuan, between China and Vietnam in September 1990.

The summit meeting (to which Thach was not invited) included Premier Li Peng and Party Secretary Jiang Zemin for China, and Premier Do Muoi and Party Secretary Nguyen Van Linh for Vietnam, as well as the party elder Pham Van Dong. China and Vietnam drew up a secret memorandum of agreement on Cambodia and resolved in principle other obstacles to normalization. "The Chengdu summit marked China's abandonment of its 'bleed Vietnam white' policy and the start of Sino-Vietnamese normalization," according to Carlyle Thayer. "When news of the summit and its deliberations became public both the Khmer Rouge and Norodom Sihanouk were shocked."[79] Normalization was not consummated until November 1991, after Vietnam's 7th Party Congress reshuffled leadership and removed Nguyen Co Thach, and after the final approval of the UN plan for Cambodia at the second session of the Paris Conference on October 23, 1991.[80] In the meantime China had distanced itself from the Khmer Rouge and Hun Sen's rebaptized "State of Cambodia" had distanced itself from Vietnam, and therefore the Sino-Vietnamese relationship was no longer triangulated through Cambodia.

Recall that the period of serious negotiation between China and Vietnam, 1989–91, was also a period of dramatic and profound changes in the communist world. When the vice foreign ministers first met in January 1989, China and Vietnam were two of fourteen communist countries, and the Tiananmen Spring was not even a glimmer on the horizon. When Do Muoi and Vo Van Kiet visited Beijing in November 1991 for the normalization ceremonies, there were many more independent states in the area formerly known as the communist world, but only five of them were still communist. The Chinese and Vietnamese communist parties were thus in similar political situations of

[78] Carlyle Thayer, "Sino-Vietnamese Relations: The Interplay of Ideology and National Interest," *Asian Survey* 34:6 (June 1994), pp. 513–28; Xinhua News Agency, "Nguyen Co Thach Is at It Again," August 28, 1990, in *BBC Summary of World Broadcasts*, August 30, 1990.

[79] Carlyle Thayer, "Sino-Vietnamese Relations," p. 517.

[80] See Xinhua, "China and Vietnam issue joint communiqué," *BBC Summary of World Broadcasts*, November 10, 1991.

anxious conservatism in tension with commitments to continuing economic reform and international openness.

While the situation of remaining communist countries in a post-communist world influenced the articulation of normalization, it would be implausible to argue that China and Vietnam were brought back together by their communist conservatism. First, the actual rhythm of normalization did not match political developments. Second, shared political anxieties did not necessarily make the two countries mutually attractive. Domestic stability was the priority, and Vietnam had little to offer China in this regard, while China's actions at Tiananmen hardly made it attractive to Vietnam.[81] Third, both countries were quite pragmatic in dealing with regime change in the post-communist states as well as in expanding their relations with non-communist states. Thus, while China and Vietnam may have become more similar, what brought them together was a complex process of negotiation.

Both sides could claim "victory" in the resumption of normal relations after thirteen years of hostility. China could claim that it had successfully demanded a Vietnamese withdrawal from Cambodia, and Vietnam could claim that it had stood up to Chinese pressure and had eliminated the Khmer Rouge threat. In fact, normalization was a policy success for both, but only in contrast to thirteen years of hostility. While hostility had emerged from a vicious circle of misperceptions against a background of conflicting illusions of victory, normalization emerged from the sober realization of the limits of one's own capacities and a more realistic appraisal of the threat posed by the other. Vietnam was the first to come to this realization. From 1985 its promise of unilateral withdrawal implied a conditional abandonment of its control of Cambodia, and from 1988 its top policy goal became international openness. China had the luxury of moving more slowly, since the general success of its reform and openness policies did not depend on abandoning the Khmer Rouge. However, China did have to rethink its policy when the United States abandoned the Khmer Rouge, and in 1990–91 it traded the dark satisfactions of *Schadenfreude* for the small but real advantages of normalization.

The Cycle of Systemic Misperception

Sino-Vietnamese relations from 1975 to 1991 present a classic example of the full cycle of systemic misperception resulting from asymmetry. From 1975 to 1979, Vietnam's oversensitivity to China's actions and China's insensivity to Vietnam's security concerns led to a vicious circle of Vietnamese escalation and Chinese bullying, culminating in the border war. The failure of the larger side to dominate the smaller side by a show of military force led to stalemate. The smaller side recognized that stalemate was disadvantageous

---

[81] Although the Vietnamese government closely followed the official Chinese version of Tiananmen, privately Vietnamese officials were shocked by the killings.

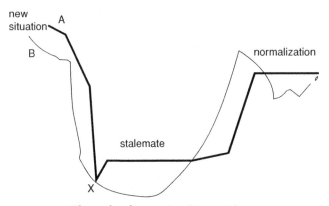

FIGURE 9.1. The cycle of systemic misperception

and changed its policies, and eventually the larger side also agreed to normalization. Normalization is usually rather stable because it is founded on the sobering experience of stalemate. However, normalization, as we shall see in the next chapter, is not a simple situation of friendship.

Figure 9.1 illustrates the general characteristics of the cycle. The cycle begins when a situation is perceived by one or both not to be governed by the routine expectations of the relationship. The line for B is lower than A and more variable because B is usually more suspicious of the relationship than A and adjusts its policies more rapidly and more often. For A, to reorient policy is more of an effort and B is less significant to it, so A's policy changes tend to be less frequent and more abrupt.

The negative complementarity of systemic misperception results in the attempt to resolve the conflict by force (point X). But in most situations, as in our case of China and Vietnam, A cannot simply force its will on B, although it can inflict considerable damage. After the initial attempt to force a resolution, a situation of stalemate emerges in which neither side is able to prevail, but the grounds of negotiation have not yet been restored. B is more at risk than A in hostility and suffers proportionally more damage and deprivation, and therefore has reason to be more emotionally anti-A than A is anti-B. However, because it suffers more from stalemate, it is more likely to begin adjusting its policies to create the grounds for negotiation.

Although stalemate does not serve a positive purpose for A, the situation is stable and B is suffering more. Therefore A is more inclined to continue with stalemate and to enjoy the satisfaction of B's suffering. B's first attempts at negotiation will be gratifying, but it will be harder for A to move from a climate of hostility in the relationship to one based on negotiation. B will vary in its tactics from expressions of its alienation from A to offering more than it really wants to give in order to get A to move. When A does move, B will be faced with new dimensions of vulnerability (for instance, trade imbalance), and therefore will be more cautious and suspicious in the new, normal relationship. By contrast, A will be likely to settle into a climate of cooperation, though with memories and resentments of the recent hostility. Despite the lingering coolness of the normalized relationship and the hesitations of B, neither side is likely to push differences to the point of re-awakening hostility. Both sides have learned from the experience of stalemate that the costs of hostility are greater than the gains. As normalcy continues and develops, it creates its own expectations of negotiation and controlled conflict that make vicious circles of misinterpretation less likely. Thus the situation of normalcy is not simply a return to the starting point of "new situation" and the beginning of a new cycle of an endless series of misunderstandings. To the extent that A and B learn from stalemate, the end situation of normalization is less naive but more stable than the beginning situation.

10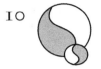

From Normalization to Normalcy

The normalization that China and Vietnam announced in November 1991 was profoundly important. It was a decisive move beyond hostile stalemate. The climate of the official relationships between states and between communist parties changed from a zero-sum confrontation to one emphasizing common ground and cooperation. Practically speaking, however, normalization is a process rather than an event. Gradually the heat of hostility cools down and permits a readjustment of relations, and thus normalization starts from a cold and distant situation in which recent resentments and tensions are pushed out of official view but are not forgotten. The relationship is stable because the alternative of hostility is all too familiar. But it is a new relationship, and each side will be suspicious of the other and will hedge against the other. Bullying and paranoia continue, but under a general flag of truce.

Eventually, however, memories of hostility fade and new challenges are faced together. The economic relationship begins to grow and to displace security concerns in the calculations of both sides. The new bilateral relationship affects the structure of regional relations. The new context of normalization is accepted as a continuing reality, and pursuit of opportunities displaces hedging. Normalization evolves into normalcy.

Normalcy might be called "mature asymmetry" because it is grounded in a learning experience and it has the capacity to be long term and stable. In mature asymmetry, the deference of B to A and A's acknowledgment of B's autonomy become embedded in mutual expectations. Asymmetry continues to affect the relationship, but both sides become practiced in handling the perspective and interests of the other. Only an event that would redefine the situation as novel could create the conditions for a serious crisis.

This chapter describes the passage of Sino-Vietnamese relations from normalization to normalcy and concludes with a general analysis of mature asymmetry. In a sense, the normalization process began in 1985, and formal normalization in 1991 was the midpoint rather than the beginning or end of the process. But new opportunities did begin to open up in 1991, and new problems as well. Vietnam's entry into the Association of Southeast Asian Nations (ASEAN) in 1995 as well as the improvement of relations with Europe and the United States provided an important buffer that could absorb some of the tensions of the bilateral relationship with China. The contrast between China's behavior in the Asian financial crisis of 1997 with that of the United States, Japan, and the international financial organizations helped to transform Southeast Asia's attitude toward China as a rising regional power. Although Vietnam was less affected by the crisis than most of its neighbors, the regional change supported the bilateral trend toward closer relations. The key turn in the Sino-Vietnamese relationship from normalization to normalcy was Party Secretary Le Kha Phieu's visit to China from February 25 to March 3, 1999. The new stage has been marked on the Vietnamese side by the decision in principle to resolve or marginalize remaining sovereignty disputes and to allow and encourage economic relations with China on the same terms as economic relations with other countries. For China's part, it has upgraded its judgment of the importance of its relations with Southeast Asia, and it has been careful to treat the autonomy of Vietnam and Southeast Asia with respect.

Normalization, 1991–1999

The passage from hostile stalemate in 1985 through formal normalization in 1991 to the general acceptance of normalcy by 1999 was a complicated one, even if in general the trend was in the same direction. In the last chapter we saw that China was the slowest participant to respond to the change of context in Cambodia initiated by Prince Norodom Sihanouk's decision to negotiate with Phnom Penh. Meanwhile Vietnam wanted to normalize relations with China, but it did not want to be isolated from other countries. There were speculations in 1990–91 that China and Vietnam might form a close alliance of brother socialist countries, but any such leap from hostility to friendship would have been unrealistic.[1]

It is not surprising that a relationship as novel as normalization with China would engender hopes and fears in Vietnam. The previous non-hostile relationship had been the brotherly intimacy of 1950–75, and few Vietnamese wanted to go back under China's wing. On the other side, China was bitterly

---

[1] When I visited Vietnam shortly before the 7th Party Congress in May 1991 there was considerable anxiety about the impending improvement of relations with China. Alexander Vuving argues that a "red option" of a defensive socialist alliance between China and Vietnam was proposed by Party Secretary Nguyen Van Linh and President Le Duc Anh, but rejected by China. Vuving, "The Two-Headed Grand Strategy: Vietnamese Foreign Policy since *Doi Moi*", paper presented at "Vietnam Update 2004: Strategic and Foreign Relations," Singapore, November 2004. See also Carlyle Thayer, "Sino-Vietnamese Relations: The Interplay of Ideology and National Interest," *Asian Survey* 34:6 (June, 1994), pp. 513–28.

TABLE 10.1. *Normalization*

China	Vietnam
Normalization announced November 1991	
Deng's "Southern Journey" 1992	Vietnam joins ASEAN 1995
	U.S.-Vietnam normalization 1995
	Rail link restored 1996
	Asian financial crisis 1997–98
Deng Xiaoping dies February 19, 1997	
Do Muoi visits Beijing July 1997	
Prime Minister Phan Van Khai visits Beijing October 1998	
Hu Jintao visits Hanoi December 1998	

aware that its earlier sacrifices for Vietnam had not bought permanent friendship and gratitude. According to President Jiang Zemin, the situation of mutual hostility was abnormal, but returning to a condition like that of the 1950s was also not possible.[2] For China, "socialist internationalism" now meant that each socialist country pursued its own interest.[3] Moreover, the new relationship with Vietnam was seen in the context of China's newly normalized relations with the entire Southeast Asian region. Normalization with Vietnam was ranked by the Chinese press as the eighth of the top ten Chinese news stories of 1991, just above the readjustment of grain prices because of bumper harvests.[4] In short, China and Vietnam wanted a new relationship, but not a special one.

For both countries the chief advantage of formal normalization in 1991 was the cessation of hostilities. For Vietnam, this permitted further demobilization of the army and the beginning of reconstruction in border areas. Economic renovation, *doi moi,*[5] had been adopted in 1986, but reform had been hampered by the occupation of Cambodia, international isolation, and hostility with China. With all three obstacles removed, the Vietnamese economy began to grow despite the cessation of Soviet aid in 1990. For China,

---

[2] Jiang as summarized in Guo Ming, ed., *Zhong Yue guanxi yanbian sishi nian* 中越关系演变40年 [The 40-year evolution of Sino-Vietnamese relations] (Nanning: Guangxi Renmin Chubanshe, 1992), p. 221. See also "Chinese, Vietnamese Leaders Announce Normalization of Ties," Xinhua, November 5, 1991.

[3] See the discussion of this in Guo Ming, *Zhong Yuo* pp. 232–61.

[4] "China's Top Ten News Stories Selected," Xinhua, December 27, 1991.

[5] The ideological change involved in *doi moi* is analyzed carefully in Eero Palmujoki, "Ideology and Foreign Policy: Vietnam's Marxist-Leninist Doctrine and Global Change, 1986–96," in Carlyle Thayer and Ramses Amer, eds., *Vietnamese Foreign Policy in Transition* (New York: St. Martin's Press, 1999), pp. 25–43.

ending the hostility with Vietnam meant that it had normal relations along its entire border. Moreover, economic reform in Yunnan and especially in Guangxi had been delayed because these were frontline provinces. Now, after a ten-year delay, these two provinces could join the rest of China in pursuing decentralization. But the most important security effect for China was that hostility toward Vietnam had been the exception to its reform-era foreign policy. Now it could pursue a regional strategy in Asia based on peace and economic cooperation with no exceptions.

The more concrete advantage of economic relations was significant but problematic for Vietnam, and for China it was significant only for the border areas. The sudden availability of Chinese consumer and light industrial goods in the early 1990s transformed the markets of northern Vietnam.[6] From beer to pesticide sprayers, the goods now coming over the border from Guangxi were better and cheaper than local products or imports from elsewhere.[7] But Chinese products brought three acute problems for Vietnam. First, they created a balance of payments problem, since there were few Vietnamese products to sell in return. Most Vietnamese exports to China in the 1990s were raw materials and produce, and Vietnam was concerned about the siphoning off of its natural resources. Sharp increases in the trade deficit led to reductions of trade volume in 1993, 1996, and 1998.[8] Second, the influx of Chinese goods led to the ruin of many local Vietnamese producers of competing goods, and therefore Vietnam tried to protect its industries against Chinese competition. The most significant of these efforts was an import ban on seventeen categories of goods imposed in September 1992 that was reduced to a ban on three categories in April 1993. The list was remarkably broad and clearly aimed at consumer goods from China. It included bicycles and spare parts, electric fans, common lightbulbs, electronic goods, thermos flasks, garments and knitwear, textile fabrics, household items made of porcelain and glass, paper, cosmetics, household plastic goods, and batteries.[9] Third, smuggling was endemic, estimated to be equal in value to official trade. As a result, the import ban was ineffective, and more generally Vietnam has been unable to control border trade.

As Beresford and Phong observe, border trade also had positive structural effects on the Vietnamese economy.[10] Although the Chinese goods did undercut local production, in most cases local production was inadequate

---

[6] Brantly Womack, "Sino-Vietnamese Border Trade: The Edge of Normalization," *Asian Survey* 34:6 (June 1994), pp. 495–512.

[7] For a detailed description, see Melanie Beresford and Dang Phong, *Economic Transition in Vietnam: Trade and Aid in the Demise of a Centrally Planned Economy* (Cheltenham, UK: Edward Elgar, 2000), pp. 130–39.

[8] Gu Xiaosong and Brantly Womack, "Border Cooperation between China and Vietnam in the 1990s," *Asian Survey* 40:6 (December), pp. 1042–58, especially p. 1049.

[9] Vietnam Ministry of Commerce, circular of October 24, 1992, as published in the *Saigon Newsreader*, October 29, 1992, pp. 1–2.

[10] Beresford and Phong, *Economic Transition in Vietnam*, pp. 137–9.

TABLE 10.2. *China's Vietnam trade*

	1992	1995	1997	2003
Amount (U.S.$ billon)	.558*	1.052	1.436	4.639
Share of Chinese total trade	.4%	.37%	.44%	.54%
% of China-Thailand	44%	31%	41%	37%

* Estimated value.
Sources: *China Statistical Yearbook*, 1993, 1996, 1998, 2004.

for demand, and rationing was endemic. Before Chinese beer came pouring over the border, for instance, beer shops all had long queues to buy a single glass, and on a hot day the black market price of a bottle was four times the state price. Chinese goods undercut domestic monopolies, satisfied demand, and stimulated local producers to be more customer-oriented. Moreover, the goods initially sold to China over the border were often agricultural goods and scrap metals. The former brought money to rural producers, and the informality of border trade bypassed the state trading companies. Similar market forces had long been operative in the south, but the border trade gave a special stimulus to private trade and production in the north.

Table 10.2 illustrates the growth of trade between China and Vietnam but also its continued relative insignificance at the national level. At less than half of 1 percent of China's overall trade, official trade with Vietnam in 1997 was at the same level as with South Africa and Switzerland. Trade with Vietnam was considerably more important for the provinces of Guangxi and Yunnan, however, and it transformed the economies of towns and counties on the border.[11]

As one might expect, bilateral investment was not significant in the 1990s. As developing countries and as new fledglings in the Asian flock of economic geese, both China and Vietnam were both heavy and willing recipients of Asian and global investment. Nevertheless, it should be noted that Vietnam was initially quite hesitant concerning even small-scale investment from China, even though Hong Kong and Taiwan were among its top investors. Although Vietnam generally welcomed investment in most sectors, investment from China was the exception. Vietnam's hesitation with regard to Chinese investment was particularly evident in the border area, and development on the China side far outpaced restoration and development on the Vietnamese side. In general, with regard to border development and cooperation in order to facilitate trade, China pushed and Vietnam resisted.

Most of the public conflict between China and Vietnam in the 1990s related to conflicting sovereignty claims. As we have seen, sovereignty claims

---

[11] See Gu Xiaosong and Womack, "Border Cooperation."

were by no means the major issue in the 1970s, but as the other issues faded in the late 1980s, sovereignty conflicts became more evident. The naval incident of March 1988 in which seventy Vietnamese sailors died was the last of the bloody incidents, but it presaged continuing confrontations over the Spratlys, the land border, and claims of territorial waters.[12]

The 1991 normalization agreement prescribed peaceful negotiations as the mode of resolution for territorial problems. Item number 5 of the eleven-point joint communiqué issued on November 10, 1991 states:

> The two sides agreed to continue to take the necessary measures to maintain peace and tranquility along the border and encourage the border inhabitants to restore and develop traditional friendly exchanges so as to turn the Sino-Vietnamese border into a border of peace and friendship. The two sides signed the provisional agreement concerning border affairs. Both sides agreed to settle the boundary and other territorial issues peacefully through negotiations.[13]

Interpreted narrowly as an agreement to avoid military confrontation over disputed territory, both sides abided by the communiqué. However, there was little progress in actually resolving territorial conflicts through negotiation. On the land border there were few new incidents,[14] but Vietnam resisted any border cooperation that involved disputed territory. The most notable case was that of the major railroad between China and Vietnam. Its opening was delayed until 1996 because Vietnam claimed that China had occupied 300 meters of Vietnamese territory.[15]

The disputes that gained world attention involved maritime territorial claims, especially those concerning the Spratly Islands.[16] From the initial confrontation between China and Vietnam in 1988, the Spratlys became the symbol of the threat that China's growing power posed to all of Southeast Asia. In February 1992, three months after normalization, China announced that it had signed an agreement with Crestone Energy Corporation for oil and gas exploration in the area of the Spratlys closest to Vietnam.[17] Vietnam protested and pursued countervailing contracts. By the mid-1990s the Philippines became even more vocal and belligerent than Vietnam in

---

[12] The specific conflicts are detailed in Ramses Amer, "Sino-Vietnamese Relations: Past, Present and Future," in Thayer and Amer, eds., *Vietnamese Foreign Policy*, pp. 68–130.

[13] Xinhua, "China and Vietnam Issue Joint Communiqué," *BBC Summary of World Broadcasts*, November 10, 1991.

[14] The most serious of the border confrontations involved construction that allegedly affected the flow of a boundary stream in a remote area in 1997–98. See Amer, "Sino-Vietnamese Relations," pp. 93–5.

[15] *Ibid.*, pp. 75, 83.

[16] There is a vast literature on the Spratly Islands controversy. See, for instance, the special issue on the Spratlys in the *Asian American Review* 12 (Fall 1994).

[17] See Ramses Amer, *The Sino-Vietnamese Approach to Managing Boundary Disputes* (International Boundaries Research Unit, Maritime Briefing 3:3, 2002), pp. 8–11.

contesting Chinese construction and fishing in the Spratlys, even though the historical claim of the Philippines was weak.[18] There were also confrontations between China and Vietnam in the Tonkin Gulf. In general, the form that "peaceful negotiation" took in maritime disputes in the 1990s was that one party, often but not always China, would take a unilateral action, then a public objection would be raised by the other side, and finally an adjustment would be made in the initial action. While this process was better than war, it was not quite peace.

The most important advance in Sino-Vietnamese relations during the 1990s was indirect. Essential for the normalcy of the bilateral relationship was its inclusion in a matrix of supportive regional relations. With the end of the conflict over Cambodia and Sino-Vietnamese normalization, Southeast Asia had to face the challenge of how to reconstitute itself as a region and how to relate to China. The outcome of each of these problems was by no means obvious in 1991, when, as in the mid-1970s, the conclusion of a major regional conflict gave Southeast Asia the uncomfortable feeling of being in a "vacuum" attractive to larger powers.

During the 1980s the Association of Southeast Asian Nations (ASEAN) had become more cohesive and had been treated with unprecedented respect by the United States and China. However, ASEAN had flourished as an entente against Vietnam, and its future was unclear in an era of peace. If it continued to exclude Vietnam, Cambodia, Laos, and Myanmar, then it would confirm itself as a "Group of Six" relatively well-off states in Southeast Asia rather than becoming an inclusive regional organization. This would have created an awkward division within Southeast Asia and, as a group rather than a regional organization, ASEAN would have found it difficult to remain a focal point and venue for the global relations of Southeast Asia. On the other hand, if it expanded to include the others, the economic and political disparities within ASEAN would be magnified. Unlike NATO or the European Union, ASEAN could not require its new members to meet a high threshold of conformity. Vietnam, Cambodia, Laos, and Myanmar would

---

[18] The claim of the Philippines is based on an assertion that the islands were discovered in 1956 by a Filipino maritime entrepreneur and lawyer, Tomas Cloma, who claimed the islands for himself and called them "Freedomland." By 1971 the Philippines had occupied five of the islands. Cloma was imprisoned by Ferdinand Marcos and forced to cede his private claim to the Philippines on December 4, 1974, for the price of one peso. Marcos renamed them "Kalayaan." Eventually Cloma received the highest military award of the Philippines in 1996, at the age of ninety-one, and he died shortly thereafter. See Lee Lai-to, "The People's Republic of China and the South China Sea," Department of Political Science, the National University of Singapore, Occasional Paper no. 31 (Singapore: Chopmen Enterprises, 1977), pp. 10–11. Also *Asiaweek*, January 5, 1996. Also Venus Olivia Cloma (grandniece of Tomas Cloma), "The Spratly Islands Dispute," http://www.geocities.com/vomcloma/thespratlys.htm.

have to be admitted "as is," or be left outside the gate.[19] Fortunately ASEAN took up the challenge of becoming a truly regional association and admitted Vietnam in 1995, Laos and Myanmar in 1997, and Cambodia in 1999.

The second problem, that of Southeast Asia's relationship with China after the resolution of the Cambodian problem, was at least as difficult. Although China and ASEAN had been informal allies against Vietnam during the 1980s, it was not a close relationship, and China's rapid economic and military growth made that country an implicit threat to the region. In 1979 China's GNP was only two-thirds that of Southeast Asia; by 1993 the economies were roughly equal, and in 2001 China's was roughly half again as large.[20] Even more alarming, China's military budget was already equal to the aggregate military budget of Southeast Asia in 1989 and then began a rapid increase after Tiananmen. Southeast Asia responded in the mid-1990s with a military push of its own, but then fell back because of the Asian financial crisis. By 1999 China's estimated military budget was 167 percent of the region's.[21]

From the perspective of realist international relations theory, Southeast Asian states should have either balanced against China by forming tighter alliances with the United States, or they should have bandwagoned with China as China became more powerful. Instead, Southeast Asia did both. On the one hand, Southeast Asia energetically developed its relations with the United States both as individual states and as a region, and with Japan and Europe as well. The occasional meetings of ASEAN with other dialogue partners became common in the 1990s, and the formation of the security-oriented ASEAN Regional Forum (ARF) in 1995 provided a new venue for extensive security consultations. It is clear that China's growth provided the major incentive for these activities, and the continuing controversy over the Spratlys became the symbol of regional concern about China's power and intentions. But China was not excluded from ASEAN's expanded contacts. In 1990 Indonesia began a series of international workshops under the series title "Managing Conflicts in the South China Sea"; the thirty-two meetings held from 1990 to 1998 helped to develop an "epistemic community" for the management of regional maritime conflicts. After some initial hesitation China became a founding member of ARF, and China became a dialogue partner with ASEAN in 1996.[22] ASEAN had applied its traditional, inclusive

---

[19] See Leszek Buszinski, "ASEAN's New Challenges," *Pacific Affairs* 70:4 (Winter 1997–1998), pp. 555–77.

[20] See Brantly Womack, "China and Southeast Asia: Asymmetry, Leadership and Normalcy," *Pacific Affairs* 76:4 (Winter 2003–4), pp. 529–48.

[21] Calculated from data provided by the Stockholm International Peace Research Institute (SIPRI), http://databases.sipri.se/.

[22] Joseph Y. S. Cheng, "China's ASEAN Policy in the 1990s: Pushing for Regional Multipolarity," *Contemporary Southeast Asia* 21:2 (August 1999), pp. 176–202.

approach of meetings, consensus, and conflict avoidance to the new challenge of a powerful neighbor.[23]

A general reorientation of China's regional politics was essential for the evolution of normalcy in the 1990s. At the highest level, China reevaluated the relative significance of its global and regional relationships after Tiananmen.[24] It appreciated Asia's relative tolerance of its behavior in contrast to the American-led condemnations, and the simultaneous collapse of European communism made the global picture cloudy at best. China developed a theory of multipolarity that both criticized the growing American tendency of unilateral action and promoted international cooperation.[25] The most obvious practical consequence in Asia was the completion of regional normalization. This resulted in normalization of relations with Laos in October 1989, with Indonesia in September 1990, with Singapore in October 1990, with Brunei in September 1991, with Vietnam in November 1991, and with South Korea in August 1992. In conjunction with improving bilateral relations China became more involved with multilateral regional organizations such as ASEAN, Asia Regional Forum (ARF), and Asia Pacific Economic Cooperation (APEC).[26]

China's regional normalization with Southeast Asia, like its bilateral normalization with Vietnam, moved from normalization to normalcy during the 1990s. Initially Southeast Asia was anxious about China's power and suspicious of its motives. China's steady drumroll of official visits and reiterations of its commitments to peaceful coexistence and multipolarity provided background for a gradual change in public attitudes. Shared concerns about American unilateralism were expressed in such common causes as the promotion of "Asian values" and the emphasis on cooperative implementation of human rights concerns embodied in the Bangkok Declaration of April 1993.[27] The rapid development of trade and investment between China and ASEAN warmed the relationship by adding the sunshine of opportunity.

[23] See Alice Ba, *ASEAN's Ways: A Study of the Association of Southeast Asian Nations and the Regional Idea in the Politics of Southeast Asia* (Ph.D. dissertation, University of Virginia, 2000).

[24] See Quansheng Zhao, "Chinese Foreign Policy in the Post-Cold War Era," *World Affairs* 159:3 (Winter 1997), pp. 122–4; Brantly Womack, "China's Southeast Asia Policy: A Success Story for the Third Generation," *Cross-Strait and International Affairs Quarterly* 1:1 (January 2004), pp. 161–84.

[25] See Chen Qimao, "New Approaches in China's Foreign Policy: The Post-Cold War Era," *Asian Survey* 33:3 (March 1993), pp. 237–51; also Brantly Womack, "Asymmetry Theory and China's Concept of Multipolarity," *Journal of Contemporary China* 13:40 (August 2004), pp. 351–66.

[26] See Hongying Wang, "Multilateralism in Chinese Foreign Policy," *Asian Survey* 40:3 (March 2000), pp. 475–91.

[27] The Declaration was a product of the Asia regional preparatory meeting of the UN-sponsored World Conference on Human Rights. Text available at: http://law.hku.hk/lawgovtsociety/ Bangkok%20Declaration.htm.

The Asian financial crisis of 1997–99 became a critical juncture in China's relations with ASEAN. Especially during the first year of the crisis, China's declaration that it would not devalue the renminbi and its support of the Hong Kong dollar showed a commitment to regional stability that was sorely lacking in the International Monetary Fund, the United States, and Japan.[28] The favorable impression created by China's economic diplomacy was crucial because, as Alice Ba has pointed out, the Asian financial crisis led to a dramatic increase in Southeast Asia's asymmetry with China.[29] Not only did China continue to grow, but the crisis stimulated a major shift of foreign investment away from Southeast Asia and toward China. Had China disregarded the interests of Southeast Asia and devalued the renminbi, its relative gains during the crisis would have been attributed to its self-interested action, and the region would have faced the question of how to defend itself from the Chinese economic threat. As it was, China demonstrated both credible political leadership and the strength of its economy, and Southeast Asia could begin to formulate the question of how to protect itself by forming a closer relationship with China.

Vietnam was not as severely affected by the Asian financial crisis as were most of its neighbors. Nevertheless, the change in the regional climate was a prerequisite for Vietnam's own move to normalcy with China. Vietnam's membership in ASEAN from 1995 was of deep significance in relieving its sense of isolation and in decreasing its feeling of vulnerability to China. For Vietnam to move closer to China in isolation would seem more risky than to do it at the same time that neighboring states were doing the same thing, and the framework of China-ASEAN relations provided even more cohesion. As a Vietnamese foreign ministry official explained even before entry into ASEAN, "Sino-Vietnamese relations will be meshed within the much larger regional network of interlocking economic and political interests. It is an arrangement whereby anybody wanting to violate Vietnam's sovereignty would be violating the interest of other countries as well."[30] The peculiar pace of normalization with the United States also helped to foster relations with China. The formal establishment of U.S.-Vietnam relations in 1995 decreased Vietnam's global isolation, while the slow pace of the subsequent exchange of ambassadors and of trade discussions must have discouraged

---

[28] Perhaps the best example of the attitude of the "Washington Consensus" is the speech by Michel Camdessus, Director General of the International Monetary Fund, at the UN General Assembly on October 31, 1997, "The Asian Financial Crisis and the Opportunities of Globalization." For Japan's role see Wimonkan Kosumas, *Half a Hegemon: Japan's Leadership in Southeast Asia* (Ph.D. dissertation, University of Virginia, 2000).

[29] Alice Ba, "Sino-ASEAN Relations: The Significance of an ASEAN-China Free Trade Area," in T. J. Cheng, Jacques deLisle, and Deborah Brown, eds., *China under the Fourth Generation Leadership: Opportunities, Dangers, and Dilemmas* (Singapore: World Scientific Press, 2005).

[30] Nguyen Hong Thach, quoted in Thayer, "Sino-Vietnamese Relations," p. 528.

those who thought of ties with the United States as an alternative to ties with China.[31]

The key area signaling the move to normalcy was the transition in sovereignty disputes from peaceful contention to problem containment. Although the remaining land border problems, the demarcation of the Gulf of Tonkin, and control of the Paracels and Spratlys were important concrete issues, even more important for the confirmation of a normal relationship was the shift in attitude. In a relationship that is peaceful but also cold, distant, and suspicious, the border and its demarcation are the constant test of the relationship. Public outrage over alleged violations is proof to the other side and to domestic audiences that peace does not mean surrender. However, as the normalcy of the relationship comes to be accepted, then sovereignty disputes lose their trip-wire function. The task then becomes how to contain the disputes so that the credibility of both sides is maintained and yet the whole relationship is not inconvenienced by the remaining differences. In contrast to the transition from hostility to normalization, when Vietnam took the lead because it had the most to gain, in the move from normalization to normalcy Vietnam was the more hesitant player, because it felt more at risk.

The shift in sovereignty disputes was a long process and not without its tense moments. Its most important aim was dispute containment rather than a complete solution. The process began with a visit by Vietnam Communist Party Secretary Do Muoi to Beijing on July 14–18, 1997. He discussed territorial issues with Jiang Zemin and both agreed that disagreements over the land border and the Gulf of Tonkin should be settled "at an early date."[32] Unofficially, they agreed to sign the relevant documents by 2000.[33]

Despite the "agreement to agree," disputes and minor crises continued both on the land border and in maritime areas into 1998. The determination to settle the boundary issues and the Tonkin Gulf differences by 2000 was publicly announced during Prime Minister Phan Van Khai's visit to Beijing in October 1998. During Vice President Hu Jintao's visit to Hanoi in December, the formula shifted to settling the boundary issues "before 2000" and the

---

[31] See Bui Thanh Son, "Vietnam-U.S. Relations and Vietnam's Foreign Policy," in Thayer and Amer, eds., *Vietnamese Foreign Policy*, pp. 202–14.

[32] Amer, *The Sino-Vietnamese Approach*, pp. 21–2.

[33] See the later statement by Le Kha Phieu, "Party Leader Views Results of China Visit; Border Issue "Discrepancies" Narrowed," Voice of Vietnam, March 2, 1999, in *BBC Summary of World Broadcasts*, March 4, 1999. Japanese media quoted Foreign Minister Cam that "It can be understood that those two problems must be settled in the year 2000 at the latest." *BBC Summary of World Broadcasts*, July 21, 1997. However, the *Beijing Review* article reporting the 1997 meeting merely expressed the hope that the disputes would be settled "soon" and conveyed Qian Qichen's comment that "China is ready to resolve the issue of demarcation of land borders as well as sea borders in the Beibu Gulf," *Beijing Review* 30 (August 4, 1997).

Tonkin Gulf issue "not later than" 2000.[34] These meetings were precursors to a visit to Beijing of Party Secretary Le Kha Phieu on February 25–March 3, 1999, twenty years after China's border attack.

Le Kha Phieu viewed his summit meeting with Jiang Zemin as the consummation of Do Muoi's 1997 summit, and further as the continuation of the process begun by the (now publicly acknowledged) secret summit of September 1990.[35] In its general summary of relations between China and Vietnam, China's Ministry of Foreign Affairs agreed with Phieu:

> During the official and goodwill visit to China of Le Kha Phieu, General Secretary of the Central Committee of the Communist Party of Vietnam, the General Secretaries of the two parties defined the framework for further developing the relations towards the new century between the two countries, namely to build long-term, stable, future-oriented and all-round cooperative relations, which marked a new stage of development of the bilateral relations between China and Vietnam.[36]

Despite the importance attached by both sides to the meeting, the concrete results appeared limited, and perhaps for that reason it attracted little international media attention.

The results of the meeting were twofold. First, a "16 Word Guideline" was adopted for guiding Sino-Vietnamese relations in the future: "long-term, stable, future-oriented, good-neighborly and all-round cooperative relations" [Changqi wending, mianxiang weilai, mulin youhao, quanmian hezuo, 长期稳定, 面向未来, 睦邻友好, 全面合作 *Láng giềng hữu nghị, hợp tác toàn diện, ổn định lâu dài, hướng tới tương lai*]. Friendly as the Guideline is, it is worth noting that the order of the terms is different in Chinese and Vietnamese. The Vietnamese version lists good neighborliness first, followed by cooperation, stability, and future orientation. Even normalcy has its different perspectives and priorities.

Second, the signing of the border treaty was now scheduled to coincide with the national days of both countries, that is, by September or October 1999. As it turned out, the treaty was not even ready by the time of Premier Zhu Rongji's visit to Hanoi in early December, and was finally signed by the respective foreign ministers on December 30.

The "16 Word Guideline" has been recited at every subsequent summit meeting. It was referred to as "the line for the two countries' relations in the 21st century" at the summit between President Tran Duc Luong and President Jiang Zemin in December 2000. At that summit, a "Joint Statement for Comprehensive Cooperation" was adopted that paralleled the Joint

---

[34] Amer, *The Sino-Vietnamese Approach*, p. 26.
[35] The most extensive report on Phieu's attitude toward the meeting and its accomplishments is Le Kha Phieu, "Party Leader Views Results of China Visit."
[36] Ministry of Foreign Affairs of the People's Republic of China, *China and Vietnam* (revised April 2003).

Communiqué on normalization of November 1991 in spelling out the expectations of normalcy.

The non-spectacular summit meeting between Le Kha Phieu and Jiang Zemin was an appropriate beginning for an era of normalcy. Normalcy is the opposite of war in its processes as well as in its content. It does not have a clear and exciting beginning. It is marked by the adjustment of both parties to an ongoing and stable framework for the relationship. The "16 Word Guideline" puts it quite well: "long-term," not limited in intent to a stage in the relationship; "stable," routinization of problem solving; "future-oriented," setting aside the potentially explosive issues of history; "good-neighborly," expectation of openness and cooperation in interactions; "all-round cooperative relations," comprehensive interactions rather than restricted or arms-length relations. Nevertheless, normalcy is not nirvana. Problems are expected to continue, and crises will emerge. But both sides commit themselves to the expectation that the mutual benefit of the relationship outweighs its negative consequences and that differences can be handled within a peaceful framework.

The evolution from normalization in 1991 to normalcy by 1999 involved the development of patterns of management for stable asymmetric relations. First, normalization restored the framework of formal diplomatic relations. A pattern of annual summit meetings was established in 1991 and the meetings became more frequent from 1999. Besides the summit meetings, exchange visits were encouraged at every level. In 2000 more than 300 official visits occurred, of which 100 were at the vice ministerial level or above. Second, the rhetoric of normalization, that of peace and respect for sovereignty, was an inclusive rhetoric. The "16 Word Guideline" presents this rhetoric at its simplest, but in general official discourse from 1991 on did not force one side into a discourse that was favorable to the other. Rhetoric, of course, is not reality, and China and Vietnam were quite competitive in many of their interactions, especially concerning the Spratlys.

Third, there were increasingly successful attempts to contain, neutralize, and resolve areas of disagreement. In my opinion China deserves special credit for not reacting to various Vietnamese defensive measures such as the 1992 goods embargo. If China had engaged in a tit-for-tat counter-embargo, the progress of cross-border relations would have been retarded. Even in areas of conflict where resolution is unlikely, such as the Paracel and Spratly disputes, progress was made in containing and neutralizing points of conflict. Joint expert discussions on territorial issues began in October 1992, and official talks began in August 1993, leading to a preliminary agreement on principles for managing the land border and Tonkin Gulf disputes in October.[37] Moreover, in conjunction with the workshops sponsored by Indonesia and

---

[37] Amer, *The Sino-Vietnamese Approach*, pp. 36–58.

other regional and international activities, an epistemic community of expertise has developed regarding South China Sea issues.

Last, as normalization continued, China and Vietnam developed new expectations of each other's likely behavior in crisis. After the bloody conflict in the Spratlys in 1988, both sides must have been prepared for the worst. But after subsequent confrontations did not lead to escalation and bloodshed, the expectations of both sides gradually changed. A new "common sense" of the relationship developed in which hostile escalation now appeared unlikely.

Beyond these developments in the four areas of the management of bilateral asymmetry, the relationship of China and Vietnam was greatly facilitated by improving relations of both to ASEAN and its component nations. Vietnam's membership in ASEAN from 1995 brought it into the institutions of Southeast Asia for the first time, and the success of China's regional diplomacy provided an encouraging context for the improvement of bilateral relations. In the new context of Southeast Asia, normalcy was normal.

Normalcy

If we compare the content of the communiqué on normalization of 1991 to the Joint Statement on Comprehensive Cooperation nine years later, it is clear that the relationship between China and Vietnam had become thicker and closer, and that a new norm of mutual expectations had evolved.

The key points of the 1991 agreement were the establishment of normalization, the commitment to promoting cooperation, and the pledge to avoid armed conflict in remaining disputes. In 2000, the Joint Statement includes such provisions as "to imbue the young generations of the two countries with the traditional friendship by increasing the exchange of friendly visits between them, thus helping enhance mutual trust and friendship and hand down the long-standing bonds, trust and cooperation between the two countries to the future generations." The article on cooperation is broken down into nine subdivisions that cover a full range of economic and other activities, and Article 5 provides for "multi-level military exchanges." The discussion of remaining differences emphasizes that they should be handled properly "in order not to allow disputes to impede the normal development of bilateral ties" (Table 10.3).

The 2000 Joint Statement did not contradict the 1991 normalization communiqué, but there are two fundamental differences between them. First, the communiqué defined the rules for a distant and limited relationship, while the later document facilitates a close and comprehensive relationship, and clearly expects it to become even thicker. Second, the communiqué defined a new context of behavior, peaceful cooperation, while the Sino-Vietnamese relationship in 2000 was already in the midst of the evolution made possible by the communiqué. In the later document, the whole problem area of

TABLE 10.3. *Normalcy*

China	Vietnam
Le Kha Phieu visits China February–March 1999, "16 Word Guideline" issued	
Zhu Rongji visits Hanoi December 1999	
Land Border Treaty signed December 30, 1999	
Joint Statement on Comprehensive Cooperation December 2000	
Tonkin Gulf Agreement December 2000	
Hu Jintao named Party Secretary November 2003	Nong Duc Manh named Party Secretary April 2001
Agreement on Conduct in South China Sea November 2002	
ASEAN-China Free Trade Area 2002	
China accedes to ASEAN Treaty of Amity October 2003	
China launches manned spacecraft October 2003	

conflicting sovereignty can be put to the side of the relationship because of confidence in the mainstream of cooperation. The Joint Statement promotes comprehensive cooperation because both sides have experienced improving relations for nine years and are expecting a stable, peaceful relationship. Normalization has succeeded.

The first test of success in establishing a new era is leadership succession. Le Kha Phieu was considered a conservative, pro-China party secretary, and so his somewhat premature replacement by Nong Duc Manh at the 9th Party Congress in April 2001 led some to expect a distancing from China. However, the first words of the new party secretary regarding China policy were reassuring:

Now as before Viet Nam will do its best to consolidate and develop the Vietnamese-Chinese traditional friendship and cooperation on the principle of building long-term, stable, future-oriented, good-neighborly and all-round cooperative ties in the 21st century for the benefit of each nation as well as for peace, stability and development in the region and the world at large.[38]

This repetition of the "16 Word Guideline" by the new leader confirmed the policy initiated by Le Kha Phieu as a general commitment rather than the personal preference of one leader. Manh made his first official visit to China in December 2001 and reaffirmed continuity, and the first boundary stone of the new border was laid in the same month. As far as leadership succession in China is concerned, there is no reason for worry in the

---

[38] Vietnam News Agency, April 23, 2001.

leadership succession from Jiang Zemin to Hu Jintao. Hu has been rather closely involved with Vietnam since 1999, and he led the Chinese delegation to the 9th Congress of the Vietnam Communist Party. In fact, it was to Hu Jintao that Manh addressed the reassurance quoted earlier. Hu had made similar friendly remarks, also incorporating the "16 Word Guideline," in interviews at the beginning of the Congress.[39]

The establishment of normalcy does not mean the end of serious disagreements, but it does shift the context of disagreement from public (but peaceful) confrontation to negotiation out of the spotlight, and it favors the resolution of as many issues as possible. The best examples are the territorial disputes: the land border, maritime rights in the Gulf of Tonkin, the Spratlys, and the Paracels.

Officially, the problem of the land border was resolved by the Treaty on the Land Border signed on December 30, 1999. However, the delay of the signing to the penultimate day of the promised year of 1999 is a symptom of hard bargaining behind the scenes over remaining differences. Moreover, the text of the treaty was not immediately available, and the process of placing the eighty-eight boundary markers is expected to last until 2005.[40] These facts reflect in part the technical difficulties of allocating the contested border areas. These stretch over 450 kilometers of the 1,350 kilometer border, comprising 227 square kilometers. Ultimately 114 square kilometers went to China and 113 to Vietnam.[41] The disputed 300 meters that had delayed the opening of the railroad through Friendship Gate for five years was settled in a similar fashion, with the border being marked 148 meters north of the line originally claimed by China. The even splitting of the differences reflects the sensitivity of relinquishing even relatively minor territorial claims, and there were protests within both countries that each government had yielded too much.

Since the Tonkin Gulf disputes involved maritime zones of control rather than land they were somewhat easier to resolve, at least in principle, and the Tonkin Gulf Agreement signed on December 25, 2000, provides the coordinates for exclusive economic zones and maritime boundaries. The Tonkin Gulf Fishing Accord, signed the same day, not only delineates exclusive and common fishing areas but also stresses sustainability of fishing by limiting the number of boats and amount of harvest in common areas. Nevertheless, regardless of governmental agreements, fishermen, smugglers and the

---

[39] Vietnam News Agency, April 19, 2001.

[40] The first marker was planted with great ceremony at Mong Cai-Dongxing on December 27, 2001. The fourth was planted at Lao Cai-Hekou on April 11, 2003. At the rate of three markers per year, the process would be complete in 2031 rather than in 2005. Vietnam News Agency, April 11, 2003.

[41] A very useful and detailed account of the problems and process of border demarcation is provided by an interview with Deputy Foreign Minister Le Cong Phung, in Vietnam News Agency, September 14, 2002.

exigencies of foul weather do not always respect invisible lines of control, and boat seizures have continued in the Gulf.

The multilateral nature of the Spratly Islands dispute takes some of the pressure off the bilateral relationship. Disagreements and minor confrontations occur among all parties, not simply between China and Vietnam or between China and the rest. Although so many overlapping claims make resolution virtually impossible, the complexity also implies that the negative consequences of unilateral action will undoubtedly exceed the possible gains. Therefore the situation of stalemate may well be permanent, and the most likely breakthrough would be a series of multilateral agreements on cooperative utilization. In the meantime, a code of conduct covering all parties is the most effective way to prevent and contain potential confrontations. The Declaration on the Conduct of Parties in the South China Sea signed by China and the ASEAN countries in Phnom Penh in November 2002 is a major accomplishment in this regard.[42] Two major provisions of the agreement are commitments to refrain from occupying presently uninhabited features and to cooperate and provide prior notification before engaging in scientific or other activities. These address two of the major sources of tension during the 1990s. The declaration is a prerequisite for future cooperative activity but it is a long way from providing a platform for cooperation.

Last, the dispute over the Paracels is usually overshadowed by the Spratlys because it is only bilateral, and therefore there are not as many interested parties or as many occasions for confrontation. Here the commitments of China and Vietnam to avoid conflict leave China in possession of territory also claimed by Vietnam. There is no cooperative solution that would be advantageous to China, since it already controls the territory, and there is no obvious compromise or trade-off that could induce Vietnam to give up its frustrated claim. Since there is no likelihood of confrontation beyond verbal differences, the Paracels dispute is likely to remain a cyst in the relationship, not endangering the rest of the relationship but lingering for Vietnam as a symbol of victimization by China.

Generally speaking, mutual reassurance on security matters has been the dominant feature of normalcy. As Carlyle Thayer observed in an overview of Vietnamese military diplomacy, China is second only to Laos in the number of high-level military delegations exchanged with Vietnam from 1990 to 2004.[43] But asymmetry has prevailed – Vietnam's defense minister has visited China four times, with only one return visit from China. More important, reassurance is necessary because of the continuing sensitivity of the security relationship. China is conspicuously absent from Vietnam's list of military

---

[42] Declaration on the Conduct of Parties in the South China Sea, www.aseansec.org/13163.htm.
[43] Carlyle Thayer, "Vietnam's Foreign Relations: The Strategic Defense Dimension," in David Koh, ed., *Vietnam's Strategic and Foreign Relations* (Singapore: Institute of International Relations, 2005).

procurement partnerships.[44] Under the influence of history and geo-politics, Vietnam's security identity is braced against China. Regardless of normalcy, Vietnam sleeps with its China eye open.

Economics has replaced security as the central concern of the normalcy era. Already during Do Muoi's summit meeting of 1997 he complained of the slow pace of development of trade and investment between China and Vietnam. The earlier anxiety about exposing Vietnam's economy to the much greater capacities of the Chinese economy was displaced by a desire to maximize Vietnam's opportunities in its relations with China. In part, the change of heart was due to the real risk of economic disaster evidenced by the Asian financial crisis. In part, it was based on Vietnam's greater confidence in its regional and global position.

Table 10.4 both clarifies the transformation of the economic relationship between China and Vietnam and indicates the continuing importance of asymmetry. Vietnam's imports from China in 1999 and 2001 still show the restrictive influence of Vietnam's balance of trade deficit. The trade pattern of the 1990s was one in which trade and the deficit would expand and then the following year they would fall back. But a major difference in recent years is that Vietnam's exports are rising fast.

Clearly the most rapidly rising Vietnamese export to China is crude oil. In 1998 China was not considered even a major prospect for oil sales by Vietnam, but by 2001 China was a major customer, buying over one-fifth of Vietnam's oil exports. The reason for the change lies in part in China's increased demand for oil, which has led in turn to a diversification of its oil sourcing. In 2000–02 China's crude oil imports from Vietnam have run at roughly 10 percent of its imports from the Middle East. Even though Vietnamese oil cannot possibly replace oil from the Middle East, the fact that it can be covered by an existing trade surplus (and thereby encourage more trade) is a plus for China, and Vietnamese oil is less susceptible to regional and global conflicts. But importing oil from Vietnam is only one of a number of policy initiatives aimed at broadening and stabilizing China's oil import base.[45]

From Vietnam's point of view, having China as a solid customer for 20 percent of its oil is convenient because of the reduction in transportation costs, but the greatest utility is that China is the best and cheapest supplier of so many consumer and light industrial goods, and oil revenues can help pay for the imports. As the 1990s demonstrated, when Vietnam is

---

[44] *Ibid.*

[45] The most important initiatives involve Kazakhstan and Russia. China is also a major purchaser of Indonesian oil, but Indonesia may become a net oil importer by 2015, and Malaysia in 2010. However, Southeast Asia will become a more important source of natural gas. Li Wei 李玮, "Zhongguo shiyou anquan zhong de dongnanya yinsu 中国石油安全中的东南亚因素," [The Southeast Asian element in China's petroleum security], *Dongnanya zongheng* 东南亚纵横 : 10 (October), pp. 19–23.

TABLE 10.4. *Sino-Vietnamese trade in the normalcy era*

	1998			1999			2000			2001		
	TOTAL	V to Ch	Ch to V	TOTAL	V to Ch	Ch to V	TOTAL	V to Ch	Ch to V	TOTAL	V to Ch	Ch to V
Vietnam's China Trade												
amount (million U.S.$)	955.1	440.1	515	1419.5	746.4	673.1	2937.5	1536.4	1401.1	3047.2	1418.1	1629.1
% annual increase				48.6%	69.6%	30.7%	106.9%	105.8%	108.2%	3.7%	−7.7%	16.3%
% total	4.6%	4.7%	4.5%	6.1%	6.5%	5.7%	9.8%	10.6%	9.0%	9.8%	9.4%	10.1%
% oil					6.3%			48.9%			53.3%	
% total oil exports					8.0%			20.5%			19.8%	
Trade Rank	5	6	7	5	3	5	3	2	5	3	2	5
China's Vietnam Trade												
amount (million U.S.$)	1245.7	217.4	1028.3	1218.2	354.3	863.9	2466.4	929.2	1537.3	2815.2	1010.8	1804.5
% annual increase				−2.2%	63.0%	−16.0%	102.5%	162.3%	78.0%	14.1%	8.8%	17.4%
% total	0.4%	0.2%	0.6%	0.3%	0.2%	0.4%	0.5%	0.4%	0.6%	0.6%	0.4%	0.7%
% total oil imports								4.6%			5.6%	
% of Thai trade	33.9%	17.3%	42.6%	28.9%	24.7%	31.1%	37.2%	41.4%	35.1%	39.9%	43.2%	38.3%
Trade Rank	30	24	38	31	26	40	30	22	34	29	22	32

V to Ch, Vietnam to China; Ch to V, China to Vietnam.

Sources: Calculated from *China Statistical Yearbook 2000, 2002*, various reports from World Bank, Xinhua, and Vietnam News Agency. The difference in trade statistics reflects the discrepancy in the official data for China and Vietnam.

cash-starved and hungry for Chinese goods, smuggling is encouraged. But the long delay in selling oil to China may well be evidence of a sensitivity linked to the Spratlys. The major reason for interest in the Spratlys was the possibility of oil there, and Vietnam's oil is produced from offshore fields on its continental shelf but fairly close to the Spratlys. Confidence in the bilateral relationship had to develop before Vietnam could feel comfortable selling oil to China.

Overall, from 1998 to 2001 total trade between China and Vietnam tripled. Indeed, it had already tripled by 2000, and then 2001 was a year of consolidation. According to Chinese statistics there was another 16 percent increase in trade in 2002. The announced goal of both sides is to reach U.S. $5 billion in total trade by 2005, and with 2003 trade at $4.64 billion, it appears too modest. China now represents 10 percent of Vietnam's trade and is its third-largest trading partner, after Japan and Singapore.[46] Chinese tourism in 2001 was more than ten times its 1995 figure. The 675,700 Chinese visitors were by far the largest national group, comprising 29 percent of all visitors to Vietnam.[47]

China is now important to Vietnam's economic prospects, but Vietnam is not likely to become economically dependent on China. First, Vietnam's trading pattern is diverse. Although trade with China is likely to continue increasing, Chinese goods are unlikely to displace the goods Vietnam imports from Japan and other regional partners, especially since China imports the same goods from them. Second, China's investment in Vietnam is weak. China ranked twenty-sixth among cumulative foreign investors in Vietnam in 1988–2001, behind Canada, Bermuda, and the Bahamas as well as Indonesia, the Philippines, Malaysia, Singapore, and Thailand.[48] China began to encourage external investment only in November 2000, and from 2001 to mid-2003 Chinese firms have invested in 822 projects worth $1.4 billion in Southeast Asia.[49] Given China's domestic capital needs and opportunities, however, China is unlikely to compete with developed countries in profit-driven investment elsewhere, including Vietnam. China has greatly increased its global strategic investment in foreign resource suppliers, but Vietnam is likely to remain a hesitant partner in such ventures. China's foreign aid to Vietnam consists of small amounts of disaster assistance and support for Chinese cultural studies. Last, crude oil, the mainstay of Vietnam's exports to China, is not a niche product. Oil is sold at global market prices and it can easily be diverted from one market to another. It may be convenient

---

[46] Since Vietnam does not yet have operating refineries, it buys much of its petroleum products from Singapore.

[47] Adding visitors from Taiwan would raise the share to 38 percent, explaining the popularity of Chinese language study in Vietnam. See *Nien Giam Thong Ke 2001* (Hanoi: Statistical Publishing House, 2002), p. 381.

[48] *Ibid.*, pp. 336–8.

[49] Xinhua, August 18, 2003.

for both sides to allocate production, but allocation does not involve a restructuring of the industry. Moreover, as Vietnam's refinery capacity rises China might shift to importing refined petroleum products, since it imports a somewhat greater value of these than it does of crude oil.

For China, the increased trade with Vietnam is a positive development, and access to Vietnam's oil is a useful diversification of its sourcing. However, in general the economic effects of normalcy are considerably less significant for China than they are for Vietnam. Because China's world trade continues to rise rapidly, Vietnam's rank as a trading partner has moved only one place in 1999–2001, from thirty to twenty-nine. In 2001 Vietnam was just behind Spain and the United Arab Emirates and just ahead of Mexico and Switzerland. Even with the most optimistic expectations for Sino-Vietnamese economic relations, Vietnam will not reach 1 percent of China's total trade.[50] Trade with Vietnam is considerably more important for the border provinces of Guangxi and Yunnan, but even in these areas the dynamic of China's domestic economy is far more significant than border trade.

In general, the bilateral economic relationship has been transformed since 1999, but its asymmetry has not decreased. The opportunities and risks of the relationship are more acute for Vietnam than for China. But China cannot now dominate Vietnam economically, nor is it likely to be able to in the foreseeable future.

For both China and Vietnam, regional integration has been fundamentally important in framing and stabilizing the bilateral relationship. We have seen in the previous section that Vietnam's entry into ASEAN and China's more active regional initiatives after Tiananmen were important in deepening normalization, and that the Asian financial crisis was the catalyst for a regional shift in attitude toward China. In a world in which global institutions and the United States were indifferent to the vulnerabilities of smaller states, and a world that was dividing itself into the powerful trading blocs of the North American Free Trade Association (NAFTA) and the European Union, leaving the rest on the outside, Southeast Asia had to work together and look for opportunities specific to its situation. Clearly, China was such an opportunity. Moreover, as China entered the World Trade Organization (WTO) in 2002, Southeast Asia ran the risk of losing its opportunity.

Again, ASEAN rose to the challenge. In 1997 the "ASEAN +3 (China, Japan, South Korea)" framework of consultation and cooperation was initiated, and it was confirmed by the Joint Statement on East Asian Cooperation in November 1999.[51] Providing advice on regional cooperation was the East

---

[50] If Sino-Vietnamese trade had achieved its 2005 target of U.S. $5 billion already in 2001, it would still be slightly less than 1 percent of China's total trade.

[51] In the current context of ASEAN discussion, "East Asia" refers to East and Southeast Asia, with the cloudy areas of North Korea, Taiwan, and East Timor, since their governments are not participants in the consultation.

Asia Vision Group, formed of eminent intellectuals from ASEAN, China, Japan, and Korea, which made its report to the ASEAN Summit of 2001 and recommended the goals of establishing an East Asia Free Trade Area and an East Asia Summit. The East Asia Study Group (EASG) was then formed, consisting of officials from all concerned countries and tasked with assessing the recommendations of the Vision Group and the feasibility of an East Asia Summit.

The EASG report was delivered at the Phnom Penh Summit in November 2002. It made twenty-six specific recommendations, including, in the medium and long term, the creation of an East Asian Free Trade Area and an East Asian Summit. The latter would evolve out of cooperative measures undertaken in the ASEAN + 3 framework. It argued that "East Asian cooperation is both inevitable and necessary, that the deeper integration of an East Asian community is beneficial and desirable, and that such integration in East Asia will evolve over time."[52] However, it noted "concerns that ASEAN may be marginalized if the transition towards an East Asian Summit moves too fast."[53]

In contrast to the broad vistas but cautious pace of the EASG initiatives, the China-ASEAN Free Trade Area (CAFTA) agreed on at the Phnom Penh Summit was quite detailed. The World Bank has called it "the most significant" of the various preferential trade agreements under discussion in East Asia.[54] It would create a free trade area with a population of 1.7 billion and a collective GDP of U.S. $2 trillion, half that of Japan.[55] Not only did the process of implementation start in 2003, but there is a special set of policies called "Early Harvest" that create a fast track for mutually beneficial adjustments ahead of schedule. In October 2003 China and Thailand eliminated tariffs on 200 farm products, and beginning in 2004 China eliminated tariffs on 500 types of agricultural products from the six original ASEAN members.[56] Vietnam plans to join the Early Harvest program by 2008 and has already cut tariffs on agricultural produce bound for China.[57] However, given the similarities of the Chinese and Vietnamese economies, some Vietnamese economists expect that CAFTA will be more significant for more advanced ASEAN economies.[58] CAFTA is scheduled to be in full

---

[52] *Final Report of the East Asia Study Group* (Phnom Penh: ASEAN +3 Summit, November 4, 2002), p. 5.

[53] *Ibid.*

[54] Kathie Krumm and Homi Karas, eds., *East Asia Integrates: A Trade Policy Agenda for Shared Growth* (Washington: World Bank, Advance Edition June 6, 2003), p. 79. World Bank lists thirty-six preferential trading proposals affecting East Asia. *Ibid.*, p. 83.

[55] *Ibid.*, p. 79. It is noted that at current rates, the growth of CAFTA would equal Japan in five to ten years.

[56] "Asian Integration Process Picking Up Speed," Xinhua, December 25, 2003.

[57] "Vietnam to Cut Tariffs on Exports to China," Xinhua, November 27, 2003.

[58] Do Tien Sam [杜进森], "Zhongguo-Dongmeng ziyou maoyiqu beijing xia de Yue Zhong jingji hezuo zhanwang" 中国东盟自由贸易区背景下的越中经济合作展望, [The Influence of

effect in 2010, with the less-developed Southeast Asian countries on board by 2015.

The report that was the basis of the proposal is a lengthy and sober economic analysis of the effects of China's membership in the WTO on ASEAN and the possible consequences of a CAFTA.[59] The conclusion of its economic modeling is that CAFTA would greatly increase China-ASEAN trade, significantly increase their GDP growth, but with some displacement of trade with the rest of the world.[60] In some respects the most interesting parts of the report are the national reports separately prepared by economists from ASEAN's member states. These show a full awareness of the problems of competing with China in trade and in attracting foreign investment, but ultimately they conclude that their own competitiveness will be strengthened by integration.[61] Although the World Bank considers China's entry into the World Trade Organization the biggest event in East Asia since the Asian financial crisis in 1997, for ASEAN the CAFTA may well be more important.[62] It would be risky for ASEAN simply to sit next to China on the global market shelf, but it would be advantageous to be part of an East Asian cluster with China.

On the security front, not only did China and ASEAN address the major confrontational issue by adopting the Declaration on the Conduct of Parties in the South China Sea in 2002, but in 2003 China started a trend of non-ASEAN members acceding to the Treaty of Amity and Cooperation in Southeast Asia (TAC). TAC amounts to, in the words of a leading Chinese expert on Southeast Asia writing in *China Daily*, "joining a mutual non-aggression treaty."[63] India and Japan also acceded to the treaty in 2003. Thus the regional context of Sino-Vietnamese relations has been completely transformed in the course of little more than a decade.

The general situation created by normalcy is one in which the deferential cooperation of ASEAN and Vietnam will play an important role in China's international self-concept, and an important role in China's international economy. For ASEAN and especially for Vietnam, China has become the keystone in a pattern of regional relations that represents very serious strategic expectations of mutual cooperative interaction. Normalcy does not imply harmony, but only the embedded assumption that differences will be negotiable and will be less significant than the relationship as a whole. It is by no means an exclusive relationship. Indeed, neither the bilateral relationship

CAFTA on Prospects for Sino-Vietnamese Economic Cooperation], *Dongnanya Zongheng* 东南亚纵横 [Around Southeast Asia] 7 (July 2004), pp. 1–4.

[59] *Forging Closer ASEAN-China Relations in the Twenty-First Century* (2001), prepared for ASEAN by the ASEAN-China Expert Group on Economic Cooperation. Available at www.aseansec.org.

[60] *Ibid.*, Annex 2, pp. 150–2.

[61] See, for instance, Vietnam's national report by Tran Dong Phuong, in *ibid.*, pp. 134–44.

[62] See Krumm and Karas, *East Asia Integrates*, p. 2.

[63] Zhang Xizhen, "Treaty Develops Relations with ASEAN," *China Daily*, September 8, 2003.

of China and Vietnam nor the regional relationship between China and ASEAN would be conceivable if they were not buffered by healthy relations with other countries. China proved itself in the 1990s not to be a jealous partner, and this was a precondition of closer relations.

It is reasonable to expect that normalcy between China and Vietnam will be "long-term" and "stable," as promised in the "16 Word Guideline." However, it may be too optimistic to expect, in Le Kha Phieu's words, "an eternal neighborly and friendly relationship."[64] But the relationship should be able to weather any storm as long as the crises do not redefine the relationship as a "new" relationship, one not governed by the embedded expectations of a successful past.

Mature Asymmetry

The experience of China and Vietnam in the process of normalization and the establishment of normalcy may not be typical of every relationship of mature asymmetry, but at a minimum it does demonstrate features that are compatible with a stable asymmetric relationship.

Most simply, normalization does not mean surrender, and normalcy does not mean domination, or even alliance. What both China and Vietnam yielded in their transition from hostility to normalization was their expectation of victory over the other. Normalization is indeed the opposite of one side prevailing over the other; normalcy is a *modus vivendi*, not a *modus dominandi*.

China is more powerful than Vietnam, in the sense of having greater capabilities, and the disparity of capabilities shapes the difference of interests in the relationship. But normalcy is a negotiated relationship, not an imposed one. Negotiation implies different interests and perspectives – if there were a pre-existing harmony, negotiation would not be necessary. Successful negotiation implies that a consensus is reached on a resolution that is not necessarily identical to the interests and perspective of either side, so yielding and accommodation are involved. But the outcome of negotiation must be consensual. A coercive act by either side would challenge the basis of normalcy.

Mature asymmetry can involve alliance, but the cases of China and Vietnam, and of China and ASEAN demonstrate that the relationship need not be exclusive or directed against other states. Indeed, we have seen that in terms of both security and economics the asymmetry of the relationship was more tolerable to the smaller side because it could be buffered by relationships with other states. Superficially, the external activities might seem similar to the balancing of smaller states against larger ones in order to maintain a "balance of power," but this is not a case of "balancing against," but rather "balancing with." The efforts of Vietnam to join WTO or to improve

[64] Voice of Vietnam, March 2, 1999, in BBC *Summary of World Broadcasts*, March 4, 1999.

ties to the United States, or ASEAN's efforts to establish an East Asia Summit that would include Japan and South Korea as well as China are neither actions against China, nor actions against China's interests, nor actions that China itself would disapprove of or would not engage in. The enmeshment of a bilateral asymmetric relationship in a larger matrix of relations does not neutralize the asymmetry or weaken the relationship, but it lessens the sense of risk of the smaller side and, ironically, permits a more intimate bilateral participation.

The key to a stable asymmetric relationship is the larger side's expectation of deference and the smaller side's expectation of autonomy. Deference is partly rhetorical and symbolic. It is probably not an accident that the major summit meetings between China and Vietnam occurred in China, though China reciprocates with numerous high-level visits to Vietnam. Vietnam's ideological style has returned to paralleling China, beginning with the commitment to "Marxism-Leninism and the Thought of Ho Chi Minh" at the 7th Party Congress in 1991. The essence of deference, however, is the confident expectation on the part of the larger side that the smaller will act in accordance with the realities of the asymmetric relationship. Conversely, precisely because of the asymmetry of the relationship, the smaller side must have the confident expectation that its autonomy and its interests will be respected. Autonomy and deference are not simple matters of well-defined commitments by each side but rather expectations with frontiers of ambiguity. The habits of inattention on one side and overattention on the other persist, but conflict is at the fringe of a solid relationship. As conflicts become more serious, both sides expect the other to dampen escalation and to negotiate.

The most basic reason for the emergence of mature asymmetric relationships is that previous attempts to dominate or eliminate one another have failed, and a situation of stalemate emerged. Stalemate is not desirable for either side, though it is usually more acutely inconvenient for the smaller side. Normalization is the process of changing the climate of the relationship from hostility to peace, and normalcy is the end stage of the process. Of course, stalemate is not the only possible result of conflict. One side can be eliminated, as in the case of the indigenous inhabitants in most of the Americas, or one side can be defeated and its organization destroyed, as in the case of many colonization efforts, including the French in Vietnam. But these are not normal cases in the modern world. Moreover, even the defeat of one side does not mean that domination will be long-lasting, stable, or worth the continuing and increasing effort. After all, the French eventually left Vietnam and now enjoy a normal relationship with their former colony. The reason that peaceful, negotiated relationships are the norm is not only that peace is morally preferable to war and that the economic advantages of peace are attractive, but that war often has unintended consequences and disappointing results. Mature asymmetric relationships are often founded on the painful experience of this truth.

Given that mature asymmetry is more often the result of sober experience with the alternative rather than mutual benevolence, it is not surprising that there are continuing and also novel problems of asymmetry in a normal relationship. A normal relationship is closer than a cold or hostile one and involves more transactions on many different dimensions, and many of these transactions are affected by differences in capacity. If we consider a normal bilateral relationship such as that between the United States and Canada, for instance, there are some issues that pose acute problems for Canada and yet are peripheral to the United States, such as timber and fisheries. In many cases, Canada's greater attentiveness has enabled it to be more adroit and quite successful in negotiations.[65] But even Canada has to be careful and deferential in its confrontations with the United States.

Lastly, asymmetric bilateral relationships form regional patterns of relations that add to the stability of the individual dyad. Even if ASEAN did not exist, the similarity of Sino-Vietnamese relations to Sino-Thai, Sino-Lao, and so forth creates a common context in which the other interrelations within the region will be formed. An existing regional pattern would strengthen the expectations of continuity in each of its component relationships. If we add to the regional pattern of stable bilateral relations a multilateral organization of the smaller states such as ASEAN that can negotiate with the larger power on a more equal footing, then each participant has a greater confidence in its autonomy. At the most general level of global relations, membership in the United Nations and in other world institutions based on sovereignty provides ultimate assurance of autonomy. Under the general assurance of autonomy, a complex matrix of particular relationships can emerge.

---

[65] See Robert Keohane and Joseph Nye, *Power and Interdependence* (Boston: Little, Brown, 1977), ch. 7.

Change and Structure in Asymmetry

Three Kingdoms, the first Chinese novel and part of the cultural heritage of both China and Vietnam, begins with the famous lines, "The empire, long divided, must unite; long united, must divide. Thus it has ever been."[1] Our review of the vicissitudes of the relationship between China and Vietnam could yield the same conclusion concerning asymmetric relations. The relationship has experienced an impressive variety of forms. Given the changes in the past, one must ask whether the present age of normalcy is the final resting place of the relationship or merely the most recent phase.

Of course, reviewing the grand sweep of history can cause a loss of existential perspective. If normalcy lasts only as long as French colonialism in Vietnam, it would frame the life experience of three generations. If it lasts as long as the phase of traditional unequal empires, then it would end when the millennium that we are now beginning has grown old. Moreover, although normalcy does not resolve the tensions inherent in asymmetry, it also does not have an obvious internal contradiction that would shorten its span. It would be far more reasonable to predict, as Alexander Woodside did in 1979, that a period of hostility would lead to a mutually frustrating stalemate and thence to a (relatively) early normalization.[2] If we are to try to gauge when "mature asymmetry" might pass into old age and death, we will have to locate an aging process or to analyze what factors might cause it to have a fatal accident.

In order to cope with such problems we must address questions of change and structure in asymmetric relations. In Chapter 4 we considered the patterns of interests, perception, and management of asymmetric relations, and this model of the process of asymmetric interaction was used in the

---

[1] Luo Guanzhong, tr. Moss Roberts, *Three Kingdoms*, 4 vols (Beijing: Foreign Languages Press, 1995), vol. 1, p. 1.
[2] Alexander Woodside, "Nationalism and Poverty in the Breakdown of Sino-Vietnamese Relations," *Pacific Affairs* 52:3 (Autumn 1979), pp. 381–409.

subsequent chapters. In this chapter we will begin with a general consideration of the variety of asymmetric relations, and then consider their deep
structure. Finally, we will return to the task of analyzing the factors that
might affect the current era of Sino-Vietnamese normalcy (Table 11.1).

Varieties of Asymmetry

The first task is to summarize and generalize the variety of asymmetric relations that we have seen in the history of China and Vietnam. This is necessary
in order to enrich asymmetry theory, but it is also a necessary precondition
to considering structural characteristics that are not parts of the process of
interaction but rather are valid for all phases and that condition the transition
from one to another.

Although the Sino-Vietnamese relationship does not exhaust the range of
possible asymmetric relationships, it has covered a variety that is amazing for
a single relationship. Moreover, these are not abstract modalities created by
rotating the variables in a theoretical model; they are historical experiences.
Here we will define each phase, recall the characteristics of the phase in the
Sino-Vietnamese relationship, and then consider possible analogues from the
experiences of other states.

We will follow the historical stages of Sino-Vietnamese modalities of
asymmetry, but their sequence should not be mistaken for a necessary path.
Although some paths might seem more natural than others – for instance,
to move from internal asymmetry to a more independent stage – there are
certainly instances of developments in the opposite direction. The counter-
instances would include not only cases of one state incorporating another, but
also the evolution of voluntary associations of states into larger sovereignties. The unifications of Italy and Germany are good examples of the latter,
while Yugoslavia and Czechoslovakia provide examples of movements in
both directions in the twentieth century.

Amorphous asymmetry relies on the judgment of the observer, because
the two regions are not self-constituted as political communities but rather
are externally defined. This does not make "amorphous asymmetry" a subjective category. The geographic contiguity and capacities are real, but the
observer must argue for a latent relationship rather than point to a self-
conscious interaction. With China and Vietnam in the pre-Qin period, we
must ask ourselves whether we are actually dealing with the pre-history of
a relationship, one that would be meaningless if China and Vietnam did not
congeal as political communities later on, or a stage that is meaningful in
itself.

I think amorphous asymmetry is a useful category as a heuristic device for
imagining possible geographical sets of interest. It is similar to the analysis
of economic classes in cases where the ascribed class status is not (yet) self-
conscious for its members. For example, the American mountainous area of

TABLE II.I. *Varieties of Sino-Vietnamese asymmetry*

	Type	Definition	China and Vietnam	Other Examples
I	Amorphous	Between regions that are not organized as political communities	Before the Qin unification of China and the incorporation of Vietnam into China	Appalachia and Atlantic coastal, urban America
2	Internal	Between a central government and an organized part, or between two parts	Vietnam as part of China, AD44–967	Texas and United States; Lyon and Paris
3	Subjugated	Between a dominant unit and a distinct subordinate community	Ming occupation, 1407–27 French Indochina, 1883–1954	Colonies and occupied territories; United States in Iraq
4	Role	Between autonomous units arranged in an explicit structure of superiority and inferiority	China and Vietnam after the failure of the Ming occupation, 1427–1858	Most feudal systems that impose a hierarchy but presume that the nobility controls its domains
5	Disjunctive	Between units so disparate in values and political culture that collision is the major form of contact	Opium War in China, French in Vietnam	United States and Native Americans; the western Mongol empire (Ilkhanate)
6	Distracted	Between units, both of whom have other, more important relations to worry about	China and Vietnam from 1840 to 1950	Thailand and Cambodia in colonial period
7	Dependent	One unit does not have a feasible alternative to compliance with the preferences of the other; a kind of systemic duress	Vietnam 1950–75	United States and Japan
8	Hostile	Between units that are perceived as denying minimal levels of autonomy or deference to the other	China and Vietnam 1975–91	United States and Cuba
9	Normalized	Between units confident of the acknowledgment of their basic interests by the other and in which the management of the relationship is institutionalized	Normalization 1991–	United States and Canada

Appalachia is in an asymmetric relationship with the urban Atlantic coast, and one could imagine an analysis of the mutual interaction in terms of asymmetry even though neither region exists as a political entity and each would have to be defined by the observer. As with the analysis of "non-conscious" classes, there is the danger that the ascribed latent reality will be taken to be the "true reality," and society as it actually exists and interacts will be described in terms of "false consciousness"[3] or "artificial boundaries." Nevertheless, current reality hardly exhausts its own possibilities, and the hypothetical redrawing of social and political maps can highlight patterns that are plausible not only to external observers but might even appear valid to the proposed inhabitants as well.

Internal asymmetry is less dependent on the observer, but it is not at the level of international relations. It is an especially useful modality because it broadens the scope of analysis to include relations that are not even hypothetically between states. Internal asymmetry can exist between a national government and an organized part, or between two asymmetric parts. In the case of China and Vietnam from the defeat of the Trung sisters in AD 44 to independence in 967, it is important to avoid the retrospective anachronisms of "China occupying Vietnam" or "China in control of Vietnam"; at this time Vietnam was part of China. Nevertheless, there was certainly an asymmetric relationship between the two, and it led eventually to the formation of a local self-consciousness and a local elite that was separatist.

One could analyze the relationships of internal asymmetry in terms of center and periphery, but I think that the introduction of questions of disparity of scale and capacities and the consequent differences of perspective give a richer and more appropriate texture to the analysis.[4] Moreover, there are many non-state asymmetric relationships – especially among asymmetric parts – that do not fit a center-periphery pattern. The relationship of Texas to the United States might appear to be center-periphery, but the relationship of Texas to Oklahoma is also asymmetric, as is the relationship of Fort Worth to Dallas. Even though these are not international relations, they are not metaphorical applications of asymmetry because the units actually do interact with one another and the interactions and mutual attitudes show evidence of asymmetric effects. It is even possible to analyze asymmetry between units that are not geographical, for instance, between a provincial police department and the national police.[5] Of course, interaction between

---

[3] The term *false consciousness* [falsches Klassenbewußtsein] was originally introduced by the Hungarian activist and scholar Georg Lukacs in *Geschichte und Klassenbewußtsein* (Berlin: Malik, 1923).

[4] See Edward Shils, *Center and Periphery: Essays in Macro Sociology* (Chicago: University of Chicago Press, 1975).

[5] I gave a talk on international asymmetry to the FBI Academy, and afterward some participants pointed out that they saw the same traits in the relationship between the FBI and the state police.

sovereign states is quite different, but attention to the difference specifies the salience of sovereignty in asymmetric relations.

Subjugated asymmetry involves the use of the superior capacities of the stronger state to dominate and control the weaker. Subjugation is difficult to maintain because it implies the application of a constant and credible threat of compulsion against the weaker population. While the stronger side is likely to realize some benefit from domination and may imagine that it is providing some service to the weaker by "civilizing" it, it is rare that the motivation to dominate is as intense as the desire to be free of subjugation. Weaker armies may be defeated and weaker regimes destroyed, but if a population views itself as a repressed political community it will strive to be free.

The dilemma of subjugation is that the exercise of force by the stronger underlines the difference between itself and the weaker. Even a population without an army and without organized leadership will use the "weapons of the weak" to resist and to frustrate alien masters.[6] Unless the difference in capacity is vast indeed, or the indigenous population is rendered insignificant by extermination or the settlement of colonists, the resistance to subjugation will increase to the point that domination becomes more trouble than it is worth for the stronger, and a dialectic of compromise and consolidation ensues. Liberation does not require that the subjugated become stronger than the dominators but rather that the effort of domination exceeds its rewards. Thus there is often a sense among the dominators of the inevitability of retreat, well expressed by Rudyard Kipling, the poet laureate of imperialism:

> Far-called, our navies melt away;
> On dune and headland sinks the fire;
> Lo, all our pomp of yesterday
> Is one with Nineveh and Tyre![7]

In the cases of Vietnam and Ming China or Vietnam and France, subjugation ended with an acknowledgment of Vietnam's autonomy. However, another path would be the incorporation of the subjugated unit into the more powerful state. In the decolonization debates of the twentieth century this path was called "romanization," after the Emperor Caracalla's decision in AD 212 to grant Roman citizenship to all freemen within the Roman Empire.[8] France and Portugal were leading exponents of this approach. However, the twin problems in incorporating subjugated territory are that subjugation produces alienation and that asymmetry continues to generate differences of interest and perception. In the case of Portugal, for example,

[6] James Scott, *The Weapons of the Weak: Everyday Forms of Peasant Resistance* (New Haven: Yale University Press, 1985).

[7] Rudyard Kipling, "Recessional" (1899). Nineveh and Tyre were the capitals of the defunct Assyrian and Phoenician empires, respectively.

[8] Adam Watson, *The Limits of Independence* (New York: Routledge, 1997), pp. 58–9.

the difficulties of sustaining the fiction that Angola and Mozambique were overseas territories led to the alienation and radicalization of the Portuguese army and eventually to the overthrow of the post-Salazar regime by the army in 1974.

Role asymmetry exists between autonomous units arranged in an explicit structure of superiority and inferiority. It characterizes the entire period of Sino-Vietnamese relations from 967 to 1885, but the clearest example is the period after the Ming occupation until the arrival of the French. It is a pattern based on the inequality of the units and on the acceptance of the different roles of superior and inferior. Despite the inequality, the framework of role asymmetry does provide for the autonomy of the weaker state as well as for deference to the stronger, and thus it meets the minimum requirements of both and can be sustained by mutual – though different – interests.

Role asymmetry stabilizes expectations in asymmetric relations, and this is a fundamental contribution. However, it assumes that the relationship is a distant one, and it does not encourage a closer or thicker relationship. The relationship must be distant because the ruler of the weaker country must acknowledge his inferiority in the capital of the stronger, but he must maintain his authority in his own capital. We have described the various subterfuges that Vietnamese rulers used to disguise their relationship to Beijing. If CNN-TV had existed in the eighteenth century, the Vietnamese emperor would have experienced considerable embarrassment to have his obeisance to the Chinese emperor televised to his subjects at home. Of course, it would have caused even more embarrassment to Beijing to see pictures of the Vietnamese emperor in Hanoi and to realize that they were entertaining an impostor. Moreover, role asymmetry replaces the open discussion of international problems with a cumbersome process of petitions and decisions. Last, it is a relationship between rulers rather than between states, and it does not encourage the development of economic and societal contacts beyond the exchange of tribute gifts.[9]

Feudalism provides many examples of role asymmetry, and the largest feudal systems, such as the Holy Roman Empire, provide the best examples because of the greater autonomy of the parts from the suzerain. In the modern world the presumption of sovereign equality makes explicit role asymmetry impossible. There are, however, patterns of international interaction that informally resemble roles, for instance, the British affinity for American leadership since the Suez crisis in 1956. Once a pattern of deference and autonomy is established, it naturally develops characteristic habits of expression and interaction, and both sides find satisfaction in affirming the relationship. This is often called "bandwagoning," but the weaker state

---

[9] The ideology and ritual of China's tribute practice is well described by James Hevia, *Cherishing Men from Afar* (Durham: Duke University Press, 1995).

is not necessarily picking sides in a great power conflict, nor is it simply submitting voluntarily to whatever the stronger decides.[10] Although one could make the case that *disjunctive asymmetry* existed between Vietnam and early Han China and led to the revolt of the Trung sisters, the best example that we have considered is the relationship between Vietnam and France. If the values and political culture of political communities have nothing in common, then their mutual perspectives not only will differ according to the scale of their disparities, but also there will be no common ground for understanding or empathy. There is not necessarily a lack of mutual information, but there is no foundation for the credibility presumed by negotiation. Contact is reduced to collision, and the larger side usually wins, at least initially.

Despite the tendency of disjunctive asymmetry to result in subjugation, the two should be distinguished. After all, the Ming subjugation of Vietnam was not disjunctive, and neither were Napoleon's conquests in Europe. Moreover, the wars encouraged by disjunction do not have to be wars of conquest. John Owen's thesis that regimes of similar types are less likely to go to war than dissimilar regimes expresses the same basic idea as disjunctive asymmetry.[11] In contrast to Samuel Huntington's "clash of civilizations," however, it should be noted that contact is a learning process, even when it involves collisions and subjugation.[12] In the process of French colonization, not only did Vietnam learn about France, but France learned about Vietnam. The historical personalities of each were shaped by the encounter. Perhaps the best example of a disjunctive asymmetric encounter morphing into a unique blend would be the course of the Mongol empire, which especially in Persia followed initial destruction with a transformative blend of cultures.[13]

Distracted asymmetry occurs when both sides of an asymmetric relationship have to confront more important relationships. China and Vietnam were both distracted by their encounters with the West, and as a result they stood for the first time shoulder to shoulder in their relationship facing others. Asymmetry does not cease to be relevant in such a situation; China and Vietnam remained big and little brothers. But the relationship as a whole moved from the center of attention, and it could be utilized to serve common, other-directed interests. The Chinese and Vietnamese communists were

---

[10] Kenneth Waltz, *Theory of International Politics* (New York: McGraw-Hill, 1979), pp. 125–7.

[11] John Owen, "Transnational Liberalism and U.S. Primacy," *International Security* 26:3 (Winter 2001–2002), pp. 117–52.

[12] Samuel P. Huntington, *The Clash of Civilizations and the Remaking of World Order* (New York: Simon and Schuster, 1996).

[13] For the Ilkhanate in Persia, see Linda Komaroff and Stephano Carboni, eds., *The Legacy of Genghis Khan: Courtly Art and Culture in Western Asia, 1256–1353* (New Haven: Yale University Press, 2002).

truly "tongzhi" [同志, tong chi, comrades, "sharing a common will"]; they could be intimate friends because they themselves were not one another's major problem.

An extreme example of distracted asymmetry was the relationship between Thailand and Cambodia during the colonial period. Until the arrival of the French, Thailand and Vietnam were fighting over the carving up of Cambodia and Laos. With the arrival of France, Thailand suddenly faced a more powerful opponent, and it had to negotiate its own freedom of action between the British in Burma and the French in Indochina. Bangkok became the seat of various Southeast Asian independence groups, and its border with Cambodia became the locus of various Khmer political movements from the 1940s to 1991.

It is a common observation that the Cold War's bipolarity suppressed regional conflicts and these returned to prominence in the post–Cold War period. The Sino-Vietnamese experience suggests that we should examine more closely the modality of the regional asymmetric relations in times of distraction. The distracted relationship does not go into hibernation. The presence of a greater, common problem can produce unique opportunities for cooperation.

We considered two forms of *dependent asymmetry* in Chapter 8: the DRV (North Vietnam) in its relation to China, and South Vietnam in its relation to the United States. In both cases, the weaker side was under the duress of not having a feasible alternative to compliance with the stronger side. This situation pre-empted real negotiation and put the apparent discretion in managing the relationship in the hands of the stronger partner. The crucial difference was that China respected the autonomy of the DRV, while the United States used its leverage to control South Vietnamese policy and personnel. South Vietnam was a "bad puppet," but it was not allowed to be a disobedient one. By contrast, sharp differences of opinion arose between China and the DRV, and the DRV defied China's preferences and was not punished.

As the results of the American war in Vietnam suggest, the discretion enjoyed by the stronger partner is only apparent. If the stronger utilizes the dependence of the weaker to maximize its preferences, then it is implicitly subjugating the weaker. The subjugation appears voluntary, but only because the weaker side faces a greater threat. Domination by the stronger of its partner pre-empts the autonomy and legitimacy of its partner, and it is thus hardly surprising that the United States was dragged into a quagmire of increasingly direct involvement in Vietnam. Of course, the divergence of priorities between Beijing and Hanoi also created suppressed resentment and alienation, especially after 1964. But the autonomy of the DRV was not called into question by its relationship to China.

The post-war relationship of the United States and Japan could be considered one of dependent asymmetry. Although the relationship does not have the sharp external focus that the Vietnamese examples have, the presence of the American security umbrella and the radical dependence of the Japanese economy on world resources create a situation in which Japan has had no feasible alternative to compliance with American strategic priorities. In contrast to its relationship with Saigon, the United States has respected Japanese autonomy. However, there is also evidence of the systemic duress inherent in dependent asymmetry. Japan's foreign policy even with third countries must be articulated within the constraints of American foreign policy; it can discreetly push the edges of the envelope, but it cannot openly confront the United States. The reason that "Japan cannot say no" is not primarily cultural - it was not a shy country before 1945 – but that dependence creates inhibitions.

Hostile asymmetry occurs when one or both sides are perceived as denying minimal levels of autonomy or deference to the other. As this definition suggests, hostility is almost always blamed on the other side. Thus it is not surprising that both China and Vietnam in 1979 produced long and detailed accounts of the relationship in which the other side was the malevolent actor. The negative complementarity of the bullying of the stronger and paranoia of the weaker was described in Chapter 4, and the resulting stalemate and possibility of normalization was covered in Chapter 9. Mutual misperception is the engine of the "down cycle" of hostility, while stalemate, the inability of either side to achieve its objectives, is the precondition for the "up cycle" of normalization.

As the example of the United States and Cuba suggests, there is no necessary progression from stalemate to normalization. The stronger is not threatened by hostility, merely inconvenienced, whereas the weaker side is much more aware of threat. Therefore the stronger side can enjoy the suffering of the weaker – *Schadenfreude* – and not feel compelled to move beyond stalemate even though it derives no positive benefit from hostility. The weaker side is in a more acute dilemma, but the sense of national crisis can strengthen popular support. In itself, therefore, stalemate is not unstable. The general motive to move beyond stalemate stems from its lack of positive benefit and the dwindling expectation that continued hostility can achieve its original aims.

Normalized asymmetry does not imply a completely harmonious relationship but rather a stable one based on the general expectation of mutual benefit. Normalcy presupposes a mutually satisfactory framework for cooperation and negotiation, and that implies in turn the acknowledgment by the stronger side of the autonomy of the weaker side and deference of the weaker toward the stronger regarding the real disparity of capacities. Unlike role asymmetry, normalized asymmetry presupposes the formal equality of states. In contrast to role asymmetry's fiction of the generosity of the superior and the suppliant gratitude of the inferior, normalized asymmetry creates the contrary fiction of two equal sides at the negotiating table.

Since normalized asymmetry is expected to encourage cooperation and mutually beneficial contact, the venues for negotiation provided by formal sovereign equality are essential for the management and development of the relationship. The major purpose of role asymmetry was to avoid conflict by securing an international order; normalized asymmetry aims at maximizing individual benefit within a framework of encouraging mutual benefit. The states must coordinate their regulatory roles and be able to articulate their differences. Greater interaction requires more explicit institutionalization of mechanisms for neutralizing areas of potential conflict and reaffirming the solidity of the relationship.[14] Nevertheless, asymmetry will continue to engender differences of interest and perspective. Normalized asymmetry does not function by pre-empting asymmetric differences, but by managing their consequences.

Both role asymmetry and normalized asymmetry can be termed *mature* asymmetries for two reasons. First, as in the case of China and Vietnam, they often result from prior experience of the futility of conflict. As relational stages based on the sober experience of the alternative to peace, they can be considered more mature. Second, although role asymmetry and normalized asymmetry do not "solve the problem" of asymmetry, they both provide for its management. The relationship is not fragile. The longer a peaceful relationship continues, the more stable it is likely to be. But the problem remains of different interests, differently perceived.

China and Vietnam have lived up to their promise of providing a broad spectrum of varieties of asymmetry. Nevertheless, there are other patterns that could be explored. China and Japan, for instance, present an interesting case of countervailing asymmetries of demography and economics. More generally, I expect that the detailed exploration of European and inter-American relationships could yield not only confirmations of some of the patterns we have discussed but also additional variations. Also to be explored are problems specific to asymmetries of different capacities (demographic, economic, and military as separate disparities, for instance) and of the salience of the scale of disparity. By concentrating on one dyad, we have held constant many of such factors. Nevertheless, the variety displayed by the Sino-Vietnamese throughout its history certainly demonstrates that asymmetry merits careful study.

Asymmetry's Deep Structure

Despite the variety of asymmetric relationships, asymmetry itself is not a situation of dynamic disequilibrium. China hasn't become smaller, and Vietnam larger, nor has either disappeared, despite the efforts of the Ming dynasty. The long-term coexistence of large and small states demonstrates a certain

---

[14] The mechanisms of management are detailed in Chapter 4.

underlying stability in asymmetry. What we now seek to understand is how the modalities of the relationship persist and change.

The Sino-Vietnamese experience makes some sequences more plausible than others, but there is no apparent cycle of asymmetric relations. A cycle requires either repetitive regularity or an unchanging underlying dynamic. Variety itself is not proof of a cycle; it merely demonstrates that asymmetry does not always produce the same relationship. Clearly, change is possible with any modality because change has occurred before. But there is no underlying explanation for change, like the source of seasonal changes in the earth's tilted trip around the sun, nor is there a general rhythm or pattern.

It does seem that subjugated and hostile asymmetry are inherently less stable than the others. Subjugation requires the constant threat of force, and the actual resources of stronger states – and their interest in continued subjugation – are usually limited. Likewise, hostile asymmetry is essentially a lose-lose situation, and one might expect states to pursue more beneficial arrangements. There is no inexorable logic that requires a shift to a different relationship, and there are a number of international relations that persist in hostility,[15] but there is the gentle pressure of frustration. Moreover, although the transition from a force-based modality to a mature, mutually beneficial relationship seems quite reasonable, one could well imagine a sequence in which subjugation leads to hostility, or vice versa.

If the situation of asymmetry is not inherently unstable and the modalities of asymmetric relations are not linked in a cycle, then we must examine the factors that sustain and transform modalities. I propose that there are three categories of basic conditioning factors: identity, context, and leadership.

The role of identity is particularly evident in amorphous and internal asymmetry. The lack of formed communities in amorphous asymmetry prevents interaction. The lack of separate identities in internal asymmetry creates a tension between the localism of the part and the broader interests and greater power of the center. But beyond these obvious cases, the integrity and continuity of the identity of the political communities is always a sustaining factor. The disintegration of China between the Tang and the Song created the opportunity for Vietnam's independence. The decision of Chinese emperors not to recognize the separatist regimes of the Mac and the Nguyen preserved the Sino-Vietnamese relationship forged after the Ming occupation.

Identity is also interactive with relationships. The challenge of the Mongol invasions led to the elaboration of a Vietnamese cultural identity separate

---

[15] Continuing patterns of bilateral conflict have been awarded the name and acronym "Enduring International Rivalries" (EIR). See Zeev Maoz and Ben Mor, *Bound by Struggle: The Strategic Evolution of Enduring International Rivalries* (Ann Arbor: University of Michigan Press, 2002).

from that of China, and the Ming abandonment of its attempt to subjugate and incorporate Vietnam contributed to a more introverted identity for China. More generally in the modern era, the emergence of revolutionary regimes produced a sharp change in identity that required the reformulation of external relations. France in 1789 and Russia/Soviet Union in 1917 are the most obvious examples. Other massive ideological changes, such as religious conversion, can also produce a change in external identity. The conversion of Shah Ismail (1499–1524), founder of the Safavi Dynasty, to Shi'a Islam transformed Persia's relation with Turkey.[16] The disintegration of a state presents the interrelated problems of the disappearance of a larger, old identity and the emergence of newer, smaller ones, though the original framing of the political community can remain important, as in the case of China during the warlord era. The amalgamation of small states into a new, larger one produces a different and usually more worrisome set of novelties for its neighbors. The founding of the Qin Empire is the obvious case from our study, and more modern examples would be the unifications of Italy and Germany.

The second sustaining factor of asymmetric relations is the broader international context. Distracted asymmetry is defined by the presence of a more pressing external concern, and the reason for dependent asymmetry is often, but not always, a looming third-party threat to the weaker side.[17] But whether or not external context poses a focused, major problem, it is always an essential element in the stability or change of relational modalities. In the case of China and Vietnam, one reason that this relationship presents such an archetypal case of a long-term asymmetric relationship is that there were no major distractions until the arrival of the French.

Globalization has created a sea change in the role of context in international relations. The importance of economic interaction has risen to the point that economic security requires continued and increasing integration with the rest of the world rather than defensive isolation. New vulnerabilities and frictions are created, and demographic asymmetries can be dwarfed by economic asymmetries, but the rest of the world is very much more present to any bilateral relation than was the case two hundred or even twenty-five years ago. At the time of their hostility in 1979, neither China nor Vietnam was a part of an important and sensitive fabric of international economic relations that could be stressed or torn by conflict. Now they are. Globalization

---

[16] Rouhollah Ramazani, *The Foreign Policy of Iran, 1500–1941* (Charlottesville: University of Virginia Press, 1966).

[17] In the case of small, underdeveloped states, economic and even diplomatic security might require a dependent relationship with a larger state. This is particularly evident in former colonies, but also occurs regardless of previous colonial relationships (Haiti and Panama, for instance). See Robert Jackson, *Quasi-States: Sovereignty, International Relations and the Third World* (New York: Cambridge University Press, 1990).

does not preclude war but it profoundly affects its reverberations and therefore its calculus.

The last sustaining factor in asymmetric modalities is leadership. Because
asymmetry is not a problem to be solved but rather a situation to be managed,
the relationship poses constant challenges to the leaderships of both sides. In
some respects the diplomatic relationship is competitive, but in times of peace
both sides also have a common interest in avoiding conflict and promoting
mutually beneficial cooperation. In times of subjugation or hostility, the
chief strategic task of leadership – if, as in most cases, final resolution of the
relationship through force is impossible – is to minimize losses and eventually
to move beyond stalemate.

Because of the interactive sensitivity of asymmetric relations, leadership
is not simply a question of the competent or incompetent execution of set
tasks. Provocative behavior by one side can lead to misinterpretation and
thus escalating behavior on the other side, and that in turn can start a cycle
of negative complementarity. On the positive side, leadership is essential in
creating the atmosphere for peaceful relations and in securing the benefits of
cooperation.

There are many examples of the specific effects of leadership on Sino-
Vietnamese relations. To begin with the positive, Le Loi's expressions of deference toward Beijing after he defeated the Ming occupation was essential for
a smooth transition to a mature role-based autonomy, and Le Thanh Ton's
creative sinification of governance utilized the advantages of the relationship
to China without sacrificing Vietnam's autonomy. More recently, the "Third
Generation" of Chinese leadership has provided remarkably consistent and
successful guidance in the normalization of relations with all of China's
neighbors, including Vietnam.[18] China's regional policy after 1989 was conditioned by the domestic trauma of June 4 and its international repercussions,
but it was not inevitable that China would launch a good neighbor policy.
Good leadership must be appropriate to the situation, and ironically, when
appropriateness is achieved, good leadership looks "natural" or even "easy."
But good leadership is effortless only in the Daoist sense of non-activity [wu
wei无为, vô vi] in following the way, and it is never inevitable.

The most impressive example of the effect of a single leader's action on the
general diplomatic context is Prince Sihanouk's decision to negotiate with
Hun Sen in 1987. At the time of his action, all sides were rather comfortably
settled into a stalemate of isolating but not challenging Vietnam's occupation
of Cambodia. Although Sihanouk's individual action was key to breaking
the logjam of stalemate, actions by both the Chinese and Vietnamese leaderships were essential in creating the opportunity. Sihanouk's action was a
response to Vietnam's 1985 declaration of a unilateral withdrawal by 1990,

[18] Brantly Womack, "China's Southeast Asia Policy: A Success Story for the Third Generation,"
Cross-Strait and International Affairs Quarterly 1:1 (January 2004), pp. 161–84.

and China could have made Sihanouk's decision considerably more difficult by threatening personal sanctions for breaking with China's policy. Even the most noteworthy single actions of leadership require a supporting interactive context in order to be effective.

Negative examples of leadership are not difficult to find in the Sino-Vietnamese relationship. The incompetence and greed of the Han administrator Su Ting led to the uprising of the Trung sisters. The Mongols' insatiable pushing of the margin of their power led to frustration in Vietnam and eventually to the collapse of their dynasty. In the 1960s the radicalism of the Cultural Revolution alienated Vietnam despite increasing Chinese support. More recently, the arrogance of Le Duan contributed significantly to the emergence of a hostile relationship with China.

If correct leadership is important for the stability of asymmetric relations and the possibility of misperception is always present, then how do we explain the long periods of stability in the Sino-Vietnamese relationship? Surely the leadership of neither China nor Vietnam was consistently good from the end of the Ming occupation to the arrival of the French. There are three factors that contribute to the apparent stability of leadership. The first is true only of mature modalities, namely, the previous experience of the frustration and inconvenience of hostility. For instance, it became part of the lore in China that one should avoid fighting in Vietnam, and it became the habit of Vietnamese leadership to avoid antagonizing China. Second, the tribute system was part of the ritual framework of leadership in traditional East Asia, and it included acknowledgment of the legitimacy and autonomy of lesser states as well as their deference to China. Thus each new leader did not have to reinvent the wheel of asymmetric management; he merely had to keep it rolling. Third, the appearance of stability is somewhat misleading. There were minor and major crises in the Sino-Vietnamese relationship, the last and most spectacular being the Chinese invasion of Vietnam in 1788. From a distance and in retrospect things look quieter than they appeared at the time. Nevertheless, the education of each leader by the history of the relationship and his encapsulation in ritual tended to keep the pre-modern individual decision maker within the groove of the established relation.

In both traditional and modern times, a situation perceived as new, one not bound by immediate precedent, put a special burden on the leadership of both countries. Ho Quy Ly's overthrow of the Tran dynasty created a new situation in the eyes of the Ming, as did the Tay Son revolution in 1788. The founding of the People's Republic of China created a new potential of intimacy in the relationship. Most important, the victory of Vietnam in 1975 ended the colonial era in Southeast Asia and the existing structure of Indochina, and at the same time removed the necessity of a dependent asymmetry with China. Unfortunately, a most delicate time in the relationship was perceived as an opportunity to solve the problem of asymmetry. The novel situation of normalization in 1991 was dealt with more soberly and more carefully by the leaderships of both sides.

Challenges to Normalcy

In 1991 there was no doubt on the part of China or Vietnam - or on the part of external observers - that a new phase in the relationship was being launched. At the same time, however, it was generally assumed that the new relationship would be stable and would not fall backward into renewed hostility or fall forward into an intimate alliance. Over the following decade both of these assumptions have proven true. Normalcy is quite different from the intimate dependency of the 1950s, and yet the possibility of a hostile relationship seems even more remote. We conclude our study with a consideration of the factors that sustain normalcy, and then of possible transformations of the factors that might produce new challenges.

First, the most foreseeable aspect of the foreseeable future is that the relationship between China and Vietnam will remain asymmetric. The demographic and economic disparities outlined in Chapter 1 will remain roughly the same regardless of relative rates of growth, or even economic or political disasters. Vietnam cannot aspire to parity with China in overall capacities, neither will it sink into insignificance.

Furthermore, the current era of normalcy is solidly supported by identity, context, and leadership. Identity is not an issue in the current bilateral relationship. Not only is there formal mutual recognition, but the recent experience with hostility confirmed for Vietnam the necessity of peaceful relations with China, and it confirmed for China that Vietnam was beyond its control. The reality of sovereignty is the underlying fact of the relationship.

Context also supports normalcy. The expansion of ASEAN into a regional association including Vietnam has provided reassurance for the Sino-Vietnamese relationship. The other Southeast Asian countries are in the same situation of asymmetry with China, and their regional organization lessens the individual feeling of exposure and vulnerability. Moreover, ASEAN has gained diplomatic respect and recognition from the rest of Asia as well as from the United States and Europe. Instead of balancing against China, ASEAN provides stability to the individual bilateral relations by making them part of a regional and even global texture.

From China's perspective, an even broader supportive context exists. Since 1989 China has been pursuing regional "good neighbor" policies all around its borders. The transformation of relations with Southeast Asia is perhaps the greatest success, but in general China's prestige as a cooperative regional leader has increased. The "Shanghai Five" was formed with Russia and the new Central Asian states in 1996 for fairly narrow, security-related purposes. By 2001 it had expanded into the Shanghai Cooperation Organization, and China's economic involvement in Central Asia is increasing. Similarly, China has played a major integrative role in handling the crisis concerning North

Korea that ballooned in 2002, and it has improved its relations with India in 2003 without losing its long-standing ties to Pakistan. Normalcy with Vietnam thus fits into not just a policy toward Southeast Asia, but into a broad commitment to increasing China's prestige by means of policies of cooperative engagement with neighbors.

The current global international context is also favorable to Sino-Vietnamese normalcy. Both China and Vietnam – and, more discretely, the rest of Asia – are concerned about the implications of America's status as the sole superpower, but generally their policies toward the United States stress engagement and cooperation. American interest in human rights and democratization is seen as intrusive by both. The post-September 11 issue of global terrorism is not a major concern for either country, although China has ongoing problems with ethnic separatists in Xinjiang.

The leaderships of both countries have been very careful in developing the bilateral relationship, and the bilateral relationship is in harmony with the regional and global priorities of both. Although there are elements of private opinion in China resentful of Vietnam, and even broader elements in Vietnam suspicious and fearful of China, neither government has been pushed by domestic forces into a confrontational position. Both have weathered the determination of the land border, which was a sensitive issue for both sides. The venue of the Spratlys controversy appears to have moved to a multilateral framework. The Paracels remain a standing bilateral issue that is unlikely to be resolved, but there is no inherent reason for the disagreement to produce an acute crisis.

There is fundamental ideological resonance between the two leaderships. Most obviously, they are now the world's first- and second-largest communist countries. They stand together against international pressures to change their political systems to multi-party, competitive politics, and meanwhile they are both striving for greater rule of law and accountability within their party-state systems. Second, the commitment to economic reform and international openness is an important shared commitment. Not only do these commitments create a common set of priorities, but they direct diplomatic attention away from zero-sum confrontations and toward mutually beneficial cooperation. Last, the Chinese doctrine of multipolarity, although ambiguous in some important respects, suggests a stable framework of states rather than American domination or an inevitable competition for hegemony. It does not appear likely, therefore, that China's activities as a global actor would upset its bilateral relationship with Vietnam.

Thus Sino-Vietnamese normalcy rests on a solid foundation of identity, context, and leadership. But what are the hypothetical permutations of these foundations, and how might changes in identity, context, and leadership affect normalcy? Although it is as certain as the future can be that the relationship will remain asymmetric, and there are no internal contradictions or impending crises evident in its current foundations, it is worth considering the salience for the relationship of imaginable changes in basic factors.

Essentially, the question is whether a situation can be imagined in which changes would lead to a redefinition of the relationship from one of mature normalcy to a "new" relationship. Of course, this exercise is simply a speculative consideration of the possible effects of hypothetical changes and not in any sense a prediction.

We start with leadership, since it is the most variable of the factors. Since the retirements of Le Duan, Nguyen Co Thach, and Deng Xiaoping, the leaderships of China and Vietnam have not been abrasive or confrontational toward one another. Certainly the return of abrasive leadership is possible hypothetically, and as the leaderships in both countries are more exposed to domestic public opinion they may feel constrained to be more assertive. However, the likely targets of Chinese assertiveness are Taiwan, the United States, and Japan rather than Vietnam. China is a more likely target for Vietnamese assertiveness, though others are also possibilities. In any case, assertiveness is far more likely to lead to minor crises or a temporary cooling of normalcy rather than to a breakdown.

What if currently shared ideological commitments changed? As unlikely as a regime change appears to be in either country, the examples of European communism make the question worth considering. If the political system of one country changed while the other did not, the tone of the relationship might be affected but not the basic normalcy. Both China and Vietnam retained normal relations with the European post-communist states, and indeed Jiang Zemin developed a close relationship with Boris Yeltsin. There would be mutual influences. In my opinion, for Vietnam to become post-communist would not in itself be a crucial influence on Chinese politics, but if China became post-communist it would be surprising if Vietnam remained the world's largest communist country for long. As we have seen in Chapter 3, Vietnam is quite cosmopolitan in its attitudes, and it is more likely than China to respond to international developments. If the domestic politics of both countries were transformed, the presence of so much domestic political novelty might influence international relations, but on the other hand it might also lead to political introversion.

Contextual changes are even less likely than changes in leadership, but if they occurred they might pose more significant challenges for Sino-Vietnamese normalcy. If, for instance, ASEAN collapsed, Vietnam would feel more isolated and more vulnerable in whatever relationship it had with China, and if regional hostilities emerged in Southeast Asia then China might have to choose between normalcy with one country or another, or it might distance itself from conflict by cooling its relations with all hostile parties. A crisis between China and Taiwan would probably not have a direct effect on relations with Vietnam. A hostile relationship between China and Japan would certainly not be welcome in Southeast Asia, but the most likely posture would be regional solidarity and equidistance rather than individual bandwagoning.

The most significant imaginable contextual change would be the emergence of bipolar global hostility between China and the United States. Given the anxieties among American neo-conservatives concerning China's increasing strength and the continuing possibility of confrontation over Taiwan, a zero-sum relationship between the United States and China is impossible to rule out. Global hostility in itself would not have an immediate effect on Vietnam or on Southeast Asia more generally. They would be more secure maintaining normal relations with both. However, it is imaginable that the United States might try to "contain" China by building exclusive relations with Southeast Asian countries. Although some states might respond to American incentives, with the possible exception of the Philippines none would willingly choose sides.[19] However, another possibility would be that China would pressure its neighbors to stand either with it or against it. Faced with such a choice, many would choose the United States because China would be the closer threat. In general, the side that tries to force Vietnam into its camp is likely to lose Vietnam's support because the attempt to force Vietnam's position would be evidence of threat.

The last fundamental factor is identity. As long as China and Vietnam remain unitary actors, identity will support normalcy. But given the history of both states over the past hundred years, the possible effects of national disintegration are worth considering. It is highly unlikely that China would fall apart.[20] If it did so, and did so by provinces, a minimum unit would be the combination of Guangdong, Hong Kong, and Guangxi. The strength of this unit and the uncertainties of internal Chinese turmoil would probably constrain Vietnam to a role of cautious supporter of its neighbor. The possibility of separatist tensions in Vietnam is also unlikely, but perhaps less unlikely. Vietnam's recent history has created regional identities, and these are amplified by geography and the uneven distribution of resources. If changes in the political system allowed regionally based competitive parties to develop, it is possible that southern politicians could make demands that would be unacceptable to the north or to the national government. Some overseas Vietnamese groups might encourage a radically regionalist movement. Such a development is by no means inevitable, even with multi-party politics.

If a confrontation developed in Vietnam between a national government located in the north and radical regionalism, effectively separatism, in the south, both China and ASEAN would be quite concerned. Neither would favor a separatist movement, and if Vietnam's solidarity with China and

---

[19] I do not mean to imply that the Philippines is pro-American, but rather that American pressure could lead to another Marcos era of military rule and that government could become an American client.

[20] This possibility was considered – and largely rejected – in Richard H. Yang, Jason C. Hu, Peter K. H. Yu, and Andrew N. D. Yang, eds., *Chinese Regionalism: Security Dimensions* (Boulder: Westview, 1994).

ASEAN held, it is possible that separatism would fail or would become an ineffective radical current. But the leadership in Vietnam would certainly be dealing with a novel and dangerous situation, and it is possible that a situation could emerge in which southern separatism secured a foothold and other states would have to choose between supporting an established separatist state and supporting the national government's attempt to maintain or to reestablish unity. Given the history of China's relations with Vietnam, it would seem more likely, though not inevitable, that China would support the national government. However, regardless of the decision, a new situation different from normalcy would have been created, and the potential for redefinition and for significant misperceptions would be heightened.

It is important at this point to remind ourselves that we have been engaged in speculations akin to Harry Potter looking into the magician's mirror. The purpose has not been to see around the bend of the future, but to assess the stability of Sino-Vietnamese normalcy if there were hypothetical changes in its foundation.

The overall conclusion is that normalcy is remarkably stable. Not only are its current foundations of leadership, context, and identity quite solid, but imagining variations in these three factors does not produce an inevitable or sudden change. Normalcy's framework for handling asymmetric relations would probably remain sturdy and functional despite more confrontational leadership, and even through major ideological change. Although normalcy is supported by the current regional and global environments, it is not contingent on current multilateral relations. In the event of renewed global bipolarization there might be problems if China leaned on its neighbors, including Vietnam, to choose sides, but bipolarization itself is unlikely to recast the relationship. Successful separatism in either country would of course require a redefinition of the relationship, but the relationship would remain asymmetric.

Despite such optimism, it is well to remember that normalcy does not solve the problem of asymmetry, it merely provides the patterns for managing an asymmetric relationship for mutual benefit. Asymmetry remains a negotiated relationship, and the strength of normalcy is its explicit recognition of this fact. Increased economic, political, and societal interactions have created and will continue to create new common interests, but they also create new frictions. Differences of perception will occur constantly, and the temptation will remain for China to nudge Vietnam into compliance with its wishes, and for Vietnam to react allergically to Chinese pressure and to downplay the reality of China's greater capacities. The capacity of normalcy to neutralize and negotiate differences, and to contain crises through diplomatic ritual and the overall momentum of the relationship, is the secret of its stability. Normalcy is not a smooth road, but rather a sturdy vehicle.

Appendix

Glossary of Terms

English	Vietnamese	汉字	Pinyin
Places			
In China			
China	Trung Quốc	中国	Zhongguo
Beijing	Bắc Kinh	北京	Beijing
Guangdong	Quảng Đông	广东	Guangdong
Guangxi	Quảng Tây	广西	Guangxi
Dongxing	Đông Hưng	东兴市	Dongxing
Nanning	Nam Ninh	南宁市	Nanning
Pingxiang	Bằng Tường	凭祥市	Pingxiang
Yunnan	Vân Nam	云南	Yunnan
Hekou	Hà Khẩu	河口市	Hekou
Chengdu	Thành Đô	成都市	Chengdu
Lingnan	Lĩnh Nam	岑南	Lingnan
In Vietnam			
Vietnam	Việt Nam	越南	Yuenan
Hanoi	Thủ đô Hà Nội	河内首都	Henei shoudu
Ho Chi Minh City	T. P. Hồ Chí Minh	胡志明市	Hu Zhiming shi
Cao Bang	Cao Bằng	高平	Gaoping
Lai Chau	Lai Châu	莱州	Caizhou
Lang Son	Lạng Sơn	谅山	Liangshan
Haiphong	Hải Phòng	海防市	Haifang shi
Quang Ninh	Quảng Ninh	廣寧	Guangning
Mong Cai	Móng Cái	芒街	Mangjie
Thai Binh	Thái Bình	太平	Taiping
Thanh Hoa	Thanh Hoá	清化	Qinghua
Dien Bien Phu	Điện Biên Phủ	奠边府	Dianbianfu
Cam Ranh Bay	Vịnh Cam Ranh	金兰湾	Jinlan wan
Saigon	Sài Gòn	西贡	Xigong

English	Vietnamese	汉字	Pinyin
Historic			
Annam	An Nam	安南	Annan
Nan Yue	Nam Việt	南越	Nan Yue
Champa	Chăm-pa	林邑	Linyi
Co Loa	Cổ Loa	古螺	Guluo
Empire of Vietnam	Đại Việt	大越	Da Yue
Empire of Vietnam	Đại Cồ Việt	大瞿越	Daiju Yue
Funan	Phù Nam	扶南	Funan
Hundred Yue	Bách Việt	百越	bai yue
Jiaozhi	Giao Chỉ	交趾	Jiaozhi
Jiuzhen	Cửu Chân	九真	Jiuzhen
Lac Viet	Lạc Việt	雒越	Luo Yue
Thang Long (Hanoi)	Thăng Long	昇隆, 昇龙	Shenglong
Treaty zone	Tô giới	租界	zu jie
Van Lang	Văn Lang	文郎	Wenlang
Disputed			
Paracel Islands	Hoàng Sa	西沙群岛	Xisha qundao
Spratly Islands	Trường Sa	南沙群岛	Nansha qundao
Elsewhere			
Australia	Ô-xtrây-li-a	澳大利亚	Aodaliya
Burma (Myanmar)	Mi-an-ma	缅甸	Miandian
Rangoon	Răng-gun	仰光	Yangguang
Cambodia	Cam-pu-chia	金埔寨	Jinbuzhai
Phnom Penh	Phnôm-pênh	金边	Jinbian
Europe	Châu Âu	欧洲	Ouzhou
France	Pháp	法国	Faguo
Geneva	Giơ-ne-vơ	日内瓦	Rineiwa
Hong Kong	Hồng Công	香港	Xianggang
Japan	Nhật Bản	日本	Riben
Korea, South	Hàn Quốc	韩国	Hanguo
Korea, North	Triều Tiên	朝鲜	Chaoxian
Laos	Lào	老挝	Laowo
Vientiene	Viêng Chăn	万象	Wanxiang
Malaysia	Ma-lai-xi-a	吗来西亚	Malaixiya
Philippines	Phi-lip-pin	菲律宾	Feilübin
Singapore	Xinh-ga-po	新加坡	Xinjiapo
Thailand	Thái-lan	泰国	Taiguo
Bangkok	Băng-cốc	曼谷	Mangu
United States	Mỹ	美国	Meiguo
Washington	Oa-sinh-tơn	华盛顿	Huashengdun
People			
Chinese			
Chiang Kaishek	Trưởng Giới Thạch	蒋介石	Jiang Jieshi
Deng Xiaoping	Đặng Tiểu Bình	邓小平	Deng Xiaoping

English	Vietnamese	汉字	Pinyin
Dong Zhongshu	Đồng Trọng Thư	董 仲 舒	Dong Zhongshu
Hu Jintao	Hồ Cẩm Đào	胡 进 涛	Hu Jintao
Jiang Zemin	Giang Trạch Dân	江 泽 民	Jiang Zemin
Li Peng	Lý Bằng	李 鹏	Li Peng
Liu Shaoqi	Lưu Thiếu Kỳ	刘 少	Liu Shaoqi
Lu Bode	Lộ Bác Đức	路 博 德	Lu Bode
Ma Yuan	Mã Viện	马 援	Ma Yuan
Mao Zedong	Mao Trạch Đông	毛 泽 东	Mao Zedong
Nong Zhigao	Nùng Trí Cao	儂 智 高	Nong Zhigao
Emperor Qin	Tần Thuỷ Hoàng Đế	秦 始 皇 帝	Qin Shi Huangdi
Ren Yan	Nhâm Diên	任 延	Ren Yan
Sima Qian	Tư Mã Thiên	司 马 迁	Sima Qian
Su Ding	Tô Định	蘇 定	Su Ding
Sun Yatsen	Tôn Dật Tiên	孙 中 山	Sun Zhongshan
Wang Mang	Vương Mãng	王 莽	Wang Mang
Yuan Shikai	Viên Sỹ Khải	院	Yuan Shikai
Zhao Tuo	Triệu Đà	赵 佗	Zhao Tuo
Zhou Enlai	Chu Ân Lai	周 恩 来	Zhou Enlai
Zhu Rongji	Chu Dung Cơ	朱 镕 基	Zhu Rongji
Vietnamese			
King An Duong	An Dương Vương	安 陽	An Yang
Bao Dai	Bảo Đại	保 大	Bao Dai
Dinh Bo Linh	Đinh Bộ Lĩnh	丁 部 领	Ding Buling
Do Muoi	Đỗ Mười	杜 梅	Du Mei
Ho Quy Ly	Hồ Quý Ly	胡 季 縭	Hu Jili
Le Van Huu	Lê Văn Hưu	藜 文 休	Li Wenxiu
Le Duan	Lê Duẩn	黎 笋	Li Sun
Le Duc Anh	Lê Đức Anh	藜 德 英	Li Deying
Le Kha Phieu	Lê Khả Phieu	黎 可 漂	Li Kepiao
Le Loi	Lê Lợi	黎 利	Li Li
Le Thanh Ton	Lê Thánh Tôn	黎 神 宗	Li Shenzong
Ngo Dinh Diem	Ngô Đình Diệm	吴 庭 艳	Wu Tingyan
Nguyen An	Nguyễn An	阮 安	Ruan An
Nguyen Co Thach	Nguyễn Cơ Thạch	阮 基 石	Ruan Jishi
Nguyen Hue	Nguyễn Huệ	阮 攸	Ruan You
Nguyen Khac Vien	Nguyễn Khác Viện	阮 克 员	Ruan Keyuan
Nguyen Trai	Nguyễn Trãi	阮 鹰	Ruan Zhi
Nguyen Van Linh	Nguyễn Văn Linh	阮 文 灵	Ruan Wenling
Nguyen Van Thieu	Nguyễn Văn Thiệu	阮 文 绍	Ruan Wenshao
Nong Duc Manh	Nông Đức Mạnh	农 德 孟	Nong Demeng
Pham Quynh	Phạm Quỳnh	梵 琼	Fan Qiong
Pham Van Dong	Phạm Văn Đồng	范 文 同	Fan Wentong
Phan Boi Chau	Phan Bội Châu	潘 佩 珠	Pan Fengzhu
Phan Van Khai	Phan Văn Khải	潘 文 凯	Fan Wenkai

English	Vietnamese	汉字	Pinyin
Tran Hung Dao	Trần Hưng Đạo	陈兴道	Chen Xingdao
Tran Duc Luong	Trần Đức Lương	陈德良	Chen Deliang
Trung sisters	Hai Bà Trưng	微姐妹	Zheng jiemei
Truong Chinh	Trường Chinh	长征	Chang Zheng
Vo Nguyen Giap	Võ Nguyên Giáp	武元甲	Wu Yuanjia
Vo Van Kiet	Võ Văn Kiệt	武文杰	Wu Wenjie
Terms			
All under heaven	thiên hạ	天下	tianxia
Asymmetry	bất đối xứng	非对称	fei duichen
Chaos	loạn	乱	luan
City people	thị dân	市民	shi min
Domestic dependency	nội phụ	内附	neifu
Ethnic Vietnamese	Kinh	京	Jing
Essence-utility	thể-dụng;	体用	ti-yong
Gulf of Tonkin Incident	Sự kiện Vịnh Bắc Bộ	北部湾事件	Beibu wan shijian
Loose reins policy	cơ mi	羁縻	ji mi
Non-action	vô vi	无为	wu wei
People as root	dân bản	民本	minben
Southern push	nam tiến	南进	nan jin
Tay Son rebellion	Khởi nghĩa Tây Sơn	西山起义	Xishan qiyi
Zhuang	Tráng (Choang)	壮族	Zhuang
Expressions			
"As close as lips and teeth"	gắn bó như môi với răng	唇齿相依	chun chi xiangyi
"Long-term, stable, future-oriented, good-neighborly and all-round cooperative relations"	Láng giềng hữu nghị, hợp tác toàn diện, ổn định lâu dài, hướng tới tương lai	长期稳定, 面向未来, 睦邻友好, 全面合作	Changqi wending, mianxiang weilai, mulin youhao, quanmian hezuo

Bibliography

Books

Anderson, Benedict. *Imagined Communities: Reflections on the Origin and Spread of Nationalism.* London: Verso, 1991.

Asia-Africa Speaks from Bandung, Proceedings from the 1st Non-Aligned Movement Conference. Jakarta: Ministry of Foreign Affairs, 1955.

Ba, Alice. *ASEAN's Ways: A Study on the Association of Southeast Asian Nations and the Regional Idea in the Politics of Southeast Asia.* Ph.D. Dissertation. Charlottesville: University of Virginia, 2000.

Bao, Ninh. *The Sorrow of War* [Than phan cua tinh yeu], tr. Phan, Tanh Hao. New York: Pantheon, 1993.

Barlow, Jeffrey. *The Zhuang: A Longitudinal Study of Their History and Their Culture.* http://mcel.pacificu.edu/as/resources/zhuang.

Bauer, Wolfgang. *China und die Hoffnung auf Glück.* Munich: Carl Hanser Verlag, 1971.

Beresford, Melanie, and Phong, Dang. *Economic Transition in Vietnam: Trade and Aid in the Demise of a Centrally Planned Economy.* Cheltenham, UK: Edward Elgar, 2000.

Blumer, Giovanni. *Die Chinesische Kulturrevolution.* Frankfurt: Europäische Verlagsanstalt, 1968.

Burchett, Wilfred. *The China–Cambodia–Vietnam Triangle.* Chicago: Vanguard Books, 1981.

Buttinger, Joseph. *Vietnam: A Political History.* New York: Praeger, 1968.

Buzan, Barry, and Little, Richard. *International Systems in World History: Remaking the Study of International Relations.* Oxford: Oxford University Press, 2000.

Chanda, Nayan. *Brother Enemy: The War after the War.* New York: Macmillan, 1986.

Central Intelligence Agency. *The World Factbook,* Various years. http://www.odci.gov/cia/publications/factbook. html.

Chan, Anita, and Unger, Jonathan, eds., *Popular Protests in China: Reports from the Provinces.* Armonk: M.E. Sharpe, 1991.

Chang, Pao-min. *Beijing, Hanoi and the Overseas Chinese.* Berkeley: Center for Chinese Studies. China Research Monograph, no. 24, 1982.

Chen, Jian. *China's Road to the Korean War.* New York: Columbia University Press, 1994.

Chen, Jian. *Mao's China and the Cold War.* Chapel Hill: University of North Carolina Press, 2001.

Chen, King. *Vietnam and China 1938–1954.* Princeton: Princeton University Press, 1969.

Chen, Zhihong. *Die China-Mission Michail Borodins bis zum Tod Sun Yatsens.* Münster: Lit Verlag, 2000.

Cheng, Zhongyuan, Wang, Yuxiang, and Li, Zhenghua, eds., *Zhongguo 1976–1981* 中国 [China 1976–1981]. Beijing: Zhongyang Wenxian Chubanshe, 1998.

Ch'i, Hsi-Sheng. *Warlord Politics in China, 1916–1928.* Stanford: Stanford University Press, 1976.

Communist Party of Vietnam 4th National Congress Documents. Hanoi: Foreign Languages Publishing House, 1977.

Creel, Herrlee. *The Origins of Statecraft in China,* vol. 1. Chicago: University of Chicago Press, 1970.

Dang, Nghiem Van, Chu, Thai Son, and Luu, Hung. *Ethnic Minorities in Vietnam.* Hanoi: The Gioi, 2000.

Dangdai Zhongguo di Guangxi 当代中国的广西 [Contemporary China's Guangxi], vol. 1. Beijing: Dangdai Zhongguo Chubanshe, 1992.

de Tréglodé, Benoît. *Héros et Révolution au Viêt Nam.* Paris: L'Harmattan, 2001.

Diem, Bui, with Chanoff, David. *In the Jaws of History.* Boston: Houghton Mifflin, 1987.

Diguet, Colonel Edouard J. J. *Les Montangards du Tonkin.* Paris: A. Challomel, 1908.

Dittmer, Lowell. *Liu Shao-ch'i and the Chinese Cultural Revolution: The Politics of Mass Criticism.* Berkeley: University of California Press, 1974.

Duiker, William. *Ho Chi Minh.* New York: Hyperion, 2000.

Duong, Van Mai Elliott. *The Sacred Willow: Four Generations in the Life of a Vietnamese Family.* New York: Oxford University Press, 1999.

East Asia Analytical Unit. *Overseas Chinese Business Networks in Asia.* Canberra: Australian Department of Foreign Affairs and Trade, 1995.

Fall, Bernard. *The Two Vietnams: A Political and Military Analysis.* New York: Praeger, 1967.

Feinberg, Richard, Echeverri-Gent, John, and Müller, Friedemann. *Economic Reform in Three Giants.* New Brunswick, NJ: Transaction Books, 1990.

Fforde, Adam, and Vylder, Stefan. *From Plan to Market: The Economic Transition in Vietnam.* Boulder: Westview Press, 1996.

Fforde, Adam, and Paine, Suzanne. *The Limits of National Liberation.* New York: Croom Helm, 1986.

Fitzgerald, C. Patrick. *The Southern Expansion of the Chinese People.* New York: Praeger, 1972.

Fitzgerald, Frances. *Fire in the Lake: The Vietnamese and the Americans in Vietnam.* Boston: Little, Brown, 1972.

Fox, Annette Baker. *The Power of Small States: Diplomacy in World War Two.* Chicago: University of Chicago Press, 1959.

Gill, Stephen, and Mittelman, James, eds., *Innovation and Transformation in International Studies*. New York: Cambridge University Press, 1997.

Gross, John, ed. *The Oxford Book of Essays*. Oxford: Oxford University Press, 1992.

Guo, Ming, ed. *Zhong Yue guanxi yanbian sishi nian* 中越关系演变40年 [The 40-year Evolution of Sino-Vietnamese Relations]. Nanning: Guangxi Renmin Chubanshe, 1992.

Haldane, John Burdon Sanderson. "On Being the Right Size," in Haldane, John Burdon Sanderson. *Possible Worlds*. New York: Harper and Row, 1928.

Hall, D. G. E. *A History of Southeast Asia*. 4th ed. New York: St. Martin's, 1981.

Hayslip, Le Ly. *When Heaven and Earth Changed Places*. New York: Penguin, 1990.

He, Xin. *Sikao: Wo di zhexue yu zongjiao guan* 思考: 我的哲学与宗教观 [Reflections: My Philosophical and Religious Viewpoint]. Beijing: Shishi Chubanshe, 2001.

Heilig, G. K. *Can China Feed Itself?* IIASA (International Institute for Applied Systems Analysis, Laxenburg). CD-ROM Vers. 1.1, 1999.

Hevia, James. *Cherishing Men from Afar*. Durham: Duke University Press, 1995.

History of the Indochina Incident, 1940–1954. Washington: Historical Division, Joint Secretariat, Joint Chiefs of Staff. Originally prepared February 1955, 2nd ed. 1971, declassified edition 1981.

Ho, Chi Minh. *Selected Writings*. Hanoi: Foreign Languages Publishing House, 1977.

Hubei Provincial Museum, ed. *Zeng Hou Yi mu wenwu zhenshang* 曾侯乙幕文物珍赏 [Appreciating the Cultural Relics of the Zeng Hou Yi Tomb]. Wuhan: Hubei Fine Arts Publishing House, 1995.

Hucker, O. Charles. *China's Imperial Past: An Introduction to Chinese History and Culture*. Stanford: Stanford University Press, 1975.

Huntington, P. Samuel, *The Clash of Civilizations and the Remaking of World Order*. New York: Simon and Schuster, 1996.

Huntington, P. Samuel, and Nelson, Joan. *No Easy Choice: Political Participation in Developing Countries*. Cambridge: Harvard University Press, 1976.

Ikenberry, G. John. *After Victory: Institutions, Strategic Restraint, and the Rebuilding of Order after Major Wars*. Princeton: Princeton University Press, 2001.

International Energy Agency. *Key World Energy Statistics* 2003. http://www.iea.org/statist/key2003.pdf.

Jackson, Robert. *Quasi-States: Sovereignty, International Relations and the Third World*. New York: Cambridge University Press, 1990.

Jervis, Robert. *Perception and Misperception in International Politics*. Princeton: Princeton University Press, 1977.

Kant, Immanuel. *Zum ewigen Frieden*. Königsberg: Friedrich Nicolovius, 1795.

Katzenstein, Peter. *Small States in World Markets: Industrial Policy in Europe*. Ithaca: Cornell University Press, 1985.

Kaup, Kate. *Creating the Zhuang: Ethnic Politics in the People's Republic of China*. Boulder: Lynne Reinner Publishers, 2000.

Kenny, J. Henry. *Shadow of the Dragon: Vietnam's Continuing Struggle with China and Its Implications for U.S. Foreign Policy*. Washington: Brasseys, 2002.

Keohane, O. Robert. *After Hegemony: Cooperation and Discord in the World Political Economy*. Princeton: Princeton University Press, 1984.

Keohane, O. Robert, and Nye, S. Joseph. *Power and Interdependence.* Boston: Little, Brown, 1977.

Kindleberger, P. Charles. *World Economic Primacy, 1500–1990.* New York: Oxford University Press, 1996.

Kindleberger, P. Charles. *The World in Depression, 1929–1939.* Berkeley: University of California Press, 1973.

Komaroff, Linda, and Carboni, Stephano, eds. *The Legacy of Genghis Khan: Courtly Art and Culture in Western Asia, 1256–1353.* New Haven: Yale University Press, 2002.

Kosumas, Wimonkan. *Half a Hegemon: Japan's Leadership in Southeast Asia.* Ph.D. Dissertation. Charlottesville: University of Virginia, 2000.

Kuhn, Philip. *Rebellion and Its Enemies in Late Imperial China.* Cambridge, MA: Harvard University Press, 1970.

Krumm, Kathie, and Karas, Homi, eds. *East Asia Integrates: A Trade Policy Agenda for Shared Growth.* Washington: World Bank, 2003.

Lattimore, Owen. *Inner Asian Frontiers of China.* Hong Kong: Oxford University Press, 1988. Originally American Geographic Society, 1940.

Le, Thanh Khoi. *Le Vietnam.* Paris: Editions de Minuit, 1955.

Leng, Tse-kang. *The Taiwan-China Connection: Democracy and Development across the Taiwan Straits.* Boulder: Westview Press, 1996.

Lenin, V. I. *Imperialism, The Highest Stage of Capitalism. Lenin Collected Works.* Moscow: Progress Publisher, 1976, Volume 22, pp. 185–304.

Levenson, Joseph. *Liang Ch'i-ch'ao and the Mind of Modern China.* Berkeley: University of California Press, 1959.

Li, Gu. *Cong en'en yuanyuan dao pingdeng huli: Shiji zhi jiao di Zhong Yue guanxi yanjiu* 从恩恩怨怨到平等互利:实际之交的中越关系研究 [From Graciousness and Resentment to Equality and Mutual Benefit: Research on Sino-Vietnamese Relations at Century's End]. Hong Kong: Honglan Chuban Gongsi, 2001.

Li, Tana. *The "Inner Region": A Social and Economic History of Nguyen Vietnam in the 17th and 18th Centuries.* Ph.D. Dissertation. Canberra: Australian National University, 1992.

Lin, Shangli. *Guonei zhengfu jian guanxi* 国内政府间关系 [Domestic Intergovernmental Relationships]. Hangzhou: Zhejiang Renmin Chubanshe, 1998.

Lindblom, E. Charles. *Politics and Markets: The World's Political Economic Systems.* New York: Basic Books, 1977.

Lloyd, Seton. *Ancient Turkey: A Traveller's History.* Berkeley: University of California Press, 1989.

Lukacs, Georg. *Geschichte und Klassenbewußtsein.* Berlin: Malik, 1923.

Luo, Guanzhong. *Three Kingdoms*, vol. 4, tr. Roberts, Moss. Beijing: Foreign Languages Press, 1995.

Luu, Van Loi. *Fifty Years of Vietnamese Diplomacy.* Hanoi: The Gioi Publishers, 2000.

Lynch, Allen. *How Russia is Not Ruled. Reflections on Russian Political Development.* Cambridge, UK: Cambridge University Press, 2005.

Maddison, Angus. *Chinese Economic Performance in the Long Run.* Paris: OECD Development Centre, 1998.

Mannikka, Eleanor. *Angkor Wat: Time, Space and Kingship.* Honolulu: University of Hawaii Press, 1996.

Mao, Zedong. *Minzhong de da lianhe*民众的大联合 [The Great Union of the Popular Masses]. June 1919.

Maoz, Zeev, and Mor, Ben. *Bound by Struggle: The Strategic Evolution of Enduring International Rivalries.* Ann Arbor: University of Michigan Press, 2002.

Marr, G. David. *Vietnam 1945: The Quest for Power.* Berkeley: University of California Press, 1995.

Marr, G. David. *Vietnamese Tradition on Trial 1920–1945.* Berkeley: University of California Press, 1981.

Mearsheimer, J. John. *The Tragedy of Great Power Politics.* New York: Norton, 2001.

Moise, E. Edwin. *Land Reform in China and North Vietnam.* Berkeley: University of California Press, 1983.

Morgenthau, J. Hans. *Politics among Nations: The Struggle for Power and Peace.* 5th ed. New York: Knopf, 1973.

Morse, Hosea Ballou. *The International Relations of the Chinese Empire*, vol. 3. London: Longmans Green, 1910–1918.

Möller, Kay. *China und das wiedervereinte Vietnam.* Bochum: Studienverlag Brockmeyer, 1984.

National Academy of Sciences. *Cooperation in the Energy Futures of China and the United States.* Washington: National Academy of Sciences, 2000.

Nguyen, Du. *The Tale of Kieu,* tr. Thong, Huynh Sanh. New Haven: Yale University Press, 1983.

Nguyen, Huy Lai Joseph. *La Tradition Religieuse Spirituelle Sociale au Vietnam.* Paris: Beauchene, 1981.

Nguyen, Khac Vien. *Vietnam: A Long History.* Hanoi: The Gioi, 1993.

Nguyen, Ngoc Huy, and Ta, Van Tai. *The Le Code: Law in Traditional Vietnam.* Athens, Ohio: Ohio University Press, 1987.

Nguyen, Van Hua. *Hoi An.* Danang: Nha Xuat Ban Da Nang, 1999.

Niebuhr, Reinhold. *The Irony of American History.* New York: Scribner's, 1962.

Niên Giám Thống Kê [Viet Nam Statistical Yearbook]. Hanoi: Statistical Publishing House, Various Years.

Nye, S. Joseph. *Bound to Lead: The Changing Nature of American Power.* New York: Basic Books, 1990.

Nye, Joseph. *Soft Power: The Means to Success in World Politics.* New York: Public Affairs, 2004.

Owen, M. John. *Liberal Peace, Liberal War: American Politics and International Security.* Ithaca: Cornell University Press, 1997.

Pei, Jianzhang, ed. *Zhong Hua Renmin Gonghe Guo Waijiao shi 1949–1956* 中华人民共和国对外关 [History of the foreign relations of the PRC 1949–1956]. Beijing: Shijie Zhishi Chubanshe, 1994.

Powell, Robert. *In the Shadow of Power.* Princeton: Princeton University Press, 1999.

Qian, Qichen. *Waijiao shi ji*外交十记 [Ten stories of a diplomat]. Beijing: Shijie zhishi Chubanshe, 2004.

Race, Jeffrey. *War Comes to Long An.* Berkeley: University of California Press, 1972.

Ramazani, Rouhollah. *The Foreign Policy of Iran, 1500–1941.* Charlottesville: University of Virginia Press, 1966.

Richardson, Sophie. *China, Cambodia, and the Five Principles of Peaceful Coexistence: Principles and Foreign Policy.* Ph.D. dissertation, University of Virginia, 2004.

Ross, S. Robert. *The Indochina Tangle: China's Vietnam Policy, 1975–1979.* New York: Columbia University Press, 1988.

Rossabi, Morris. ed. *China among Equals: The Middle Kingdom and Its Neighbors, 10th–14th Centuries.* Berkeley: University of California Press, 1983.

Rostovtseff, M. I. *The Social and Economic History of the Hellenistic World.* Oxford: Oxford University Press, 1941.

Sayer, Geoffrey Robley. *Hong Kong 1862–1919: Years of Discretion: A Sequel to Hong Kong-Birth, Adolescence, and Coming of Age.* Hong Kong: Hong Kong University Press, 1975.

Scott, C. James. *The Weapons of the Weak: Everyday Forms of Peasant Resistance.* New Haven: Yale University Press, 1985.

Shawcross, William. *Sideshow: Kissinger, Nixon and the Destruction of Cambodia.* New York: Simon and Schuster, 1979.

Shils, A. Edward. *Center and Periphery: Essays in Macro Sociology.* Chicago: University of Chicago Press, 1975.

Smith, Richard J. *Mercenaries and Mandarins: The Ever-Victorious Army in Nineteenth Century China.* Millwood: KTO Press, 1978.

Stoessinger, John. *Nations in Darkness.* 2nd ed. New York: Random House, 1975.

Sun, Pin. *Military Methods: History and Warfare,* tr. Sawyer, D. Ralph. Boulder: Westview, 1995.

Swaine, Michael, and Tellis, Ashley. *Interpreting China's Grand Strategy: Past, Present and Future.* Santa Monica: Rand, 2000.

Szuma, Chien (Sima, Qian). *Records of the Historian,* tr. Yang, Hsien-yi (Yang, Xianyi), and Yang, Gladys. Hong Kong: Commercial Press, 1974.

Taylor, Keith Weller. *The Birth of Vietnam.* Berkeley: University of California Press, 1983.

Tonnesson, Stein, and Goscha, Chris. *Le Duan and the Break with China.* Dossier No. 3. Washington: Cold War International History Project, Woodrow Wilson International Center for Scholars, 2001. http://cwihp.si.edu/tonviet.htm.

Toynbee, J. Arnold. *A Study of History.* Oxford: Oxford University Press, 1947.

Tran, Van Don. *Our Endless War: Inside Vietnam.* San Raphael, California: Presidio Press, 1978.

Truong, Buu Lam. *Patterns of Vietnamese Response to Foreign Intervention: 1858–1900.* New Haven: Yale University Southeast Asia Studies Monograph Series, no 11, 1967.

Tsai, Jung-fang. *Hong Kong in Chinese History: Community and Social Unrest in the British Colony, 1842–1913.* New York: Columbia University Press, 1993.

Tsou, Tang. *Ershi shiji zhongguo zhengzhi: Zong hongguan lishi yu weiguan xingdong jiaodu kan* 二十世纪中国政治：從宏观历史与微观行动角度看 [Twentieth Century Chinese Politics: From the Macro-Historical and Micro-Behavioral Perspectives]. Oxford: Oxford University Press, 1994.

Tư Liệu Kinh Tế-Xã Hội 61 Tỉnh và Thành Phố [Socio-Economic Statistical Data of 61 Provinces and Cities in Vietnam]. Hanoi: Nhà Xuất Bản Thống Kê, 1999.

United Nations Development Programme. *National Human Development Report 2001: Doi Moi and Human Development in Vietnam.* Hanoi, 2001. http://www.undp.org.vn/undp/docs/2001/vnnhdr2001/index.htm.

United Nations Development Programme. *Vietnam Development Goals: Closing the Millennium Gaps 2003.* Hanoi, 2003. http://www.un.org.vn/undocs/mdg03/mdg03e.pdf.

Vu, Tu Lap, and Taillard, Christian. *An Atlas of Vietnam.* Paris: Reclus, 1994.

Wallace, Henry. *Toward World Peace.* New York: Reynal and Hitchcock, 1948.

Wallerstein, M. Immanuel. *The Modern World System.* New York: Academic Press, 1974.

Waltham, Clae, ed. *Shu Ching: Book of History.* Chicago: Henry Regnery, 1971.

Waltz, Kenneth. *Man, the State, and War: A Theoretical Analysis.* New York: Columbia University Press, 1959.

Waltz, Kenneth. *Theory of International Politics.* New York: McGraw-Hill, 1979.

Wang, Gungwu. *The Chinese Overseas: From Earthbound China to the Quest for Autonomy.* Cambridge: Harvard University Press, 2000.

Watson, Adam. *The Limits of Independence: Relations between States in the Modern World.* London: Routledge, 1997.

Wen, Fong, ed. *The Great Bronze Age of China.* New York: Knopf for the Metropolitan Museum of Art, 1980.

Wendt, Alexander. *Social Theory of International Politics.* Cambridge: Cambridge University Press, 1999.

Westad, Odd Arne, Chen, Jian, Tonnesson, Stein, Nguyen, Vu Tung, and Hershberg, James G., eds. *77 Conversations between Chinese and Foreign Leaders on the Wars in Indochina, 1964–1977.* Washington: Woodrow Wilson Center, Cold War International History Project Working Paper. no. 22, May 1998.

Whitehead, Alfred North. *Process and Reality.* New York: Harper, 1929.

Whitmore, John. *The Development of Le Government in 15th Century Vietnam.* Ph.D. Dissertation. Ithaca: Cornell University, 1968.

Will, Gerhard. *Vietnam 1975–1979: Von Krieg zu Krieg.* Hamburg: Mitteilungen des Instituts für Asienkunde, 1987.

Wittvogel, Karl. *Oriental Despotism: A Comparative Study of Total Power.* New Haven: Yale University Press, 1957.

Womack, Brantly. *The Foundations of Mao Zedong's Political Thought, 1917–1935.* Honolulu: University of Hawaii Press, 1982.

Womack, Sarah. *Colonialism and the Collaborationist Agenda: Pham Quynh, Print Culture, and the Politics of Persuasion in Colonial Vietnam.* Ph.D. Dissertation. Ann Arbor: University of Michigan, 2003.

Woodside, Alexander. *Vietnam and the Chinese Model: A Comparative Study of Vietnamese and Chinese Government in the First Half of the Nineteenth Century.* Cambridge: Harvard University Press, 1971.

World Bank. *Vietnam Development Report 2002.* Hanoi: World Bank, 2001.

World Bank. *World Development Report 2003.* New York: Oxford University Press, 2003.

World Bank. *World Development Report 2001.* New York: Oxford University Press, 2001.

Yang, Richard H., Hu, Jason C., Yu, Peter K. H., and Yang, Andrew N. D., eds. *Chinese Regionalism: Security Dimensions.* Boulder: Westview Press, 1994.

Zhai, Qiang. *China and the Vietnam Wars, 1950–1975.* Chapel Hill: University of North Carolina Press, 2000.

Zheng, Yi. *Scarlet Memorial: Tales of Cannibalism in Guangxi*, tr. Sym, T. P. Boulder: Westview Press, 1996.

Zhongguo Tongji Nianjian 中国统计年鉴 [Statistical Yearbook of China]. Beijing: China Statistics Press, various years.

Zhonghua Renmin Gonghe Guo duiwai guanxi shi (chu chao), di si zhang: Zhong Mei guanxi kaishi zhengchanghua zhi Sulian junshi ruqin Afuhan di duiwai guanxi (1972/2 zhi 1979/12) 中华人民共和国对外关系史(初抄): 第四章:中美关系开始正常化止苏联入侵阿富汗的对外关系 [History of External Relations of the PRC (first draft): Chapter 4: from the Beginning of Sino-American Normalization to the Soviet Military Invasion of Afghanistan (February 1972 to December 1979)]. N.p., n.y.

Book Chapters and Articles

Amer, Ramses. "The Chinese Minority in Vietnam since 1975," *Ilmu masyarakat: Terbitan Persatuan Sains Sosial Malaysia* [Sociology: Proceedings of the Malaysian Social Science Association] 22. 1992.

Amer, Ramses. *The Sino-Vietnamese Approach to Managing Boundary Disputes.* International Boundaries Research Unit, Maritime Briefing 3:3, 2002.

Amer, Ramses. "Sino-Vietnamese Relations: Past, Present and Future," in Thayer, A. Carlyle, and Amer, Ramses, eds. *Vietnamese Foreign Policy in Transition.* New York: St. Martin's Press, 1999.

Anderson, James. "From Tribute to Trade: Examining a Pivotal Period in Middle Period Sino-Vietnamese Relations." Paper presented at the Annual Meeting of the Southeast Conference of the Association for Asian Studies, 2003.

Ba, Alice. "Sino-ASEAN Relations: The Significance of an ASEAN-China Free Trade Area," in Cheng, T. J., deLisle, Jacques, and Brown, Deborah, eds., *China under the Fourth Generation Leadership: Opportunities, Dangers, and Dilemmas.* Singapore: World Scientific Press, 2005.

Bairoch, P. "International Industrialization Levels from 1750 to 1980." *The Journal of European Economic History* 11:2. Fall 1982.

Brocheux, Pierre. "Vietnamese Communism and the Peasants," in Turley, S. William, ed., *Vietnamese Communism in Comparative Perspective.* Boulder: Westview Press, 1980.

Bui, Thanh Son. "Vietnam-U.S. Relations and Vietnam's Foreign Policy," in Thayer, A. Carlyle, and Amer, Ramses, eds., *Vietnamese Foreign Policy in Transition.* New York: St. Martin's Press, 1999.

Buszinski, Leszek. "ASEAN's New Challenges." *Pacific Affairs* 70:4. Winter 1997–1998.

Cederman, Lars-Erik. "Back to Kant." *American Political Science Review* 95:1. March 2001.

Chan, Ming. "All in the Family: The Hong Kong-Guangdong Link in Historical Perspective," in Kwok, Yin-Wang, and So, Alvin, eds., *The Hong Kong-Guangdong Link.* Armonk: M.E. Sharpe, 1995.

Chen, Jian. "China and the First Indochina War, 1950–1954." *China Quarterly*, no. 133. June 1993.

Chen, Jian. "China's Involvement in the Vietnam War, 1964–1969." *China Quarterly*, no. 142. June 1995.

Chen, Jian, "Personal-Historical Puzzles about China and the Vietnam War," in Westad, Odd Arne, Chen, Jian, Tonnesson, Stein, Nguyen, Vu Tung, and Hershberg, James G., eds. *77 Conversations between Chinese and Foreign Leaders on the Wars in Indochina, 1964–1977*. Washington: Woodrow Wilson Center, Cold War International History Project Working Paper. no. 22, May 1998, pp. 21–33.

Chen, Qimao. "New Approaches in China's Foreign Policy: The Post–Cold War Era." *Asian Survey* 33:3. March 1993.

Chen, Yonghua. "Liang Song shiqi Zhong Guo yu Dongnanya de Maoyi 两宋时期中国与东南亚的贸易" [Trade between China and Southeast Asia during the North and South Song Dynasties]. *Dongnanya Zongheng* 东南亚纵横 [Around Southeast Asia] 2004:5 May.

Cheng, Joseph, Y. S. "China's ASEAN Policy in the 1990s: Pushing for Regional Multipolarity." *Contemporary Southeast Asia* 21:2. August 1999.

Cheng, Joseph Y. S. "Sino-ASEAN Relations in the Early Twenty-first Century." *Contemporary Southeast Asia* 23:3. December 2001.

Chiu, Hungdah. "China's Legal Position on Protecting Chinese Residents in Vietnam." *American Journal of International Law* 74:3. July 1980.

Cloma, Venus Olivia. "The Spratly Islands Dispute." www.geocities.com/vomcloma/thespratlys.htm.

Coedes, George, Vella, Walter. ed., *The Indianized States of Southeast Asia*, tr. Cowing, Susan. Honolulu: East-West Center Press, 1968.

Cooke, Nola. "The Myth of Restoration: Dang-Trong Influences on the Spiritual Life of the Early Nguyen Dynasty, 1802–1847," in Reid, Anthony. ed., *The Last Stand of Asian Autonomies: Responses to Modernity in the Diverse States of Southeast Asia and Korea, 1750–1900*. New York: St. Martin's, 1997.

Cuong, Tu Nguyen. "Rethinking Vietnamese Buddhist History," in Taylor, Keith, and Whitmore, John, eds., *Essays into Vietnamese Pasts*. Ithaca: The Southeast Asia Program, Cornell University, 1995.

Dauphin, Antoine. "La frontière sino-vietnamienne de 1895–1896 à nos jours," in *Les Frontières du Vietnam*. Paris: Éditions L'Harmattan, 1989.

Do, Thi Thanh Huyen. "Xiandai yueyu zhong de Hanyu Jieci 现代越语-中的汉语借词" [Chinese loan words in modern Vietnamese]. *Dongnanya Zongheng* 东南亚纵横 [Around Southeast Asia] 2004:5 (May).

Do, Tien Sam[杜进森]. "Zhongguo-Dongmeng ziyou maoyiqu beijing xia de Yue Zhong jingji hezuo zhanwang中国东盟自由贸易区背景下的越中经济合作展望," [The Influence of CAFTA on Prospects for Sino-Vietnamese Economic Cooperation]. *Dongnanya Zongheng*东南亚纵横 [Around Southeast Asia] 2004:7 (July), pp. 1–4.

Duiker, William, "China and Vietnam: The Roots of Conflict," Berkeley: Institute of East Asian Studies. Indochina Research Monograph. no. 1, 1986.

Duiker, William. "Vietnamese Revolutionary Doctrine in Comparative Perspective," in Turley, S. William, ed., *Vietnamese Communism in Comparative Perspective*. Boulder: Westview Press, 1980.

Du, Peng, and Tu, Ping. "Population Aging and Old Age Security," in Peng, Xizhe, ed., *The Changing Population of China*. Oxford: Blackwell, 2000.

Fourniau, M. Ch. "La fixation de la frontière Sino-Vietnamienne 1885–1896," in *Etudes indochinoise: Frontières et contacts dan la Peninsule Indochinoise*. Provence: Institut d'histoire des pays d'outre-mer, *Études et documents no. 13*, 1981.

Furuta, Motoo. "A Survey of Village Conditions during the 1945 Famine in Vietnam," in Kratoska, Paul, ed., *Food Supplies and the Japanese Occupation in Southeast Asia*. New York: St. Martin's Press, 1998.

Gerring, John. "What Is a Case Study and What Is it Good For?" *American Political Science Review* 98:2. May 2004.

Goscha, Christopher. "The Borders of the DRV's Early Trade with the Chinese during the War against the French: 1945–1950." *Asian Survey* 40:6. December 2000.

Goscha, Christopher. "La survie diplomatique du Parti Communiste Indochinois et l'importance de la Chine communiste (1945–1950)". Ms.

Gu, Xiaosong, and Womack, Brantly. "Border Cooperation between China and Vietnam in the 1990s." *Asian Survey* 40:6. December 2000.

Jencks, Harlan. "China's 'Punitive' War on Vietnam: A Military Assessment." *Asian Survey* 19:8. August 1979.

Kang, David. "Getting Asia Wrong: The Need for New Analytic Frameworks." *International Security* 27:4. Spring 2003.

Kang, David. "Hierarchy, Balancing, and Empirical Puzzles in Asian International Relations," *International Security* 28:3. Winter 2004.

Karube, Keiko. "Japan's Desire to be a Major Political Power and Historical Burdens," *Southeast Review of Asian Studies* 16. 1994.

"Keng Piao's [Geng Biao's] Report of the Situation of the Indochinese Peninsula," delivered January 16, 1979, for high-level internal circulation. *Issues and Studies* (January 1981), pp.78–96.

Kenny, Henry. "Vietnamese Perceptions of the 1979 War with China," in Ryan, Mark, Finkelstein, David, and McDevitt, Michael, eds., *Chinese Warfighting: The PLA Experience since 1949*. Armonk: M.E. Sharpe, 2003.

Kerkvliet, Ben. "Authorities and the People," in Hy, Van Luong, ed., *Postwar Vietnam: Dynamics of a Transforming Society*. New York: Rowman and Littlefield, 2003.

Lafont, Pierre-Bernard. "Les archipels Paracel et Spratly: Un conflit de frontières en Mer de Chine méridionale," in *Les Frontières du Vietnam*. Paris: Éditions L'Harmattan, 1989.

Lake, David. "Leadership, Hegemony and the International Economy." *International Studies Quarterly* 37. 1993.

Langlet, Philippe. "La frontière Sino-Vietnamienne du xviiie xixe siècle," in n. a. *Les frontières du Vietnam: Histoire des frontiers de la pénninsule indochinoise*. Paris: L'Harmattan, 1989.

Langlois, John. "Introduction." Langlois, John, ed., *China under Mongol Rule*. Princeton: Princeton University Press, 1981.

Lee, Lai-to. "The People's Republic of China and the South China Sea." Department of Political Science, the National University of Singapore. Occasional Paper. no. 31. Singapore: Chopmen Enterprises, 1977.

Lewis, John. "Some Consequences of Giantism: The Case of India." *World Politics* 43:3. April 1991.

Li, Jiazhong. "Zhong Yue guanxi zhengchanghua qianye de liang guo fu wai zhang cuoshang中越关正常化前夜的两国副外长磋商" [Negotiation between Vice Foreign Ministers on the Eve of Sino-Vietnamese Normalization], *Dongnanya Zongheng* 东南亚纵横 [Around Southeast Asia]. 2003:4. April 2003.

Li, Wei. "Zhongguo shiyou anquan zhong de dongnanya yinsu 中国石油安-全中的东南亚因素" [The Southeast Asian Element in China's Petroleum Security]. *Dongnanya Zongheng* 东南亚纵横 [Around Southeast Asia]. 2003:10. October 2003.

Li, Yongping, and Peng, Xizhe. "Age and Sex Structures," in Peng, Xizhe, ed., *The Changing Population of China*. Oxford: Blackwell, 2000.

Lin, Ziping. "Ping Yuenan changpian lishi xiaoshuo 'Hu Jili' 评越南-长篇历史小说胡季犛." *Dongnanya Zongheng* 东南亚纵横 [Around Southeast Asia]:5 May 2003.

Mantienne, Frédéric. "Military Technology Transfers from Europe to Lower Mainland Southeast Asia (c. 16–19th centuries)." Paper presented at the Annual Meeting of the Association for Asian Studies, Washington, DC, April 2002.

McGregor, Charles. "China, Vietnam, and the Cambodian Conflict: Beijing's End Game Strategy" *Asian Survey* 30:3. March, 1990.

Merli, Giovanna. "Socioeconomic Background and War Mortality during Vietnam's Wars." *Demography* 37:1. February 2000.

Nguyen, Khac Vien. "Confucianism and Marxism," in Nguyen, Khac Vien. *Tradition and Revolution in Vietnam*. Berkeley: Indochina Resource Center, 1974.

Nguyen, The Anh. "Attraction and Repulsion as the Two Contrasting Aspects of the Relations between China and Vietnam." *China and Southeast Asia: Historical Interactions. An International Symposium*. University of Hong Kong, July 2001.

Nguyen, The Anh. "Japanese Food Policies and the 1945 Great Famine in Indochina," in Kratoska, Paul, ed., *Food Supplies and the Japanese Occupation in Southeast Asia*. New York: St. Martin's Press, 1998.

Nguyen, The Anh. "La frontière Sino-Vietnamienne du xiᵉ au xviiᵉ siècle," in n. a. *Les frontières du Vietnam: Histoire des frontiers de la pénninsule indochinoise*. Paris: L'Harmattan, 1989.

Nguyen, Truong To. "Memorial on Eight Reforms Urgently Needed (1868)," in Truong, Buu Lam. *Patterns of Vietnamese Response to Foreign Intervention: 1858–1900*. New Haven: Yale University Southeast Asia Studies Monograph Series. No. 11. 1967, pp. 92–3.

O'Harrow, Stephen. "Nguyen Trai's *Binh Ngo Dai Cao* of 1428: The Development of a Vietnamese National Identity." *Southeast Asian Studies* 10:1. March 1979.

Owen, M. John. "Transnational Liberalism and U.S. Primacy." *International Security* 26:3. Winter 2001–2002.

Palmujoki, Eero. "Ideology and Foreign Policy: Vietnam's Marxist-Leninist Doctrine and Global Change, 1986–96," in Thayer, A. Carlyle, and Amer, Ramses, eds., *Vietnamese Foreign Policy in Transition*. New York: St. Martin's Press, 1999.

Porter, Gareth. "The Transformation of Vietnam's World View." *Contemporary Southeast Asia* 12:1 (June 1990), pp. 1–19.

Qu, Xing. "Zhong Yue zai Yinzhi zhanzheng wenti de zhanlue yizhi yu celue chayi 中越在印支战争问题的战略_致与策略差异" [The strategic unity and tactical differences of China and Vietnam regarding the Indochina war]. *Guoji Luntan* 国际论坛 [International Forum] 2:3. June 2000.

Rudolph, Suzanne. "State Formation in Asia: Prolegomenon to a Comparative Study." *Journal of Asian Studies* 46:4. November 1987.

Sakurai, Yumio. "Peasant Drain and Abandoned Villages in the Red River Delta between 1750 and 1850," in Reid, Anthony, ed., *The Last Stand of Asian*

Autonomies: Responses to Modernity in the Diverse States of Southeast Asia and Korea, 1750–1900. New York: St. Martin's, 1997.

Sit, Victor. "Industrial Transformation of Hong Kong," in Kwok, Yin-Wang, and So, Alvin, eds., *The Hong Kong-Guangdong Link.* Armonk: M. E. Sharpe, 1995.

Taylor, Keith Weller. "Kao Pien/Cao Bien and the Vicissitudes of Being Remembered in Vietnam." Paper presented at the Annual meeting of the Association for Asian Studies, 1997.

Thayer, A. Carlyle. "Sino-Vietnamese Relations: The Interplay of Ideology and National Interest." *Asian Survey* 34:6. June 1994.

Thayer, Carlyle. "Vietnam's Foreign Relations: The Strategic Defense Dimension," in Koh, David, ed., *Vietnam's Strategic and Foreign Relations.* Singapore: Institute of International Relations, 2005.

Truong, Buu Lam. "Intervention versus Tribute in Sino-Vietnamese Relations, 1788–1790," in Fairbank, K. John, ed., *The Chinese World Order.* Cambridge: Harvard University Press, 1968.

Tsou, Tang. "Reflections on the Formation and Foundations of the Communist Party-State in China," in Tsou, Tang. *The Cultural Revolution and Post-Mao Reforms: A Historical Perspective.* Chicago: University of Chicago Press, 1986.

Turley, William, S. and Womack, Brantly. "Asian Socialism's Open Doors: Guangzhou and Ho Chi Minh City." *China Journal*, no. 40. July 1998.

Ungar, E. S. "The Struggle over the Chinese Community in Vietnam, 1946–1988." *Pacific Affairs* 60:4. Winter 1987–1988.

Vuving, Alexander. "The Two-Headed Grand Strategy: Vietnamese Foreign Policy since *Doi Moi*." Paper presented at "Vietnam Update 2004: Strategic and Foreign Relations," Singapore, November 2004.

Wang, Guixin. "The Distribution of China's Population and Its Changes," in Peng, Xizhe, ed., *The Changing Population of China.* Oxford: Blackwell, 2000.

Wang, Gungwu, "The Rhetoric of a Lesser Empire: Early Sung Relations with Its Neighbors," in Wang, Gungwu. *The Chineseness of China: Selected Essays.* Hong Kong: Oxford University Press, 1991.

Wang, Hongying. "Multilateralism in Chinese Foreign Policy." *Asian Survey* 40:3. March 2000.

Whitmore, John. "Chu Văn An and the Rise of 'Antiquity' in Fourteenth-Century Đài Viêt," *The Vietnam Review* 1. 1996.

Whitmore, John. "Communism and History in Vietnam," in Turley, S. William, ed., *Vietnamese Communism in Comparative Perspective.* Boulder: Westview Press, 1980.

Whitmore, John. "Literati Culture in Dai Viet, 1430–1840." *Modern Asian Studies* 31:3. July 1997.

Wolters, O. W. "Assertions of Well-Being in Fourteenth-Century Vietnam: Part I." *Journal of Southeast Asian Studies* 10. September 1979.

Wolters, O. W. "Assertions of Well-Being in Fourteenth-Century Vietnam: Part II." *Journal of Southeast Asian Studies* 11. March 1980.

Wolters, O. W. "Historians and Emperors in Vietnam and China: Comments Arising out of Le Van Huu's History, presented to the Tran Court in 1272," in Reid, Anthony, and Marr, G. David, eds., *Perceptions of the Past in Southeast Asia.* Singapore: Heineman Educational Books, 1979.

Wolters, O. W. "Le Van Huu's Treatment of Ly Than Ton's Reign (1127–1137)," in Cowan, C. D., and Wolters, O. W., eds., *Southeast Asian History and Historiography*. Ithaca: Cornell University Press, 1976.

Womack, Brantly. "Asymmetry and Systemic Misperception: The Cases of China, Vietnam and Cambodia during the 1970s." *Journal of Strategic Studies* 26:2. June 2003.

Womack, Brantly. "Asymmetry Theory and China's Concept of Multipolarity." *Journal of Contemporary China* 13:40. August 2004.

Womack, Brantly. "China's Border Trade and Its Relationship to the National Political Economy." *American Asian Review* 19:2. Summer 2001.

Womack, Brantly. "China and Southeast Asia: Asymmetry, Leadership and Normalcy." *Pacific Affairs* 76:4. Winter 2003–4.

Womack, Brantly. "China's Southeast Asia Policy: A Success Story for the Third Generation." *Cross-Strait and International Affairs Quarterly* 1:1. January 2004.

Womack, Brantly. "How Size Matters: The United States, China and Asymmetry." *Journal of Strategic Studies* 24:4. December 2001.

Womack, Brantly. "Ke chixu de guoji lingdao quan: Lai zi chi 968–1885 nian zhong yue guanxi do jingyan jiaoxun 可持续的国际领导权：来自持 968–1885 年中越关系的经验教训" [Sustainable International Leadership: Lessons from the Sino-Vietnamese Relationship, 968–1885], *Shixue Jikan* 史学季刊 [Collected Papers of History Studies] 2004:1. January 2004.

Womack, Brantly. "The Party and the People: Revolutionary and Post-Revolutionary Politics in China and Vietnam." *World Politics* 39:4. July 1986.

Womack, Brantly. "The Phases of Chinese Modernization," in Chin, S. K. Steve, ed., *Modernization in China: Selected Seminar Papers on Contemporary China, III.* Hong Kong: Hong Kong University Press, 1979.

Womack, Brantly. "Sino-Vietnamese Border Trade: The Edge of Normalization." *Asian Survey* 34:6. June 1994.

Womack, Brantly. "Stalemate in Indochina: The Case for Demilitarization." *World Policy Journal* 4:4 (Fall 1987),675–93.

Womack, Brantly. "The United States, Human Rights, and Moral Autonomy in the Post–Cold War World," in Fatton, Robert, and Ramazani, Ruhi, eds., *The Future of Liberal Democracy: Thomas Jefferson and the Contemporary World*. London: Palgrave, 2004.

Womack, Sarah. "The Remakings of a Legend: Women and Patriotism in the Hagiography of the Trung Sisters." *Crossroads: An Interdisciplinary Journal of Southeast Asian Studies* 9:2. Spring 1997.

Woodside, Alexander. "Conceptions of Change and of Human Responsibility for Change in Late Traditional Vietnam," in Wyatt, David, and Woodside, Alexander, eds., *Moral Order and the Question of Change: Essays on Southeast Asian Thought*. New Haven: Yale University Southeast Asian Studies, 1982.

Woodside, Alexander. "Early Ming Expansionism, 1406–1427: China's Abortive Conquest of Vietnam." *Papers on China* 17:4. 1963.

Woodside, Alexander. "Nationalism and Poverty in the Breakdown of Sino-Vietnamese Relations." *Pacific Affairs* 52:3. Autumn 1979.

Woodside, Alexander. "The Relationship between Political Theory and Economic Growth in Vietnam, 1750–1840," in Reid, Anthony, ed., *The Last Stand of Asian*

Autonomies: Responses to Modernity in the Diverse States of Southeast Asia and Korea, 1750–1900. New York: St. Martin's, 1997.

Zhao, Quansheng. "Chinese Foreign Policy in the Post–Cold War Era." *World Affairs* 59:3. Winter 1997.

Zhang, Xiuhua. "Changqi hunxiao di jige zhongyao guannian–nongcun geju, junshi da benying he nongcun geming genjudi di guanxi zhi wo guan 长期混淆的几个重要观念农村割剧,军事大本营, 和农村革命根据地的关系之我见" [Several Important Concepts that have been Confused for a Long Time – My Opinion about Rural Separatist Rule, Military Strongholds and Revolutionary Rural Bases], *Shixue Jikan* 史学季刊 [Collected Papers of History Studies]. 2002:3, no. 88. July 2002.

Zhang, Xiumin. "Ming dai jiaozhi ren zai Zhongguo neidi zhi gongxian 明代交趾人在中国内地之贡献" [The Contributions of People from Jiaozhi inside China during the Ming Dynasty], in Zhang, Xiumin, *Zhong Yue guanxi lunwen ji* 中越关系史论文集 [Collected Essays on Sino-Vietnamese Relations]. Taipei: Wen Shi Zhe, 1992.

Zhang, Xizhen. "Treaty Develops Relations with ASEAN." *China Daily*, September 8, 2003.

Zhao, Quansheng. "Chinese Foreign Policy in the Post–Cold War Era." *World Affairs* 159:3. Winter 1997.

Index

Made in the USA
Las Vegas, NV
02 April 2021